First Lady of Versailles

LUCY NORTON

FIRST LADY
OF VERSAILLES

Marie Adélaïde of Savoy
Dauphine of France

J. B. LIPPINCOTT COMPANY
PHILADELPHIA AND NEW YORK

3-3-79

To Elizabeth

Contents

Illustrations

Acknowledgement

I should like to express my gratitude above all to Christopher Sinclair-Stevenson for the skill and patience which he devoted to editing this book, and for his unquenchable faith in my ability to write it. My thanks go also to my friends Betty Askwith and Micherl Holroyd who have supported me with their encouragement and wise advice, and to Francine Yorke for the great help she has given me in tabulating my notes and revising the text. To the staff of the London Library my thanks go also for their unfailing courtesy, interest and kindness.

Some Books Consulted

This book is meant for readers to enjoy and not primarily as a
reference book for students. I have therefore not wanted to clutter
the pages with notes giving the exact reference for every quotation.
The sources from which these come are the following books.

Historical Memoirs of the Duc de Saint-Simon (whose spirit pervades
  this book). Translated by Lucy Norton. In three volumes, London, 1967, 1968, 1972

Philippe Marquis de Dangeau, *Journal*

Marquis de Sourches, *Mémoires Secrètes et Inédites de la Cour de
  France*

Marquis de Proyart, *Mémoires*

Katherine Prescott-Wormley (editor). *Correspondence of Madame,
  Princesse Palatine, of Marie Adelaide, Duchesse de Bourgogne, and
  of Madame de Maintenon,* 1898

Mme de Caylus, *Souvenirs*, Paris, 1806

Madame, The Letters of. Stevenson G. Scott, 2 vol. London, 1924

Fénelon, *Letters*. London, 1964

Mme de Maintenon, *Lettres inédites à la Princesse des Ursins*

Mme de Maintenon, *Correspondance*, Paris 1865

Ducs de Bourgogne et Beauvilliers, *Lettres inédites*, 1700–1708, ed.
  Vogüé

Mme de Lafayette, *Histoire de Madame Henriette d'Angleterre*, Paris,
  1853

G. P. Othenin de Cléron d'Haussonville, *La Duchesse de Bourgogne*,
  Paris, 1908

René de Froullai, Comte de Tessé. *Lettres*

Nancy Mitford, *The Sun King*, London, 1966

Mme Saint René Taillandier, *La Princesse des Ursins*, Paris

'Small details seldom find a place in memoirs; but more than anything else they give the essential flavour of what we seek to find, the true atmosphere of a bygone age.'

Saint-Simon, *Mémoires*

The Family of Louis XIV

Children of marriages who play no part
in this book, are omitted.

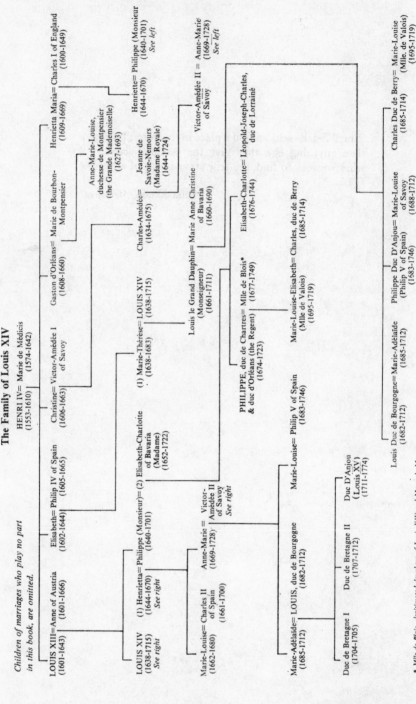

* Mlle de Blois - legitimated daughter of Louis XIV and Mme. de Montespan.

I

Childhood

THE LIFE stories of royal personages make fascinating reading because, at least until recently, they were regarded as a race apart, superior to the rest of humanity, and considered so to be in God's eyes as well as in their own. Describing the character of the Duc de Bourgogne, whom Adelaide of Savoy went to France to marry, Saint-Simon tells us that 'from his celestial height he thought of other men as of atomies bearing no resemblance to himself. Even his brothers, supposed to be his equals, he considered, at best as mere go-betweens twixt himself and the rest of the human race'. Old Mme de Meilleraye, tut-tutting with her gossips over the lamentable fate of a dead, debauched, distant cousin of Louis XIV, earnestly stated, 'It is my considered opinion that with people of his birth God thinks twice before damning them'. Even Queen Victoria was not entirely unaffected. 'I do so strongly believe,' she wrote to the Princess of Prussia, 'that in the eyes of God we are all equal.'

To strengthen this sense of their difference, royal children, at any rate in France, were taken from their mothers soon after birth, to be trained by governesses or governors in separate establishments, brought up to be the centre of their private universe, bereft of family life and maternal love. 'My son is only two months old,' wrote Adelaide to her grandmother, in Turin, 'but I scarcely ever see him, lest I become too fond of him.' French princesses, exposed for years to the flattery and intrigues of their households, entered Society proud, ignorant, arrogant, unable to meet on equal terms any but their closest relations, whom they generally hated. So long as they feared and obeyed the King and their confessors, made a suitable show of piety, and were healthy enough to make desirable marriages, their governesses were thought to have done well by them. Their characters, principles and general education went for nothing. What they learned to cling to for dear life was the crazy structure of rank and precedence on which the very existence of Louis XIV's rule depended, and without which France would have been in chaos. To them rank was vital; witness the Duchesse de Chartres, the King's legitimated daughter, so proud that they called her Madame Lucifer, who remembered, even upon her chaise-percée, that she was a daughter of France.

Marie Adelaide, the little Princess of Savoy, who was sent to France at the tender age of eleven to marry Louis XIV's grandson, and became the mother of Louis XV, provides a notable exception to this crew of arrogant princesses. Pitchforked from a quiet country life into the world's most brilliant court, to find herself suddenly the centre of attention, the first lady, the future queen, subjected to the torturing constraints of etiquette, and the splendours, pleasures, and depravities of Court life, it seems incredible that she should not have been ruined by the spoiling and the flattery which she received. Three things may have helped to save her: firstly her own nature, for she was essentially kindhearted. She seems, all through her life, to have had a genuine love for people, rich or poor, high or low, with an intense desire to please and help everyone, beginning with the King himself. In letter after letter her contemporaries bear witness to this quality in her. 'Kindness came naturally to her,' says Saint-Simon, 'she showed it to all, even to the members of her own household.' 'She feared to do the least hurt to anyone,' wrote another who knew her. 'She was eager to serve, oblige, and content others, and her sweet ways brought all hearts to her feet.' Voltaire, after her death, wrote that 'her gracious and appealing ways made her the idol and model of the Court'.

Secondly, she was given a very good start. At home, she was neither crushed nor spoiled, but loved, and very well brought up, and, until her great adventure, lived a tranquil, happy country life with her mother and younger sister. From her father, Victor Amadeus II, who did not welcome her at first, but soon saw her capabilities, she received an admirable training. He taught her something of statecraft and diplomacy (some believed that he taught her to spy for him). It was said that no princess going to a foreign court had ever been so well prepared. She had, moreover, proved a marvellously quick and intelligent pupil, and was so well instructed in the modes of the French court that, from the first, she knew her role perfectly, and was thus able to be happy at Versailles.

Yet it was probably to her mother, Anne of Orléans, and to her grandmother, Marie Anne Baptiste de Nemours (called Madame Royale), that Adelaide owed the biggest debt, for Duchess Anne was said to have left her heart behind her when she crossed the Alps, and Madame Royale's court at Turin was a necessarily pale reflection of the pleasures, the beauty, the immorality of the Versailles she had known and loved in Louis XIV's glorious youth. Together they persuaded Adelaide (as they believed was true) that the French court was still the happiest, gayest, most beautiful place on earth, and that she was the luckiest little girl in all Christendom. They told her that her great uncle the old King and all her French family would love her dearly, provided only that she was good; and, best of all, that in Mme de Maintenon the King's unofficial wife she would find a second and most kind mother, to whom she might turn in every trouble. And so, marvellous to relate, it happened. Adelaide, at first sight, fell in love with her, yielding to the enormous charm that children of all kinds found captivating and, in their intimate daily tête-à-têtes, felt securely protected from any hint of jealousy or unkindness. A loving attachment was very quickly established that ended only with Adelaide's tragic death. On the princess's side, the relationship was one of light-hearted affection. Mme de Maintenon, who was not a warm-hearted woman,[1] came to feel for the little girl a love and devotion which she gave to no one else, save perhaps to her unattractive nursling the Duc du Maine.

Between them all, they spoiled her abominably. The King idolised her for her gaiety and the spontaneous affection which she showed him, and could deny her nothing. To Mme de Maintenon's infinite relief he ceased to be bored, and grew young again in the child's innocent company. No one was allowed to cross or reprove her, no

[1] Since Mme de Maintenon was essentially frigid (Fénelon accused her, in a letter, of being 'dry, cold, and tactless', and the Italian players ruined themselves by a sketch of her, entitled *The Prude*), it seems odd that the epithets of her arch enemies, Madame and the Duc de Saint-Simon, were all such as 'the old bitch', 'the old bag of filth', referring to her supposed immorality in the days when she was 'Widow Scarron'. It is hardly likely that, had her life been notably scandalous, Mme de Montespan would have chosen her for her children's governess, or the King, who was a great stickler for morality in others, allowed it. One possible explanation is that Scarron had a sister Françoise, who figured prominently in the elegant, intellectual, but frankly debauched circle, at the house of the crippled poet. There were thus two Françoise Scarrons, and in later years, the names may well have been confused and the exploits of the one attached to the other. The poet's wife, the future Mme de Maintenon, had been so well brought up, imbued with such very high principles, it seems difficult to imagine her otherwise than prim and virtuous.

matter what the provocation, for fear lest she lose her charming confidence, and sulk with him, or be troublesome, and thus after a time she became ungovernable. The wonder is that she ever recovered. That she did reform was due perhaps to Mme de Maintenon's tact and good sense; perhaps also to the strength of her own character and the good principles instilled into her by her mother. Perhaps her gentle heart was kept warm by the protective affection of her household and her servants, who seem all to have loved her— Domingo, for example, her Spanish butler, a proud man, far above his station, would have gone through fire for her, and refused ever to marry, '*pour ne se point partager*'. She was touched by his devotion and treated him as a friend, allowing him, in private, to speak to her very frankly. When she died he took to his bed, saw no one except his confessor, and died himself less than a year later. Be that as it may, Adelaide's nature was not permanently warped by spoiling and flattery. When she grew up and troubles came, she suddenly and completely reformed, as Madame, her fiercest critic, was the first to admit. Abandoning her wild hunt after pleasure, she met real adversity with courage and intelligence.

Adelaide of Savoy was born at Turin, on 6 December 1685, the daughter of Victor Amadeus II, Duke of Savoy, and of Marie Anne d'Orléans, the second child of Louis XIV's brother Philippe d'Orléans by his first wife, Henrietta of England, with whom the King had once been over head and ears in love. When Adelaide came to his court so many years later, with all her grandmother's irresistibly appealing charm, the old King fell in love all over again, and relived with the little girl the happy days of his young manhood. He probably loved her more than he loved anyone else in his whole life, as much indeed as he was capable of loving. His thwarted paternal affection found an outlet in her, and for a long time his chief object in life was to make her happy.

Duchess Anne, Adelaide's mother, inherited neither the beauty nor the charm of Henrietta. She was pleasant to look at, no more; not conspicuously intelligent, but most certainly good and high-minded. Her life shows her to have been remarkably sweet-natured, more than a little dull, and rather irritatingly emotional, as she struggled in vain to ingratiate herself with a bored and selfish husband. Born on 11 May 1669, scarcely a year before her mother's death, she was brought up by her stepmother the redoubtable second Madame, Elizabeth Charlotte of the Palatinate, who with characteristically good-hearted firmness took charge of the tiny orphan and her seven-year-old sister. Madame took her task seriously (she was more successful with girls than with boys) and was both proud and pleased to see them grow into amiable and accomplished princesses, full of dignity and most excellent principles. When the time came for them to make royal marriages, she parted with them in real sorrow, Marie Louise the elder to marry, in 1679, Charles II of Spain, and Marie Anne, just a month before her fifteenth birthday, to be the wife of Victor Amadeus of Savoy. Needless to say that for many years they kept up a lively correspondence. Madame wrote to them both several times a week, as she did to so many of her relations. Unhappily the letters have been lost, or were destroyed by her orders, the fate of much of her correspondence, apart from those which she wrote to her aunt the Electress of Hanover.

It was on 9 April 1684, immediately after a proxy-wedding, at Versailles, before the King and the entire Court, with the Duc du Maine representing the absent bridegroom, that Adelaide's mother, newly created Duchess of Savoy, set out to meet her husband. The meeting took place on 6 May, near Chambéry, at a picturesque village named Pont-de-Beauvoisin, through which ran the little river Guiers that used to be the boundary between Dauphiné and Savoy.

During the short period of her engagement, Anne had been thoroughly instructed by Madame, and by the King himself, on her duties as the wife of a reigning duke, and her rights as a princess in the royal line of France. During the long journey, trundling in the royal coach with its military escort along the dusty roads, the Ambassador to Savoy sat beside her and gave her further instruction, especially in the intricate ceremony of formal presentation to her unknown husband, and the ritual to be observed in bidding farewell to her French household, and greeting the nobles and gentry of Savoy. Anne was well prepared to be dignified; yet, horrible to relate, as soon as she saw Victor Amadeus smiling at her, looking so very handsome with his golden hair and blue eyes, in an elegant wasp-waisted uniform that set off his princely figure to perfection, her dignity deserted her. Ignoring all the rules of procedure, the two masters of ceremony, the nobility, office-holders, and members of both retinues, she ran forward and flung herself straight into his arms. Everyone was appalled, except Victor Amadeus himself. He seemed not to mind and, 'for some moments,' as one of his gentlemen recorded, 'spectators were privileged to observe those first sentiments of the love that beats in all youthful hearts'. It was none the less very shocking, for the Court had been told that their new duchess was every inch a princess, yet here was an exhibition of manners totally lacking in the demure repose that marks good breeding. Worse, it was profanity, an attack on the sacred edifice of etiquette, on which the rights and functions, and to a large extent the livelihood, of every courtier depended.

But Anne, unfortunate girl, had fallen, at first sight, passionately, desperately in love with Victor Amadeus, a man with whom she had no chance of happiness. His exterior was attractive enough; his personal character was far otherwise. Moody, contemptuous, heartless, consumed with ambition, nothing was further from his mind than playing the devoted husband to an inexperienced girl. For a couple of months he was charming to her; he then returned to his official mistress, the Comtesse de Verrua,[1] to his army and his ambitions, where his heart had always been. Thereafter he took little notice of his wife, except to scold and nag her for being either too extravagant, at Turin, or else too quiet and dull at her country house. When he received, as he very often did, reproachful letters from Monsieur and Louis XIV, he turned upon her furiously. His French relations were much concerned at his unkindness to her, and Madame, in 1688, wrote to the Electress that 'her husband is so savage that I fear he will end by going out of his mind'.

Anne nonetheless continued to love him passionately. She was in agonies whenever he was with the army, and wrote to him daily, until he told her that her letters bored him, and that in any event he had no time to answer them. Thereafter she wrote every day to his secretary, begging for news, in case he fell ill, which he very often did. Perhaps one of her happier moments was when he contracted smallpox, and graciously allowed her to come and nurse him. 'Only give me your consent,' she had written, 'it will be the strongest proof of your love. I promise not to embarrass you. Only two ladies shall come with me. It will be enough just to be near you; and you shall see that I love you more than life itself.' Permission was granted, and he may have been thankful, for Duchess Anne wrote to Madame Royale that there were no doctors in his suite. It is even possible that

[1] 'The loveliest of the Duc de Luynes's four lovely daughters', about whom Dumas wrote a novel entitled *La Dame de Volupté*. She is said to have composed her own epitaph.

> 'Here lies in peace profound
> La Dame de Volupté,
> Who, so as to be quite secure,
> made her paradise here on earth.'

he was grateful; but as soon as he recovered he left her. All that he required from his wife was an heir, and, with that in mind, he kept her busily employed with motherhood, for she gave birth to eight children, and had several miscarriages before achieving the desired result. Only four babies survived their infancy: Marie Adelaide, her eldest, born on 6 December 1685; Marie Louise Gabrielle, three years younger, who married Philip V of Spain; and, much later, two sons, the elder, a good-looking, intelligent boy, who died in his sixteenth year, the younger a pitiable contrast, both in mind and body, who lived to succeed his father.

At Adelaide's birth, which very nearly killed her sixteen-year-old mother, Victor Amadeus surprised everyone by being quite unusually kind. He had his camp-bed taken into his wife's room so as to spend the nights beside her and, according to d'Arcy, the newly-arrived French envoy, was always running upstairs during the daytime to look at his baby daughter. He was none the less bitterly disappointed, for he had the fireworks and bonfires cancelled, together with all the other ceremonies of congratulation and rejoicing. Years later, Adelaide wrote from Versailles to Madame Royale her grandmother, 'I believe, dear Grandmamma, that I did not give you much joy thirteen years ago, because you would have preferred a boy; but from all the kindness you have always shown me, I cannot doubt that you have forgiven me for being a girl.'

Duchess Anne only briefly enjoyed her husband's company. His army soon required his presence, and once again he left her lonely and neglected. What Victor Amadeus lived and worked for, the cause to which he devoted his considerable intelligence and all the energies not expended on his mistress, or in quarrelling with his totally francophile mother,[1] was the extension of his territory and the glory of his House. All his forebears, the previous Counts and Dukes of Savoy and Piedmont, stemming from the sinister-sounding Humbert of the White Hands (980–1048), had very skilfully exploited the natural advantages of their country's geographical position by playing off the great powers, France and Austria, one against the other. Time after time, they had been successful, selling their alliance in the continual wars to the side that at any moment appeared to be winning, and changing sides whenever that seemed desirable. Victor Amadeus II, using the same methods, excelled

[1] Madame Royale, in 1687, when Savoy was an ally of the Emperor and fighting against France, kept up a running correspondence with Louvois, telling him all that was happening in Turin, even down to details of the finances.

them all. He became notorious for never finishing a war on the side where he had started and, during one campaign, he changed sides twice. Where his ancestors had succeeded, he triumphed. He married his daughters to the King of Spain and the heir to the throne of France, and gained for himself the kingdoms of Sicily and Sardinia.

Considering the smallness and poverty of Savoy, it does seem extraordinary that Louis XIV, the most powerful, most glorious monarch in Europe, should have sought there a bride for his eldest grandson and heir presumptive. The secret lay in Savoy's geographical situation, covering as it did both sides of the mountain frontiers of Italy. Both France and Austria needed to take their armies across the Alps and through the passes in every campaign, and the ruler of Savoy could give free passage, or deny it, to either side. Hence the huge importance of Savoy, and of Victor Amadeus II, its ruling duke. He was an ally worth paying a high price for; but, as events proved, hard to secure, and as slippery as any eel. His grandfather, Victor Amadeus I (1587–1637), had been the ally of Spain against France; his father Charles Emmanuel II (d. 1675) had joined Louis XIII against the Austrians. Thus, when Victor Amadeus II succeeded to his dukedome at the age of ten, Savoy was the ally of France. Ten years later, just a year after his marriage in 1685, Victor Amadeus joined the powerful League of Augsburg, when Austria, Holland, Spain, England, and Sweden banded together to prevent the further expansion of France. There seemed, at that time, no possibility of their failure.

At that time, however, the French armies and generals were the best in Europe, and the Allies suffered a series of humiliating defeats. When General Catinat captured Nice and overran Savoy itself, Victor Amadeus began to think of selling his friendship back to France. With a great French army encamped in the foothills threatening to descend upon the plain, and destroy the mulberry trees whose loss would mean ruin for the silk industry, on which Savoy's finances depended, he felt a great need for peace. In previous years he had seen his finest châteaux burned and looted, and many of his smaller country houses, where, following the lead of Louis XIV, he had found pleasure in 'improving nature and revealing true beauty.'[1]

[1] The motto which Le Nôtre, the great landscape architect, kept hanging over his drawing board: 'To improve nature and reveal true beauty, at the lowest possible cost.'

For the next few years he shilly-shallied, making tentative approaches to the King, with elaborate precautions to observe secrecy, lest rumours of impending desertion should reach the Emperor's ears. It was the French victory of La Marsaille, in 1693, that decided him. He agreed to receive the visit of Louis XIV's envoy, the Marquis de Tessé, a diplomat of great charm and sagacity, and to begin the preliminaries of peace negotiations. There was one condition; Tessé must come in the guise of a hostage, a status which the poor man did not much relish, for he wrote to the minister for war, pleading not to be left long in that unenviable situation, since he recollected that 'by some unfortunate mis-understanding, not rectified in time, one such hostage had recently been hanged'. Meanwhile the fighting continued furiously, until, at last, a two-month truce was arranged, and Tessé returned, not this time as a hostage, but still incognito.

Louis XIV himself badly needed peace, and had decided that the best means of gaining it was to weaken the League by detaching from it one or other of the Allies. He had fixed on Savoy as being the state in most urgent financial difficulties, and the one most irked by Imperial tyranny. That, indeed, had been the reason for Catinat's threatening presence on the foothills above Savoy, and for his very obvious preparations to descend upon Turin. Louis was willing to pay a great price for peace; but he intended to secure compliance and found Victor Amadeus very ready to comply. Negotiations proceeded. Savoy would receive Nice; the restitution of all the territories captured during the war, and a very large sum of money in compensation for damage. Insignificant to modern notions, but far from meaningless to a seventeenth-century duke on the road to glory and a kingship, was a clause to the effect that Savoy's ambassadors should in future receive royal honours, and Victor Amadeus, himself, be saluted as a royal Highness.

The most important condition of the treaty was the marriage of the Princess Adelaide of Savoy to the young Duc de Bourgogne, the Dauphin's son and heir, who stood only two steps from the throne of France. She was to go to France to be brought up there as a French princess, rather, perhaps, in the nature of a warranty for her father's good faith, his rejection of the Austrian alliance, and his firm intention to be the friend of France. That, at least, was what Louis XIV devoutly hoped. In the event, it happened otherwise, for in 1703 Victor Amadeus returned to his Austrian alliance, thus confirming his reputation for inconstancy.

While the negotiations continued, secrecy was of prime importance. Envoys came and went incognito, and Victor Amadeus's
resourceful mind conceived the brilliant notion of gaining better
terms by offering Princess Adelaide also to the Emperor's eldest
son, the thirteen-year-old King of Rome. When the Emperor
refused on the rather odd grounds that, if his son were obliged to
wait another four years before consummating his marriage, he
might be driven to immoral conduct, Victor Amadeus capitulated
completely and turned openly to France.

It had been a cruel and costly war, waged with that extraordinary
mixture of barbarity and politeness that was the way of the seventeenth century. Towns were destroyed, villages burned, fields
ravaged, peasants ruined, large tracts of country desolated, yet all
the time, the opposing generals were sending one another presents
of fruit and game, allowing private letters to pass unopened, and
constantly inquiring about each other's health. When Victor
Amadeus had been dangerously ill, Tessé had written assuring him
of the King's deep concern, offering to send the best French doctors, and passports, should he wish to convalesce at a French spa.
Alternatively, the mineral waters of his choice could be bottled and
dispatched to him, at Turin, together with some particularly holy
relics, in which Duchess Anne had always placed great faith. On his
recovery, King Louis had sent hearty congratulations and his best
wishes.

Duchess Anne, meanwhile, was living a quiet and lonely life.
'She spends her time in almost complete retirement,' wrote Madame
Royale to her friend Mme de La Fayette, in Paris. 'We never see her
unless we meet on the Mall, or when we go to church.' The war
with France, her native country, made her wretched, almost to the
point of despair; but she remained loyal to Savoy, and took no part
in her mother-in-law's political intrigues. More and more she had
come to hate life at the gloomy ducal palace of Turin, where she
was continually humiliated by the insolence of her husband's mistress, bedecked with jewels far more resplendent than any which she
possessed as his wife, and fawned upon by his courtiers. At the
palace of Madame Royale, where the cream of Piedmontese society
encircled that still beautiful, gay, and witty lady, she felt neglected
and out of place. It was there that such pleasures as Turin could
provide were to be found, inspired by a bevy of the prettiest girls
imaginable, Madame Royale's famous maids of honour, drawn from
the best Piedmontese families; all of them eager to be more than

agreeable to their young duke and the noblemen of his suite. Their open immorality was deeply shocking to Duchess Anne, who had been strictly brought up, and her husband's constant complaining, about her supposed extravagance, served to discourage her completely.

No wonder she gave up the struggle to please him, and began to absent herself from him and from his capital for longer and more frequent periods, finding consolation in motherhood, and devoting herself to the education of her little daughters. She first sought refuge at *La Venerie*, the country residence of the Dukes of Savoy, built after the model of Versailles; but finding even that oppressive, she retired to a charming little house, deep in the country, which the peasants called 'La Vigna di Madama', surrounded by vineyards and farms, set in wooded slopes running down to the Po. The children had an official governess, the Principessa della Cisterna, and, to teach them the three Rs, an under-governess, Madame Desnoyers, a lady with a great reputation for her learning, who had already written several books on the education of young ladies. With Adelaide, however, she was singularly ineffectual, for in all her life, that princess never learned to write or spell correctly, even by the lax standards of the period. One of Mme de Maintenon's first actions, after her arrival in France, was to give her a writing master, who, according to Adelaide herself, 'took an immense amount of trouble with very little result'. Two years later, when she was nearly thirteen, she confided to her grandmother, 'It is high time I learned to write properly; they often tell me that a married woman should be ashamed of needing a master for something so easy'.

With her moral education it was very different. 'She was imbued with most excellent principles by her virtuous mother,' wrote Madame, 'and when she first came to France appeared remarkably well brought up. Mme de Maintenon was entirely responsible for her subsequent relapse, which might have been foreseen, in the circumstances of the King's blind adoration.' It was indeed Duchess Anne who personally undertook the religious instruction and moral training of her two daughters. She taught Adelaide to fear God, and Louis XIV as his regent, to obey her confessor, and to exercise, at all times in public, that composure and dignity which was the first duty of a princess. Adelaide took her religion seriously, and Mme de Maintenon describes her relief when she discovered that she had only to say, 'That would be sinful', for the headstrong little girl to reply 'Then I will not do it'.

In every way, apart from her books, Adelaide was quick and eager to learn, especially when she could see the point, as she did when it came to absorbing the duties and behaviour required of a very great lady, at the Court of Versailles. It was again her mother, assisted by Madame Royale, who undertook, even from babyhood, that part of her training, in the hope, so precious to all of them, that it might be their little girl's high destiny one day to become queen of their beloved France. There is reason to think that Adelaide herself was not unaware of that splendid possibility, for after her recovery from scarlet fever, as a very small child, the Dauphine[1] had written to Madame Royale, expressing her pleasure, 'not only because she is our cousin, but because we are given to understand that she says she will never be happy unless she marries our son'. Versailles was presented to her as a fairy palace, where everybody was young and gay and happy, and whose lord and master was her kind old great uncle, the Sun King, the most glorious and powerful monarch in all Christendom. The Versailles which Duchess Anne remembered was not the Versailles of 1696; but Adelaide did not know that; to her, the future was a beautiful dream, and sad thoughts of parting may not have loomed very large in the mind of an excited little girl, with a light and cheerful nature.

When Savoy had gone to war with France, the royal duchesses had been in despair; but the truce of 1692 had given them fresh cause to hope, and Tessé's reappearance, though still incognito, sent Adelaide's mother into such an ecstasy of delight that her emotions were too much for her. High politics demand secrecy and restraint; but restraint was more than Duchess Anne could manage, and Tessé wrote pathetically to the King, 'She displays her intense, her almost frenzied joy, and although she has been warned not to let the allied commanders see where her heart lies, she cannot contain herself. She takes every opportunity to converse with me, speaks of Your Majesty, of her raptures, of her past wretchedness and mortification.' It is plain that he found her most embarrassing.

Adelaide's training was now proceeding in earnest. She was given instruction by her father, who joined his family when he could spare the time, on the meaning and purpose of the endless

---

[1] The wife of le Grand Dauphin, and mother of Louis XIV's three grandsons, the Duc de Bourgogne, the Duc d'Anjou (later Philip V of Spain, and the ten-year-old (in 1696) Duc de Berry.

ceremonies at the French Court, and their vast importance. He taught her something of statecraft, and of the discriminating politeness due to precedence, birth, and age in every rank and grade. Something else she learned from him, which astonished Louis XIV, and made him supremely grateful—how and when to hold her tongue. Silence was his own method, by which he ruled his courtiers and avoided reproach. They might speak to him; but he never replied, except with the words, 'I shall see', accompanied by a pleasant smile. To find that he could rely on the little princess not to make trouble with her chatter was a great asset, and an even greater one was that she had been indoctrinated with that strange belief, the lofty, terrifying conception of the divinity of the King, God's regent upon earth. She had learned that his word was God's law; that to obey, and content, him in everything would be her first and bounden duty, and that, at Versailles, it was required of a great lady, at all times, to please and be pleased. Not that pleasing presented any problem to Adelaide. She was naturally friendly and affectionate, and had inherited with her English grandmother's charm, a great desire to serve people and make them love her. As for being pleased herself, it was her ambition to enjoy everything and to get the greatest possible fun out of life.

To please and be pleased was the supposed aim of all ladies at Versailles. It was part of a code of manners designed to create harmony and prevent people from flying at each other's throats. Another requirement, harder to put into practice, was for gentlemen to be at all times brave and gallant, and for ladies, for the general good, to conceal personal griefs and discomforts, and not to complain of the unavoidable. This unselfish code may possibly have been aimed at producing a company of angels; but it certainly did not have that result at the Court of Versailles. The underlying theory was that each individual had a great number of dear friends and relations (probably some two hundred), a number of whom would certainly be ill, or otherwise distressed at any given time. To put on a sorry countenance for their sake would dampen the spirits and spoil the enjoyment of everyone else. In the same way, it would be pure selfishness to upset other people by drawing attention to the smaller miseries of life, caused by draughts, too much standing, tight stays, boredom, headaches, or a thwarted inclination to seek relief in a privy. The King was strict with himself, or was made less miserable by such matters. If he ever appeared other than equable, pleasant, and courteous, it was an astonishing event, to be recorded

in the journals; and attributable to his sufferings from gout, or the
boils that sometimes afflicted him and, on rare occasions, made him
irritable. His desire was to see happy, cheerful faces at his Court,
and his courtiers complied with his wishes; they dared not do otherwise.

He particularly enjoyed coach-parties, with all the windows down,
and the ladies making merry on cakes and fruit, while he pressed
on them a variety of delicious drinks, contained in the pockets of
the doors. He took nothing himself, for although he ate enormously,
he did so only at meals; but he liked to see others enjoy themselves,
and would have been much offended by a refusal. He never seemed
to feel the needs of nature, and would have been so shocked and so
indignant had anyone asked him to stop his coach, that no one, no
one at all, had ever dared to make the request.[1] 'It was not exactly
that he was selfish,' wrote poor Mme de Maintenon (who had long
established it that she did not travel with the King), 'but he had
been King since he was four, and had been trained to consider only
himself. . . . His every wish was instantly acclaimed; for instance,
when he wanted the windows opened wide, in January, everyone
immediately discovered that they had been feeling too hot. It never
struck him that other people might be different from himself.'
Towards his family, Louis XIV was not often unkind, rather the
reverse, unless of course they obstructed his sport or his pleasures,
when he could be cruel. He liked women to be laughing, witty,
and in good health. 'At Versailles,' said Saint-Simon, 'happy
beauty was the best dowry of all.'

Adelaide was certainly no beauty; she was, indeed, distinctly
plain; but she had a freshness, and a charm that was better than
classical beauty. When her great adventure began, in 1696, she was
not quite eleven years old, yet she seems to have bowled over every
member of the party sent to form her new household, responsible
for the impression she would make on her state journey to France
and her first meeting with the King. She was so eager to please
them, so friendly, what the French called '*franc du collier*', like a
willing horse that throws all its weight into the collar, when an

---

[1] In the reign of Louis XIII, one aged courtier once dared to desire a stop;
and he was not immediately executed. He had pleaded that it would not give
the King pleasure to see him burst. Incidentally, a recent survey of the toilet
facilities at Windsor Castle describes them as being 'woefully inadequate',
offering as a possible reason that 'visitors were too much inhibited by the nearness
of royalty to want to spend a penny'.

effort is required. Her freshness and innocence came as a complete surprise to them. What the French ladies and gentlemen had expected was a spoiled and arrogant princess. What they found was a good little girl, with an affectionate, happy nature, and a great determination to learn her part and play it well. No wonder they came to love her.

Adelaide, indeed, had been very sensibly brought up. Although book learning had not penetrated, she had had an extremely active out of door life, involved with every kind of handiwork that had brought her into contact with the people, working on the farm, in the vineyards, the dairies, and the still-rooms. She had innumerable hobbies and handicrafts and dolls that were very dear to her. 'There is nothing the Duchesse de Bourgogne cannot do,' Mme de Maintenon told the girls of Saint-Cyr. 'She can spin wool and silk and flax, and knows how to work with a loom. The other day she made and embroidered a yellow taffeta dress. There is nothing left for me to teach her. Would you believe it, she even understands fevers? When I feel poorly she comes and feels my pulse, and what she says is sure to be just what the doctor tells me later on.'

The quiet country life at La Vigna suited the children well enough when they were small; but as they grew older, it seemed to them very dull. They saw few people, and nothing interesting happened. Years later, when she was Queen of Spain, Adelaide's sister Marie Louise wrote to her grandmother, 'So you are alone at Turin now that my mother and brothers have gone to La Vigna. It does not surprise me to hear that she has taken scarcely anyone with her; it was the same in our time.' All the brilliance and gaiety were at Madame Royale's palace, where laughter was heard all day long, from the witty and amusing people who gathered around the children's still fascinating and beautiful grandmother. Best of all to them were the games in which everyone joined, after formal occasions, when restraint was abandoned and etiquette thrown to the winds. The most popular was blind man's buff, with its opportunities for surreptitious flirting, amid cascades of squeaks and laughter. Another game which Adelaide enjoyed and certainly played at Versailles, though probably not in her grandmother's drawing-room, was 'sledging', when, gripped by the ankles, she was whirled at breakneck speed over the polished floors of the state apartments. Madame Royale's court appeared to the children like a dream, a glimpse of that great beautiful world to which they would one day belong, and that lady herself was the person whom Adelaide loved best. For Duchess Anne and her father she had a strong affection[1]; but her letters to them are far more formal, and less spontaneously loving than those written to her grandmother.

[1] She had a pet name for him, 'Le Grand' (the Great Man).

2

The Betrothal

IN JUNE 1696, Duchess Anne's dream became a reality. Victor Amadeus decided finally (or at least until circumstances should suggest otherwise) to become the ally of France, and Tessé reappeared to put the last touches to the peace treaty and the arrangements for Adelaide's marriage. This time he did not pose as a hostage but, secrecy still seeming desirable, as a servant of the Adjutant-general of Savoy, wearing a huge black wig, which he had borrowed for the occasion. A fortnight of hectic bargaining followed; then, on 16 June, concealment was abandoned, and he was allowed to make a triumphal entry into Turin, wearing his own fair wig, as the envoy of the Sun King, in a golden coach with painted panels, drawn by eight beautiful horses, with an escort of gentlemen superbly dressed and mounted, and a train of thirty baggage mules, laden with rich and elegant gifts for Adelaide, the bride to be. In a moment she became the centre of interest and admiration, the most important person in all her world. It is a wonder that she did not lose her head. That she kept it was largely due to her parents and her training. It was due also to Tessé, his kindness and good sense.

René III de Froulley, Comte de Tessé, was one of the nicest men at the Court of France. Even the captious Duc de Saint-Simon could find nothing very bad to say against him, although he was a friend of Mme de Maintenon, the little duke's abomination. He was tall, good-looking and extremely well-bred, with a gentle, kindly manner, and a desire to serve that made him much liked. He was also a delightful raconteur, and one of the most charming letter-writers of his day. On the other hand, he was not clever, and often embarrassed people with foolish remarks. Saint-Simon, who may have been jealous, said that he was a toady, ready to go to all lengths for promotion, and 'playing his hand so extraordinarily well that he rose to be a Maréchal de France without ever hearing a musket fired'. Later, Saint-Simon corrects himself, saying that Tessé had, in fact, been present at some of the most spectacular sieges, and had even been wounded at the Siege of Veillane, in 1690, by the bursting of a grenade 'no larger than the egg of a small-sized hen'. Be that as it may, he was a delightful character, and a true friend to Adelaide, supporting her with sympathy and understanding, and encouraging her when the moment of parting came. She, on her side, loved and trusted him. One of the very rare occasions when she dared to make a scene with Louis XIV was when she thought Tessé had been passed over for promotion—her dear Tessé, who had brought her safely to Versailles, and to so much love and happiness.

It is easy to imagine the excitement, the cheering at Turin, as the people rushed into the streets to watch the procession. They were tired of war longing for peace with France, ruined and exhausted by the pillaging and depredations of two armies, for the imperial troops had lived off the country with no more restraint than the French, and had been far more disliked. The rumours of a royal wedding gave them new heart, bringing hopes of better times to come and a revival of trade and industry.

The royal ladies, too, were in seventh heaven. Duchess Anne, with Adelaide half-hidden behind her, had watched Tessé's arrival from a balcony, and that same evening, the elder ladies received him in raptures. After the formal presentations had been made (as though Tessé were making his first appearance), Madame Royale was all smiles and flattery, expressing a most tender affection for King Louis and all his family. As for Duchess Anne, needless to say she was nearly weeping for joy; indeed, so much so that Tessé himself was on the verge of tears. Only Adelaide was upset. Meeting Tessé unexpectedly in one of the corridors, she did not recognise him in his fair wig, mistaking him for Count Mansfeld, the Austrian Commissioner for Italy. 'Oh! Heavens!' she exclaimed to Duchess Anne. 'Why is he here? You will see that Papa will listen to him, just as he did before. He has no business with us now. Why won't he leave us in peace?' Adelaide was not altogether wrong, for the Emperor, on second thoughts, was making one last effort to keep Savoy loyal, and had sent Mansfeld with an offer for Adelaide's hand, on behalf of his son the King of Rome. Victor Amadeus, however, was not to be moved, and must have enjoyed composing a snubbing reply, which began by saying 'that the inclinations of both mother and daughter are against profiting by this most advantageous offer'. Adelaide could breathe again, and dry her tears. Both she and Tessé remembered the incident; long afterwards, when he was writing to her, at Versailles, he reminded her of how, that first day, she had run away from him in tears, mistaking him for an Austrian.

Tessé himself was not overjoyed to find, on his arrival, that the court of Turin was still full of his country's enemies; but next day he felt able to write to King Louis, 'In the end, Sire, even the best of friends must part; the Imperial troops, the Spanish contingent, the Calvinists, and the auxiliaries have all separated from the army of M. de Savoie.' Tessé, if he felt embarrassed for Adelaide's father, need not have concerned himself, for Victor Amadeus was equal to any occasion. He had summoned the Allied officers and had delivered the following address. 'Messieurs,' he had said, 'our paths now somewhat diverge . . . but I shall find occasion to show you marks of my esteem. I have done everything possible to secure for you good winter quarters; I hope, in future, you may find even better ones; but please, not in Italy. . . . It is time for my country, and, if possible, for the princes, my neighbours, to enjoy the rest which I have endeavoured to procure for them. I trust your masters will consent . . . Should they refuse, to my great regret, I shall proceed against you, at the head of a French army, and with all the vigour that has won your respect hitherto. Yet, Messieurs, since I hope to retain your friendship, let us, pray, dine together.' No reply came from the Austrian officers, only profoundly respectful bows. No one stayed to dine, and they were seen no more. That same evening, Victor Amadeus was telling the ladies of his court, 'You may be sure of one thing, from now onwards we are all French'. For the present all seemed happily settled; there remained only the future to be made secure by the signing of the marriage contract between the Princess Adelaide and the Duc de Bourgogne. To that end Tessé now turned his whole attention, for there were many difficulties to be overcome, and many ceremonies to be gone through.

First of all, after recognition of his official status as Louis XIV's envoy, he had to be introduced publicly and formally to all the people with whom he had been secretly closeted for the past weeks. Moreover, he had to have a formal presentation to the two duchesses, and to Adelaide, whom he had already met in her father's study in his various disguises; but who, well-instructed, gave not the slightest sign of recognising him. They then settled down to the business in hand. The first problem was an affair of State, concerning an oath renouncing the succession to her father's estates. It was a matter of some importance because, in 1696, the duke still had no male heir, and was not expected to enjoy a long life—although, in fact, he lived to a great age, and later had two sons. The two parties had previously agreed that Adelaide should take the oath customary for foreign brides, giving up all claim to her father's dukedom, should he die before her. It was the form of the oath, and the question of whether it should be part of the marriage contract, according to the wishes of Louis XIV, or be inserted in the peace treaty, as Victor Amadeus desired, that provoked the controversy. This may seem of relatively small importance; but to the Savoyards, who had no wish to see their small, independent country become a part of France, publication in an international treaty appeared to make the declaration more binding. In the end, Victor Amadeus was obliged to give way. The renunciations were made part of the contract; but he saw to it that they were surrounded by the most complicated guarantees imaginable, with the result that this clause was as long as, if not longer than, all the other ten clauses put together. One difficulty was Adelaide's age, for she had not yet reached the 'age of puberty', and thus could not legally take, or be bound by, an oath. It was not considered sufficient for her father to take it on her behalf, and there the matter rested for some days. At last, a special dispensation was allowed her because 'she is gifted with knowledge and discernment far beyond her years, and states that she well understands the advantage to herself and her descendants of a marriage which gives her just hope of becoming Queen of France, and, her descendants, of succeeding to that throne'.

Tessé had nothing to do with the wording of the contract, of which he sent a copy to the King, saying, 'Your Majesty will find in the enclosed draft of Mgr le Duc de Bourgogne's marriage contract all manner of unfamiliar words, and references to local practices, it would have been difficult in the extreme to get the people here to adopt our ways.' Yet he did manage to slip a few words into the clause, which made a very great difference. After a sentence in which the Duc of Savoy promised never to permit his daughter or her descendants to have the right of succession at any future time to the dukedom of Savoy, Tessé added '*au prejudice des masles de la maison de Savoie*'. 'By this means,' he wrote to the King, 'should all the princes of Savoy die, our princess will not lose her rights, and by those few words, the succession remains open to her.' By all of which it may be seen that the advisers of Victor Amadeus were right to have their suspicions of France, and to hedge the renunciations about with every kind of safeguard.

The remaining clauses presented less difficulty, especially since the impoverished Duke of Savoy was not required to produce a dowry for Adelaide. As a face-saving device, an appropriate sum was mentioned in the contract; but it was arranged, by the peace treaty for an equivalent amount to figure as compensation for war damage. In fact it was Louis XIV who gave Adelaide her dowry, with a princely sum to buy 'rings and jewellery', and a very large income to enable her to keep up her State. Victor Amadeus wrote delightedly to Pope Innocent XII that he was marrying his daughter without it costing him a penny, and, according to Tessé, was observed, wreathed in smiles, striking exultant attitudes before the long mirror in his bedroom.[1]

What Victor Amadeus did contract to provide for his daughter was a 'fardel', or wedding bundle, in other words, her trousseau, the bills for which were still being sent to him fifteen years later, when he had become King of Sicily. The entire sum amounted to fifty-three thousand, nine hundred and five francs. There was a matter of twenty-four thousand, two hundred and ten francs for lace and linen; thirteen thousand for brocades, worked in gold and silver thread, on backgrounds of cloth of silver and gold. The gold and silver appointments of her dressing table cost nine thousand, and her embroidered petticoats nearly three thousand. Her shoes, the only items made at Turin, came to a mere hundred and six francs; there were also small additional sums for ribbons and panniers, and for a dressing-case made of violet-wood. The list ends with an item of sixteen hundred and eighty-two francs for a new carrying chair, and repairs to the chairs for ladies of her suite. Fifteen years seems a long time for the tradesmen to wait for their money, and there appears to be no proof that they were paid even then. Perhaps the glory of providing for royalty was then considered sufficient reward. The trousseau was adequate, not princely, for times were hard, in Savoy. Five years later, when Victor Amadeus married his younger daughter to the King of Spain, the wedding-bundle cost double as much.

[1] He might well be pleased with himself. After six years of devastating war and a succession of defeats, he saw his dukedom freed, friendship re-established with France, and his daughter betrothed to a prince who seemed likely to become the most powerful king in Christendom.

At last all was arranged; the marriage contract was drawn up, ready to be signed, and 16 September was appointed for the betrothal ceremony. It was a great day for Turin. Between six and eleven o'clock in the morning, the entire court, dressed in their very best and wearing all their jewels, assembled in Duchess Anne's salon, at the ducal palace. There they found the Duke, in a powdered wig, a particularly elegant coat, and robes trimmed with ermine. Madame Royale was decked out, said Tessé, with every piece of jewellery that she possessed, while Duchess Anne sparkled with joy and a sufficiency of diamonds. Between them stood the tiny figure of the ten-year-old Adelaide, dressed in cloth of silver, embroidered in gold, with diamonds flashing in her pretty light brown hair, and her person bedecked with all the crown jewels of the royal House of Savoy. Plain Adelaide might be, but she had a beautiful figure and quick graceful movements, as well as natural dignity and a most disarming smile. 'I can assure Your Majesty,' wrote Tessé, 'that she was perfectly composed, and carried out her duties with a facility that really astonished me.'

Everyone complimented her, and then, in all their finery, the ducal family, with their guests and courtiers, went in procession to mass, with Tessé, newly appointed her master of horse, leading her by the hand. When mass was over they returned in procession to Duchess Anne's apartments where, after the princes and princesses, the nuncio, and the Archbishop of Turin had entered, the door was firmly closed to the remainder of the noble company. The Marquis de Saint-Thomas, Savoy's first minister, then read aloud the marriage contract, with all its complicated clauses. Next, a Bible was held before Adelaide, who placed her hand upon it, solemnly swearing to abide by its terms; and Tessé, deputising for the Duc de Bourgogne, did the same, where it was indicated. 'After this,' continued Tessé in his report, 'we signed in the order which Your Majesty will note. I wish with all my heart that Your Majesty could have seen how bravely, modestly, and with what dignity this young princess made her curtseys and appended her signature.' The actual writing of it betrayed her, however, for it was clearly a most laborious business, with the letters childishly shaky and ill-formed.

When all was done, the doors were opened and the crowds poured in to kiss Adelaide's hand. Everyone seemed quite overcome with joy, and they all began kissing and embracing. 'I must say,' concluded Tessé, 'that I have never witnessed anything more resembling a turmoil than the sight of those hundred women and more than two hundred men, kissing one another indiscriminately, and showing all the signs of heartfelt joy.' Later, that same evening, Tessé gave a party, with open house and a banquet supper for all comers. So great was the crush (including beggars and sweepers), so many roads were blocked by the coaches, such was the hubbub, that he was obliged to take refuge in the house next-door, in order to finish his report.

He was very busy; his advice was sought by both sides on every possible question, especially by the King of France on the subject of the presents, for Louis XIV was determined to do the thing in style. From the Marquis de Saint-Thomas down to the lowest servant no one was forgotten, all were satisfied, and Tessé was able to report that 'Your Majesty is as much master of all hearts here, as he is in the realm of France'. Saint-Thomas's present, in particular, had taken a great deal of thought. So much was owed to him, not only for drawing up the contract, but for being a staunch friend during the past three years of negotiation. 'I have been pondering Saint-Thomas's present,' wrote Tessé to the King, 'in order to discover what would please him best. I do not think that money, however much he may need it, would be quite suitable, for there is always a kind of shame attached to accepting money. I understand, from what he himself has said, that a portrait of Your Majesty, set in precious stones of a value commensurate with your grandeur, would be most agreeable to him.' The King inquired whether he would prefer silver plate to diamonds; to which Tessé replied, 'Allow me, Sire, to answer you in the manner of children when asked which they love best, their fathers or their mothers. Generally, they say that they love both equally. Since Your Majesty does me the honour to inform me that the value of the present will amount to twenty, or twenty-five thousand écus, may I suggest that a portrait with diamonds worth ten or twelve thousand écus, and the same value in silver would please him best; for silver is a man's best friend.' In due course Saint-Thomas duly received both plate and portrait, and was made very happy.

Meanwhile, the thoughts of Princess Adelaide, her family, the Comte de Vernon, master of ceremonies, the Princesse de La Cisterna, her governess, and all the other people concerned, were turned to the complicated arrangements for her ceremonial departure and State journey through France. It very soon became apparent that Victor Amadeus (whether because he loved his little daughter and did not want to part with her, or thought it advantageous to keep her as a hostage now that she belonged to France) was most unwilling to fix a date, and the long-suffering Tessé became involved in a new series of negotiations that lasted until well into September.

All this time, streams of letters were coming to him from the King, with a whole questionnaire of intimate inquiries regarding Adelaide. Not about her character—no one was much interested in that, for a good confessor would keep her under sufficient control. It was her appearance, health, and physique that were important to the King, her only functions being to breed children to assure the succession, and enhance the dignity and beauty of State occasions. Fortunately Tessé was able to reassure the King on every point. 'The more I see of her,' he wrote, 'the more convinced I become that she is healthy and possesses a good constitution'; and he tactfully added, 'Whenever I have the honour of seeing her, she blushes, as though the sight of me reminded her of Mgr le Duc de Bourgogne.' Tessé was evidently becoming fond of her; indeed, it is hard not to love a child who tries its best to be helpful and to please, and Adelaide was doing her utmost, and succeeding brilliantly.

He sent back to Versailles all manner of portraits, and personal belongings to satisfy the eager curiosity—miniatures from Duchess Anne to her father Monsieur, the King's only brother; a full length portrait to the King; the 'body' or stiff foundation of one of her dresses to Mme de Maintenon, with a smaller portrait and a length of silk ribbon, to show the size of her slender waist. The Parisian *modistes* were set to work designing, stitching and embroidering rich, and marvellously beautiful dresses, in the French style. Mme de Maintenon played a great part in choosing them. In her early days, when she was very poor, but moving in the great houses, she had been noted for the elegance of her clothes which, though few, were strikingly handsome. For a long time past she had worn only 'decent black', but her excellent taste remained, and her interest in other people's clothes.

One thing which greatly puzzled both her and the King was the colour of Adelaide's hair. Tessé had said in his first letter that it was black; but all the portraits had shown it to be a bright chestnut brown. Inquiries were made, and Tessé wrote apologising for his error. The painters were right, he said, but, owing to an excessive amount of colour having been sprayed on the princess's hair when he first met her, it had appeared darker than it really was. His letter was addressed to Barbezieux the minister for war. It may seem strange that all the parcels, and Tessé's letters to the King, should have been directed to him, but France and Savoy were technically still at war. It was not until 10 September that the Peace of Savoy was officially declared, and Louis XIV, writing to the Archbishop of Paris, announced the glad news, and ordered *Te Deums* and public rejoicings.

In France, the King and Mme de Maintenon were not alone in rejoicing over the peace and the wedding, or in being eager to hear every detail about Adelaide. The entire Court was agog with excitement over the imminent arrival of the little princess who would one day, so they believed, be their Queen and their mistress. Life had been for years so dull, so boring, the war had dragged on and on, with the men all away campaigning during the summers, and no royal princess at the Court, since the death of the Dauphine, six years earlier, to provide an excuse for revelry.[1] Versailles was not what it once had been. The poet La Fare, writing his memoirs in 1669, said that after the death of Adelaide's enchanting grandmother Henrietta of England, the taste for pleasures of the intellect swiftly declined at Louis XIV's brilliant Court, and soon there remained nothing but gambling, disorder, and discourtesy. Some pleasures of the mind might still perhaps be found at Saint-Maur and Sceaux, the houses of the King's legitimated daughters; at Versailles, towards the end of the century, there was only drunkenness, bassette, and lansquenet.[2] It was the Court of an elderly King, preoccupied with fears of death and damnation, and life there had become inexpressibly tedious. The advent of a new era and a new personality was as welcome as it could possibly be; the

[1] Queen Marie-Thérèse had died in 1683 (two months later Louis XIV's secret marriage to Mme de Maintenon had taken place); the Dauphine died in 1690, and neither of these depressed and virtuous ladies had been of the kind to revive the gaieties of the early days.

[2] Madame, in 1695, had the same impression: 'Here, in France,' she noted, 'as soon as people meet they sit down to play *lansquenet*; the young ones do not care to dance any more. I do neither. I'm much too old to dance, and have not done so since my father died; and I never gamble, for two excellent reasons. First, I have no money; secondly I don't care for cards. Here they play for terrifyingly high stakes; and behave like lunatics. One person shrieks, another hits the table so hard that the entire room re-echoes; a third curses in a way to make one's hair stand on end; they all appear to take leave of their senses, and look most alarming.'

young looked forward to parties, theatricals, and other excitements; the ambitions to jobs; the old to power and money for their children, and, for themselves, brilliant State occasions, and delightful intrigues. Everyone, except the King's daughters, whose noses would be put out of joint by a princess of higher rank, was eager to give Adelaide, young as she was, an enthusiastic reception.

The King himself was bored and frightened; taking every possible precaution to ensure his soul's salvation. He was fifty-eight years old. Two illnesses, the heads of the Church, and more especially, the great Bossuet, Bishop of Meaux, had combined to warn him of the approach of death, and to convince him, as most men of his century firmly believed, that this life, in which he had been so criminally immoral, was a mere curtain-raiser to an eternity of torment or bliss. He had just occasion to be uneasy, for his sexual appetites had been as keen as his appetite for food, and in both he had been and still was greedy. Since Mme de Maintenon had effected his conversion there had been no mistress to enliven and amuse him; nothing but statecraft, building, hunting, and gardening to take his mind off his troubles, with a shared, and quite genuine interest in the school she had founded at Saint-Cyr. She was his sole support; the one he relied on to see him safely into Paradise—or at least to Purgatory. He depended on her practical piety for his guidance, and on her body alone for the relief of his desires. It may have been good for his soul, but it was certainly not good fun. The arrival of Adelaide and all the planning for the little girl's life and happiness were a godsend, an innocent pleasure which he could enjoy in partnership with his old wife, for one of her great attractions, for him, was her love of children, and her sweetness with them. His paternal instincts, by force of circumstances, had been thwarted; he foresaw that kind of pleasure ahead, and could scarcely bear to wait. Perhaps he remembered how much he had loved Adelaide's grandmother. Above all, he saw ahead an absorbing task, well worth the attention of a great King, the training, from the beginning, of a perfect Queen. There was no doubt of the eager, loving reception which Adelaide would get from him.

Mme de Maintenon, too, was looking forward, full of hope and tender expectation, to Adelaide's arrival. She was sixty-one years old, and excessively worried about the King who, very evidently, was neither happy nor amused, when it was essential for him to be both. 'If he gets bored with me,' she wrote to her friend Mme de Brinon, 'he will seek other society.' She feared a relapse into mistresses; and did not at all relish, though it was only for conversation, the idea of elderly and witty ladies of the Court being shown up to his study by the backways, or the cackles of laughter that could sometimes be heard through the closed doors. Her own life was not a little boring, especially in his company. She felt she had much to put up with, as she confided, once again to Mme de Brinon: 'When we are alone I have to listen to his troubles, if he has any, and endure his moods and his peevishness. Sometimes he weeps, for he cannot control his tears; often he feels unwell; he has no conversation.' They were an elderly couple, soon wearied by each other's company, what a descent for the Sun King! Mme de Maintenon built great hopes on the innocent distraction that a little child would provide. But there was another reason for joyful anticipation. She genuinely loved to be with children and children loved being with her. All her life she contrived to be surrounded by them for she adopted and took more than one little girl into her home, and when she was over eighty, she wrote to a friend about the visit of a child, 'Do not be afraid to send her; children never tire me'. She had made up her mind to love, educate, and protect this lonely child, and to being loved in return, so that, when Adelaide grew up, she would find in her a friend, not a jealous rival for the King's affection. Mme de Maintenon's hopes were fully realised in the years to come, and the little princess, when she arrived, went straight into her protective arms.

As for the people of France, the *Mercure* might speak of 'general rejoicings' at the ending of the 'Savoy War', but they were utterly exhausted, and Voltaire wrote that 'they died of hunger to the sound of *Te Deums*'. The *Mercure de France*, on the other hand, said that although they may have longed for peace, the people neither petitioned, nor even desired it against the King's will. The burdens of the war had been enormous, the taxes crippling, the casualties huge; yet the news of even this much peace and of a royal wedding did serve to raise people's spirits, and the fact of Adelaide's having a French mother, and coming from Savoy, their late enemy but traditional ally, seemed to promise at least a long respite and better times to come. In Paris, therefore, along the roads of France, and in the towns through which she would pass on her State journey to Versailles, people were ready to welcome her enthusiastically.

3

The Appointment of the Household

AT THE Court of Versailles, it was not so much the peace that fired people's enthusiasm as the prospect of the royal wedding. Despite the mourning for the young men killed, the nobility were by no means tired of the war and the chances it brought of fame and advancement, and there were whispered criticisms of the treaty. Vauban, the great expert on sieges, wrote confidentially to the historiographer royal, who happened to be Racine, that the restitution of so many fortresses to Savoy was the greatest military disgrace since Henri II. But the great majority of the courtiers turned with joy to thoughts of balls, new clothes, and the arrival of the little princess. Everyone wanted to hear about Adelaide and to see her portrait, and when news came that the Duc de Bourgogne had a charming and most speaking likeness of her in his schoolroom, they flocked there to see it. The little princes, his brothers, were no less curious, especially the youngest.[1] 'To turn for a moment to lighter issues,' wrote Barbezieux to Tessé, 'let me tell you what the young Duc de Berry said to the Duc d'Anjou. He had been asking his eldest brother if he was looking forward to being married, and whether his wife would be happy.' Having received a firm 'Yes' to both questions, he turned to the Duc d'Anjou, asking what he would do if his wife tried to stop his hunting; to which came the gentle reply, ' "In that case, I should not hunt." This brought a furious protest that he ought to be ashamed of letting his wife wear the trousers, and that if he himself ever married, his wife might do as she pleased at home; but if she got in the way of his pleasures he would soon show her who was master. No one knows what the Duc de Bourgogne said.'[2]

[1] The Duc de Bourgogne was fourteen, the Duc d'Anjou thirteen, and the Duc de Berry, a lively, merry little boy of whom Madame was very fond, ten.

[2] Tessé, who loved a joke, must have been very much amused. Everyone

On Sunday 2 September, amid triumph and bitter disappointment, the list of Adelaide's French household was published. A
craving for power, office, and money had set up an intense rivalry
between the ladies of suitable rank; everyone had been involved in
some intrigue or other, to discover how best to canvass for jobs or
favour. Anonymous letters buzzed about like flies, blackening characters, reviving ancient scandals, slandering with false reports. It was
of no avail; in the end, the entire business was settled out of hand
by the King and Mme de Maintenon, and they had plenty of opportunity to confer privately because the King was ill in bed (a rare
event for him), with a carbuncle upon his neck that had turned to
anthrax, and was causing him acute pain. The surgeons had several
times lanced it, one operation entailing 'eight snips of the scissors'
and of course no anaesthetic. He had been very patient and courteous to the doctors, but was miserable, and had been sleeping so
badly that Racine had been sitting up with him all night reading
aloud from Plutarch's *Lives*. All through the long days Mme de
Maintenon sat at his bedside, only leaving him when he felt strong
enough to allow his courtiers to enter. They thought him irritable,
in fact this was one of the occasions when they expressed astonishment at not finding him his usual calm self.[1]

In these circumstances, it is probable that most of the work of
choosing suitable ladies was done by Mme de Maintenon. The King
had the deepest, perhaps too much, admiration for her 'sanctified
commonsense' and her capabilities as an educator. She was to him
the perfect example of what a great lady should be, with manners
as exquisite as his own, and it was his desire that she should be in
sole charge of Adelaide's further education. That also was Mme de
Maintenon's intention, for it was the wish of her heart to be the
little girl's mother and governess, in all but name. A genuine love
of children, and a desire for the King's happiness may have been
her prime motives; but she was an ambitious woman and loved

knew how furious the King, his grandfather, got when his hunting was interfered with; the little duke was showing himself to be a chip off the old block.

[1] 'Except at his meals, the King is seeing no one but his family, the doctors,
and Mme de Maintenon. As for me, I only visit him now-a-days for a few minutes between a quarter to one and one o'clock, never any longer. The rest see
him three times a day. He shuts himself up in his study, and never sees members
of the Court. After meals we all go our own ways. There is no Court any more.
It is all vastly irregular; I have never seen anything like it in my whole life.
Everyone complains of boredom. The King is recovering from his anthrax.'
Letters of Madame to the Duchess of Hanover, 6 September 1696.

power, discreetly used. She was also worried about the King's health, and no doubt felt insecure. Unpopular as she was with most of the royal family, the thought of gaining the Duc de Bourgogne's affection may have struck her as a matter of prime importance.

For such reasons and probably many others she saw to it that Adelaide was surrounded by ladies who were bound to her by the strongest ties of friendship and advantage, or else of such limited understanding that they presented no danger. In the event, her choice could scarcely have been bettered, for Adelaide's ladies, though they would not have qualified as a beauty chorus and were not very young (the youngest was twenty-nine), were all of them kind, sensible women, not too old to enjoy active games and childish fun. What is more, they could all be trusted to give indulgent protection to the little princess whom they were appointed to serve. They gave her much more, for they gave her their love. Adelaide took to them at once; treating them as friends, with none of the arrogant rudeness that was the way of other royal princesses. For their part, they seem to have been quite bowled over by her simple kindness. They found her eager to co-operate, fair-minded, uncorrupted by the cynicism of court-life, with a capacity for giving affection, unrestrained by prudence or calculation, and showing a touching gratitude for the friendship they offered her. Indeed, she showed such precocious good judgment, such clear common sense, that her sudden flashes of spoiledness and selfishness took them aback, reminding them that she was, after all, no more than a young child.

The published list was as follows:

The Marquis de Dangeau, First Equerry (Chevalier d'Honneur);
The Duchesse du Lude, First Lady (Dame d'Honneur);[1]
The Comtesse de Mailly, Mistress of the Robes (Dame d'Atours);[2]
The Comte de Tessé, Master of the Horse.
Palace ladies, in the following order:

[1] The highest post of all, whose fortunate possessor took precedence over, and sat in a more comfortable chair than, any lady not of the blood royal, or the wife of a royal prince. She went everywhere with her princess and rode in the King's coach.

[2] The Dame d'Atours ranked below the Dame d'Honneur, but above the Dames du Palais. She had charge of everything connected with dress and toilet, and had the privilege of holding the saucer on which her princess placed her rings and other jewellery before going to bed.

Mme de Dangeau;
The Comtesse de Roucy;
Mme de Nogaret;
Mme d'O;
The Marquise du Châtelet;
Mme de Montgon;
and, as her personal maid, Mme Quentin.

The appointment of Dangeau, courtier, soldier, poet, gambler, author of the famous Court Journal, and the best dancer in France, was a surprise and an inspiration. He was the King's friend, and the same age; but until his marriage with that almost royal lady the Comtesse de Loewenstein, which allowed him, to everyone's fury, to couple the arms of the Palatinate with his own on the doors of his carriages, he had been regarded as a nobody, and something of a bounder. Yet everyone was disarmed by him; Mme de Montespan used to say in earlier days that no one could help liking him or teasing him. He did not mind; he was handsome, jolly, and had a way with him, and Mme de Maintenon saw that he would be able to make Adelaide laugh (not very difficult, as it turned out), and correct her without upsetting her. There was just the shadow of an excuse to appoint him because he was attached to the late Dauphine, and had been out of employment since her death. What was remarkable about Dangeau, apart from his famous journal, was that, without ever being suspected of cheating, he amassed so vast a fortune playing cards, that he was one of the very few courtiers able to play at the King's table against that reckless gambler Mme de Montespan, leaving her time and again with an empty purse, but no hard feelings. 'I watched him play,' said Mme de Sévigné, in 1676, 'and realised what innocents we all are in comparison with him. He concentrates on the game to the exclusion of all else, and neglects nothing which he can turn to his advantage. His judgment far outweighs his luck, and 200,000 francs in ten days, 100,000 écus every month, go into the credit side of his account book.'

His wife, aged thirty-two, was a great friend of Mme de Maintenon, and of the Saint-Simons also. Mme de Sévigné said of her: 'She was, of all the Court-ladies, the loveliest, the slenderest, the most charming, most nymphlike.' One is left with the impression that she was the nicest woman imaginable, without malice or arrogance.

Tessé's appointment was the reward of all his hard work, and both he and Adelaide were delighted. In the event, however, they were extremely disappointed because the King sent orders for him to remain in Turin until the next campaigning season, so as to keep an eye upon Victor Amadeus, and prevent any backsliding. Poor Tessé, who had to give up the idea of a triumphal return with his princess! Poor Adelaide, who was temporarily losing a good friend, on whom she was learning to rely!

Mme de Mailly, Mistress of the Robes, was Mme de Maintenon's first cousin, dependent on her, and deeply attached. She was a young widow, twenty-nine years old, and had been most unhappy in the service of that pea-hen the Duchesse de Chartres. She was thus thankful for release as well as gratified by promotion. Saint-Simon disapproved of the appointment, on the usual grounds of low birth—'a mere gentlewoman of Poitou, not from the top drawer, and without a shift to her back'; but even Saint-Simon had to admit that she was kind and sensible, and she proved a very good friend to Adelaide. Although Mme de Mailly did not shine at her job, and ran up enormous bills with little to show for them, her personal maid, who succeeded her six years later, was even worse, for she set out to line her own pockets, and the bills became astronomical.

Of the other ladies, Mme de Roucy, the daughter of one of Mme de Maintenon's oldest friends, was appointed only to please her mother,[1] who had been disappointed of the post of lady-in-waiting. She is polished off in the Memoirs as 'plain but amusing'. Mme de Nogaret, whom Adelaide called her 'Nanny', and came to love, was also 'exceedingly plain, fat, always laughing, but with an expression that redeemed all'. When, later, things became too much for poor Adelaide, she would (like many children in future generations) make a rush for her privy, seizing hold of Mme de Nogaret, and in that quiet and private place, would tell her all, and be cuddled and comforted.

Another appointment of tremendous benefit to Adelaide was that of Mme Quentin, as her personal maid. This was a thoroughly nice and motherly woman, wife of the King's barber-valet, and sister-in-law of La Vienne the King's masseur, who could get the King's ear

---

[1] Her mother, the Duchesse d'Arpajon, far from being placated, was perfectly furious. Not only was she losing the job she coveted, but also her daughter and companion, who would now be in the royal circle, leaving her mother in the cold. It is said that she never got over it, and died six years later of boredom and resentment.

at his least royal and most receptive moments. Mme Quentin knew everything worth knowing of the modes of the Court and Society, and of everyone that mattered. She also knew her place, and kept it politely but resolutely. No better guide could have been found for a newcomer to the Court, and she was able to put in a steadying word at quiet moments.

Adelaide seems to have genuinely liked all her ladies, and enjoyed their company. She chattered to them, calling them '*Mes puits*', 'my wells' (of silence, presumably), because they never made mischief. What she did not know was that every morning they told all to Mme de Maintenon. Had that lady been an enemy, or loved her less, Adelaide's story might have been very different. As it was, the road was smoothed for her, and many dangers and difficulties averted, of which she remained quite unaware.

The Court received news of the appointments with modified approval and relative calm. Only the choice for the lady-in-waiting provoked a rumpus. The Duchesse du Lude had not even been considered, for the Duchesse d'Arpajon, Mme de Maintenon's dear friend, was apparently more suitable, and had been thought a certainty. But Mme du Lude coveted the post, and by underhand intrigue had filched it. She had access, through her maid, to Nanon Balbien, Mme de Maintenon's ancient servant and crony, who wielded enormous influence, and, immensely dignified, kept herself invisible, and inaccessible, 'a kind of second-rank fairy', acting, very occasionally, behind the scenes. Mme du Lude's maid had known Nanon from the old days, when Mme de Maintenon was no more than the widow Scarron, and they used frequently to meet for little chats. They had a little chat regarding this matter also; Mme du Lude's wealth had a dazzling effect; sixty thousand livres changed hands, and the job was done. It came as a complete surprise.

The day before the list appeared, Monsieur (the King's brother), dying of curiosity, had been to see the King, who was sitting up but still in a good deal of pain and not in the best of tempers. His nights were rather better, but Racine's camp-bed was still in his bedroom, and the readings from Plutarch's *Lives* continued. They had got as far as Alexander the Great, but were not making much progress because the King kept on dropping off to sleep. Monsieur tried by every means to discover the names, one by one, but with little success, and they had reached the lady-in-waiting when he saw through one of the windows the Duchesse du Lude crossing the courtyard in her chair, on her return from mass. 'There is someone,' he said to the King, 'who is dying for the job.' 'Yes, indeed,' said the King, 'she would be marvellous for teaching the princess to paint and wear patches,' and followed that with a most disagreeable comment. Monsieur said no more, being perfectly convinced of her exclusion because, since his conversion, the King had become extremely severe over such matters. Next day when an usher came to tell Monsieur of the appointments, he, thinking that he knew best, believed her name to be no more than a rumour. After a crowd of people had entered his study, full of the same news, he was so much astonished that he told two or three of them all that had happened on the previous day. Thus the plot was unmasked and it was discovered that the whole affair had been settled only the evening before. 'That,' said Saint-Simon, 'is typical of the Court; a Nanon with power to sell the highest and most coveted posts, and a rich, high-born duchess, free, independent, without children, who is willing to sell herself into slavery for 60,000 livres.'

That is his story, but as so often where Mme de Maintenon is concerned, Saint-Simon is not entirely reliable. The Duchesse du Lude would appear to have had a very good case on her own merits, without needing Nanon's intervention. Not only was she a very great lady, both by birth and marriage, but she also was popular, and a famous hostess, admired for her exquisite manners and amiable disposition. She was still beautiful in 1696, with a fine presence[1] and, best of all, she was untouched by scandal even after spending all her life at the Court; moreover, she knew all that there was to know of the intricate ceremonial, and the degrees of rank. The worst of her was that she was fussy, always concerned with draughts and the dangers to her complexion. Until this moment, Mme de Maintenon had never seemed to care for her; as for the King, he had positively disliked her, and had not once invited her to Marly. Adelaide, though she wrote the contrary to her grandmother (perhaps because she knew her letters were opened), found her irritating and teased her unmercifully, so much so indeed that it was remarked upon. Mme du Lude, herself, was enchanted at her triumph and the new importance that it gave her, the unaccustomed intimacy with the King and Mme de Maintenon, the opportunity to shine. Though she may later have regretted her servitude, she filled her role with distinction, saved her unappreciative little charge

---

[1] Of the Duchesse du Lude, Mme de Sévigné's cousin Mme de Coulange said, 'The years flow over her like water over oilskin'.

from many blunders, and lent beauty and dignity to her household.[1]

At this point a quite unexpected storm blew up between Victor Amadeus and the King. It had been the firm rule that foreign princesses, coming to marry princes of the royal blood of France, should bring with them no one from their own countries. An exception had been made, with most disastrous consequences, for the late Dauphine, a German princess who spoke little French. The German lady who was allowed to accompany her, La Bessola, as she was known in France, gradually gained such an ascendancy over her mistress that, whenever either of them was ill, they shut themselves up together for days and nights on end, refusing to emerge, or to admit anyone, no matter who they might be.[2] Louis XIV fully imagined that the rule was well known and had been accepted by the Duke of Savoy, and he was therefore outraged to learn that three waiting-maids and a doctor were being sent with Adelaide. A stream of letters flowed between Barbezieux, at the War Ministry, and Tessé, at the Court of Savoy, who found himself in considerable difficulties because on this one occasion he could not bring himself to side wholeheartedly with the King. 'Monsieur de Savoie and Madame la Duchesse,' he wrote on 26 July, 'agree, in principle, with the King about the two or three women whom they wish to send to France with the princess. Yet she is only a child, and will cry at the least little thing, and they believe she will be sooner comforted by women whom she knows, if only to hand her her chamber-pot. Everyone finds comfort in not having to keep up appearances before servants whom they know more or less intimately.'

This brought a reply dictated by the King himself. 'You must stick to your orders and insist on her being unaccompanied by anyone from Savoy. The pain at parting will be just as great after the three or four months which they suggest. She will much more quickly become accustomed to the ladies given her here if there are no others better known to her. As for the doctor, when once he has informed those in my service regarding her constitution, his presence will be extremely unhelpful.'

---

[1] It was indeed a kind of slavery for Mme de Lude, without respite or appeal. Very soon after she joined Adelaide, the King ordered her to share her princess's bedroom, not a comfortable arrangement for an elderly duchess.

[2] There were rumours regarding their friendship which, so people said, was '*une affection excessive qui tenait de la passion*'. The poor Dauphine was plain, lonely, and unhappy, at the Court, where Monseigneur, after the first few years, paid little attention to her. She was fond of Mme de Maintenon, who was motherly to her, and used to brush her hair.

Tessé launched a fresh attack on Victor Amadeus, but found him inflexible. As a last resort, he showed him the King's letter, but all that this evoked was a cry of anguish from the paternal heart. 'This prince,' wrote Tessé to the King, 'who claims to be above personal considerations, was moved to tears, and I must confess that my own eyes filled also when, with a heavy sigh, he said, "I shall never see my daughter again, and when she reaches France, there will be no one she knows well to give her a chamber-pot and make her clean".' Tessé was in some perplexity. He was well aware that Victor Amadeus would find spies in the royal circle extremely useful; on the other hand, the father's cry seemed real enough, more especially since Tessé himself was full of a compassion for Adelaide, of which, at that moment, she did not feel the need. On the whole, he was inclined to give Victor Amadeus the benefit of the doubt. There can be no question that the little girl had a capacity for arousing lasting and deep affection in those people with whom she had dealings. To attribute it simply to inherited charm is not enough; she had a strong personality that revealed itself in later years, when adversity struck her. At the time when she went to France, people were disarmed by her freshness and friendliness, her eager desire to do her duty, her refusal to quarrel or make mischief. There was, too, in her public manner, a mixture of seriousness, shyness and reserve, which they found very moving. It was such a complete contrast with her irrepressible high spirits, when she was at leisure with her ladies.

Tessé certainly loved her; he ended his reply to the King with an impassioned appeal. 'Once again, I do entreat Your Majesty to allow a few waiting-women (no more than two) to accompany her, and the doctor who understands her health. All here are agreed that they should return in six months time or, at the very latest, after her marriage. I can assure Your Majesty that this trifle has caused me more distress and anxiety than far more difficult matters. Moreover, it truly appears to me that in all this Monsieur de Savoie has no other purpose than a misplaced tenderness for his daughter. She is still a young child who will cry, and the prince seems unable to overcome his, perhaps rather puerile, fear that she will need some familiar servant to save her embarrassment in the early days, at moments of weakness, dirtiness, or indisposition. In every other respect he thinks and speaks in exact accord with Your Majesty's desires, and accepts all you say as being reason itself. What he fears most is that his daughter, when she arrives at your Court, will be transported in such an ecstasy of delight that she may, so to speak, forget the mechanism of the human body unless some intimate woman is there to calm her in such moments of weakness.'

That was the kind of language to which Louis XIV was accustomed, and it had its effect. Yet he still had his suspicions, and Tessé's less tactful reference to possible tears brought a very frosty reply, dictated by the King himself. 'It would be far better for the princess that any tears occasioned by the parting should be dried before she meets me.'

There were other communications from Tessé in the same vein; then there arrived a letter in the King's own august hand that seemed to put an end to the whole affair. 'I had reason to suppose that, when he knew my mind, the Duke of Savoy would order all the women and other servants attached to the princess to return to Turin as soon as she came under the care of those ladies whom I have appointed to attend her. Since I now learn that he still speaks of letting them remain, you must state clearly that my desire for her happiness forbids me to consent. The Duke of Savoy himself says that he knows what disastrous consequences result from such misplaced compassion for princesses going to foreign countries. The pain his daughter may suffer at parting from the women who brought her up will certainly be forgotten when she arrives at Fontainebleau. She will learn, during the journey, to be happy with the ladies charged with her care, and the Duke of Savoy may rest assured that every attention will be paid to her upbringing once she arrives at my Court.

'A skilled hand will complete the task of forming the intelligence, of which the princess already gives proof. She will have the knowledge and enlightenment becoming to her future rank, and examples of the most perfect virtue will daily inspire her to love her duties.[1] I have reason to believe that she will be guided by the principles thus instilled into her, and she will be taught those others that will ensure her a happy life. I persist in concluding that she would be greatly harmed by the counsels of women who accompanied her from Savoy, and since I am firmly resolved to send them all back, together with any officers, no matter what their rank, you must make every effort to persuade the Duke of Savoy to forbid their

---

[1] Torcy, in his accompanying letter: 'I do not think I need explain to whom His Majesty is referring. A far less perceptive mind than yours could guess who is to take charge of the education of Madame la Princesse de Savoie.' (9 September 1696)

going further than the Pont-de-Beauvoisin.[1] Indeed, if he imagines that his daughter will be distressed at parting from them, it will be far better to allow her time to recover during the journey, than to cause her that unhappiness at the moment when she meets me.'

The correspondence then ceased, but Victor Amadeus stubbornly persisted, and in the end seems to have won, for Adelaide, when she finally reached Fontainebleau, had in her retinue both her doctor and Mme Marquet, her confidential maid. The doctor's services were not required and he very soon returned but, strangely enough, the maid was a distinct success, and two months later the duke's ambassador[2] was writing to his master: 'His Majesty has been speaking to me of Mme Marquet, saying that she is a quiet, sensible woman who has asked permission to return to her family. She may do as she best pleases because there is no fear of her giving bad advice, such as the infamous Bessola gave to Madame la Dauphine, which caused the King so much unhappiness.'

The oddest thing about the whole affair is that Duchess Anne, a far better mother than Victor Amadeus was a father, attached no importance to the issue, and asked Tessé to give the King a message to that effect. Odder still, Adelaide herself said that she did not mind one way or the other. Perhaps she was too much excited to care; perhaps they had so instilled into her the need to please the King that she was determined to obey him at all costs; perhaps, since she was precociously open to reason, she may have seen his point. On the other hand, she may have said no more than the truth, for although her affection for the people around her was quite sincere, and her goodwill all-embracing, her love did not always go very deep.

The great matters of the household and the retinue now being settled, the King fixed the day of their departure for the frontier of

---

[1] The Duchesse du Lude also received orders to 'turn back at the frontier everyone who has accompanied the princess, no matter what the uproar'. It must have been embarrassing for her, more especially since she was likewise commanded to return everything Adelaide was wearing, even down to her pocket handkerchief. 'France wants her naked,' wrote the ambassador to Saint-Thomas.

[2] The ambassador was the Comte de Govon whom Victor Amadeus had sent to Versailles immediately after the signing of the treaty. Saint-Simon says that he was 'a clever man, witty, and polite, made for life at Court, and extremely popular with everybody. The King took a liking to him and distinguished him with invitations to Marly, something he had never done for any foreign minister, and never did for any other'.

Savoy. He was feeling a good deal better, though still not out of pain; but his neck was healing; he was able to dress, and Racine and his camp-bed had been removed from the royal bedroom. Before the ladies left, the King had a long interview with them, impressing on them the honour and the responsibility, and the great trust reposed in them. 'You are old friends,' he said, as he bade them farewell, 'from now onwards you must be united.' Louis XIV believed in doing things in style, and this was certainly a moment for splendour. He arranged for the Duchesse du Lude to take truly magnificent presents of jewellery and precious stones for Adelaide's retiring household, and a princely sum of money for distribution among the officers and servants who had accompanied her from Turin. At the last moment he added a further very large sum for Adelaide herself to give in charity on her way through France.

It was a long procession that, on Tuesday, 11 September, set out for the Pont-de-Beauvoisin. The Comte de Govon, Madame Royale's equerry, who passed it on the road, reported that it was 'in every way fit for a queen' and far more numerous than the one sent to escort Madame Royale to the frontier, in 1675. 'They are preparing to receive her like the dove with the olive branch,' he added. It was, indeed, a great company, six hundred people, all in royal coaches, and in the private carriages of the ladies and officials of the household. Five royal coaches headed the procession. In the first sat the Duchesse du Lude and other ladies; in the second the haughty Comte de Brionne,[1] acting as the King's representative, and Dangeau. The coach destined for Adelaide came third, draped with a violet cover and lined with violet silk because the Court was in mourning for the old Duchesse de Guise.[2] The stream of equipages that followed contained the King's secretary the Sieur Desgranges, his personal physician, his surgeon-in-chief, his apothecary, many officers and pages, and the servants of the King's kitchen. The party was escorted by an unusually large detachment of the household cavalry, and a company of the King's own bodyguard. The list of lower officers of the King's household who were sent with the reception party comprised: a chaplain and clerk; a master of horse and his deputy; 6 pages; 10 footmen; coachmen, postillions,

---

[1] Henri de Lorraine, Comte de Brionne (1661–1712). Like the other princes and princesses of Lorraine, he carried on a running fight to take precedence over the French dukes.

[2] Elizabeth d'Orléans, daughter of Gaston d'Orléans, and the King's first cousin. French Kings wore violet mourning for members of the royal family.

and grooms as necessary; a major-domo, 3 gentlemen-in-waiting
and their lackeys; 8 waiting maids; a controller; 2 ushers; 2 tap-
estry-hangers; 3 furniture removers; 25 officers from the Gobelin
factory, as many from the King's kitchen, and a great number of
serving men; 4 officers for firewood and kindling; 37 officers from
the fruit and vegetable larder, the bakery, the butlers' pantry, and
the household's kitchen; a baggage-master and his assistant; 2
billeting officers and 4 couriers; an officer of the watch; 2 mounted
brigadiers and 2 under-officers; an officer and 8 men of the Swiss
Guard; an officer of the watch and 2 guards of the provost-
marshal's establishment; 4 door-keepers; also a small orchestra
to play during Adelaide's meals. If all these were considered
necessary to accompany a mere princess, the thought of what
the King's own journeys must have cost is horrifying. Partly,
perhaps for that reason, during the last twenty-five years of Louis
XIV's reign it was only the princes of the blood who joined the
campaigns and they took with them only their personal servants.
It was a sign of retrenchment.

The deputation could scarcely have been more splendid had the
King himself been making a progress. Moreover, Desgranges, as
master of ceremonies, had orders to accord to Adelaide a rank and
precedence far higher than that which she could rightfully claim as
a 'foreign princess'; for instance, she was to eat alone and not with
her ladies, and to be served by the King's own officers. In every
room, she alone would sit in a chair with arms, while everyone else,
no matter what their rank or age, would be accommodated with a
backless stool. As a foreign princess, she had no rank in France,
and would normally have sat on a *tabouret* in the Duchesse du
Lude's presence, and far below her at the dinner table. So it would
have continued at the Court, until her marriage to the Duc de
Bourgogne made her the first lady of France, and raised her, in
precedence, above all other ladies, even above the King's sister-in-
law, the redoubtable Madame. Adelaide's rank and standing were
thus urgent matters, requiring much consideration, yet needing a
quick settlement, if only for the sake of the provincial nobility and
the civic authorities in the towns and villages through which the
procession would pass.

The King consulted Monsieur, who said that Madame would not
mind stepping down, for it would be simplest to treat Adelaide as
though she were already the 'First Lady', and so it was decided.
Madame said, 'Now it has been resolved that she will have pre-

cedence of me, it matters little whether it is sooner or later; except for precedence, no other benefits have accrued to me from being the first lady in the land.' She changed her mind after a few days and took offence, perhaps because the King did not thank her.[1] The King's daughters were also much annoyed and attacked Monsieur who went into a black sulk, made worse when he discovered that Adelaide, his own granddaughter, was not to be allowed to mix with the immoral company at his court of Saint-Cloud.

The reception party, nearing the frontier, were thankful to have the matter of precedence settled and done with; they would be spared from making endless trivial decisions, all of them time-consuming, all liable to cause ill-feeling, envy, and resentment in some person or other. But, indeed, the King seemed to have thought of everything; he was a man whose chief delight lay in the details of a plan, and everyone had precise orders. The Comte de Brionne, in particular, was well coached. He was to tell Adelaide 'how eagerly the King looked forward to her coming, and his real joy in hearing of her good qualities'. He was to say that already the King felt he loved her dearly, and that he meant to prove his love in all possible ways; and Brionne was to impress over and over again upon Adelaide that, even before her marriage to his grandson, she would find in Louis XIV not only a great King, but a very loving and tender grandfather.

Meanwhile the line of coaches had been trundling along at a snail's pace. It was not until 30 September that it reached Lyons, where the party were greeted with fireworks, illuminations, cheering crowds, and loyal addresses. Dangeau says that, at this point, the Duchesse du Lude displayed her exquisite manners and high breeding by begging to be excused from hearing the speeches, asking, like the great lady she was, for them to be reserved for the princess on the return journey.[2] She did condescend, however, to accept as gifts numerous boxes of delicious crystallised fruit.

---

[1] Later, in the same letter to the Duchess of Hanover, she said: 'The love he bears that woman [Mme de Maintenon] is quite astonishing. Everyone in Paris believes that the marriage will be proclaimed and that she will take her rank as soon as the peace is concluded. That is another reason why I consider myself lucky to be no longer the first lady. At least I shall be walking behind someone well-bred, and not be forced to hand that old garbage-bin her shift and gloves.'

[2] Good manners, indeed; but at the age of fifty-three, after a long, dusty, bumpy journey, one may imagine that the Duchesse du Lude was thankful for any excuse to seek her bed and repair the ravages to her complexion.

They had expected to remain only a day or two at Lyons, waiting for news that Adelaide had left Turin on her way to the frontier; but there were long delays and, as often happens, contradictory orders. They were still waiting on 6 October, and Dangeau was writing to Torcy, 'This morning we were all ready to start, and the ladies were considerably upset at losing two hours' sleep. Most of them have now gone back to bed; but others, who had their beds sent on ahead, are greatly inconvenienced; yet they all prefer to remain here until tomorrow, rather than go on to wait at Pont-de-Beauvoisin'.

There had been delays for all kinds of aggravating reasons; this final one was caused by the fireworks and celebrations, and the unusually lengthy poems and addresses to which Adelaide had had to listen, in the loyal towns and villages, on the Savoyard side of the frontier. The local gentry had turned out to greet her in splendid new uniforms, mounted on beautiful horses. There had been theatrical performances and contests in oratory, with appeals to the gods and goddesses, nymphs and zephyrs, to shed their blessings upon her and her bridegroom. Even the birth of Louis XV was predicted, who would grow up to be 'a Mars in battle, with the face of Cupid the God of Love'. All these rejoicings were, no doubt, highly gratifying to her parents; but to Adelaide herself, at ten and a half, they would seem likely to have been tiring and something of a trial to her patience, though she probably enjoyed the fireworks.

4

The Journey

TESSÉ MEANWHILE had been having an exasperating time with Victor Amadeus, who could not, or would not, bring himself to name the date of Adelaide's departure. Day after day, he had produced some fresh excuse, until even Tessé lost patience with him. 'Regarding the departure of Madame la Princesse de Savoie,' he wrote to the King, 'it is the way they have in this country of putting everything off until the last moment; and Monsieur le Duc de Savoie acting on that principle, or from parental affection, desires me to remind Your Majesty that his daughter is very young, and the season very far advanced. He wonders whether it would not be best to wait until the spring before making her cross the Alps. I offered no hopes as to that, seeing that all she will need is six vests and a warm cloak to protect her from the elements. I pressed and shall continue to press him for her departure, and I beg Your Majesty to send me word that your eagerness to see the princess is such that you can accept no further delay.'

Louis XIV responded nobly. In letter after letter, he demanded to be given a date, finally expressing his intention of going all the way from Versailles to Fontainebleau, to meet Adelaide on her journey. At that season of the year, he said, the damp of the forest was bad for his health, and he hoped not to be obliged to prolong the excursion. That was enough. 'After some painful sessions, which he and the duchess spent weeping together,' wrote Tessé, 'the Prince sent for me to say that the Princess would leave whenever Your Majesty gives the word. Although affairs in this country are not easily brought to a head, I believe that Your Majesty may safely order the reception party and the coaches to go to Pont-de-Beauvoisin, though I conclude that the Princess could not depart before the first days of October.'

Policy no doubt entered into it. While Adelaide remained in

Savoy, her father still had some influence with Louis XIV. On the other hand, in spite of Victor Amadeus's exasperation with Duchess Anne because of her doglike devotion and her nerve-storms, and his ferocious quarrels with Madame Royale, their letters show them to have been an affectionate family, and the parting with Adelaide was a grief which they were inclined to put off as long as possible.

The day finally appointed was 7 October. During the interval, there were banquets, receptions, illuminations, fireworks along the river, dancing in the streets, and fountains running wine. On the sixth, while all Turin was on holiday, Adelaide stood for hours, grave, smiling, a little shy, beneath a silken canopy, in Madame Royale's great audience chamber. She wore a dress of cloth of silver with a long train, and listened, one after another to complimentary addresses from the Nuncio, the Council, the Senators in scarlet robes, the City Fathers in black, and the guilds and corporations of the city, dressed in their very best. When the last speech, couched in most elegant and flowery Latin, was finished, all the members of the various deputations stepped forward to be presented and to kiss her hand. It was probably the grandest moment of her life. All the reports speak of her dignity and her graciousness; but what a test of patience and good manners for a child who, off duty, was darting here, there and everywhere.[1]

That same evening, her father kissed her goodbye. He did not stay to see her go, next day. Perhaps he dreaded an emotional scene; perhaps he could not bear to see her drive away. She cried bitterly when she kissed him and her sister for the last time; but recovered her poise when she said farewell to the ladies of her mother's and grandmother's households. The ladies had probably been asked to restrain themselves, but at least one of them shed tears, for two years later Adelaide wrote to the Comtesse de Grésy, a member of Duchess Anne's household, 'I have not written to you since I became Duchesse de Bourgogne; but I love you still the same. You were the only one of my mother's ladies who cried when I left home and, believe me, I shall never forget that.'

Next day, after the company had been to mass, a line of coaches and carriages was drawn up at the door of the ducal palace. Adelaide, in tears, stepped into the great violet travelling-coach with her governesses, the Princesse de La Cisterna and Mme Des-

---

[1] Saint-Simon said of her after her death that her nymphlike grace carried her everywhere, like a whirlwind, filling many places at once, and setting them all alive and in movement.

noyers, and rolled away on her long journey to Versailles. Her mother and grandmother had not intended to go with her, but the little girl had been so much upset at parting that they impulsively followed her to Avigliano, the end of the first stage, so as to be with her one more night, and watch over her while she slept. Many ladies and gentlemen of the court came after them in carriages and on horseback, and, on the following day, the farewells were a great deal more cheerful.

The rest of the journey was comparatively uneventful. The Comte de Vernon, her master of ceremonies, and the opposite number to Desgranges who acted on the French side, reported thus to her father (13 October 1696):

'Most illustrious, most excellent Lord, my most beloved master. This evening the most serene princess has arrived at Chambéry in perfect health, having met with no other mishap than the accidental entry of a gnat into her left eye, near Montmélian, which has caused her some annoyance but little loss of time. Although this evening she still suffers somewhat from the effects, I trust that by tomorrow she will have entirely recovered ...

The demonstrations of love and affection have been all that one could possibly desire, and in this town greater than on any previous occasion; I shall reserve the full description for an audience. On Monday, the Princess will sleep at Echelles, where she will breakfast on Tuesday morning, and will reach Pont-de-Beauvoisin on Tuesday evening. These two easy stages have been arranged in order that the Princess may not be too tired on her arrival. We consider that it would not be to her advantage to cover the remainder of the way in one long journey. May I beg Your Excellency to honour me with a continuance of your powerful protection. I think you will believe in my respect and devotion, which will endure as long as I live.

> Your Excellency's very humble, very obedient,
> very grateful servant.'

Adelaide soon began to feel more cheerful, and perhaps to enjoy her great position. When they reached Montmélian, the frontier fortress which the French had captured during the war and were still occupying, the governor paraded the garrison for her inspection and, according to the custom, begged her to choose a password for the day. She seems to have behaved heroically, at that point, for drying her tears, she turned upon him a ravishing smile, stoutly declaiming what must surely have been a set-speech: 'I choose Saint-Louis, because from now onwards he is my patron Saint.'

At Chambéry, Adelaide was lodged in the old palace of the dukes of Savoy. It was on the boundary between France and Savoy, and it was from there, at the centre of the humpbacked bridge over the river Guiers, by the neighbouring village of Pont-de-Beauvoisin, that she was to meet her French household and cross the line into her new country, severing the last links with her old home. So far all had gone according to plan; and when Desgranges arrived to take charge of the important ceremonies of farewell, welcome, and introduction, it seemed that only details remained to be settled. It was, however, of paramount importance that neither France nor Savoy should encroach upon the other's territory, or gain the smallest advantage that could be used later as a sign of superiority. Difficulty piled upon difficulty, and when the bridge was found to be too narrow to take two coaches side by side, the problem, for a time, appeared insoluble, and it looked as though Adelaide would be doomed to permanent immobilisation on the wrong side of the border.

There was, however, a precedent, for, in 1684, Victor Amadeus had crossed that same narrow bridge into France to fetch his young wife away. Hopes were raised; but although, at the time, his action had been hailed as the eagerness of a young lover, it was later condemned as a shocking breach of etiquette. Desgranges pointed out that there had been some excuse on that occasion, since Duchess Anne had already been married by proxy, and was thus already a Savoyard, whereas Adelaide was a foreigner, merely the betrothed of the Duc de Bourgogne. It took genius to find a solution, with the brilliant notion of backing the French coach up the steep slope of the narrow, hump-backed bridge, so that while the back wheels were in Savoy, the horses and front wheels remained in France, and the doors opened onto neutral territory above the exactly central line.

At this moment, M. de Brionne himself created trouble by advancing a claim for special treatment, on account of his rank. He was a Prince of Lorraine, a so-called foreign prince, and on that pretext demanded equal rank with Adelaide, and the right to an exactly similar armchair on which he would sit whenever she was seated—notwithstanding that, after her marriage to a Grandson of France, he would be allowed nothing whatsoever to sit on in her presence. He continued to be obstructive, until the King's order regarding her status arrived in the nick of time to close all argument.

Nonetheless he took offence and was preparing to be thoroughly unpleasant to all concerned, when Desgranges was inspired so to arrange matters that whenever M. de Brionne and Adelaide met no chairs were forthcoming, and both had to stand. Etiquette was thus satisfied; the princess could once more be set in motion, and nothing remained but to order for this ten-year-old child, as soon as she set foot in France, royal salutes, the ringing of church bells, reviews of troops, the very highest honours which any princess could be accorded, with the Duchesse du Lude, a sure guide to direct her faltering steps, the only person allowed to sit, even on a *tabouret*, in her presence.

Adelaide had arrived at Chambéry on the evening of the thirteenth. A long procession of coaches containing the local nobility had driven out to meet her on the road, and a troop of eighty young gentlemen in new scarlet coats, mounted on fine horses with scarlet saddle-cloths to match. There were illuminations, and the most dazzling fireworks that Adelaide had yet seen. All along the streets troops in their best uniforms lined the way, and in the courtyard of the old castle a great company of ladies and gentlemen were waiting to be presented. They said that she greeted them *benignissimamente* (with the utmost graciousness and kindness), and shyly whispered her thanks for their congratulations.

Next morning, after mass, she had stood and listened attentively to flowery Latin addresses from the bishop and clergy of Chambéry and, in the afternoon, had endured a chain of ceremonies, like the ones at Turin, as the Senate of Chambéry, the Chamber of Commerce, the members of the various guilds and corporations had advanced one after another to deliver their harangues; but were not, on this occasion, allowed to kiss her sore little hand.[1] At three o'clock, in the afternoon of 16 October, she had reached Pont-de-Beauvoisin and the frontier, and was taken to the Carmelite convent, to change her dress for the ceremony to come, to have a rest, and enjoy a collation.

They did not leave her quiet for long, only the time needed for the mounted gentlemen to line the road, with a couple of trumpeters to sound a fanfare, and a beautifully embroidered standard, displaying the arms of Savoy. At four o'clock, in a carrying chair, preceded by footmen, and escorted by a detachment of the ducal

[1] The audiences at Turin had made her hand sore, and Desgranges had ordered that on the remainder of the journey only the highest-born of each group should be allowed to kiss it.

bodyguard, Adelaide started on the short journey to the bridge.
Behind her, in other chairs, came the Princesse de La Cisterna and
Mme Desnoyers, with a large contingent of Piedmontese nobility
following on horseback.

At the end of the bridge, Adelaide stepped down; one of her
father's pages took up her long train, and she walked the few steps
up the steep slope towards the royal coach perched upon the sum-
mit. At the further end, beginning to advance towards her, was the
Comte de Brionne, with Dangeau, the Duchesse du Lude, and the
ladies who were to be members of her new household, her guides
and playfellows, in the strange, glorious, frightening world that
would soon confront her. On the French side of the bridge, as far
as the centre, the King's bodyguard with their kettledrums and
trumpets lined the way, and, as Adelaide set her toe for the first
time on French soil, there came a burst of cheering, to the accompaniment of a fanfare, a roll of drums, and deafening cannon-
fire, all designed to honour one particular little girl, because she
carried in her body the possibility of continuance for the line of
the Bourbon Kings of France.

The momentous ceremony proceeded; the page holding her
train handed it, sobbing as he did so, to one of the King's pages[1];
the Marquis de Dronero stepped forward with the Comte de
Vernon, holding Adelaide's hands. M. de Brionne advanced to
present Dangeau, the Duchesse du Lude, and the other ladies. He
and Dangeau then took her hands and helped her into the coach,
with the Duchesse du Lude and the Princesse de La Cisterna
sitting beside her. A mishap occurred at this point because Mme
Desnoyers was prevented from entering, and was extremely mortified. It was the fault of Tessé, who had mistakenly cited her as
the 'under-governess', thus ranking her no higher than a servant;
but the Comte de Vernon immediately put matters right, explaining
that she was governess-proper, with the privilege of eating with her
princess, and Mme de Dangeau invited her into the second coach
with such charming courtesy that all her distress was forgotten.

To the sound of cheering and shouts of '*Vive le Roi et Madame
la Princesse de Savoie*', on the French side, and sobs and cries from
the Piedmontese left on the other, Adelaide proceeded to the house
where she was to spend her first night in France. One oversight,
deliberately engineered by M. de Brionne, spoiled the stately har-

[1] He was said to have shed 'abundant tears' which was 'noticed with all the
attention merited by that gentleman's kind heart'.

mony. Still furious that his opposite number, the Marquis de Dronero, should be a man of lower rank, he cancelled the order for a third coach, lest he be obliged to sit beside him. Thus when they reached the French bank, he and Dangeau mounted their horses, leaving the unfortunate Dronero to follow on foot. The snub was understood as an insult typical of the Lorraines and caused much offence.

A crowd of twenty thousand people, or so they said in the gazettes, was present when Marie Adelaide, Princess of Savoy, stepped from the coach and was conducted to her apartments. The *Mercure de France* reported that she appeared not the least nervous or shy, and, that when the officers of her escort were presented to her one after another, she smiled on them all with most genuine kindness. 'From what she said,' continued the report, 'and from her general appearance, she seems much older than her age. She has a beautiful figure and great amiability. Her face shows her noble birth, with a lovely complexion, and a colouring that is all her own. Her eyes are very fine, her hair a beautiful *blond cendré*.[1] Among her many charms, the princess shows a readiness to please, and a liveliness of mind that are truly astonishing.'

After a short rest they all went in to supper. Adelaide sat at table with the Princesse de La Cisterna and Mme Desnoyers, while the Duchesse du Lude and M. de Brionne headed tables each laid for twelve guests, chosen from among the ladies and gentlemen of Savoy. Dronero had been so much hurt by his ill-treatment that he had thought of refusing to attend the supper; but in the end he came, and wrote next day to Victor Amadeus that he had seen Adelaide gossiping with her French ladies as happily as though she had known them all her life.

The ice was further broken when the Comte de Brionne distributed the King's magnificent presents, which staggered the Piedmontese officers and ladies by their costliness and beauty. The Princesse de La Cisterna had a piece of jewellery worth 31,000 livres; the Marquis de Dronero a box of fifty diamonds worth 14,000; Mme Desnoyers a set of bracelets worth 11,000, and the Comte de Vernon, diamonds worth 8,000. That, at least, was the actual cost of the stones; 'but,' wrote Desgranges to Torcy, 'you may well imagine that the price of them was not mentioned, and

[1] The disagreement about the colour of her hair was probably caused by the colour-rinses and dyes then in fashion. In France, people called it chestnut-brown.

that I raised the amount somewhat to anyone who was curious.' All
the rest of Adelaide's retinue and escort, down to the lowest of the
servants, received a present of money. No one was forgotten; all, or
nearly all, were highly gratified.

As in all the fairy-tales, in spite of every precaution, someone was
displeased, as usual someone of vital importance, in this case, the
Comte de Maffei, Victor Amadeus's first equerry and bosom friend—
the very last person whom Desgranges would have wished to offend.
Horrible to relate, however, when presented with a handsome piece
of silver plate, he had returned it, saying with extreme haughtiness
that, unhappily, it was beneath his rank to accept silver or money.
When pressed, he had allowed it to be known that a diamond-hilted
sword would not be unacceptable, but the last sword had already
been given away. The situation seemed desperate until Dangeau
stepped forward, offering his own sword, which had a particularly
beautiful and costly hilt. That solved the problem, and Maffei was
later observed to be handing it round in a state of ecstasy for the
admiration of the company.

'As for M. de Dangeau,' wrote Desgranges to Torcy, 'I cannot
speak too highly of him, he is charming to everybody, everywhere
at once, doing the honours with much grace; everyone is delighted
with him. If I may say so, he is a man of the utmost goodwill, with
a most agreeable manner, very capable of filling a high post.'

That night, the Duchesse du Lude once again showed her exquisite manners by waiving her rights and allowing the Princesse de la
Cisterna and Mme Marquet, Adelaide's old friends, to sleep beside
the little girl. Next morning, 17 October, the Duchess accepted all
her responsibilities. Adelaide was heroically brave, she even remembered, when letters from the Court were brought her, to ask Mme du
Lude to open them, saying that it would not become one of her age
to open letters without first showing them for inspection—'a
courtesy which,' according to the *Mercure de France*, 'was accompanied by compliments and tokens of budding affection from
both ladies.' Adelaide may also have recollected that royal persons
were trained never to open letters, accept presents of gloves, or
smell the flowers offered to them for fear of poison.

When the last goodbyes had to be said, the Duchesse du Lude
suggested cutting them very short so as to spare her distress. But
although Adelaide was very near to tears, she insisted on seeing
separately all her Piedmontese ladies and gentlemen, and her servants. One of them tactlessly asked her if she would not miss her

friends and her old life. She hesitated, murmured something inaudible, and finally admitted that she had hated leaving her dolls and playthings. This innocent reply so much touched the King that he sent special orders to Paris, for dolls and games of such supreme beauty and charm that they would put the old ones quite out of her mind.

The farewell to the Princesse de La Cisterna was dreadful for her, and she broke down completely; but, when it was over, she turned smiling to the Duchesse du Lude, saying, 'Now I won't be unhappy any more.' She also sent Tessé a message, when a French officer on his staff arrived to welcome her to France. 'She did me the honour to say,' he wrote to the King, 'that she had remembered my telling her not to mind if she cried; and that she had cried very much. But she had also remembered my adding that when she ceased crying she must laugh, recollecting her great position, and how happy she was going to be.' No wonder if the King and Mme de Maintenon were moved.

Then the great travelling coach, with the violet lining and the eight horses, drew up at the door. The four other coaches for the ladies and gentlemen of the household, and the conveyances for the chaplains, doctors, surgeons, butlers, secretaries, cooks, valets and servants, lined up behind. Adelaide stepped in, to sit between the Duchesse du Lude and Mme de Dangeau. The doors slammed; the footmen climbed aboard; the jingling mounted escort formed up around them, and they set off on the second part of the long journey to Versailles, through Lyons, where they spent three nights, and stopping thereafter at Roanne, Moulins, Nevers, and La Charité.

It was a royal progress, the intention of which was to display the new member of the royal family to her future subjects—and to acquaint her with local dignitaries and conditions. It was the occasion for ceremonial entrées, loyal addresses, flowers and garlands strewn along the way, feasting and dancing, illuminations and fireworks. Adelaide was feeling much more cheerful. At ten years old unhappiness does not usually last very long; the French ladies were kind and amusing; Dangeau was unbelievably jolly, and the excitement was intense, as they passed through village after village, with church bells pealing, young lords galloping out to meet her, cheering crowds lining the streets and the roads outside, sometimes for a distance of two miles in both directions. What was more, she had bags of money to throw among the children and the poor, and could

watch them scrambling to pick up the gold and silver pieces. On
the long stretches between the towns, they played spillikins, at
which Adelaide was adept, and in the evenings, at her lodgings,
they all, even the Duchesse du Lude, played blind-man's buff with,
according to Dangeau, 'much activity, and even more laughter'.

They stopped for three nights, from 17 to 20 October, at Lyons,
where everything was formal, and crowded with ceremonies.
Adelaide's courage and good manners never failed, but despite the
vigilant care of Mme du Lude she was getting very tired. She
stood to receive interminable harangues, dressed in white and silver,
beneath a silken canopy; she smiled on each speaker when they had
finished, gently murmuring, 'I shall tell the King of the honour that
you have done me'; she visited churches and convents, and was
received everywhere with ceremony and musical honours; she was
complimented by the noble company of the Count-canons of Lyons
who, to be so appointed, needed to show sixteen quarterings. At the
Carmelite Convent she gave the habit to a novice on her profession;
at the Jesuit College she heard the boys recite verses composed in
her honour by the Fathers, and did not forget to beg them to be
given a holiday. She was at all times splendidly dressed, sparkling
with jewels and, in her hair, which was powdered in the French
fashion, she wore sprays of diamonds.

Time and again she had to show herself to the eager crowd, for
whose gratification the Duchesse du Lude made her drive in her
coach along the ramparts, amidst wild cheering. In the middle of
the day, she dined alone, and in public, wearing a rose-pink dress.
There was the same ritual as for the King's State dinner, 'with the
bâton and the cadenas',[1] as Desgranges wrote to Torcy. Mme du
Lude served her on silver dishes, with that gliding gait and supremely
graceful curtseys that were the admiration of visitors to the Court of
France. The King's personal steward directed with his bâton, at each
stage of the service, tapping the plates that were to be handed to
Adelaide, following an ancient tradition supposed to ward off evil
spells. The doors of the room were left wide open, in order that the
public might enter and see the glory of France and the splendour
of its Court. Beneath the thousands of candles in the lustres and

---

[1] The *bâton* was the wand of office, with which the major-domo indicated the
dishes to be served. The cadenas was a locked box, containing the table silver
(knife, forks, spoons) of a royal person. It was placed before them on the table,
and was one way of protecting them from poison. It was also a much prized
mark of rank.

candelabra, the flashing diamonds, the magnificent silk dresses, the brilliance of the men's coats and uniforms, the ordered movements of the attendants, presented a scene of great beauty, while the entire orchestra of the Lyons opera house played during the meal. The people of Lyons had probably never imagined such splendour.

As for Adelaide, whose table manners, in private, were not her strongest point, she behaved as a princess should, eating daintily and moderately, receiving with politeness and suitable gravity the ministrations of the Duchesse du Lude, remembering her training, smiling on those presented to her with that friendly, disarming smile, that was particularly her own, and won her affection everywhere. At this period of her life, she was quite unspoiled, and her French household expressed their gratitude to her parents for the way in which she had been trained.[1]

In the evening they drove out to see the illuminations and returned to watch the fireworks. Every window in the great square had been covered with paper, painted with the arms of France and Savoy, and behind each window a flaming torch gave the effect of stained glass. The fireworks were the best that had ever been seen. At this point one may imagine Adelaide and her ladies enjoying the innumerable and beautifully decorated boxes of crystallised fruit, and other sweets, that were pressed on them in every town and village.

During the remainder of the time at Lyons, there were still more addresses to be received, including one, delivered by the Chief Magistrate, which was greatly admired for its elevated sentiments and refined language. 'Madame,' he had concluded, 'Heaven could have reserved for you no higher destiny . . ., for you bring to an armed Europe the long-desired peace which for so long has been banished by the fury of war. With that thought in mind, Madame, all France prepares to rejoice in the fruits of a union of the two noblest bloodstreams in the world, and we are truly happy to be first to demonstrate the joy which you bring to the entire nation.' The language may sound flowery, but it was a time when oratory was the fashion and rhetoric greatly admired. The compliments were not empty flattery, but a true expression of the general feeling,

[1] Dangeau and the ladies, writing back to Mme de Maintenon, all spoke, as did Saint-Simon, of her eagerness to co-operate with them, and of the great help they were receiving from her careful upbringing. As Saint-Simon said, 'It had taught her the only way to be happy at our Court'.

for over and over again in letters, gazettes, and ambassadors' dispatches, Adelaide is described as a 'dove of peace', the 'long-awaited olive branch', the 'Princess of Peace', bringing relief to a people rendered almost desperate by the hardships and miseries of war.

By this time she had become something of an expert in receiving harangues, and dealing with nervous speakers. When, at her departure from Lyons, the Lieutenant-Governor addressed her at the door of her coach there was an embarrassing moment when he dried up completely. Nothing daunted, Adelaide rose ever so slightly in her seat, and gently whispered the concluding sentence, thanking him afterwards with such a kind and sympathetic smile that he was her slave for life. Dangeau said that she managed the mishap with a grace and presence of mind that would have become a much older and more experienced lady. His praise of her had, until that incident, been carefully measured. He had written to Torcy that although she appeared exceedingly amiable, he would say no more for fear of saying too much. He now allowed himself more freedom, describing her good sense, and quick wits, her grace and charm of manner, her tactful greetings and replies. He stressed also that, beneath her public manner, she was still very much a child, full of laughter, and with a great love of children's games.

Mme de Maintenon was not much impressed by the glowing reports. She wrote to Dangeau 'we are of course delighted to have news of the Princess, and all the letters from your little court make us impatient to see her', adding that she was glad to hear that Adelaide was still a little childish, 'since the many tales of her precocity have somewhat alarmed us'. There was not very much else for Adelaide's household to rave about, for the little girl was almost exhausted by the fatigues of the journey and her constant public appearances. Perhaps the Duchesse du Lude had not sufficiently protected her, yielding too easily to the clamour for her to be seen (for example, when she had sent her for that unscheduled drive along the crowded ramparts of Lyons). Be that as it may, what good looks Adelaide had possessed were fading. Her lovely skin, inherited from Henrietta, her English grandmother, no longer had the 'purity of a lily, the colour of a rose', her eyes no longer sparkled. No one any longer wrote of her pretty ash-blond hair, and the beautiful eyes with their long, dark lashes, her gaiety, her laughter, her kind and gentle smile. No more was said of her appearance than that she was agreeable, elegant, well shaped.

Mme de Maintenon decided, from the letters, that she was downright ugly, and became distinctly unnerved, since everything, in her view, depended on this child—her own future, the King's happiness, his continuance in the path of virtue, her power over him. What she had hoped was that, in the years before her marriage to the Duc de Bourgogne, Adelaide would provide a new hobby for the King and for herself, a mutual interest and pleasure, a grandchild to train for the greatest of futures. What she could not foresee was that both she and the King would immediately fall beneath the spell of Adelaide's irresistible charm, that the King would love the child as he had loved no one else, that she would become his pet, his favourite companion, and that for the next ten years her rule at Versailles would be absolute. As for Mme de Maintenon, by nature so cold, her heart also would be immediately and profoundly touched. Her love for Adelaide, begun at first sight, turned, despite much provocation, to an enduring maternal affection that never failed her throughout her pitifully short life.

5

The Arrival

IT WAS Dangeau's stream of enthusiastic letters that finally reassured Mme de Maintenon. 'You may confidently expect,' he wrote as they left Lyons, 'a princess with a most delightful appearance, nature, and manner. The more we know of her, the higher our opinion rises. She is only a child, but she displays so much good sense, and has a gentle spirit. She speaks only when necessary, and is full of kindness.' Desgranges also praised her, but in a rather different vein. 'They talk of nothing but her kindness and docility; I say that she is not like a child of ten, but behaves like a reasonable person, quite capable, even now, of managing a household.'

Mme de Maintenon was relieved, indeed in raptures. 'You are giving us,' she wrote to Dangeau, 'a most charming impression of the princess; we are all impatient to greet her. You are clearly a man of many parts, as the story of the diamond sword, and now of blindman's buff, amply proves. If the princess is not deceiving us, we are fortunate in having a child with a sweet nature to bring up, and I am glad to hear that she is still babyish, because I do not think precocious children ever go far in life. All you tell me of her occupations seems perfect; if her ladies continue to amuse her with this mixture of word games, active games, and a few serious lessons, they will not waste their time. Charades will accustom her to making conversation, and teach her to speak out; proverbs will sharpen her wits; blind man's buff will keep her healthy, and spillikins make her dexterous. Truly, it all sounds excellent to me, especially since she plays these games with intelligent people, who will instruct as they amuse her.'

It was all most encouraging, and Mme de Maintenon continued her preparations with renewed vigour. She worked out the details of Adelaide's education at Saint-Cyr, where she was to be a day-girl—studying religion above all; then Roman history, classical mythology, the clavichord, dancing, and writing (her worst, and never-to-be-mastered subject). That was not all; for Mme de Maintenon next proceeded to do something, for her quite unprecedented, by summoning the Comte de Govon, the Duke of Savoy's ambassador, to a private audience,[1] saying that although she had never before given an audience, not even to the nuncio bearing a papal bull, she wished to question him closely about Adelaide's early life, her health and character, her lessons, her likes and dislikes. Nothing would be too trivial for him to relate (both Mme de Maintenon and the King set great store by details), and when Govon described to her the quiet family life at La Vigna di Madama, she was lavish with her praise. Card-playing, she said, operas, balls and suchlike were not the amusements for a child.

She then spoke of Madame Royale's letters, of her deep love of her little grandchild; her anxiety regarding her future happiness, and of how she had expressed the hope that Adelaide's character would 'tend towards goodness'. Mme de Maintenon declared that she meant to interpose herself between the princess and the world, until such time as she had learned its ways, as she needs to do before entering Society. More especially, she would keep her far from the fashionable, immoral company at Monsieur's court, at Saint-Cloud, and would try to gain her affection. Continuing, Mme de Maintenon stated that she would make every effort to ensure that religion had a part in the illustrious task to which the child had been called, so that in future years she would shine out as an example to all France. 'At which point,' wrote Govon, 'she launched forth into reflections of so high-flown a nature that neither my pen nor my memory are equal to their expression.'

That was typical of Mme de Maintenon. She was a born governess, with a perfect mania for delivering homilies, in that flutelike voice that was one of her chief attractions. Small children loved her for them, she had such a coaxing, comical way of sugaring her pills; young people found them irritating; but the King relied upon them to keep him in the narrow path of salvation. Witness the letter she had written him in the brief period of his unhappiness after the

---

[1] 'I shall never,' wrote Govon, 'forget that incomparable lady telling me, as she bade me farewell, that she had never hitherto given an interview, not to the nuncio himself, even when he bore a papal bull, nor to ambassadors or ministers. She did not wish, she said, to be so reserved with me. She gave me to understand that the King was glad of my coming, and that she hoped it would not be the last time that I visited her. I answered her with all due humility.'

Queen's death. 'The Queen must not be pitied; she died like a saint, and now Your Majesty has a friend in heaven to pray God to forgive your sins, and send you the grace you require. Reflect, Sire, on this, and be as good a Christian as you are a great king.' No one else had ever spoken to Louis XIV like that. He loved her for it—'as much as he was capable of loving anyone', said Mme de Maintenon, and he depended on her quite as much as on his confessor for his soul's guidance.[1]

It is important to remember that Mme de Maintenon had been elegant and beautiful; and still retained her beauty, looking much younger than her sixty years. Her smooth, serene brow, her warm, disarming smile, the lovely white hands, with which she gestured to perfection, were attractive to those who knew her. It was said that although, at first sight, she appeared 'veiled in severity', her sudden smile and dulcet voice immediately dispersed the cloud. The King admired her, and was always praising her appearance, grace, and dignified manners.[2] It was not only as a guide and directrice that he needed her, but as a wife, a friend, and a woman, and, as such, he made constant demands upon her. As for Mme de Maintenon herself, she admits in her letters that she was frigid by nature, and from the way she speaks of the 'distasteful duties that marriage lays upon women', it is clear that she found no pleasure in them. Nonetheless, she did love the King, calmly, serenely, in moderation. 'I love him,' she said, 'like a brother, and I want to see him perfect, so that God may bless him.'

Her very coldness, her detachment, may have been, for the King, one of her greatest attractions. Yet she was bored, and, like him, desperately in need of something to love, to pet, to tease and fuss over. No wonder the reports of Adelaide's delightful qualities enchanted them, promising a shared interest, a new toy, an absorbing task for their declining years. But that was not all; behind the veil of propriety, the calm brow, there burned in the eyes of Mme de

---

[1] Madame says that if the King's confessor and Mme de Maintenon were ever at variance, it was she whom he believed, and she added that he was becoming a terrible bore, 'positively garrulous on the state of his soul'. It is amazing to think that beneath the embodiment of divine majesty there lurked a frightened little man, so fearful of his ultimate destiny that he dared not move a step without the approval of an old lady whom he regarded as the essence of sanctified common sense.

[2] In the old days, Mme de Sévigné used to find Mme de Maintenon's talk enchanting, and asked her to supper every evening, when they were both in Paris.

Maintenon an inner flame that betrayed a love of power. Madame, who missed nothing, observed it, and wrote of 'a strange light that, beneath the black coif, shines in the eyes of the sinister old witch, and makes her somewhat alarming'. Equally strange was that Adelaide, that deceptively accommodating and gentle child, whom Mme de Maintenon came to love so deeply, and who to a large extent returned her affection, should have grown up well able to match, sometimes even to defeat, the dragon upon her own ground.

As letters and reports came pouring in with stories of Adelaide's sayings and doings, the King was in what can truly be described as a state of wild excitement. Govon reported to Victor Amadeus that his 'impatience and loving tenderness were inexplicable'; but one should remember that he was recovering from an agonising operation,[1] and probably still feeling the reaction. However that may be, he talked unceasingly and to everybody of Adelaide. Monsieur de Pomponne, supervisor of the posts, said that he even interrupted Council meetings to repeat her little impromptu speeches, which he found so touching, especially the story of her kind way of dealing with the Lieutenant-Governor's verbal breakdown, at Lyons, which he said he could not have managed better himself. He sent for Govon every day, and spent long hours expatiating on his ideas for the princess's life and amusements, until that gentleman felt obliged to remind him of how quietly she had lived hitherto, and of the great need, in view of her age and high spirits, that she should lead the same kind of life in France. He even said that that would be Adelaide's own wish.

All of this had taken place at Fontainebleau, where the Court royal family—that is to say Mme de Maintenon, Monseigneur, Monsieur and Madame, their son the Duc de Chartres, the Duc du Maine, his brother the Comte de Toulouse, the three Princesses, and the young Princes[2]—had been in residence for the past three weeks, waiting for Adelaide's arrival, and allowing the 'bad airs' at Versailles to be dissipated. The atmosphere had been particularly serene, until, in the last days of October, a storm had suddenly

---

[1] Madame observed that the wound was as big as her hand, and in the shape of a cross.

[2] The Princesses were the King's legitimated daughters, the Dowager Princesse de Conti, the Duchesse de Chartres, and the Duchesse de Bourbon-Condé (called Madame la Duchesse). The young Princes were Louis XIV's grandsons, the Duc d'Anjou, and the little Duc de Berry.

blown up, which had threatened to destroy the harmony. Mme de Maintenon was much upset, fearing lest Adelaide, on her arrival, should find herself at the centre of a family row.

The trouble was, once again, the matter of Adelaide's precedence and, as usual, Monsieur was to blame, for changing his mind, standing on his dignity, and clamouring for the King to reverse his ruling At first, Monsieur had been so proud of his granddaughter's becoming the future Queen of France, that he had pestered the King to give her royal precedence, even before her marriage. He had sworn that Madame would not mind walking behind her, and on that assurance, the King, who greatly redoubted his outspoken sister-in-law, had issued his orders. Now, it seemed, Monsieur was being nagged by two of his nieces, the Duchesse de Chartres and Madame la Duchesse, and that even Madame was protesting. They complained that he was prejudicing their rights and his own by ceding precedence to a mere Princess of Savoy, who would never have had such unwarranted dignity without his intervention, and they teased him until he consented to speak to the King. All he got from his brother was a very curt refusal. Monsieur thereupon had taken umbrage, and was making himself extremely disagreeable.

The arrangements were that the King should remain at Fontaine-bleau, while Monseigneur, Monsieur, and the Duc de Chartres should meet the princess at Montargis and bring her home.[1] Madame had asked to be of the party, but had been refused. Monsieur, however, now conceived the idea of stealing a march on the others by pushing on to Briare, so as to be the first to embrace Adelaide, and, for one evening, at least, to walk in front of her. There was something else, dear to his vanity, that he wished to establish before the King could object, namely that Adelaide should be induced to call him Bonpère, instead of Grandpère, which sounded to him unbecomingly elderly. He had already left Montargis when a courier overtook him with the news of the King's sudden decision to join the reception party. Monsieur turned back immediately, either, as the tactful Marquis de Sourches suggests, to keep his brother company, or from fear of an explosion; Govon hints that he was being prudent.

What must Adelaide's feelings have been, as she rolled the last

[1] Everybody, in fact, except the bridegroom to be. He was kept in his school-room. Adelaide does not seem to have taken much interest in him. When Brionne, at Pont-de-Beauvoisin, had asked her if she had any messages for him, she only sent her love to the King and Monseigneur.

miles of her long journey? Apprehensive? Homesick, perhaps, her
short letters hint as much; but certainly not terrified. She was not
going to strangers; Monsieur the King's brother was her grandfather; the adorable Henrietta of England, his first wife, had been
her grandmother, and people said that she was extraordinarily like
her. The King himself was her great-uncle, and his Court was full
of her cousins. Duchess Anne had convinced her that the King,
and Mme de Maintenon his wife (whom she might address as
'Aunt'), already loved her dearly, and that everyone in France
wished her to be happy. What is more, she was going to be married
(that part seems not to have interested her much), and one day
would be Queen. In the meantime, all she had to do was to remember her manners, obey the King in everything, and try to act like
a very great lady.

Louis XIV's sudden change of plan spread panic among the
billeting officers. There was no royal château at Montargis, and all
the grander houses had been snapped up for lesser royalties. In the
end, they turned the chief magistrate out of his official residence,
which was pretty enough, but unsuitable, for the rooms were far
too small to be comfortable for a monarch and his huge suite,
especially as Adelaide and her ladies were also to be lodged there.

It seems that after the others had gone, the King could bear to
wait no longer. A new chapter of his life was opening and he was
eager to begin it. There is also the possibility that he wished to
prevent an intrusion by Monsieur, and to keep Adelaide from the
debauched society of Saint-Cloud. That, certainly, would have been
the advice of Mme de Maintenon. Whatever the reasons, he set off
for Montargis at half-past one on the afternoon of 4 November. It
was an act of extraordinary condescension, and a fatiguing journey—
six stages, two and a half hours of dust and jolting, even at the
breakneck speed of the King's horses. Arriving at Montargis about
four o'clock he had a short rest, and then, even though Adelaide
was not expected for another hour, went out on to the balcony,
gazing up the street to catch sight of the cloud of dust that would
herald her arrival.

As soon as that appeared, he went downstairs and out into the
road, cutting through the group of royal princes and the excited
crowd behind them, so as to be at the door of the coach when it
drew up. Stopping a moment with his invariable courtesy to
apologise to Dangeau for usurping, that one time, his official function, he lifted out the little princess himself, holding her in his arms,

and exclaiming, 'Madame, I have been waiting impatiently to greet you!' To which she demurely replied, as she kissed his hand, 'This, Sire, is the greatest moment of my life.' She tried to kneel when he set her down, but he would not have it. He was just raising her up, when Monsieur bustled forward to embrace her next, becoming unutterably furious when the King interposed, with a reminder that Monseigneur le Grand Dauphin had the precedence. At this rebuff, Monsieur turned on his heel and retired to his room in high dudgeon. It was a dismaying moment for Adelaide; in fact, the very sight of Monsieur, mincing on five-inch heels with his huge, black, curly wig, his lacquered eyebrows and cherry lips painted to re-semble Cupid's bow, not to mention his ribbons and jewellery and the clouds of scent that surrounded him, was enough to dismay anyone.[1] She had probably never seen the like of him—few people had. Cardinal Mazarin is supposed to have encouraged his frivolity and perversion, in order that his brother, the King, should not be troubled by any rivalry; nonetheless, it should not be forgotten that, despite Monsieur's flaunted homosexuality, he sired six children, and that all the Catholic royal families of Europe number him among their ancestors.

It speaks volumes for Adelaide's confidence and self-control that she did not allow herself to be embarrassed; but kissed Monseigneur, her father-in-law to be, and let the King lead her by the hand through the staring people, up the staircase, to the room that had been prepared for her. As they went, she kissed his hand gently from time to time, a trusting little gesture that completely won his heart; but he tells the story himself, in a letter which he sent that night to Mme de Maintenon, the only one of his letters to her that was not burned at his death.[2]

'I reached here,' wrote the King, 'shortly after four, but she did not arrive until nearly six. I went out to receive her at the door of her coach. She waited for me to speak, and then replied exceedingly well, with just a trace of shyness that would very much have

---

[1] Saint-Simon said: 'A little man with a big stomach, walking as though on stilts because of his high heels. Covered with rings and bracelets, like a woman, and ribbons pinned on everywhere he could find room for them.' 'It upset me,' he added, 'to remember that he was the son of that great prince Louis XIII, from whom he was so different.'—Very different also from Adelaide's father, who presented a fine manly appearance in his smart uniforms.

[2] According to Mme de Maintenon, all her letters to the King, and his to her, were burned immediately after his death.

pleased you. I took her hand and led her through the crowd up to her bedroom, from time to time making them shine the torchlight upon her face, so that the people might see her. She bore the walk and the lights bravely and modestly, and at last we reached her room, where the heat and crush were enough to kill one. Now and again, I presented to her the people nearest us, and I observed her from all sides, so as to give you my impressions. She has the most graceful bearing and the prettiest figure imaginable. She was a perfect picture, beautifully dressed, and her hair likewise. Her eyes are very bright, and very fine, with black eyelashes, very good also. Her complexion is evenly pink and white, all that could be desired; she has the prettiest fair hair in the world, and a great deal of it. She is a little thin, but that is right at her age. Her mouth is very red, with thick lips; her teeth white and long but irregular.[1] Her hands are rather red, as the hands of little girls so often are. She does not say much, so far as I have observed; but she is not embarrassed when people stare at her, and behaves altogether like one who knows the world. The curtsey is not at all good, rather in the Italian manner; indeed, there is something Italian about her face; but she is attractive, I could see that in everyone's eyes . . . Speaking to you in the way I always do, I can truly say that I find her everything that could be desired; I should even be sorry were she handsomer.

'To sum up, everything about her is perfect, save only the curtsey;[2] but I will write again after supper, when I have seen more of her. I forgot to say that she is rather small for her age. As for me, up to now I have done marvels. I only hope I may be able to sustain a certain easy manner which I have adopted until we reach Fontainebleau.'[3]

After a short time, he went back to Adelaide, and for a moment his thoughts turned to poor Duchess Anne, who would have loved

---

[1] Her teeth quite soon went black, as shining white teeth appear so often to do, and she suffered agonies of toothache all through her life. Her hair also became much darker, indeed, almost black, as she grew up.

[2] Grace in curtseying was the great test, at Versailles, of birth and rank. Awkwardness was a cause of shame, a mark of essential ill-breeding.

[3] 'A certain easy manner': Louis XIV's public demeanour, and manner with strangers, was so awe-inspiring that, when he assumed it, even his intimates were overwhelmed. He had reduced his son, the unhappy Grand Dauphin, to a state of stammering hopelessness by habitually addressing him in the manner of a sovereign, rather than as a parent. The King knew this and was determined not to alarm Adelaide.

to have come with her, but had been forbidden by Victor Amadeus. 'I wish,' he said to Monsieur, 'that her poor mother could have been here with us, so as to have seen our pleasure.' He then turned all his thoughts to making Adelaide feel at home with him. He put her into an armchair and took a low seat beside her, saying, 'Madame, this is how we must always be together, quite comfortable with one another'; and he told her that she must stop calling him 'Sire', and say 'Monsieur' when she talked to him, just as any little French girl would address any ordinary grandfather (it was a liberty he did not allow his own children). He then made her play spillikins until supper was announced, and Dangeau entered to hand her to her seat at the table, with the King and Monseigneur sitting at either side.

Adelaide ate heartily of everything set before her, appearing so comically composed and grown-up that they were charmed, and could not help teasing her a little, which she did not seem to mind. One imagines that she was enjoying herself, confidently playing the perfect lady, the part for which she had been trained. She never helped herself to a dish without courteously offering it first to the King and Monseigneur, and thanked the steward with almost excessively dignified politeness every time he handed her a plate. At dessert, the King inquired whether she did not think Monseigneur very fat; but she was well equal to that dilemma, for she gravely replied that so he had been described to her, but, seeing him, he did not appear unusually stout and, in any case, it was rather becoming than otherwise. They then held a public conversation, during which Adelaide kept her head, and answered clearly and simply.

Afterwards, the King took her to her bedroom, and sat and chatted with her while she was being undressed and having her hair brushed. He probably wanted to see what shape she was beneath the stiff foundation of her court dress and the voluminous petticoats and silken coverings. He then kissed her goodnight and retired to finish his letter:

'The more I see of her the better she pleases me. We had a conversation in public, during which she said nothing; and that speaks for itself.[1] She has an excellent figure, perfect one might almost

---

[1] The letters which the King and Mme de Maintenon received telling of Adelaide's sharp remarks during the journey, caused them to fear lest she prove to be a chatterbox. They need not have worried; Adelaide, throughout her whole life, never made mischief, nor repeated what she was told. Mme de

say, and her modesty is charming. We supped together, and she made no mistakes, being gracious and polite to everybody. To me and to my son she was absolute perfection, for she behaved just as you might have done. Everyone was watching, and observing her closely, and all appeared genuinely delighted, for she has all the air of high Society, with polished and agreeable manners. I forgot to tell you that I saw her playing spillikins, very prettily and skilfully. I am truly glad to be able to say so much in her favour. I honestly believe I may do so without flattery, indeed, the truth demands it . . .'

Next morning they were up at six, for an early start. The King came to watch Adelaide being dressed and, at nine o'clock, they went in solemn procession to the Barnabite Church, to hear mass, through a crowd of twenty thousand people. This was the moment when even Adelaide's confidence must almost inevitably have received a shock, at her first sight of Louis XIV, in majesty. She was a devout little girl, and her reverent behaviour in church that morning had been noticed with approval. What must she have felt when, at the end of the service, she saw the entire congregation turn their backs on the altar, to bow very low before God's Regent upon earth, who was also, miraculously, her kind old great-uncle!

Immediately after mass, at eleven o'clock, they dined, after which the long procession that had escorted the Princess of Savoy all the way from Pont-de-Beauvoisin was once more on the move. In the great violet-draped coach they sat in rows, as in an omnibus, the King and Monsieur at the back, Monseigneur, Adelaide, and the Duchesse du Lude in front, with a space left by the door for the thirteen-year-old Duc de Bourgogne, who was at last to see his betrothed. He and his tutor the Duc de Beauvilliers were waiting in a coach, not far from Nemours; but, when the first cloud of dust was seen, the boy could wait no longer, and, against all the rules of etiquette, jumped down to run a hundred yards along the road to greet them. They stopped and picked him up, and there was a moment of embarrassment. Then the King broke the ice with a pleasant remark, and the prince, who had deliberately been placed as far as possible from his betrothed, leaned across Monseigneur, and twice kissed her hand. He was allowed no greater liberties. Indeed, so vigilant were they that, for several months to come, all he saw of her, at Versailles, was a half-hour's interview every other

Saint-Simon said that 'secrets were safe with her'; one reason, probably, for the devotion she inspired in her ladies.

Saturday, in the presence of tutors and governesses. As for the little princes, his brothers, they saw her only once a month.

The remainder of the journey was very slow, with the heavy coach sinking and slipping in the soft sand of the forest road. Having left at mid-day, they did not arrive until five o'clock, a tedious span, compared with the King's two-and-a-half-hour gallop on the previous day. When at last they entered the gates of the palace, an astonishing sight met their eyes, for the entire Court, all those great and powerful people, with their attendants and the ladies and gentlemen of their suites, were assembled outside to meet the new princess; and all were in a state of over-mastering excitement. The highest in rank, including the young princes, stood at the top of the famous horseshoe staircase, while the courtyard,the terraces, the windows, the galleries, even the roofs were thronged with spectators.

At the coach door, when it stopped, was the Duc de Saint-Simon. Let him take up the story: 'It was a truly magnificent spectacle. The King led in the princess, so small that she appeared to be sticking out of his pocket, and after walking very slowly the length of the terrace, they entered the chapel for a short prayer, and thence to the late Queen-mother's suite, which had been specially prepared to receive her. There Madame and the other ladies were waiting. The King himself presented to her the first princesses of the blood, asked Monsieur to name the remainder for her, and to be sure to see that she was kissed by all who had that privilege (namely, dukes and duchesses, Marshals of France and their wives, ambassadors and their consorts, and all the 'sitting ladies' [those allowed to sit on *tabourets* in the King's presence]). He then retired to rest in Mme de Maintenon's apartments, while Monseigneur sought repose in the room of his crony, Mme la Princesse de Conti.[1]

For Adelaide, who had had an equally fatiguing day, there was no escape or rest, and this was perhaps the first sign of what Sainte-Beuve describes as Louis XIV's 'monumental and hideous egoism'. He neither considered nor cared for other people's well-being,

[1] The dowager Princesse de Conti, Louis XIV's daughter by Mme de La Vallière, was Adelaide's first cousin once removed, and a bosom friend of her step-brother Monseigneur. She was thirty years old, in 1696. At one time, not long before this, Mme de Maintenon had hoped she would provide a distraction for the King. Unfortunately letters of hers had been intercepted, in which she made jokes about the King's relationship with Mme de Maintenon.

and the rapid weakening of Adelaide's constitution after she left Mme de Maintenon's care, her many miscarriages and early death may partly have been due to the fact that nothing was done to protect her health or give her rest; indeed, rather the reverse. On this occasion, after the early start and long journey, she was made to stand a good two hours in her stiff court dress, receiving the presentations, curtseying, smiling, saying now and then a gracious word, with Monsieur at her side to nudge her, and whisper, 'Kiss', when a lady's rank required it.

There was an appalling crush for, as usual, when the King removed his majestic presence, tension was relaxed, and order turned to confusion. Madame, who disdained the Court, rather enjoyed the turmoil: 'I thought I should die of laughing,' she wrote to the Duchess of Hanover, 'there was such elbowing and jostling that poor Mme de Nemours and the Maréchale de La Motte were driven backwards the entire length of the room, until they finally came up against us and subsided on Mme de Maintenon. You cannot think how funny it was. If I had not put out my arm they would all have fallen down like a house of cards.' She also gave her first impression of Adelaide, more temperate, but more searching, than the King's: 'Not precisely big for her age, but has a pretty figure, like a little doll, with a great deal of lovely fair hair, beautiful black eyes with long eyelashes . . . She has a large mouth and thick lips— the real Austrian mouth and chin. She walks and holds herself well, and every movement is graceful. For so young a child, she appears very grave, and looks uncannily wise . . .'

Madame, suffering from a cold in the head and, still ruffled about her lost precedence, was not in the best of tempers, or at all inclined to join the rapturous chorus. Yet Adelaide's performance had been so perfect, that even the fault-finding Duc de Saint-Simon had found nothing to criticise. There had, indeed, been one mishap for which she could not fairly be blamed, when the Dutch ambassadress, by a piece of low cunning, had extracted an illicit kiss for her daughter, by thrusting her forward so quickly that Monsieur was caught napping. There was a rumpus, for this might have established a precedent for ambassadors' daughters, calculated to upset the delicate balance of Court etiquette. The King was not vexed with Adelaide, though much annoyed with his brother; but some of the royal family were inclined to blame her, on the assumption that a princess of her birth and breeding should have recognised the unkissable by instinct.

At last all was over, and Adelaide was allowed to retire to her room; take off the dress she had worn all day (an immensely rich one, heavily embroidered with gold thread, and studded with jewels); put on her dressing gown, and eat her supper. It was past eight o'clock. Her day had started at six in the morning; she had walked to mass, in procession with the King through a crowd of twenty thousand sightseers; received addresses from the clergy and dignitaries of Montargis; and had thereafter driven to Fontainebleau, meeting en route the boy whom she was to marry. Arriving at the château at five o'clock, she had stood 'two good hours' for the presentations. Thus for thirteen hours she had been on display, on her best behaviour, under stress of one kind or another, and was far too intelligent not to have felt the strain.

It was not yet time for her to go to bed, for shortly after her meal the Princesse de Conti arrived in déshabillé, with a patch over one eye, to pay a private visit;[1] and, after she had gone, the great double doors were once again flung open to admit the King and Mme de Maintenon, who had not been presented with the royal ladies. The King came to introduce her personally, and after the ceremonial curtseys (a graceful sweep from Mme de Maintenon, a deep, but awkward bob from Adelaide) and the usual compliments had been exchanged, he left them together to make friends. If Mme de Maintenon had been apprehensive, as she might well have been, fearing to detect in that plain little face, those big black eyes, a glint of malice or rebelliousness, she was completely disarmed. The relief is evident in the letter she wrote next day to Adelaide's mother.

'She is so polite as to be incapable of saying anything in the least hurtful. I wanted to prevent her caressing me, saying that I was too old for kisses, but she answered, "Oh no! not too old at all!" When the King had left the room, she came up to me, and did me the honour to put her arms round me; then she made me sit down, having very quickly noticed that I could not stand for long, and, settling down with a most charming smile, almost upon my lap, she said, "Mamma has told me to give you her dear love, and to ask you to love me; pray teach me all I must do to please the King." Those, Madame, were her very words; but how describe the merry look that accompanied them?'

How Adelaide should address Mme de Maintenon had presented a difficult problem which her parents had solved with extraordinary

[1] She was not appearing in public, on account of having recently had a wen removed from her eye.

tact, by telling her to say simply 'Aunt'. It was no more than the truth and, as Saint-Simon remarked, 'a manifested, charming blend of respect and affection'. More than that, it was a subtle compliment, for it was a recognition of the fact that Mme de Maintenon was the King's wedded wife, and they were both deeply moved. Although everyone at the Court guessed that the King and Mme de Maintenon were married, for they saw her daily in the chapel kneeling on the late Queen's prie-dieu and using her prayer book, her status was otherwise kept a secret. It is said that she would have wished to be made Queen, and that she made one or two attempts to persuade the King to agree, but that he always firmly refused. It was better as it was.

Adelaide, in that first all-important meeting, and in her subsequent relationship with Mme de Maintenon, was certainly obeying her parents' orders to show affectionate obedience to that august lady. A letter which she wrote to her grandmother, shows how she responded to their advice: 'I am trying to do what you told me about Mme de Maintenon. I like her very much, and have confidence in all that she tells me. Please believe, dear grandmamma, all that she says of me. I do not think that I deserve it, but I should like you to have that pleasure because I count on your love, and I do not forget all the proofs of it which you have given me.' In another letter, she wrote, 'The Duchesse du Lude has come back to me, and I am very glad of it. Truly, Mme de Maintenon sees me as often as she possibly can. I think I may flatter myself that these two ladies have become fond of me.' So far as Mme de Maintenon was concerned, Adelaide was not wrong in turning confidently to her for protection in a strange world.[1] The little princess was certainly well aware of the dangers of her new life, and of the way to protect herself. Yet she was only ten, and it is inconceivable that, newly arrived, a stranger in a strange country, surrounded by people none of whom she had known much longer than three weeks, she should not have felt shy, scared, and homesick, eager to take refuge in protective arms. Her parents had told her to trust Mme de Maintenon, and to love her; she found in her all those qualities, beginning with that wonderful smile, which children find most comfortable and reassuring—a delightful voice, pretty hands, a

[1] Mlle d'Aumale, one of Mme de Maintenon's secretaries, at Saint-Cyr, wrote, 'she has always loved children, she likes to see them behaving naturally; and children are strongly aware of her fondness, and seem more at home with her than with anyone else.'

good-humoured, funny way of talking, best of all, fastidious cleanliness and a most delicious scent. Scent was Mme de Maintenon's only personal extravagance. She spent fortunes on perfumes every year, and perhaps she needed to for, since the removal of his upper teeth, the King's breath had been very bad indeed.

After Mme de Maintenon's departure, Adelaide's day was done, and Mme Marquet was able to put her to bed. Next morning she was allowed to sleep late, and to rest until the time came for her to put on full dress, so as to be ready for the King, when he came to take her to mass. They afterwards listened to a concert given by the small orchestra that had accompanied her on her journey. She returned to eat her dinner alone; but, at half-past two, she joined the King in Mme de Maintenon's room, and, with Mme du Lude and Mme de Mailly in attendance, they drove out around the canal to watch the tame cormorants catching fish for the King's dinner.

On their return, they set Adelaide down at the foot of the steps leading to Madame's apartment, so that she might return the call which that lady had paid on her the previous day, and also visit Monseigneur, in the Princesse de Conti's drawing-room. Madame appears to have enjoyed the visit. 'Everyone here is back in the nursery,' she wrote on 8 November. 'The day before yesterday, the Princesse d'Harcourt and Mme de Pontchartrain[1] were playing blind man's buff with Monseigneur. Yesterday, Monseigneur, Monsieur,[2] the Prince and Princesse de Conti, Mme de Ventadour, my other ladies and I might all have been seen playing it. What do you think of the company I keep?' It was the kind of occasion at which Adelaide shone, and charmed. People were taken aback by her freshness, her mixture of merriment with shyness, of childishness with most precocious discretion, and the simple friendliness that made everyone her slave, just as, so many years ago, they had been captivated by her English grandmother.

[1] The Princesse d'Harcourt and Mme de Pontchartrain were two of Madame's ladies. The former was an unpleasant character, dirty and smelly, who, in later years, became the butt of Adelaide's and her husband's cruel teasing. Mme de Pontchartrain, on the other hand, wife of the controller general of finance, later made Chancellor of France, was one of the nicest women at the Court, and gave the best parties, to the annoyance of many of the duchesses, who thought that unbecoming in one of comparatively low rank.

[2] Monsieur, too, would have enjoyed himself, he liked rowdy games and annoyed Madame by the noise he made, 'shouting *Aliu!*, *ra!*, and *à la face!*, when playing bassette [a card game] so loud that the din beggars description, at least as noisy as hounds when they put up a hare'.

Everyone wrote of her, in memoirs, in their journals, in letters to friends and relations. There was general agreement about her features—sadly plain, huge staring eyes, mouth too thick, nose too short, forehead too high and too prominent—but even the most censorious were moved. Here is Sourches, one of the least flattering: 'Even her slightest actions are imbued with intelligence . . . Her manner is serious and gentle, and she already knows how to mingle high spirits with royal dignity. Yet she is still only a child, and loves to play with dolls, and at blind man's buff.' Govon, the envoy of the Duke of Savoy, was also writing to his master Victor Amadeus, a letter that cannot have failed to reassure. 'No pen in the world,' he said, 'can adequately describe the comforting, the almost excessively tender manner in which His Majesty welcomed the Princess. He has deigned to tell me several times over, since her arrival, how perfectly delighted he is with her; how exactly he finds her to his taste; how he would not have her different in the smallest detail. He never leaves her without expressing his great impatience to see her again, and is always anxious to display her, explaining her good qualities, endeavouring to prove to her his extraordinary affection by every imaginable means. Mme la Princesse responds to him amazingly well. Fully appreciating his grandeur, she realises that it would be imprudent not to merit the continuance of his favour by every possible show of love and of submission to his will . . . Monsieur's passion for the Princess is at least as great as that of the King. As for Monseigneur, when we have met, he has several times deigned to inform me (and has said the like to his intimates) that he considers his daughter-in-law even more beautiful than her late grandmother.'

Leaving Adelaide's father and mother, in distant Savoy, comforted by such glowing reports, and Adelaide herself about to embark on her new life, it would be well at this point to say something of Louis, Duc de Bourgogne, the boy she had come to France to marry. He was far more excited at the thought of meeting her than she was to see him, for the King and how to please him occupied the whole of her mind. In any event, the competition for her favour gave him no chance; for Adelaide, the focus of attention of the most polished courtiers, would scarcely have been likely to notice the charms of an awkward boy. Moreover Louis was not physically attractive, being slightly malformed, with a twisted back, and a raised shoulder that became a hump when he grew to manhood, and already made him clumsy when he rode or danced. His face was pleasant enough, and his eyes beautiful; but his hair was frizzy, and below his upper jaw, his mouth and chin receded noticeably, giving him a sad resemblance to a shark.

6

Louis de France, Duc de Bourgogne

THE DUC DE BOURGOGNE, the thirteen-year-old boy, Adelaide's betrothed, was the grandson of Louis XIV. His father, the Dauphin, the King's only legitimate offspring, had been married at the age of nineteen, on 28 January 1680, to Marie Anne Christine Victoire of Bavaria, who was just a year older than himself. They had three children, of whom the Duc de Bourgogne was the eldest.

Monseigneur, as the Dauphin[1] was called by the courtiers, and also by his father (who never referred to him otherwise, not liking to consider the possibility of his own death), was a complete nonentity, whose spirit, and such intelligence as he possessed, had been broken by the harshness, indeed cruelty of his upbringing. Louis XIV had intended to make him 'the most virtuous and accomplished prince in all Christendom', and had personally devised a system of education under the most learned and ancient scholars, none of whom was accustomed to children. He had then handed him over, straight from the nursery, to a hard and brutal governor, the Duc de Montausier, who set about, by shouting, bullying, and beating, to frighten and flog the child out of his idleness and inertia. It was a time when, perhaps because physical pain was an unavoidable part of everyday life, children, even the sons of Kings, were constantly being whipped and presumably grew accustomed to it.[2]

---

[1] Monseigneur was sometimes called '*le Grand Dauphin*', not so much for his grandeur, but because of his height. He was taller than the King, which is why, in the engravings, he is usually shown standing a step lower.

[2] There was a tradition for beating princes in order to put them in such fear of their fathers as to deter them from rebellion. Louis XIV escaped because Louis XIII died when he was only four; but Henri IV, his grandfather, wrote to his little son's governess, 'I have a complaint to make. You do not tell me that you have whipped my son. I desire and command you to whip him every time he is wilful or naughty, knowing, as I do, that nothing in the world will be more beneficial to him'.

With Monseigneur, however, they went altogether too far, for they flogged the life out of him. He left the schoolroom with such a horror of books and so deeply fixed a terror of his father, that he never afterwards recovered, but grew up stupid, apathetic, indolent— 'drowning,' as Saint-Simon describes him, 'in fat and gloomy inertia'. Yet, fundamentally, Monseigneur was neither a fool nor a coward; Madame, who thought him 'the hardest man in the world to understand', said that he was 'very far from being stupid, although, either from laziness or indifference, he tried at all times to appear so'; and although in the King's presence he was speechless with fright, he was brave enough in battle, and extremely popular with the soldiers.[1]

One attainment he acquired from his disastrous upbringing, was a perfect passion for wolf-hunting, and very great skill in the management of hounds. His entire life was devoted to the sport, and so expert did he become that wolves, to his great annoyance, became nearly extinct in the forests around Versailles and Fontainebleau. Monseigneur hunted all day long, and nearly every day in the week. People said that half his life was spent in the chase, and the other half anywhere but with his wife, the plain,[2] sickly, unhappy Dauphine. Had she possessed a stronger character she might have supported, even perhaps saved him; but she was unsociable, none too good-tempered, and full of resentment because of her lack of charm. When she first arrived at Versailles she was ready to love him, but when he left her, as he very soon did, she made no effort to gain his affection, and was rarely seen in public. She spent her life with her friend La Bessola, and one or two other women, shut away in tiny rooms at the back of her apartments, where there was little ventilation and no view. No one made any great effort to befriend her; some, particularly Monseigneur's half-sister, the beautiful Princesse de Conti, were positively nasty; but they found

---

[1] Mme de Sévigné, in a letter to Mme de Grignan, 22 October 1688: 'Monseigneur goes himself into the trenches. We heard that he got covered with mud the other day when a cannon ball exploded at his feet. He is adored for his generosity and his thought for the wounded . . . He assists those who lose their equipment, distributes money among the soldiers, and brings the officers and their needs to the King's notice, and all this because he is moved by the poverty he sees around him.'

[2] She was clearly hideous. Dangeau, in his journal, tried to make the best of her well-bred air, her well-shaped bosom, etc.; but Saint-Simon noted in the margin, 'She had never been good-looking, nor anything approaching it.'

that, nonentity though she might appear, the Dauphine had the wit to defend herself.[1]

The last years of her wretched life were spent in almost complete isolation, for the King did little to help her. He was exceedingly angry with her because she had remained loyal to her brother the Elector Maximilian, even after he had deserted France to join the League of Augsburg, and did not hide her horror at the behaviour of French troops in Germany. She became the centre of attention, however, when, shortly after dinner, on Tuesday, 4 August 1682, she felt the first pains of childbirth. She told the Queen, begging her to say nothing; but about one in the morning there was no further possibility of concealment, and the Château de Versailles began to fill with excited crowds; for by long tradition the births of children of the royal line took place almost in public, for fear of trickery, or a plot to substitute a boy for a girl. Four wet-nurses with certified good health and irreproachable conduct in religious matters had, for the past week, been living at Versailles with their babies, under strict orders to receive no visitors, especially not their husbands. A daring innovation at a royal birth was the choice of a man-midwife, a certain Clément, of whom the King highly approved, for he had most competently assisted Mme de Montespan at the secret birth of the Duc de Maine, and the King, seeing him in action, had admired his coolness and skill.

Meanwhile, along the Paris road, coaches and carriages were speeding towards Versailles. The great courtyard blazed with torches, becoming ever more crowded with the vehicles of ambassadors, ministers, foreign royalty, high officials, and their secretaries, all eager to be the first to despatch the news to their various courts. The excitement in the château was tremendous, only the King slept undisturbed. He had, as usual, gone to bed early, and they did not wake him until five in the morning, when it seemed wise to do so. He asked if the need for him was pressing, and on being told not he dressed and heard mass before making his way through the throng to the Dauphine's room, where the crowd round the door was so thick that even he had a struggle to enter. Thereafter he stayed beside her throughout her protracted, agonising labour, feeding her on chicken broth with his own hand, when her strength seemed

[1] The princess visiting the Dauphine in bed one morning, as was then the custom, found her, as she thought, sleeping: 'Look at Madame la Dauphine,' said she, 'she is just as ugly asleep as awake.' Whereupon a voice from the bed replied, 'Were I a love-child, I should be as beautiful as you.'

to ebb, comforting and encouraging her,[1] leaving her only for short intervals, to attend his council, or eat his meals. The Queen, too,[2] was kind and solicitous, even sending the holy relics of Saint Margaret, to be exposed in her bedroom, which was traditionally done solely for the accouchements of Queens of France. Only Monseigneur appeared indifferent, sitting huddled in one of the anterooms, in a kind of apathetic stupor that deprived him of both thought and action.

All through the next day (Wednesday) the poor Dauphine's pains increased with no sign of imminent delivery; but, when the King had gone to his dinner, they brought from the royal furniture depository the special accouchement bed, which had served both Anne of Austria and Marie Thérèse in their time. It was three feet wide, supplied with two mattresses separated by a board and a bolster, with a wooden peg on either side in such a position as to be easily gripped, and a wooden rail at the end to support the feet. All was now ready, and when the King returned after his supper the pains grew much stronger. He did not leave her again the whole of that night. The situation was the same on Thursday morning, but although Clément remained perfectly calm, saying that it was a long and difficult labour, but that in the end all would be well, the poor Dauphine despaired of her life. According to the *Mercure*, she said how hard it was to have found so kind a father, so good a husband, and to have to leave them so soon; to which the King replied that he did not mind if she had a girl, provided that it caused her less suffering and brought about a quicker delivery. It was clear by this time that a baby of whatever sex was at last ready to make its appearance, and accordingly the bedroom doors were flung open to admit a stream of important personages, whose privilege it was to witness a royal birth. All the royal family entered, including Monsieur and Madame's little six-year-old daughter;[3] the princes and princesses of the blood; the so-called foreign[4] princes and prin-

---

[1] The King could, when he wished, be very tender with women. His early childhood, in his mother's drawing-room had shown him the way, and so had his love for his first mistress, Mlle de La Vallière.

[2] Queen Marie-Thérèse did not die until the following year (1683).

[3] Adelaide's aunt, Elizabeth Charlotte d'Orléans, who married the Duc de Lorraine. She was the sister of the Duc de Chartres, who later became Regent of France, and grew up to be Adelaide's friend, a thoroughly nice woman, very fond of Madame, her mother.

[4] They were the inheritors of estates so large that they were, in effect, principalities; which meant that in time of war they were bound to bring a prince's

cesses; the ladies of both royal households, including Mme de Montespan (demoted from the post of official mistress, but not yet disgraced, having been created a duchess, in the traditional way, and holding the alternative post of mistress of the long-suffering Queen's household), also Mme de Maintenon, the Dauphine's lady of the bedchamber. According, once again, to the *Mercure*, everyone feared the worst, and soon the room filled with the humming of anxious voices.

The King, intent on being the first to announce the advent of a grandson and heir, had arranged a special code with Clément for that purpose. 'Is it a boy or a girl?' he would say; and Clément would reply, 'I do not know', for a girl, or 'I do not know yet', in the other eventuality. At last the moment came. 'Which is it?' inquired the King. 'I cannot tell, yet,' said Clément with a broad smile; whereupon Louis XIV turned, and called out in a loud voice, 'We have a Duc de Bourgogne'. Then, moving across the bedroom to the door, one side of which was opened for him, he made the announcement to those duchesses, whose rank had not been sufficient to allow them entry to the bedroom. At the same time, Mme de Créquy, the Dauphine's lady-in-waiting, gave the glorious news to the dukes gathered in the ante-room on the opposite side.

At that point Versailles went completely mad. Order, dignity, rank, went by the board; people fought to reach their coaches, so as to be first to bring the glad news to Paris and elsewhere. Others struggled around the Dauphine's door, and even forced their way into her room. Monseigneur suddenly recovered and began to kiss every lady within reach, an example so infectious that soon everyone was kissing everyone else, regardless of who they might be. Old enemies came together in a clasp of love, footmen kissed duchesses, everyone kissed the King who, astonishingly, did not seem to mind, refusing to check even the servants, merely saying that their joy had overcome them. He went to his private rooms to rest, and all the way was chaired on the shoulders of a happy throng eager to embrace and congratulate him. It was one of the most glorious moments of his life. Not only was he the greatest king on earth; but he had secured his line to the second generation. He was already in love with Mme de Maintenon (he married her after the Queen's death in the following year), but although deeply affected by her sermons, and those of his confessor, on the wickedness of his

army to the support of France. Their families included the Lorraines, Rohans, Valentinois of Monaco, etc.

'double adultery'¹ (his relationship with Mme de Montespan), he could feel that the Lord, at least for the moment, was not bringing him to book.

Outside in the vast courtyard there was wild rejoicing. One of the King's gentlemen shouted himself so hoarse, crying the great news from one of the windows, that he was speechless for days afterwards. A musketeer on guard duty threw out his straw mattress and set fire to it, and soon there were bonfires everywhere, fed with the builders' planks stacked outside for repairs; and the servants were throwing out chairs, tables and beds, and even the floor boards of the château. Some chairmen threw on the flames their mistresses' carrying-chairs. One footman stripped off all his clothes to add to the blaze, and ran about stark naked. But, when the King was told, all he said was, 'So long as they don't burn us!'

As for the Dauphine, there was no rest for her, since, at that time, it was thought inadvisable to allow young mothers to sleep immediately after their delivery. One of the doctors therefore sat by her bed engaging her, for the next three hours, in interesting conversation, lest drowsiness prevail. What, in itself, might have been enough to keep her miserably awake was the skinning of a live sheep, in the room next door, quite visible to her and to her ladies, who were terrified and afflicted by the sufferings of the tortured animal. The skin was immediately wrapped around her stomach, to lessen her pain, and she was given a soothing cordial, made from orange juice, and the oil of sweet almonds. For the following nine days, she was kept in almost total darkness, with the shutters firmly closed, and only the light of a single candle. Very strangely, to twentieth-century notions, they posted an usher outside her door for the next six weeks, rigorously turning away any person using scent, no matter how little; for perfumes of all kinds were considered highly injurious for new mothers, and might contain poison.

Eventually, the Dauphine recovered to live just as unhappily for the next eight years, during which she gave birth to two more boys, the Duc d'Anjou in the following year, and the Duc de Berry in 1686.² She died, aged twenty-nine, in 1690, fully convinced that the latter's birth had been the cause of her death; indeed, she said

¹ Mme de Montespan, the King's official mistress, still had a husband living. The Queen also was alive. The guilty couple were thus committing adultery twice over in their relationship.

² She said to him, 'Ah! my son, how dearly your life has cost your poor mother'.

as much to the little boy, when he was brought to receive her blessing. She was mistaken as to her illness, for she appears to have died of consumption, brought on, according to Mme de Caylus,[1] by the stuffy rooms in which she lived, her melancholy temperament, and the violent remedies prescribed by the doctors. Mme de Sévigné wondered what could be found to say of her, in the funeral oration; but decided that the three princes, her sons, 'would not unworthily furnish the main points of a panegyric'.

That all-important baby, the infant Duc de Bourgogne, was taken immediately after his birth to another room where a fire was blazing, although the month was August, and there Clément personally attended to him, washing him with a sponge dipped in warm wine, in which some butter had been melted. He was then wrapped in swaddling clothes, and brought back to the Dauphine's room, so that she might see him.

Next came baptism, at the hands of Cardinal de Bouillon the chief almoner, clad in the full regalia of cope, rochet and stole, assisted by the Curé de Versailles, who had the right to officiate at all religious ceremonies taking place at the Court. It was he who registered the birth of Louis Duc de Bourgogne, in the parish church of Versailles, where the record may be seen to this day. That done, the infant prince was handed over to the care of his kind old governess, the Maréchale de La Mothe-Houdancourt,[2] who received him on a cushion, kneeling, and bore him off in a covered chair, to his nursery, in his own suite of apartments. No sooner had he arrived there than the treasurer of the Order of the Holy Spirit appeared to place the blue ribbon around the baby's neck; for, according to precedent, royal princes became members at birth, though they were not required to take the vows until they reached maturity.

Public rejoicings took their usual course, with fountains splashing wine, casks broached in the market places, fireworks, and illuminations. One of the most brilliant was at the house of Saint-Simon's

---

[1] Marthe Marguerite, Comtesse de Caylus (1671–1729), author of *Souvenirs de Mme de Maintenon*, whose cousin and secretary she was.

[2] Louise de Prie, Maréchale de La Mothe-Houdancourt (1624–1709), had been appointed Monseigneur's official governess twenty years earlier. She continued in the post of governess to all three of the King's grandsons, and to his great-grandsons also, when their time came. She was still on active service in 1709, and was sleeping in the same room as Adelaide's baby son, the Duc de Bretagne, on the night of her death.

father—the *Mercure* mentions it especially: 'lit up to the tops of the chimneys, and the words *"Vive le Roi"* traced in huge fiery letters.' Monasteries and seminaries joined in the general celebrations, and even in the nunneries there was a little loyal jollity. What was a complete novelty, and, in view of the general poverty and distress, strangely moving, was that the people of Paris made a mass pilgrimage to Versailles to catch a glimpse of the precious baby. All that first afternoon the great courtyard was crowded with a patriotic mob, clamouring to see their prince. 'Time after time, the Maréchale obliged them,' records the *Mercure*, 'carrying the infant to the window so as to let the people see him, and by so doing she has received much praise. Those not fortunate enough to gain that distant view comforted themselves by gazing up at the nursery windows.' The prince's father did not show himself. The whole affair had been too much for him. He had quietened his overwrought emotions by disappearing on a wolf-hunt, and did not return until the following day.

For the next seven years, little Louis remained in the sole charge of his governess. Her appointment to his father had been the King's personal choice. He had a great liking for her, and an immense respect that increased with the years. In fact, she was approved and respected by everyone, from the King's haughty cousin 'La Grande Mademoiselle',[1] who condescended to say that she was 'of most pleasing appearance, with a governess's imposing presence—a very suitable kind of person to have charge of midwives and nurses, and to count the spoonfuls of milk required to make gruel properly'.[2] Saint-Simon, for once, was almost enthusiastic: 'the nicest woman imaginable, taking the greatest possible care of the royal children, and bringing them up according to their rank, with perfect manners'; though he did add that she was 'very stupid, and aware of nothing at the Court, beyond the routine of her station'. All in all, she was a kind old thing, though somewhat too much addicted to petting and spoiling. With her own three daughters she had considerable success, for although a widow, and without the possibility

[1] Anne Marie Louise d'Orléans, Duchesse de Montpensier (1627–93) was the daughter of Gaspard d'Orléans, Louis XIII's brother, and had been very prominent in the revolt of the nobles.

[2] There was a great controversy over the proper making of gruel. A mixture of milk and wheatflour, it was baked until it thickened and given to babies on the end of a finger. Doctors were concerned about it because they thought it caused indigestion if made too thick.

of offering large dowries, she married them to three dukes, and only
one of them, the Duchesse de La Ferté-Senneterre,[1] ever attracted
the least breath of scandal. As for the youngest, the Duchesse de
Ventadour, the King thought so much of her, that he appointed her
governess to the future Louis XV, after her mother's death. It was
said that the King's high regard for her came from her attempt to
strangle him, when he made an amorous advance towards her in
earlier, happier times.

The Maréchale, who was getting on for sixty when she took over
the new baby, could scarcely have found a greater contrast to the
stolid apathy of her previous charge. It was not a peaceful nursery.
The Duc de Bourgogne proved to be a handful from the very start,
indeed he was what the nurses called a 'holy terror', with the pride
of Lucifer, a will of iron, and a temper like a keg of gunpowder. One
difficulty for the biographer is that there are so many flattering
portraits of him, both by courtiers like Dangeau and Sourches,
careful to say nothing capable of giving offence; and by his confessor,
Père Martineau,[2] who glossed over his faults in childhood, in order
to extol his later virtues. Yet somehow the same picture emerges
through them all, of a highly intelligent child, with a capacity for
affection, but a most alarming temper. Saint-Simon's famous
portrait bears the stamp of truth, and is so brilliant that it is worth
quoting:—

'The Duc de Bourgogne was born furious; so ill-tempered that
he would try to break the clocks when they called him to an unwel-
come task, and flew into terrifying rages when rain prevented his
diversions. Opposition drove him frantic when he was a young

[1] Saint-Simon says of her that the duke broke with her almost at once, and
not without cause, living 'quite apart from her, and never seeing her'. The
Duchesse de Ventadour, on the other hand, was an admirable woman, who
may be seen holding the leading strings of Adelaide's son, the future Louis XV,
in the famous picture, in the Wallace Collection, of Louis XIV and his descendants.

[2] Le Père Isaac Martineau (1640–1720), who was the confessor of all three
young princes and, later, of Louis XV. Saint-Simon, with some justification,
thought his influence too great with the Duc de Bourgogne, their interviews
altogether too long, turning the prince into a bigot. 'It is a matter for some
concern,' he wrote, 'that the future administration should be inseparable from
theology . . .; that all will be a matter of religion and conscience . . .' On the
other hand, Saint-Simon did not entirely disapprove of Père Martineau himself.
'People will wish him a long life,' he said, 'not only because he is a very decent
sort of man, but because they fear the prospect of a new confessor.'

child, as I often witnessed for myself; and so violent was he that one feared lest he break every bone in his body. Headstrong to a degree, he passionately loved all pleasures, including women, with (which is rare) an equally strong partiality in another direction. He was, in very truth, a slave to every passion, and transported by all the pleasures . . .' He loved to mock, and 'his mockery was doubly cruel because, being both witty and spiteful, he pin-pointed each absurdity with absolute precision, and accompanied all this by more pride and haughtiness than can easily be described. Other people, no matter who they might be, were to him no better than insects, mere atomies bearing no likeness to himself; and though he and his brothers were supposedly brought up as equals, he treated them, at best, as his go-betweens with the rest of the human race. He was moreover dangerous in his assessments of people and ideas, quick to see any weaknesses, and arguing more fiercely and soundly than his masters. Nonetheless, once his anger had abated, reason prevailed, and he would then admit his fault, sometimes with so much violence that his rage returned.[1] As for his intelligence, it was lively and vigorous, rising to meet every difficulty, superior in every way imaginable.'

If this portrait appears exaggerated, for surely no little boy could be quite so bad, one should remember the memoirist's deep devotion for the man Louis grew up to be, and his understanding of the stuggle that went on between the generous, eager, affectionate side of the boy's nature, and the other side, rebellious, haughty, cruel, and passionate. It was a fierce internal struggle which, thanks to the extraordinary tact and sympathy of the Abbé de Fénelon, Louis's much-loved tutor, ended in a victory that, even to those who knew him best, appeared nothing short of miraculous.[2]

In the early days, in the nursery, he was a delicate child, much given to colds in the head and bouts of fever, looking, Saint-Simon records, 'puny, as though he would blow his very soul into his

---

[1] 'In the early days, I used to see him when overtaken by anger, leaning against a table or a chair, with both fists pressed tight against his cheeks, and remaining silent a long time in that posture, until he was sure that the fit of rage had passed' (Cardinal Fleury, who had been one of his under-tutors).

[2] 'God the ruler of all hearts,' said Saint-Simon, 'worked a miracle in this prince,' and Mme de Maintenon, writing at the time of his marriage to Adelaide, said, 'We have seen the faults that caused us so much concern for the future disappearing one by one. Religion has so transformed him that, though passionate by nature, he is now even-tempered, gentle, and obliging. One feels that this is his true nature.'

pocket handkerchief'. Attacks of fever, in children, were nothing out of the ordinary in those days of 'bad airs', and dirty houses; but Dangeau reports that the Duc de Bourgogne had no less than fifty such attacks in the space of a single day. It so happened that this coincided with a controversy among the doctors about a new medicine, quinine, which certainly reduced fevers, but was thought by some to be bad for children. A violent argument ensued between the Maréchale, who wished to try it, and the Dauphine, who strongly objected. The King tended to side with the Maréchale, for quinine; but the Dauphine was adamant against them both, and he decided in her favour. This was the only time that she brought herself to interfere. The mothers at the Court watched the contest with intense interest, and were greatly relieved when the prince recovered, although, as the Marquis de Sourches sagely remarked, 'In such cases the event decides. The Prince has regained his health without quinine, therefore the Dauphine was right. Had a mishap occurred, all the blame would have been hers.'

The Dauphine herself lived only a few years longer, either pregnant or in wretched health, increasingly isolated, more and more unpopular with the royal family, mourning the death of her only friend La Bessola, and becoming ever more unamiable. She died in 1690, when the Duc de Bourgogne was seven years old. He was made to attend the funeral and sprinkle Holy Water upon her coffin, but he did not follow in the interminable procession,which took her body to Saint-Denis, and kept Dangeau, in charge of the arrangements, more than twelve hours on horseback. The little prince grieved for his mother more than anyone had believed possible for, several months later, when his tutors read aloud to him one of the funeral orations composed in her honour, he suddenly slipped out of his chair and disappeared beneath the table. At first they thought he had fallen asleep, but when they picked him up, they discovered that in his proud efforts to conceal his tears, he had given himself a pain. He was a boy to take everything hardly, and very capable of loving deeply and truly, as he was to show by his devotion to Fénelon, and his tender, enduring passion for Adelaide.

He was fond also of the old Maréchale; but his career through her nursery was a stormy one, since, even at that early age, he was resisting caresses and up in arms against threats. One cannot help thinking that she was not sorry to see the last of him, when he was abruptly taken from her care and put 'under the government of men'. She could then concentrate all her attention on his more tractable younger brothers. The change took place very suddenly and in this way.

The chief distraction of the little princes was playing at soldiers, with carefully selected playmates from the ranks of the nobility. But whereas this was highly enjoyable for the Duc de Bourgogne, who always commanded and was always allowed to win, laying about him with a will in the mock charges and assaults, it had become increasingly disagreeable for his younger brothers. The gentle Duc d'Anjou supported the rough play amiably enough; but the little Duc de Berry grew positively vindictive.

It soon became abundantly clear that something must be done to bring the Duc de Bourgogne to order, and thinking it would amuse him, for a little while, to play soldiers in earnest, the King 'enrolled' him, soon after his sixth birthday, in the musketeers.[1] He was given the choice of the two companies, and chose the blacks because he greatly admired some of their young officers, and wished to drill with them. His name was accordingly entered on their roll; and he was given a beautiful little black pony as his warhorse.

If the King, imagining that the whole thing was no more than an expedient, designed to dampen the child's ardour, had expected very little from Louis in the way of effort or application, he was never more mistaken. The little duke threw himself into learning his drill with such passionate eagerness, and to such good effect, that when, on a pouring wet day, in June 1689, the King reviewed his musketeers in the great courtyard of Versailles, there was his little grandson, present and correct, mounted on his miniature black charger, in the foremost rank on the right-hand side. The rain came down in sheets all day, but, according to Sourches, 'the Duc de Bourgogne continued undismayed to exercise with his troop, showing a precision, steadiness, and skill, far beyond the usual for boys of his age'. 'It was really astounding to see a child, not yet seven,' he continued, 'behaving as coolly and confidently as young men of five-and-twenty . . . The spectators rejoiced to see such strong evidence that when he grows up, the young prince will have developed a proper inclination for war; the King, himself, was

---

[1] The regiment of musketeers was divided into two companies, the 'greys' and the 'blacks', from the colour of their horses. They went everywhere with the King, guarding his tent, during campaigns, and his private apartments at Versailles and Fontainebleau. Every gentleman had to serve as a trooper in the musketeers, before taking a commission in the regular army. The greys were the senior troop, and, rank for rank, had superiority.

deeply moved.' To the valiant Duc de Bourgogne, however, the immediate result was a most ferocious cold in his head.

Moved the King may have been, but he appears to have decided that a child who displayed such martial vigour ought not much longer to remain in the care of women. The matter came to a head when the prince created an appalling scene, which was inevitably brought to his grandfather's notice, regarding his rank in the musketeers. On a certain day, at Fontainebleau, it had fallen to him to march with a comrade from the greys to receive the order for the day from the King in person. Now the greys were the senior company and took precedence; but, when Louis discovered that he was expected to stand on the left-hand side and remain silent, he flew into a violent rage that almost led to blows. The King intervened, asking him if he would prefer to change companies, to which he replied, after a long pause, that, as heir to the throne, he rightly belonged to both, and should be given a piebald pony.

That seems to have settled the question, for the King, after publicly expressing his perfect satisfaction with the Maréchale, made the change with an abruptness typical of his methods whenever he had cause to fear tears, scenes, or recriminations. On the afternoon of 3 September 1689, he summoned the boy to his mother's bedroom, and there bade him kiss the Maréchale goodbye. He then formally handed him over to the Duc de Beauvilliers, who had been appointed only a fortnight earlier as his governor. Sourches recounts that the Duc de Bourgogne was much upset at having to leave her, and 'demonstrated his affection', but that he submitted quietly enough, and that same evening began, 'not unwillingly, to receive instruction from his new tutor, the Abbé de Fénelon'.

The appointment of the Duc de Beauvilliers was universally acclaimed. Sourches, noting that he still retained his posts of first gentleman-in-waiting, minister of State, and chief of the finance council, pronounced it 'a well-judged, brilliant reward, immediately applauded by the whole of Society'. Even the Dauphine did not object; and Mme de Sévigné wrote to her daughter that 'Saint-Louis himself could have made no better choice'.

Paul, Duc de Beauvilliers, was the King's friend, the only member of the feudal nobility whom he had taken into his councils. He was gentle, kindly, deeply religious, and a member of the French Academy. No stronger contrast could have been found to the brutal martinet who had been entrusted with the upbringing of the unhappy Monseigneur. Forty years old, in 1689, Beauvilliers was

the second son of the old Duc de Saint-Aignan and, like other
younger sons, had been destined for the Church, a life on which his
whole heart had been set, for he believed that God had called him.
The death of his elder brother, in 1664, had altogether changed his
prospects, for duty to his line required him to save his title and
name from extinction, not to mention the lucrative and hereditary
court appointments, which brought them influence and wealth. It
was a bitter wrench for him to leave the service of God for that of his
family, and a faint shadow of his disappointment may perhaps be
discerned when, long afterwards, the young Duc de Saint-Simon,
one of the most eligible young bachelors in France, made urgent
and repeated demands for the hand of the eldest of his eight unmarried daughters, who, in her convent at Montargis, aspired to
become a professed nun. 'What would you have me do?' said her
father. 'She feels it is her vocation,' and he doggedly refused to press
or trouble her, as he himself had been pressed in earlier years. He
remained, indeed, permanently saddened by the sacrifice God had
demanded of him, and more than ordinarily pious. No matter how
overburdened he might be by State affairs and Court duties, he
never failed to spend at least an hour and a half each day at his
devotions, in the chapel, and publicly took Communion twice in
every week.[1]

He had married one of Colbert's three daughters, and his sister-
in-law, the Duchesse de Chevreuse, was the wife of his greatest
friend. Their close and highly influential circle provided the pious,
respectable element at the Court. They were greatly esteemed,
particularly by the elderly, but considered by the young as more
than a little dull. Mme de Maintenon, at the time of the Duc de
Beauvilliers's appointment, was very intimate with them, and,
according to Saint-Simon, 'in the habit of dining with them once
or twice every week, in strictest privacy, with a handbell on the
table, so as to dispense with servants and permit the conversation
to flow without restraint'. She may well have encouraged the King
to choose so gentle a man for governor, since she was no advocate
of harsh methods with children; preferring the precepts, and

[1] Monseigneur tried to make trouble for him, over this, having discovered
that he did not always confess beforehand. 'He must have the devil in him
somewhere,' he remarked to the King, who might, at one time, have been
shocked, but now offered Mme de Maintenon as an example, saying that many
people took Communion twice or even three times a week, on their confessor's
advice.

milder punishments in use at her school. There is also the possibility that, none too sure of her own future, she may have welcomed
the opportunity to plant a friend in the schoolroom of the heir
presumptive.

On the day when the Duc de Beauvilliers's governorship was
announced, the names of the other members of the new household
were also published. They were not an inspiring group. The Marquis
de Denonville, a *gentilhomme de la manche*,[1] was, according to Saint-
Simon, 'a decent enough fellow, and courageous; but of an innocence not far removed from idiocy, and notoriously incapable'. Two
others, Dupuy and L'Echelles, were noted for their godliness,
'honourable, well-read, and highly esteemed, but the most boring
men in all France, relieved only by a very few clerical jokes'. There
was, however, one exception to the general mediocrity, the appointment to the all-important post of tutor, of the brilliant, the irresistibly fascinating Abbé de Fénelon,[2] whose fame would far outshine
even that of the great Duc de Beauvilliers. Fénelon was still young,
in 1689, and not known personally at the Court; but people were
beginning to speak admiringly of him, and Sourches, praising his
appointment, called him 'a man of infinite goodness and capabilities'.[3]

It is almost impossible to do justice to Fénelon's charm. Something of it may be seen in Vivien's portrait; but, as usual, it is to
Saint-Simon whom we must turn, to bring him to life. 'Tall, lean,
well-built, with a large nose, and eyes that danced and sparkled like
a torrent, a countenance, once seen, never to be forgotten . . . The
general impression was of high-thinking, wit, good-breeding, and
dignity; but, above all, of nobility . . . His manners were in keeping with all the rest, a graciousness that delighted to put people at
their ease, a poise which only frequentation of the highest Society
can bestow . . .

'Charm, that most rare of qualities, he possessed in the highest

[1] Whose duty was to hold the sleeves of toddler-princes, to prevent them
from falling.

[2] François de Salignac de La Mothe Fénelon (1651-1715). Appointed tutor
to the King's grandsons in 1689, made Archbishop of Cambrai, 1695. He was
the younger son of a noble but impoverished family. Saint-Simon who saw him
often at Court in the early years, was dazzled by his personality. There are four
portraits of him in the Memoirs, all equally admiring.

[3] It is worth noting that Montausier, Monseigneur's cruel governor did not
figure in the list. He was a very old man, but it would have been usual to give
him some consultative appointment.

degree. It kept his friends, even after his disgrace[1] wholly devoted
to him, throughout his entire life. It was the memory of that charm
that brought them together to talk of him, lament over him, and,
like the Jews who longed for Jerusalem, pine, ever hopefully, for
his return. The power of his preaching gained for him authority
over his friends and followers, and he became accustomed to ruling
them in a manner which, for all its persuasiveness, brooked no kind
of opposition.'

So it was in his relationship with his pupil. Kind, stimulating,
sympathetic, more patient than patience itself, he captured the
little boy's heart, winning from him, as from so many others, life-
long devotion. Long after they were parted, the influence of Fénelon's piety predominated in the mind of the Duc de Bourgogne,
and ruled him to an almost excessive degree; for whereas Fénelon's
religious teaching was mystical, sophisticated, directed to the soul
in a way that made Mme de Sévigné exclaim, 'pray give my religion
more substance, it becomes so aerified that it evaporates'; what the
prince clung to, like a drowning man to a plank, were the strict rules
for prayer, fasting, and conduct, laid down by the established
Church. These, he came to believe, were his one defence against
the pride, rages, and lusts of his worser nature. Perhaps he was not
so bad as he imagined, no worse, maybe, than many other boys
between the awkward ages of seven and thirteen; but his tutors put
such a sharp edge on his conscience that he became its abject
slave.

Although Fénelon, at the time of his appointment, did not carry
the rank usual for such a high post as tutor to an heir to the throne,
the Duc de Beauvilliers had had no hesitation in naming him to the
King. At this distance of time, it would seem to have been the
obvious choice. From the community of Saint-Sulpice, where the
Beauvilliers family had long confessed and to which Fénelon was
attached,[2] he would have heard nothing but praise of him. What is

---

[1] Fénelon was permanently exiled in 1697 for his patronage of Mme Guyon,
the quietist, who led the teachers at Saint-Cyr, and almost Mme de Maintenon,
herself, astray, by her preaching on grace. She set the little girls to believing
that they were mystics. They were found swooning in the corridors, and hearing
voices which the established Church thought never came from God, speaking a
kind of language that might have been spiritual, but appeared monstrously
shocking to the school's director.

[2] At Saint-Sulpice, Fénelon had the spiritual charge of the *Nouvelles Cato-
liques*, the women newly converted, or seeking instruction in the established
Church. In 1685, when the King had revoked the Edict of Nantes, there had

more, he knew him personally, for Fénelon was the intimate friend of his wife and her circle, a friend also of Mme de Maintenon, and admitted to those private dinner-parties where the talk was unrestrained by the presence of servants. It was at the request of Mme de Beauvilliers that Fénelon had written his famous treatise on education, *L'Education des Filles*, which, although not directly addressed to her, may very well have been the fruit of long conversations on the upbringing of her eight little daughters.

His ideas on education were astonishingly new at that time, and sound modern even to twentieth-century conceptions. He believed most strongly in health and hygiene, at a period when neither was regarded as important, saying that, during a child's early years, it was vital to keep his blood pure on a simple diet. 'Meals should be given at approximately the same times each day, and at fairly short intervals, as appetite requires, with nothing rich or highly flavoured, that might induce over-eating or turn him against the food that suits him best.'[1]

As regards lessons, Fénelon believed that no good ever came from cramming a child with facts, or forcing him to learn. Even the hardest things might be taught without undue strain, provided that an appeal was made to the imagination. 'Give children well-bound books,' he said, 'even books with gilt edges. Let them have good illustrations and fine printing, and be full of stories and tales of wonder. That done, have no fear that the child will not learn to read. Children love to hear absurd stories; you may see them every day in fits of laughter, or shedding tears at what you tell them. Be sure to use this to good advantage, and when you see that they are in the mood to listen, tell them some short, pretty tale. Choose animal fables that are innocent and well contrived. Narrate them quite simply, and explain the moral.'

It was on moral influence that Fénelon relied, and preached in his treatise. Harsh discipline, such as most educators advised, should be used only as a last resort, when every other method had been patiently tried, without success. Since *L'Education des Filles* was

been persecutions of protestants throughout France, and a great number of people had changed their religion.

[1] The upbringing of the little princes, as regarded their health, was strongly disapproved of by the doctors, more especially as the Duc de Beauvilliers refused to allow them to be bled or purged. He took a great responsibility upon himself in going against the usual practice; and it is a measure of the King's trust that he did not object. Madame was full of approval, she thought no child's life was safe in the hands of the doctors.

for girls alone, corporal punishment was not dwelt on, but one feels that the idea of it repelled Fénelon. 'A mind governed by fear will always be the weaker for it,' he says. The Duc de Bourgogne and his younger brothers, when they joined him in the schoolroom, were never struck or beaten. There were other punishments, such as being sent to bed, or, for bad offences, to Coventry; but for a boy who loved his master the removal of the light of his countenance was usually punishment enough. Fénelon believed in the power of love. 'There is one feeling,' he writes, 'which it is vastly difficult, but most necessary to inspire, the feeling of love. As soon as a child is capable of loving, all that is required is to turn his heart towards the people who will be of help to him. Love will lead him to do nearly all that one wants of him. It will be a sure guide to draw him to what is good, always provided that one makes proper use of it.'

Needless to say that a boy so intelligent and tempestuous as Louis, did not make an easy pupil.[1] Before very long, Fénelon was appealing to his princely honour, demanding a solemn promise of obedience, in writing, 'I promise Monsieur l'Abbé de Fénelon, on my princely honour, to do exactly what he orders, and to obey the very moment he commands. If I fail, I will submit to any kind of punishment, or disgrace. Signed at Versailles, 29 November 1689, Louis.'

There was at least one other monumental row, described by the Marquis de Louville, in his memoirs.[2] One day, the Duc de Bourgogne forgot himself. 'No, sir, No!' he exclaimed. 'I will not be ordered about. I know your place, and who I am!' Fénelon left the room without a word. Next day he returned, looking very sad. 'Do you remember saying yesterday that you knew my place, and yours? It is my duty to inform you that you know neither. You imagine yourself above me; perhaps the servants have told you so; I have no hesitation in saying that I stand far above you in learning and experience . . . You think me happy to be your tutor. You deceive yourself. I accepted the post in obedience to the King and Mon-

---

[1] 'Such spirit, and spirit of that particular variety, with such a hasty temper, and such passions, all of them extremely violent, were not easy to tame'—Saint-Simon, Memoirs. Yet tame them Fénelon and Beauvilliers between them did.

[2] Charles Auguste d'Allonville, Marquis de Louville (1664–1731) was appointed *gentilhomme de la manche* to the Duc d'Anjou, 1690, and went to Spain with him, in 1700, as head of his French household. He was also first gentleman in waiting to the Dukes of Bourgogne and Berry. He wrote a *Mémoire sur l'Education des Ducs de Bourgogne, Anjou, et Berry*, in 1696.

seigneur; not at all for the doubtful pleasure of instructing you. So that you may be undeceived, I am taking you to His Majesty to beg him to find you another tutor, whom I pray may be more successful.' As might be expected, there was a flood of tears, followed by forgiveness.

Another scene occurred, strangely reminiscent of a similar encounter between the young Queen Victoria and Prince Albert.[1] When a battering upon Fénelon's locked door, and the announcement that the Duc de Bourgogne wished to enter had produced no response, Fénelon immediately opened it to the plea that it was 'only little Louis'. He left a record of the stories he loved to tell his haughty pupil, mentioning one, in particular, the fable of Bacchus and the Faun, that may have driven home the virtue of humility. 'How dare you,' says Bacchus haughtily to the faun, 'make fun of the son of Jupiter?' 'And how dare the son of Jupiter have quite so many faults?' replies the faun.

Mercifully the boy had the saving grace of humour, and could laugh at himself; or at least Fénelon could make him do so. He was even persuaded to laugh at Fénelon's portrait of him, disguised as a fable, in the seventeenth-century way: 'Whatever has happened to Melanthe? Nothing outwardly, everything in his head. All is well with his life; everyone wants to please him. What then is wrong? He has a bad mood. Last night when he went to bed, he was a joy to all. This morning we are all ashamed of him and have to keep him hidden away. When he got up, one of his slippers was crumpled, and the entire day was spoiled; everyone suffers . . . Wait a moment, there is something more; he wants everyone round him now; they love him; he loves them too; he is sweet and charming, and wins back even those who could no longer endure him. He admits his fault, laughs at his absurdity, mimics his own conduct, and does this so well that you might believe he was really in a rage. Surely after that one would think that the devil was gone from him. No, alas! the whole thing is repeated next evening, and he will laugh at himself the day after. He never improves.' Fénelon chose the right moment to present this portrait, and it had its effect.

On another occasion, he used the same tactics, but to less permanent effect. The Duc de Bourgogne was a merciless mocker of physical handicaps, and could draw very well. One unfortunate

---

[1] Lytton Strachey describes the scene of the locked door of Prince Albert's. 'Who is there?' 'The Queen of England.' No response. Once more the knocking and the question, 'Who is there?' 'Your wife, Albert,' and the door was opened.

member of his teaching staff, a certain Abbé Geneste,[1] was afflicted by the most enormous and unsightly nose. The prince, obsessed perhaps, by his own imperfections, drew caricatures of the wretched man's nose everywhere, on scraps of paper, in his copy-books, even on the misty windows of his coach. Fénelon arranged that caricatures of the caricaturist should be found among his lesson-books: twisted shoulder, frizzy hair, receding chin, all complete. It made Louis laugh, and served to show him that he, too, might be a source of mirth. But he was not cured of cruel mimicry; for even as late as 1710, two years before the Duc de Bourgogne's death, Saint-Simon, who loved him and for a time acted as his secretary, referred in a private memorandum, written at Beauvilliers's request, to the prince's 'too often indulged-in amusement of making wax-models or, more especially, of drawing caricatures, and thus adding injury to rudeness. The more innocent-seeming and senseless such trifles appear, the more deeply they wound, and the more they provoke blasphemy.' Saint-Simon also complained of his other cruel practices, of the way Louis still loved to watch flies drowning in oil ('which makes me shudder'), or blew up frogs with gunpowder, although he eventually cured himself of these disagreeable habits, for love of Adelaide who detested them in him.

Altogether, although Saint-Simon hailed the change wrought in Louis's character as little short of miraculous, almost incredible in so short a time', he was not entirely content with the finished article. He thought the reformation had been too radical; that fear of conscience and of his carnal nature had made the Duc de Bourgogne as timid as any aspirant to the priesthood, and something of a bigot, as well. He pointed out the danger to the State, if the prince should come to rule a great country on the narrowest principles of a particular brand of religion.[2]

Yet Fénelon, though he has received from posterity all the credit for taming his rebellious pupil, did not have the final responsibility. The great Duc de Beauvilliers had that, and it would not have been

---

[1] Fénelon said of him, 'It is hard to admire piety in persons whose exterior is repellent.'

[2] The King also became anxious regarding Louis's piety; but even more he was annoyed, because the young Duc de Bourgogne was a wet blanket, refusing to go to balls or the play, if they occurred on the eve of fast-days or Church festivals. Fénelon himself came to wonder if he had gone too far. There is a letter from him, reproaching his past-pupil for trying to rule an army as though it were a monastery.

in his nature to neglect his duties, for he also was deeply interested in theories of education. In the event, they divided their responsibilities. Religious, moral, and intellectual training went to Fénelon; the organisation of the princes' daily routine, their health and physical training was in Beauvilliers's direct care. His system was spartan in its rigour, based on his conviction that since one day they would be called upon to command French armies in the field, they would be of no use if their bodies were weak. Thus he was willing to submit them to a make-or-break discipline which, according to Louville, 'no bourgeois father would have risked for his children . . . They are trained to be athletes, and the Duc de Beauvilliers will not be turned from his project by any thought of possible accidents'. Thus, ice or snow, rain or wind, the boys went bareheaded for at least two hours' hard exercise, on foot or horseback. They were encouraged to run and sweat freely, but never to change their shirts, unless they had been playing tennis. Even then, they were not rubbed down, or made to rest like other boys, and when they went hunting (their greatest pleasure), they at first followed the hounds on foot, so as to build up their powers of endurance. Coughs and colds brought them no relief; at the very most, they were dosed with quinine. Yet this hard regime seems to have done Louis no harm; for although never robust he grew up to be sufficiently healthy. The twist in his back, however, becoming increasingly noticeable, he was given special exercises, and made to wear a painful iron cross and collar. It did not prevent his running, or walking long distances; but he seemed to limp, on account of his deformed shoulder, and could not stand straight.

The princes' lot was indeed one of low living and high thinking. We have, from Louville, particulars of their diet, which was very plain indeed, far less appetising than the food of most wealthy children of that period. For breakfast, they were given dry bread and water—or wine mixed with water, if they preferred it. Dinner was boiled beef three times a week, with stewed chicken, or pheasant, accompanied by a great amount of bread (considered to be of first importance) and two glasses only of a light burgundy, beer or cider—no other wine was allowed. For their collation, the equivalent of afternoon tea, there was dry bread, or biscuits, and water. Supper consisted of stewed mutton or veal, with some game or chicken dish, and for a sweet, a marzipan cake, or a candied orange.

This diet of dry bread and water, and the banning of roasted meat, was almost certainly Fénelon's idea. He prescribed it for the girls of Saint-Cyr, with the object of keeping their blood pure, and it was the regime which he himself followed throughout his life.

Louville also recorded their timetable. Wakened at a quarter to eight, they went first to mass, then to the *levers* of their father and of the King. From nine to ten they were free; and from ten to twelve o'clock they had lessons. After that, they had three-quarters of an hour for their dinner, and either danced or drew until two o'clock, when they played tennis or some other active game. From three until five, they did lessons with Fénelon, and then rode or ran until seven o'clock, which was their supper-time. They were allowed to read with their meal, and played games afterwards, or danced with the members of their household. Bedtime was at nine o'clock—nine-fifteen if they had been good, directly after supper if they were naughty.

Four hours for formal lessons would seem a very short time; but Fénelon believed that children absorbed more in conversation, than they did when sitting at a desk. This was especially true of that restless character the Duc de Bourgogne, who could not sit still even for a moment, and could be persuaded to attend only when allowed to curl up in his chair and draw—which Madame thought had been the cause of his twisted back.

As for the lessons themselves, Louville tells in great detail what they were, and were not, taught. They learned no Greek, nor any modern languages; 'they will not travel, and all those who come to the Court will speak to them in French or Latin'. It was none the less intended for them to learn a little Spanish and Italian at some future date. Mathematics was not considered important, for there would always be someone else to do the princes' sums—yet this appears to have been a disappointment for Louis, who showed a keen interest in arithmetic. Writing verse, or playing musical instruments was strictly forbidden, because that would bring them into competition with ordinary mortals, a most undesirable event for princes who must always excel. Where the arts were concerned, dancing sufficed, or a little prose-writing.

Latin was the basis of their general education; but Fénelon eschewed the traditional method of making them learn long passages by heart, and dinning into their heads the duller rules of grammar. He wrote amusing sentences for them to parse; gave them interesting essays to write, and set them translations of anecdotes, or fables, specially composed for them by Lafontaine. It was not a good moment for Lafontaine to be dragged back to writing fables, for he had just recovered from a serious illness that had turned him to religion. 'His life,' said the Abbé Proyart, 'had become as devout and austere as many of his early writings had been abandoned . . . The poet, uniquely concerned with his salvation, would have produced no more fables, had not the Duc de Bourgogne put back the pen into his hand, and rekindled his inspiration.' In 1692, horror of the depravity of his early work, moved Lafontaine to refuse payment for a new edition that was about to appear in Holland. The Duc de Bourgogne, extremely fond of him, and almost as much concerned regarding his soul, was delighted, and expressed his joy in the usual princely manner. The Abbé Pouget, one of Lafontaine's friends, tells the story. 'Lafontaine embraced me, saying that he had good news to tell, for a gentleman had just quitted him, having been sent by the Duc de Bourgogne to inquire after his health and give him a purse containing fifty gold louis. The gentleman was commissioned to say that the prince had learned of Lafontaine's sacrifice, which did him much honour in the sight of God and of his fellow men; but contributed nothing to his purse, that was not ordinarily well-lined. The Prince thought it unfair that he should be the poorer for doing his duty, and therefore sent him this fifty louis, which was all he had, and all that was left of his pocket money for the current month.'

As well as Latin, the boys studied geography and history, and the 'art of commanding armies' (but Louville adds: 'It was the greatest pity that no one taught them strategy and the art of war itself. The want of such learning later made itself sadly evident'). As for religious instruction, it permeated everything; the idea being, 'to make of them true Christians, by inspiring them with virtuous sentiments, and removing anyone likely to set them a bad example, rather than by wearisome religious practices that most often have a contrary effect on young children, giving them a dislike, nay, a positive repugnance for piety'. This was, no doubt, wise; but, after Fénelon's exile to Cambrai, the King, among others, worried about the long periods of private prayer and meditation to which the Duc de Bourgogne had become addicted.

But life for the 'little princes', as they were called, allowed also for some pleasures and, from time to time, for treats such as excursions to Paris, and dinners at the Tuileries, after visiting Notre Dame or Les Invalides. On one such occasion, in 1694, Cardinal von Fürstenberg gave a fête for them, with shooting galleries, and all the amusements that boys most enjoy. The King himself sometimes arranged diversions, as when, 'during one of those evenings when boredom penetrates even into Versailles', he hired a famous juggler to entertain them. The unfortunate Abbé Geneste was as usual made a mock of, for the tail of his shirt trailed out of his breeches, and the juggler pretended to remove a great glass tumbler from that very spot, saying, 'Monsieur l'Abbé! You must have been most uncomfortable!' The Abbé d'Olivet, who tells this story, goes on to say that the King burst out laughing. So did the little boys, and the Duc de Bourgogne produced a caricature of the happening, which he showed next morning to the Abbé Geneste, who was too good-natured to take offence, and even wrote comic verses to accompany the sketch.

The greatest treat of all for the princes was on their journeys to and from Fontainebleau, when they stopped to dine and sleep the night at Plessis, at the house of Prudhomme, the King's old barber, with only Moreau, their much-loved personal valet, to look after them. There they were free of governors, tutors, and etiquette, free to be spoiled and perhaps to run a little wild; for Moreau was the jolliest companion imaginable. Fontainebleau itself was something of a holiday, since most of their time was spent in hunting on horseback, shooting rabbits at Noissy, in a warren which the King kept specially stocked for them, or hawking on Moret plain.

They were not an ugly trio. Even Louis had his better points, for his forehead was good and his eyes were fine, and his pleasant, alert, often kindly expression, was considered attractive by the people who came close enough to speak to him. On the other hand the lower part of his face was far from prepossessing. His nose was too long for beauty, and although his mouth was good, his upper jaw jutted out so much beyond the lower that he appeared to be trying to swallow his chin. He was said also to have the best legs and feet of any man at the Court; almost as good as the King's, whose lower limbs had been immortalised by Rigaud. Unfortunately the beautiful legs did not show to advantage on horseback. Denonville, the riding-master, despaired of all three princes, saying that, despite his efforts, they looked like nothing so much as pairs of tongs when they sat astride their horses. Altogether, although at close range the Duc de Bourgogne might pass for being charming and dignified, all that the troops and the public saw was an awkward, limping figure, with the beginnings of a hunchback.

It was a tragedy that the slightly raised shoulder of his childhood should have turned into a real deformity. He was most sensitive regarding it, bursting into furious rages if his valets appeared in any way to notice it, and equally furious if they failed to arrange his ribbons and his thick, frizzy hair so as best to conceal it.

In 1694, when the negotiations for his marriage to Adelaide of Savoy were begun, Louis was twelve years old, and no longer considered a child. He took his first Communion, at Easter 1694, in a state of holy exultation that impressed the King, and already people were noticing the 'miraculous change' which Fénelon had wrought in his turbulent nature. A week before he reached his majority, at the age of thirteen, the King was heard to say, at dinner, that France need no longer fear rule by a minor, for, as never before in history, there was a grandfather, father, and grandson, all of an age to govern.[1] What is more, by special dispensation, he allowed the Duc de Bourgogne and the Duc d'Anjou to take their solemn vows as Chevaliers of the Order of the Saint-Esprit, instead of waiting until they were twenty, which was the traditional age.

In the ceremonies and entertainments of the Court, the prince began to play the part of a grown man. He opened the ball, at the betrothal of the Duc de Chartres, and was allowed to go to the masquerade given by Monseigneur, on the last day of the Carnival of 1695. The decorous Duc de Beauvilliers also had to go, and to go masked, though he did not at all relish the prospect of rubbing shoulders with the often tipsy crowd that filled the Salles des Glaces, at the turn of the century.[2] Sourches felt for him: 'It ill became his gravity as a minister, or the piety, of which he made open profession; but, with princes, there are certain things one has to stomach, though they go against one's inclinations, and even against the proprieties.'

All this time, Fénelon had been writing his famous book, *Les Aventures de Télémaque*, the story of how Ulysses's son Telemachus journeyed, with Minerva as his guide and counsellor, in search of his father. It was an exciting story, a kind of Pilgrim's Progress, based on Greek mythology, and containing thinly veiled censure of the rule of Louis XIV[3] A great deal of *Télémaque* has to do with

[1] Dangeau records this remark; but Providence arranged otherwise, for neither the King's son nor his grandson succeeded. It was the latter's son, by Adelaide, who became Louis XV after the King's death in 1715.

[2] Masked balls were often the occasion for horse-play and practical joking, especially by the royal family.

[3] Louis XIV became increasingly suspicious of Fénelon's teaching; although

the art of government and the use and misuse of power; but there is also a great deal about true love; which gives the impression that Fénelon wished to impress on his pupil the mortal sin of adultery.

Three female characters appear, in *Télémaque*, representing the three forms of love: Calypso for the carnal love that is sinful, and must at all costs be shunned; Eucharis, representing tender, courtly love, which may be indulged in without sin, provided that, whatever the suffering, it is sacrificed when duty calls; finally Antiope, for the love that endures a lifetime, of the pure virgin who may be sought and won in marriage, with the consent of her parents. Fénelon stated that he had never intended *Télémaque* for publication; that it was meant to 'do no more than instruct Mgr le Duc de Bourgogne, while amusing him with tales of adventure'. Nonetheless, though the book was not published until 1699, two years after Fénelon's disgrace, he was writing it in 1695, and one cannot help thinking that he was preparing his pupil to fall in love with the bride chosen for him. It is surely most unlikely that the Duc de Bourgogne was unaware of the writing of the book, or that being so fond of his tutor, he did not eagerly follow the work as it progressed.

However that may have been, the boy grew up terrified of women. Saint-Simon says that, with the ladies of the Court, he was as nervous as a novice let out for a holiday. His confessor, Père Martineau, relates that he 'had not yet been seen to yield to the vices of youth', and that one of the noblemen who knew him best had stated that 'the bashfulness of even the most virtuous ladies was as nothing to the young prince's propriety'. His tutor had convinced him that, without sin, he might love no woman but Antiope, and for Antiope he was waiting. When Adelaide's portrait was sent to him he was in raptures, and Barbezieux has described the pride and joy with which he displayed it in his schoolroom.

When the day of Antiope-Adelaide's arrival came, his excitement overcame him, sending him, regardless of etiquette, running headlong up the road to greet her; then, scrambling into the huge purple

it was not until 1697 that he was banished from the Court. It is unlikely that the King would have read Louis's lesson-books; but had he done so, he would not have been amused by *Dialogues with the Dead*, featuring, among others, an imaginary conversation between Louis XII and François I, during which Louis inquired about the uses to which special taxes were put, and commented, 'I will wager that your mistresses had a bigger share of them than the officers of your army, and that is why the people are ruined, the war still rages, justice is corrupted, the Court given over to the follies of sex-mad women, and the whole country plunged into misery.'

travelling coach, to stretch across the intervening bulk of Monseigneur and kiss both her hands. Fénelon had taught him that he could safely fall in love with her, his wife to be; and fall in love he did, recklessly and immediately.

Adelaide had little attention to spare for him; in fact she seems, if anything, to have disliked him. Shy, tired, on her best behaviour, she was for the moment, and for months to come, totally dazzled by the glory and condescension of the magnificent monarch, who was her great-uncle, and her slave.

7

A Schoolgirl at Versailles

THE COURT remained only two days at Fontainebleau, after Adelaide's arrival, and then returned to Versailles. The King was especially glad to be going home, where the quarterly cleaning had been done and 'the bad airs dissipated', so that all smelled sweet and fresh. He never liked having his timetable upset, and was inclined to think Fontainebleau unhealthily damp, so late in the year.

Adelaide's last day there was one of much-needed rest. She did not leave her rooms or receive any visits, save a private one from Mme de Maintenon, who called her 'my pet', and whom she daringly addressed as 'Aunt', to the old lady's immense pleasure. They had a cosy chat that made Adelaide feel secure and comfortable. The day was quiet, but by no means dull, for the King ordered all the twenty-four violins of his private orchestra to play for her when she went to hear mass, from the curtained corner of the right-hand gallery. Better still, piqued perhaps by the handsomeness of his family's gifts, and not wishing to be outdone by them, he had sent all the crown jewels to Mme de Mailly, her wardrobe mistress, for the princess to choose those she preferred, and to wear as she best pleased. Coming from so poor a court, Adelaide had probably never seen pearls or diamonds to compare with these for colour, size, and beauty; certainly not on the dressing-tables of her mother and grandmother.

Strangely enough, Louis XIV was miserly with precious stones. In his early days he had been made to feel ashamed of the poverty of the royal family, compared with such millionaires as Mazarin and Fouquet, and his pride had been further humbled at the time of his wedding to a Spanish princess, when his gifts had seemed to him totally inadequate to the glory of France. Determined that this should never happen again, he had begun to make a vast collection of jewels and precious stones, from among which had come his astonishingly rich presents to Adelaide's Piedmontese household. To his own subjects the King seldom gave jewellery outright, most often it was on loan for life, or for a shorter period. Even his mistresses had been very promptly dispossessed when they lost his favour.

The act of handing over the crown jewels to Adelaide, even on loan, was an extraordinary mark of confidence, for despite the signing of the marriage contract, she was only on approval, and might be sent back if found unsuitable, as her son Louis XV's little fiancée was sent back to Spain, a generation later.[1] Had the King retained any doubts regarding her suitability, he, who of all things disliked scenes and disputes, would scarcely have risked future unpleasantness with her father over the contents of her baggage.

There were still important matters to be settled for her life in the year before her wedding. First the mode of addressing her, for, although treated in every way as though she were already Mme la Duchesse de Bourgogne, she could not reasonably be styled Madame while still unmarried. The King decreed that she should be known quite simply as 'the princess', and that everyone should so address her. Secondly, her place in Society. Was she to be considered grown-up and hold court and a *cercle* (which was manifestly absurd for one so young), or should she, as was customary with the royal children, be placed under the care of the old Maréchale, their governess? That, in the circumstances, could hardly be, since Adelaide already had her own household, with a lady-in-waiting, a master-of-horse, and a full complement of palace ladies, officers, and servants. This problem the King solved by ruling that the princess's life, until her marriage, should be strictly private, except for a twice-weekly public *toilette*, to accustom her to the modes of the Court; that she should otherwise live secluded with her ladies, eating her meals alone, attended only by the Duchesse du Lude and continue her education, spending all her leisure hours with him and Mme de Maintenon. This, indeed, had long been their intention. For the next two years, at least, Adelaide was to be their pet and plaything, a beloved little granddaughter, whom they would

[1] The Infanta Marie Anne Victoire, daughter of Philip V and his second wife Elisabeth Farnese. Born in 1718, and eight years younger than Louis XV, she was sent to France at the age of four, to be his future wife. The gap in their ages proved, however, too great, for Louis was showing signs of badly needing a wife before his fiancée had emerged from babyhood.

fashion with infinite care into the perfect consort for a future King
of France.

On that last afternoon, at Fontainebleau, the King went shooting,
and at his return settled down with Mme de Maintenon to write to
Adelaide's parents. His letter has unfortunately disappeared, but a
despatch to Tessé, sent by the same courier, still survives. 'Although
I have already expressed to him [Victor Amadeus] my satisfaction
at finding in her all the qualities I was promised, you may add that
I am perfectly delighted with her manners, disposition, and looks
the grace that accompanies her every movement, and the education
that she has received. I have no doubt of discovering that gentleness
of spirit, and all those other qualities needed to enable her to profit
by our care, and that being so good a subject, she will soon reach
perfection under the instruction of the lady who has prime responsibility for her training. It is certain that by following her advice, the
princess will greatly contribute to her future happiness.'

Louis XIV's letter was probably equally formal in style, but Mme
de Maintenon, writing to Duchess Anne, fairly let herself go. 'The
Princess has arrived, and I only wish Your Royal Highness could
have seen the manner of her welcome, and how much pleased the
King and Monseigneur are with her. No one could have emerged
better from that first encounter, for she was perfect in every way—
a most agreeable surprise in a young person of eleven . . . Though I
dare not add my praise to those which alone are important, I cannot
resist telling Your Royal Highness that your child is a prodigy, and
that to all seeming she will be the glory of her epoch. Your Royal
Highness does me too much honour by approving my charge of
her further education. I think we should limit ourselves to preventing her from becoming spoilt, and praying to God that he bless
this delightful marriage.'

Mme de Maintenon was evidently in the seventh heaven. Everything was turning out better than her wildest dreams, for she had
been seriously worried, not to say alarmed, by the King's low spirits.
Since his conversion he had lost his zest for life. He loved her, no
doubt of that, and depended on her for his soul's salvation, but she
could not help feeling that in other ways she had ceased to amuse
him. It was a frightening thought. Versailles was not what it had
been in the old days, and there was no one very appetising[1] among
his old friends or in the family circle. He must be kept entertained,
for 'if he gets bored with me,' wrote Mme de Maintenon, 'he will

[1] '*Il n'y avait pas grand ragout autour de lui.*'

seek company elsewhere,' and that may lead to anything, even to a mistress and his ultimate damnation.' She thought that innocent, cheerful companionship was what he needed, and that this merry, loving child, who showed no fear of him, would exactly fill the bill.

She had had apprehensions before Adelaide's arrival. Some years later, talking to the elder girls at Saint-Cyr, she said, 'Did I ever tell you that before Mme la Duchesse de Bourgogne came to France, people thought to please the King by inventing all manner of witty remarks, which they said she had made? They thought it excessively amusing, but when the King and I were alone together, we said, "The child must be a fool or a scatterbrain if she makes such retorts at her age'. And we were enchanted to find that, on the contrary, she was extremely shy, and at first scarcely uttered a word.'

Reticence was, indeed, one of Adelaide's greatest qualities. She never seems to have gossiped or made mischief, either between her own ladies, or, later, with the ministers and officials whom she met in the King's study. Saint-Simon says that they were grateful to her because she made efforts to smooth their paths and keep them out of trouble with the King; which was why, from Mme de Maintenon downwards, people felt safe with her, and why her household loved and protected her. Oddly enough, this was one reason for her becoming so spoilt, since they would never allow anyone to reproach her, or admit to her being otherwise than perfect.

The letters of this period all speak of her gentleness and charm, as was perhaps only to be expected. The one dissenting voice was that of Madame, still huffy at her loss of precedence, and fearing Mme de Maintenon's influence. Writing on 8 November, she had said, 'She walks and holds herself very well, and is graceful in everything she does—very serious for a child of that age, and uncannily shrewd. She takes little notice of her father-in-law, and hardly looks at my son or me; but the moment she sees Mme de Maintenon she smiles and rushes towards her with open arms. She does the same to the Princesse de Conti—you see how knowing she has already become.[1] Everyone who has spoken to her says that she is highly intelligent.'

There is thus a wealth of information about the impression which Adelaide made on the Court. It might be more interesting to know

[1] If the King had died, the Dowager Princesse de Conti, his daughter by Mme de La Vallière and Monseigneur's half-sister and bosom friend, would have become one of the most powerful people at the new Court.

what impression the Court made on Adelaide; but of that we have no record. The one short, formal note she had managed to write to Madame Royale says nothing; but it is so different from the dull but intimate little letters that succeeded it, that it may indicate tension. She would have been warned that her letters were likely to be scrutinised but, in all probability, she was at this time terrified of everyone, with the exception of Mme de Maintenon and the King, and particularly so of Monsieur, and Madame. They, indeed, presented an extraordinary sight. Monsieur, tiny, potbellied, apoplectic, painted, and adorned despite his fifty years with curls and jewellery, lace and ribbons; Madame, the shape and size of a grenadier, inordinately proud of her German birth, and frightening everyone with her savage temper, and biting snubs. When not out hunting, she spent all day in a room which she had chosen specially for having windows ten feet above the floor, so as to accommodate her collection of portraits of the Princes Palatine, with which the walls were lined. Every day, she spent her time writing immensely long letters in her own hand, and making copies of them to keep for her own benefit. Monsieur had done his best to persuade her to come more into Society, but it was of no avail, and he now left her solitary, resentful, and undisturbed.

To Adelaide, the King was less alarming; she was well instructed in her duty towards him. She knew that she must try to please him, and since she was a good little girl, with a natural instinct for pleasing, she set about her task with a will, and with what success we have seen. Did she love him at all? Or was Madame right in supposing her to be a hard-headed little schemer, out to do the best for herself and her family? One close observer, at least, thought otherwise. Mme de Caylus, Mme de Maintenon's first cousin and secretary, had this to say after Adelaide's death. 'It was easier for people to believe that Mme la Dauphine resembled her father, and that when she came to France at the age of ten she was just as full of schemes, and only pretended to be fond of the King and Mme de Maintenon. I, who had the honour to know her intimately, think differently, for I have seen her weeping bitterly at the thought of their great age, very reasonably supposing that they would die before her. I cannot doubt that she loved the King. Hers was not a deep nature. She very speedily became attached to people, and the King, if it suited his mood, could be kind and gentle. He was completely bowled over by her, could not bear to be parted from her a single moment.'

Adelaide's thoughts remain a secret. Her first short letters home tell us nothing. Their composition was clearly a hard labour; a few lines in a round, childish hand, filling the whole of a vast sheet of writing paper. The spelling and punctuation still showed no improvement:

> From Versailles this 12 November [1696]
> Forgive me Madame for not writing to you the fear of vexing you makes me do it now I end Madame with a kiss
>   Your very humble very obedient granddaughter
>   M. Adelaide de Savoie.[1]

If Mme de Maintenon saw this letter, as she probably did, in the usual course of the posts, it is no wonder that she thought a special writing-master was necessary. She immediately provided one, but although Adelaide was appreciative, he had little effect, for though her spelling and grammar improved with time, her writing only got worse. Her letters are all very dull and, perhaps wisely, contain no judgements; but her second, written a few weeks later, seems to show that she was settling down, but perhaps a little homesick.

An excursion to Marly prevented me from writing to you by the last courier as I had planned, my dear Grandmamma. You would never believe how little time I have. I do what you told me about Mme de Maintenon. I like her very much and trust in her advice. Please believe, dear Grandmamma, all that she writes to you about me, though I do not deserve it. I should like you to have the pleasure of it; for I count on your affection, and I never forget all the marks of it that you have given me.

The visit to Fontainebleau came to an end just a week before Adelaide managed to write this first letter. On 7 November, after his dinner, the King had set out for Versailles in a light open carriage, called a *caléche*, arriving there about five o'clock. Adelaide

---

[1] This letter is not dated 1696, but is generally believed to belong to that year because, unlike her other letters, she signed it 'M. Adelaide de Savoie', and used as seal the arms of Savoy.

No translation could do justice to the spelling of the original, which runs: 'Vous me pardonere Madame si je ne vous est pas écrit la peur de vous anuier me la fait fair je fini Madame vous embrasan

Très humble très obéisantes petite fille.'

It would be only just to add that the Duchesse du Lude's spelling was very little better.

and her ladies had left early that morning in the great travelling-coach, and had stopped at Plessis, for dinner and a rest, at the house of that same old Prudhomme who was such a favourite with the little Princes. The King had picked her up there, for he wished to be with her when she first saw Versailles, and the splendid suite of rooms, whose redecoration, according to Dangeau, he had personally supervised.[1] If the first part of her journey seemed dull to her, she would have enjoyed the remainder, for driving with the King at the racing speed he favoured, with the windows open and the dust flying, soon became one of her greatest pleasures, though the Duchesse du Lude did not find it so agreeable. Accompanying her young mistress, in the servitude for which Saint-Simon thought she had paid too dearly, she may have envied Mme de Maintenon, who had early established it that, when she travelled with the King she made the journey in her own, slow, closed carriage.

When they arrived at Versailles, the King himself lifted Adelaide down, and, taking her by the hand, led her up the steps and to her new home, the grandest set of rooms in all the great château, where the late Queen had lived, and after her Madame la Dauphine. There were four huge state-rooms, looking out over the gardens, a guard-room, ante-chamber, audience-chamber and bedroom, to which the King later added a little oratory and a closet. The last of them, the Salon de la Paix, leading out into the Salle des Glaces, became her play-room, though it was used by the courtiers at receptions, and on other State occasions. The magnificent painted ceilings; the bright gilding, recently retouched by the painter Audran and a team of assistants; the beautiful furniture, which had once been the Dauphine's; the very size and splendour of these rooms, constructed to house a queen, might have dazzled any princess. To Adelaide, knowing only the dingy palace at Turin, they may have appeared overwhelming, not to say unhomely. Some observers had the impression of a very tiny bee, lost in the centre of a gigantic golden hive.

They gave her a fortnight's holiday, in which to settle down and explore her new surroundings, before starting on the semi-serious business of her further education, and the very serious one of training her to fill her new rôle as a royal personage, the first lady of France. Meanwhile the King and Mme de Maintenon studied her,

[1] Dangeau makes a great deal of the redecoration; but in fact very little was changed.

and in her quiet way, Adelaide studied them, and how best to please them. She felt no obligation to study her husband to be. To her he was only a boy and, in any case, he already loved her. To win the heart of her old uncle the King was what she aimed at, and she did not find it difficult.

Louis XIV was a man who easily became fond of people. He needed all the time to feel loved, a requirement that remained with him after he had done with mistresses. Mme de Maintenon thought it was providential that she should have appeared in his life just at the moment when his passions were cooling. It was her mission, from God, to show him the rival charms of affection, for who could tell to what depths he might not descend without her watchful care? That was what he loved in her. When he had first seen her playing with his children by Mme de Montespan, he had exclaimed wistfully, 'She knows the way to love; it would be delightful to be loved by her.' His paternal affection needed an outlet. The little girls at Saint-Cyr, where he was always kind and gentle, provided something of the sort; but his own children were singularly unresponsive to his advances, for Monseigneur was little better than an oaf, and with his bastards there could be no reciprocity. He might treat them with fatherly love, but their rank was in his hands, and they did not dare give him their confidence. Yet he was growing old and urgently needed some object for the gentler, sweeter side of his nature, a strange mixture of pride, monstrous selfishness, and a sensibility that drew people to him, in a way they were never drawn to that cold fish Mme de Maintenon.[1] In Adelaide, he found that object ready-made.

It is scarcely surprising that such a merry, eager, loving child should have won his heart. What did surprise everyone was the immediateness of her conquest of him and the way in which she gave him back his youth. The journals of Dangeau and Sourches, which make dull reading in the previous years, spring suddenly to life, as they describe the daily adventures of Louis XIV and his ten-year-old great-niece. It is as though Versailles, Marly, and

---

[1] Fénelon, her spiritual director, wrote her a terrible letter, accusing her of being dry, cold and insensitive, and going on to say that she was proud and egotistical, only sympathetic to those who shared her views. Yet whatever effect she may have had on grown-ups, children loved her. On the other hand, when the King sent her to persuade Mlle de Fontanges, his last mistress, to leave him, her words evoked the exclamation, 'Madame, you speak of shedding a passion as though it were a chemise!'

Fontainebleau had wakened from a deep sleep, as the two of them, hand in hand, entered a wonderland of pure delight.

'The entire Court,' said Dangeau, 'now revolves around this ten-year-old child.'[1] On their first Sunday at Versailles (11 November), 'they went out walking together in the gardens; and, thinking she might be tired, the King, ordered a little pony-carriage to follow them. He showed her many of the fountains, which she thought very beautiful'. On the Tuesday, they dined at Marly, accompanied by all her ladies, and went afterwards for a very long walk, from which she returned in raptures. There was a switchback railway in the gardens, in which Adelaide and her younger companions careered downhill amid shrieks of laughter, to the King's great amusement. Next day it was the turn of Meudon; but, the weather being very bad, their walk was only a short one. Best of all, perhaps, was the day on which the King took her to see the *Ménagerie*, at Versailles, and after explaining that the princesses all had their own zoos and that he wished her to have one too, announced that he would one day give her this one, for her very own, because it was the original, and the finest of them all. Adelaide was bowled over with joy. The menagerie became her greatest pleasure, a private place, where she and her ladies went very often to cut out dresses for sewing, make cakes and butter and have picnics.[2]

In the beginning, the King sent for her every afternoon, when he was ready to go out; but, before long, when she could not bear to wait any longer for his summons, she would go flying down the length of the Salle des Glaces and into his study, regardless of the strict etiquette that enjoined scratching ever so gently with a finger-nail against the panel of the door, until admittance was granted.[3] According to Saint-Simon, the King did not mind this at all; but would rise with a comically apologetic smile to the minister with whom he was working and, taking her hand, would let her lead him, chattering, down the staircase, and out into the garden. What par-

---

[1] The remaining quotations in this chapter are from Dangeau's Journal, unless otherwise specified.

[2] Just as her grandson's wife Marie-Antoinette was to amuse herself with country pleasures in her *hameau*, her play-village and farm.

[3] Sourches says that the courtiers were dumbfounded by the King's condescension, and by 'the unimaginable liberties she took'. They were not supposed to meet until 2 o'clock; but on the slightest pretext he would send for her, or even go to find her. 'He shows the most extraordinary liking for the Princess's company. They spend hours together in his private study, or in the rooms of Mme de Maintenon.'

ticularly charmed him in her was the complete change in her bearing, from the shy, deeply respectful gravity of her public manner, and her affectionate, trustful teasing when they were alone, scrambling upon his knee, rearranging his wig, amusing him with a stream of questions and confidences, making him laugh in a way that was inconceivable with his own grandchildren.

That first fortnight was supposed to have been a holiday; but time was found for a little light instruction between the outings and the treats. Indeed, on that very first Monday morning, Adelaide was summoned by the King to be presented with a music-master for the harpsichord, and a dancing-master for that awkward curtsey, and for the processional dances, such as the *bransle*, in which she must shine, when she opened the State balls.

Harpsichords and music-masters were new in Adelaide's life (Mme Desnoyers had once again been proved inadequate), but Mme de Maintenon said that she ought to have some accomplishments, and that there was nothing the King enjoyed more than a musical evening. It is extraordinary to imagine him, whose mere presence was capable of striking terror, indulging in community singing, with a young lady at the harpsichord, playing drinking songs, Mme de Maintenon looking up from her interminable knitting to join in the chorus, and he himself, raising the echoes from his armchair, with,

> 'Vive Bacchus! Vive Grégoire!
> A tous les deux honneurs sans fin
> Vive Grégoire pour nous verser à boire!'[1]

It must also be noted that, at other times, they would chant Vespers, '*à la mode de Saint-Cyr*', the King singing every alternate verse; which would seem altogether better suited to the atmosphere generally surrounding Mme de Maintenon.

In that first week, Adelaide was called upon to perform her first State function, in receiving a courtesy visit from the ex-King and Queen of England (James II and Mary of Modena).[2] Dangeau says

[1] From the *Souvenirs* of Mlle d'Aumale (1683–1756), a former pupil at Saint-Cyr, who became Mme de Maintenon's secretary, and was thus well placed to see all that went on.

[2] Louis XIV had a genuine affection for James II and his wife, and an unshakeable loyalty to him, feeling that Mazarin's alliance with Cromwell had been the cause of some of his misfortunes. He also had an uneasy feeling that King James might be considered a martyr to his religion, and therefore safe as regarded Heaven, which King Louis did not feel sure of for himself.

that it was accompanied by a most significant breach of etiquette; for, although still unmarried, and technically a mere 'foreign princess', she was allowed to assume her future rank and precedence, and was given an armchair exactly similar to that provided for the Queen. The only difference was that Adelaide's chair was turned ever so slightly, to allow her to be on the same line, at their leave-taking. Dangeau relates that the Queen most graciously consented to this aberration, by offering Adelaide a chair of equal grandeur when, a few days later, the latter drove to Saint Germain, to return their Majesties' visit.

Adelaide also received her first official visit, from the Emperor of Morocco's departing envoy, who compared her to the morning star, and begged leave to proclaim her astonishing perfections to all the peoples of Africa. By this time she had become adept at receiving compliments graciously. Later, she grew bored with flattery and was regrettably apt to discomfit pompous visitors by disappearing behind a curtain when they made their grand entry.

Her public *toilettes* had also begun. She spent the early part of Tuesday and Friday mornings in comfortable *déshabillé*, practising dancing with Dangeau, reading fables with him, or playing the harpsichord with her music-master. Soon it was time to put on her court-dress for the solemn procession to mass, to which she went *en grand corps*. First came a shift of gossamer thin white linen, designed to show off the delicate colour of her skin; next, a tightly laced bodice, four inches apart at the top, and pulled close together at the waist; then petticoats, and the stiff body of the dress itself, with its cover of velvet or Italian silk, exquisitely embroidered. The work of dressing was slow, because it was the cherished privilege of certain of her ladies to hand her the various articles, and the rule about restrictive practices was as fiercely guarded, at the Court, as in any modern trades union. One day, for example, when the Duchesse du Lude had been delayed, another lady pulled tight the laces of Adelaide's bodice, and was tying the knot when the duchess entered. Immediately, all was torn apart, and the whole uncomfortable process had to be repeated. Another child might have rebelled; but to Adelaide, the *toilette* was part of her job; the work to which she had been called; and she respected its ritual.

At a few minutes before noon, when Mme du Lude was at last satisfied with Adelaide's appearance, the doors were flung open, and an usher cried '*Service!*', whereupon the remaining members of her household entered. Some, like Mme de Roucy, were already old friends, others she had known only for a few days. When she had greeted and kissed them all, they formed up in two smiling, welcoming lines on either side of the door, which was re-opened to admit the courtiers, who came to see her put on her jewels, and watch her hair being set in the simple style which the King and Mme de Maintenon thought so becoming. Adelaide, meanwhile, listened gracious and smiling, to the formal compliments that were the mode of the day, and received presentations. Her room soon became crowded. Forty or fifty visitors sometimes crammed themselves into it (there were often far more at the King's *lever*), for this was the first appearance of the new member of the royal family, who, in time to come, might wield immense power. Moreover, Adelaide was still a novelty, the prime topic of every conversation, and of every piece of gossip; someone to be stared at, written about, praised or criticised, torn to shreds or mocked by all the witty cynical tongues of that bored and apprehensive Court. Adelaide, perhaps, was too young to appreciate the danger. Perhaps, having always been loved, she felt a false security, for she seems to have taken all the smiles and compliments as tokens of honest goodwill, and to have felt grateful for them. It may be, however, that her very innocence moved the courtiers' hearts, for the chorus of praise in the letters and memoirs appears genuine enough.

All through her *toilette* Adelaide's private orchestra played music from the operas, until, a few minutes before a quarter to one, the visitors departed to join the crowd in the Salle des Glaces waiting to see the King take her to mass, in the chapel. Adelaide joined the stately procession, walking beside the King; his first gentleman of the bedchamber leading the way, and the captain of the guard immediately behind. Next came the princes and princesses of the blood, the high-ranking ladies all *en grand corps*, with an escort of officers, followed by a detachment of the Swiss guard. As they proceeded, an usher in the adjoining room would beat three times upon the floor with a long wand, announcing '*Le Roi*', whereupon silence fell on the double line of bowing, curtseying courtiers. The procession moved very slowly and with immense dignity through the great rooms and the crowd, with gentlemen stepping forward, now and then, to say a word into the King's wig, as he passed, or bend to breathe a compliment into the ear of the little girl, and so they arrived at the door of the royal gallery. While mass was being said, the King's twenty-four violinists played sacred music, and they heard a sermon containing a few words on the virtues of the little princess, and the bright hopes surrounding her, not forgetting, of course, a reference to the god-like King, her uncle, at which point, the entire congregation turned towards him in reverent salutation.

They then processed back, in the same order, to their dinners, which the King ate in public state, but Adelaide quite alone in her room, with the Duchesse du Lude to give her her napkin, and help her to the very simple, wholesome meal, ordered by Mme de Maintenon.

That lady had been busy making plans, an occupation in which she delighted. She had written to Duchess Anne that Adelaide was the King's darling, which was, indeed, an infinitely desirable state of affairs; but what would happen if the old King should cease to amuse Adelaide? The high-spirited, fun-loving child clearly needed playmates, and a second group of ladies was swiftly appointed to be her companions and play-fellows. Not all of them, however, were young, amusing, or capable of active games; some appointments were purely complimentary, for example the Princesse d'Harcourt, and the Duchesses of Soubise, Chevreuse, and Beauvilliers, whom Saint-Simon called 'the chaperones'. Others, including young Mme de Saint-Simon, were livelier, and there were three little girls of Adelaide's own age, Mlles de Chevreuse, d'Ayen, and Mme de Maintenon's adopted niece Françoise d'Aubigné, her brother's little daughter. Saint-Simon says that the older ladies were seldom summoned, and that when they were, they more often than not sent excuses, but the younger ones were sent for daily to accompany Adelaide, especially on the excursions. They were strictly enjoined never, on any account, to reproach or go against her, lest she become sulky or miserable, and thus annoy the King.

One thing that worried, indeed shocked Mme de Maintenon was the child's abysmal ignorance. It was all very well to praise Duchess Anne for bringing her up to be 'courteous and attentive to all', and to have good religious principles; but really she knew nothing, not even how to write. Worse still, though never rebellious, she appeared totally incapable of absorbing any teaching; for several months later (25 May 1697) she was writing to Madame Royale, 'I hope I write well enough now, dear grandmamma. I have a master who takes great trouble with me. It would be very bad not to profit by the care they lavish on me.' In the following year, she was still having difficulties. 'It is certainly time, dear grandmamma, that my writing improved. As for my style; it would be hard, feeling for you as I do, to make it more formal.'

Her education was obviously going to be a problem, and haste was needed, since she was to be married in a year's time. In the meanwhile she would attend school at Saint-Cyr, though she was fit only for the infants' class, and needed coaching to reach even that low standard. Mme de Maintenon showed insight when she turned for help to Dangeau, that jovial courtier, gambler, dancer, and bon-viveur. 'It seems ridiculous,' she wrote, 'to wish to turn you into a professor, but you are ready to do anything in a good cause, and will do more with the princess than all the tutors in the world. I think she should have two lesson-periods a day, one on mythology, the other on Roman history. You know as well as I do that it is useless to attempt making a scholar out of her; we should never succeed. It must suffice if we teach her certain subjects that enter into general conversation and her pleasures.' She selected for the history lessons a book with short chapters, 'because our princess dislikes anything long',[1] and she ended her letter to Dangeau, 'If you find an opportunity of telling her about a princess who is very polite, modest, refined, fastidious, inspiring respect, please do not let the occasion slip. I so much fear her conforming to the grossness of the present age.'[2] Dangeau makes no mention of lessons in his journal; perhaps he was too modest to speak of them. He was also the only person allowed to correct her, and had to deal with the small complaints of the Duchesse du Lude, such as her tiresome giggle that drove her ladies mad. The Duc de Bourgogne had the same fault; but he would not have giggled with the solemn Duc de Beauvilliers, and no one else dared to mention it to him.

There was one far more serious worry to disturb Mme de Maintenon. Adelaide's attitude to religion was giving cause for alarm. It was not that her religious education had been neglected, far from that. Her conduct in church, for example, even during the longest sermons, could not be faulted, and the King himself who, since his conversion, had become a stickler for reverence and watched every-

---

[1] The book's title was *L'Histoire de l'Empire Romain*, by Nicholas Coëffeteau (1574–1623), a Dominican monk.

[2] The morals of the other princesses were unsatisfactory. The Dowager Princesse de Conti had recently been the centre of a public scandal; the Duchesse de Bourbon's relationship with the Prince de Conti was no secret; the Duchesse du Maine, not long married, was already the victim of gossip. Mme de Maintenon was determined to keep Adelaide from their circle. Madame wrote, 'They keep M. le Duc de Bourgogne's fiancée in close confinement. The King forbids us to mention operas, card-rooms or plays in her presence. Poor child! I feel sorry for her.'

body, found nothing to criticise and much to praise.[1] What is more, he had come to France armed with a letter from her confessor, containing no fewer than twenty-five moral precepts.[2] Adelaide's *Sainte Mère*, as Mme de Maintenon called Duchess Anne, had certainly done her best; but something was sadly lacking for, to Mme de Maintenon's horror, the child appeared not in the least to fear God. Indeed, some weeks after her introduction to Saint-Cyr, the old lady received a shock, when Adelaide returned from school, exclaiming in fits of laughter, 'Aunt, Aunt, what do you think happened? Today we had a general confession; I never said who I was and, when the priest had heard me, he said I was worse than the Magdalen.' 'You are quite right about the Princess of Savoy,' wrote Mme de Maintenon to the headmistress. 'We must do everything possible to bring her up a Christian. They seem to have succeeded up till the present. Let us pray for her'; and she concentrated her endeavours on implanting in the child's heart the same horror of sin with which she had imbued the King.

Meanwhile, Adelaide's daily routine was taking shape. Woken at a quarter to eight, she put on *déshabillé* until it was time to dress for mass; did her short lessons with Dangeau and her other masters, and then ran out to play with her ladies, or, if it rained, busied herself with her dolls, weaving, or dressmaking. In consultation with Mme de Maintenon, whose taste was admirable, she made a dress of yellow taffetas that landed her in trouble with the King. She had sent for an embroidress to finish it, and then forgot her; so that the poor woman would have starved, had not Mme de Maintenon taken pity on her. Adelaide was very gently scolded, which surprised her somewhat; but when she told the King of it, expecting him to laugh, he did not do so, but looked very grave, adding words which made her feel his displeasure. He was learning from his old wife that there are other ways of bringing children to order than by shouting at them, as he had been used to shouting at Monseigneur.

Dinner time, for Adelaide, was one o'clock, and, at two, her outing with the King who, according to Dangeau, found every day something fresh to interest her. Sometimes they went in a coach to

[1] He required everyone to kneel upright during most of mass, and if he heard the smallest noise of whispering, delivered a personal reprimand.

[2] The first urged her not to waste time 'that vanishes like lightning and cannot be reclaimed'. The last expressed the pious hope that, after a long life full of noble deeds, she would be received in heaven 'to adore God and rejoice eternally'.

Marly, with Mme de Maintenon and the Duchesse du Lude, the children, her playmates, following in another coach that contained her ladies. When they reached the woods, and the rides were narrow, the King would take her and the excited little girls in a pony carriage, driving very fast; and they would all meet again in a clearing, for a collation, handed in through the windows of the coach because it was winter time. The greatest treat of all was when the King took her hunting, sitting beside him in his *soufflet*,[1] the light, two-seater carriage drawn by six galloping ponies, in which he followed the hunt along the forest rides. They sometimes met the Duc de Bourgogne and his brothers, on horseback, which excited Adelaide still more, for Dangeau was teaching her to ride, and the King was saying that before long she, too, would be riding to hounds on her own pony, wearing the beautiful red and blue uniform of the royal hunt. One day he took her shooting, with beaters driving the pheasants into a net. He let her fire his gun, and, between them, they managed to bring down a cock, to her enormous satisfaction. She was also learning to play billiards, for the days when it was too wet, even for the King, to go out.

These were special treats. On ordinary days, they went out on foot, or both together in the King's carrying-chair, into the gardens or the park, to watch the work in progress and talk to old Sieur Le Nôtre, the King's friend and head gardener, for whom he had true respect and affection. Sometimes they fed the animals in the *Ménagerie*, or admired the King's particular pride and joy, the orange trees in their white-painted tubs. Sometimes they visited the stables to see the pages learning to jump. Nearly always they were out of doors, for wet or fine, cold or snowing, it made no difference to the King, and few concessions were made for the health of a not too robust little girl. Adelaide's constitution was not a strong one, and her letters home began to contain references to colds and swollen gums. Yet, as Dangeau remarked, maybe with intention, 'When it is time for the Princess to go out with the King, she forgets that she has a cold'.

When they returned, about four o'clock, Adelaide would go to Mme de Maintenon's room, where the King would often follow her immediately after his *débotter* (the ceremony of publicly removing

---

[1] A kind of light carriage or wheeled chair on two wheels, with room for one or two persons; it was lined with leather or oilcloth inside, and the hood could be raised and folded back in fine weather, or stretched out as a protection against the rain.

his boots). There would then be active games like blind man's buff, or quieter ones, like hunt the thimble and spillikins, in which Mme de Maintenon could join. Often there was music from the King's fiddlers, sometimes a sing-song round the harpsichord, or dancing; very occasionally an entertainment, a juggler or a puppet-show, to which the princes would be invited. Most often the King would settle down to work with one of his ministers, leaving Mme de Maintenon and Adelaide to chat quietly together on the other side of the fire. They talked of the pleasures of the simple life, and of Adelaide's old home; and Mme de Maintenon would tell stories of the time when she also had lived in the country, at the house of her aunt; how she and a little cousin would be sent out early in the morning, wearing masks to protect their complexions, and how they were given a picnic basket and a poetry-book, entitled *The Pleasures of a Country Life*, with verses marked to be learned by heart. They carried two long sticks for they spent all day out of doors, minding the turkeys and preventing them from straying.

They also talked of clothes, about which Mme de Maintenon knew a great deal, and thought a very proper interest for a young girl, until she developed more serious, more pious concerns. She spoke of how she had been very poor when she was young, and had had to give much thought to dress, living as she did in the highest Society. She said that, when she was a widow, she had had a dress made of grey silk, very plain, but fashionably cut, and of the richest material she could afford, and that the King had thought her better dressed than anyone. Now that she was old, she had decided to wear always the same black gown and hood, but allowed herself very beautiful lace at the neck.

While they talked, Mme de Maintenon would brush Adelaide's hair, as she often brushed the hair of the younger children at Saint-Cyr. She found it a way of gaining their confidence and getting them to talk to her. Hers was not the head-jerking torment of an English nursery, but long, slow, gently caressing strokes, that comforted and reassured. Adelaide, like the other children, loved having her hair brushed as she listened to Mme de Maintenon's tales of America when she was a little girl.[1] It was really of Martinique that she spoke, but in those days it was thought of as being part of America.

---

[1] These are the stories, written down by the dames, which Mme de Maintenon told the children at Saint-Cyr. There is no evidence that she told them to Adelaide, but hard to imagine that she would not have done so. She loved to tell stories, especially if she could adorn them with a little homily.

Her family had taken several maids with them from France, but one by one they had all left to get married, even one hideous old crone with a club foot. At last, her mother had no one to wait on her, except little slave girls, too uncouth to brush a lady's hair. So little Françoise, as Mme de Maintenon then was, had had to study the art, and although so small that she was obliged to stand on a chair, her mother said that she learned quickly and did it beautifully.

'I never imagined,' said Mme de Maintenon, in the flutelike tones for which she was famous, 'that learning to brush people's hair would bring me advancement at the Court. It just goes to show that one should learn everything one can, for that was how I gained the favour of Mme la Dauphine, and became one of her ladies. She had a perfect forest of hair, always in a tangle; but I started at the ends and gently straightened it out, and I never hurt her; which was why she preferred me to all her other ladies.'

In this way a friendship was formed between Adelaide and the old lady, a comfortable intimacy, closer than that between many mothers and their daughters. Mme de Maintenon was deeply moved by the trust of this fascinating, headstrong child, on whom so much depended; she saw a second life's work in her upbringing, and eagerly accepted it. Indeed, had it not been for the loving, watchful care which she lavished on Adelaide day after day, month after month, in those early years, the nobler side of the little girl's nature might not have survived the spoiling, or showed itself so valiantly when troubles came.

Once again, did Adelaide love Mme de Maintenon? The cynical Court thought not; for her family had certainly primed her to show affection even though she might not feel it; yet the confident relationship built up in the next sixteen years could scarcely have been founded on a pretence. As Mme de Caylus said, Adelaide was a child who gave love easily and responded to kindness. For the rest of her life she went to Mme de Maintenon, not in fear, but for comfort and protection, though she could not resist teasing her now and then.

It should not be forgotten that Mme de Maintenon even in old age had many attractions. The warm smile that lit her whole face; her beauty, which was still evident; her delightful voice; her way of talking, her fastidiousness and delicious scent. Had it not been so, the King, that connoisseur of women's charms, would never have been in love with her, and love her he most certainly did. Outsiders were impressed by her kindly appearance. An English tourist who saw her setting off for Marly with the King, described her thus: 'she emerged without attendants; her dress was of some brown material, and she had a very striking head-dress. She wore no jewellery, beyond a small diamond cross suspended from her neck. She placed herself beside the King in the coach, and bowed with dignity, smiling pleasantly when she perceived an English lady among the spectators. Her eyes are very fine, and there is about her whole person an indefinable charm which old age cannot destroy. She seemed entirely occupied in seeing if the King were comfortably seated. A servant brought her needlework; she then put up the glass of the window, put on her spectacles, and began working as the coach started.' It all sounds peaceful and reassuring; but it does not tell the whole truth. Mme de Maintenon had a yearning for power, which was why many of the courtiers, notably Madame and the Duc de Saint-Simon, could not speak of her without abuse. They feared her because they saw in her eyes a love of power and believed her to be all-powerful.[1] In fact, she seems to have had little influence with the King in State affairs, although she certainly encouraged him to choose for his counsellors pious men like Pontchartrain and Chevreuse. 'Surround him with good men,' had been Fénelon's advice to her, 'and let them rule him, for that is what he needs.' That was how she had converted the King, and, for at least ten years, had made him ultra-religious. After that time, old age and disaster gradually made him indifferent to God, and even to her, whom he had once seen as the echo of the divine voice.

She had accepted that it was her mission to put the King in fear of God. Perhaps she had been inspired by the fervour of converts, for she herself, at the time of their marriage, had not long been converted from Protestantism. Saint-Simon remarked that 'a look of piety soon afterwards became her principal characteristic'. When Adelaide arrived, some fifteen years later, something of the enthusiasm had departed. Mme de Maintenon had become bored with the King and his soul, and was finding at her school of Saint-Cyr, and in the distribution of benefices, her solace and chief interest.[2]

The school, moreover, was an interest and a pleasure which she could share with the King. He had been overcome by her idea of

---

[1] Madame wrote, 'The strange light that shone in the eyes of the old witch, beneath the black head-dress, made her more than a little terrifying.'

[2] Saint-Simon says that she was 'inclined to regard herself as the Mother of the Church, and to believe that she wielded more power than she actually possessed'.

founding an academy for the daughters of noblemen impoverished by the wars[1]—'no Queen of France ever imagined such a plan,' he had said, and had gladly consented to it because it harmonised with his own intention to found a cadet-school for the sons of fallen officers. He had enjoyed all the preliminary discussions. 'What a dismal little bonnet!' he had exclaimed when Nanon put on, for his benefit, the head-dress proposed for the mistresses. He had made them alter it so as to show their curls; and on the same excuse of its being unnecessarily gloomy, he had changed the colour of their gloves from black to bronze. He loved going to Saint-Cyr and showed himself at his gentlest and kindest, coaxing the children to talk, and taking the little ones on his knee to hear their lessons. Mme de Maintenon said that he knew them all by name.

A born governess she may have been, but, as Saint-Simon said, she was incapable of looking far ahead, or of taking wise decisions in serious matters. The girls were happy enough, and well cared for, and the education, though rudimentary, not bad for the period; but she filled their heads with romantic notions, and excited them with glimpses of the Court that made them dream of great marriages and establishments, not to mention love-affairs.

Mme de Sévigné's friend Mme de La Fayette, whom she called the 'Voice of Sweet Reason', remarked, 'This place which is now the abode of virtue and piety may, in the not too distant future, become a resort of Godlessness and debauchery. For to imagine that three hundred girls can live until their twentieth birthday near a court full of lively young men without leaping over the wall is scarcely reasonable.' 'Sweet Reason' was wrong for once; there were no scandals, but though Mme de Maintenon continually warned her girls that they should fill their minds with God, because, after Saint-Cyr, there would be no more pleasures for them, and the happiest among them would find themselves far away, managing servants and a farm, even turning their hands to manual work, she did nothing to prepare them for the dull, hard life before them.[2]

As for marriage, 'Alas! my dears,' she would say, 'few men will prefer your virtue to other girls' dowries'; and would then console

---

[1] The girls had to have four degrees of nobility on their father's side, and to be free of epilepsy and the vapours.

[2] Nancy Mitford says that the life on country estates was so boring that people who retired to them got very fat, or else very thin, and died in a matter of months.

them, saying, 'If you come to face the ordeal of marriage, you will find it nothing to laugh at'. Although the King gave each of them, on leaving, a dowry of three thousand livres, they could not be regarded as good matches; but none the less some marriages were made at the school, for instance that of the future Lady Bolingbroke who, while she was still at Saint-Cyr, was first married to the ancient and very wealthy M. de Villette.

Mme de Maintenon seems to have been carried away by the overriding desire to give the King innocent pleasure.[1] He liked young people when they looked happy, and he loved girls to be pretty and well-dressed. She therefore allowed the older ones to adorn themselves with pearl necklaces and knots of flame-coloured ribbon (his favourite colour), and to sing for him the prologues and choruses from the operas.

It may have been no bad thing to avoid the pettiness and puerilities of convent schools, of which Louis XIV disapproved, thinking that they tended to make girls sour and unattractive; but, in order to please him, Mme de Maintenon went altogether too far in the other direction. The performance of Racine's plays, more especially *Andromaque*,[2] before the grandest set at the Court shocked many people, including Fénelon, who thought that girls should go from school into the world as from 'the depths of cavernous darkness into the blinding light of day'. Yet it was Fénelon who nearly brought about the closure of Saint-Cyr, and the end of Mme de Maintenon herself, by the introduction of the spell-binding Mme Guyon, with her dangerously heretical preaching on grace and pure love, her poetic mysticism, and her stories of religious ecstasies that set the girls to swooning over visions.

All that was past history when Adelaide arrived. Mme Guyon had been banished two years earlier; Mme de Maintenon was forgiven, and the whole atmosphere of Saint-Cyr had changed. It was now a convent school, with nuns for mistresses, and the King thought the standard so high that he wished his own daughters had been sent there. It was therefore reasonable, though an innovation,

[1] He hugely admired her for Saint-Cyr. He was fond of saying how wise, how sensible she was, and was apt to turn to her, saying, '*Qu'en pense Mme Raison?*' when working with a State Secretary or minister. She does not, however, seem to have been very wise about Saint-Cyr. Or did she consider the girls expendable, in the interest of keeping the King out of mischief?

[2] They acted the love-passages so realistically that Mme de Maintenon begged Racine to write another play for them, in which the morals would be impeccable—'a Bible story, or something out of history'. The result was *Esther*.

for Adelaide to attend. Young companions would keep her busy and happy, and prevent her from feeling homesick, and Mme de Maintenon would be able to keep an eye upon her. At the same time, that lady was very conscious of the danger to the school, for, one day, shortly before Adelaide's coming, she addressed the older girls. After praising them for having taken a Lenten sermon so much to heart that they had concealed their curls, she continued, 'I should feel quite in despair if the daily appearance of Mme la Duchesse de Bourgogne, with ladies whose station in life requires them to give, as it were, an air of worldliness, should revive any such tendency in you.'

She was torn apart; but Adelaide's needs were paramount, and she did not hesitate. On 25 November, just two weeks after the little girl's arrival, Mme de Maintenon took her to Saint-Cyr, for a State visit, in full court-dress. It was a glorious occasion. The entire school was drawn up on the front steps to receive her. Mme du Peyrou, the principal,[1] delivered a short address of welcome, and the girls and mistresses burst into the strains of *God Save the King*, the school hymn, especially written for them by an ex-headmistress, Mme de Brinon. Lully's tune for it has been lost, but the words are still sung by the British in their National anthem.[2] Adelaide then processed in State to the chapel for a short service, between two lines of schoolgirls, and afterwards made a tour of the whole establishment. There was a collation; and the visit ended with an entertainment. It was the normal practice, at Saint-Cyr, for the girls to act 'Conversations', on some set subject, such as prayer, the cardinal virtues, the difficulties of married life, or the dangers of keeping bad company. Sometimes, however, the dames wrote dialogues to fit a special event, and no doubt they did so on this occasion, paying the princess delicate compliments, with allusions to the tremendous honour of her visit. The Marquis de Sourches relates that she 'returned in raptures, having been enchanted by

---

[1] Catherine Travers du Peyrou (b. 1666) became a professed nun, at Saint-Cyr, in 1686. She was seven times elected its superior, and died in 1748.

[2] The French words went as follows:

Grand Dieu sauvez le Roi
Grand Dieu vengez le Roi
Vive le Roi
Qu'à jamais glorieux
Louis victorieux
Voie ses ennemis toujours soumis
Vive le Roi.

seeing the little girls in the chapel and at their play. She immediately ran to find the King, who was working in Mme de Maintenon's room, and he was particularly pleased with her eager responses to his questions, and the respect with which she tempered her childish delight'.

Thereafter she became a regular pupil, attending two or three times a week, going with Mme de Maintenon at seven o'clock in the morning, and returning about four, to be with the King. She wore the school uniform, a well-cut dress of plain brown serge, with a muslin collar and a white apron edged with red ribbon, the colour of the youngest class (for which she was too old). This dress was covered by a fur-lined cloak which, in summer, would be exchanged for one with a striped cotton lining. The dames were similarly dressed, save that they wore no aprons, and the four classes sported the ribbons of their particular colour: blue for the top class; yellow for the young ladies between seventeen and twenty; green for the eleven-to fourteen-year-olds (where Adelaide should have been), and red for the babies. Prefects, among the blues, wore flame-coloured knots in their hair. The head-dresses, a more becoming version of a nun's white coif, allowed curls to appear, and were made decorously charming with bows of the appropriate ribbon. The whole costume had been thought out to the last stitch by Mme de Maintenon.

Adelaide seems to have taken to school-life like a duck to water. She was known as Mlle de Lastic, after a former pupil, and was treated exactly like the others, except that she was allowed to see the examination questions beforehand, and was made to learn the answers by heart.[1] Mme de Maintenon ordered her dinner, every day, and she ate it in the ordinary refectory, at the reds' table. Here is the menu for a feast-day: 'She must have crayfish soup, in a silver bowl; a twisted roll of the sort she always eats; a slice of brown bread from the Ménagerie;[2] fresh butter; new-laid eggs, fried sole in a little dish, redcurrant jelly on a separate plate, cornets of pastry, a carafe of wine; water in a china jug small enough for her to lift herself, and an earthenware mug to drink out of . . .I

---

[1] The intention was to make her appear cleverer than the rest. 'If by chance the wrong question had been asked, all the preparation would have been in vain. She was frightened lest that should happen; but everyone took care not to expose her to any such humiliation.'

[2] People who had private menageries used them as a home farm, and would go there in the mornings to drink milk and eat new-laid eggs with bread.

shall eat with her in the girls' refectory, sitting at the reds' table.'

At the beginning, Mme de Maintenon went with her nearly every day, and sat with her during her lessons (reading, writing, grammar, catechism, and scripture). But lessons, despite Dangeau's coaching, did not much appeal to Adelaide, though she rather enjoyed 'Catechism', perhaps because she already knew the answers, and could show off a little. The dames said, however, that it was part of her sweetness that she was so good, always very grave and very respectful in her behaviour towards them. When it was not lesson time, they let her do very much as she pleased, and she ran through the whole convent like an eager, inquisitive, little fox-terrier, busying herself in all the different departments, helping the novices with the housework, making pies in the kitchen, running with the other children in the beautiful park which Mansart had designed for them,[1] playing hide and seek, and other running games, which she usually won because she was so quick. The other children liked her. Her rank would, in any event, have made her popular, but the dames recorded that 'though her breeding showed in all that she did, her friendly smile and merry laugh raised everyone's spirits'. She formed a real friendship with Françoise d'Aubigné, Mme de Maintenon's niece, just a year older than herself. They did everything together, kissed and quarrelled and, occasionally, came to blows. One day, just as a battle was ending, there came a message from Adelaide's confessor, bidding her come to confession. 'I would not be you for anything,' cried Françoise, 'having to confess with all that on your conscience!'; and the dames said that Adelaide blushed.

Mme de Maintenon had laid down one rule for them. They might do as they best pleased, provided that they were punctual for all their lessons and did not disturb the timetable. As to that, they were good and obedient; but they disturbed almost everything else in the convent, yet seemingly caused more amusement than annoyance. They spent a day in the novitiate, dressed up in the habit. Adelaide insisted on taking the long robe of the professed nun, with the golden cross and all the other attributes, while Françoise, to her fury, was clad like an ordinary novice. By evening, they were

[1] Jules Hardouin Mansart (1644–1708) was the nephew of the famous Mansart. He was the King's architect and, in 1699, was made director of works and gardens. The King had approved his plans for Saint-Cyr, and had himself given names to the glades and avenues—Avenue for Meditation; Avenue for Solitude; etc.

tired, and, exasperated by the need to keep total silence, they ran off together, to find a place where they could chatter.

What they particularly enjoyed was working with the house-keeper, picking over the fruit, running messages, doing all manner of little jobs; and it delighted them when she forgot their rank, and ordered them about. When they were good, she gave them dried apples and brown bread, the snack they preferred; but what they most loved was to work in the dispensary with Sister Marie, an old peasant-woman, who to their great amusement would lecture them on the vanities of this wicked world. One day, when Adelaide had a violent stomach-ache Sister Marie bound an old greasy dish-cover to the offending area, saying it would take the pain away, to the horror of Mme Quentin when she undressed her that evening. But Adelaide's life was not all play, for there were other times when she took part in the religious life of the convent; for instance, she attended a meeting of the chapter, though she did not vote; gave the veil to a newly professed nun, and held one corner of the pall at a nun's funeral.

Pious exercises and Roman history formed the greater part of the curriculum; but theatricals still figured, though on a more modest scale than in the past, for Mme de Maintenon believed that acting gave the girls the confidence and polish required to be accepted into good Society. After *Andromaque*, with its all-too-vivid portrayal of the passions, had come *Esther*, in which, according to Racine, 'the young ladies declaimed and sang with so much charm, decorum, and piety, that it would have been a crying shame to have kept it restricted to a school audience'. The King thereupon paid a second visit, bringing with him the cream of the Court, with the sad result of turning the girls' heads and provoking what was almost a mutiny by their refusal to sing Latin hymns, for fear of spoiling their accents.

Athalie followed some time later; but only the King and his family saw it, and the girls, to their great disappointment, wore their school uniforms, although a few managed to beautify them with extra ribbons and a pearl necklace. That was the last time that outsiders were admitted, and Mme de Maintenon gave strict orders for the future. 'Keep such entertainments within the school, and never, on any pretext, let them be given in public. It is always dangerous to allow men to see pretty girls, especially when they make themselves even more attractive by acting a part. Therefore let no man in, rich or poor, old or young, cleric or layman—not even a saint, if any such exist on earth.' But the acting continued and, as was only natural, a play was put on for Adelaide's benefit. On 3 January 1697, *Esther* was revived, and she was given a part. We do not know for certain which part it was; all that Dangeau says is that she played a young Israelite, but there are several such in *Esther*, who sing in the various choruses. One, however, referred to as 'the youngest of the Israelites', has the famous line, '*Ciel, qui nous défendra si tu ne nous défends?*', and that, in all probability, was her rôle. She was no actress; even the dames were silent regarding her talents; but she had acted in a play, and firmly believed herself to be a star, which, two years later, nearly caused a serious quarrel, only averted by Mme de Maintenon's supreme tact, with her friend Françoise d'Aubigné.

December came, and Adelaide's eleventh birthday. The King took her for the weekend to Marly, as an especial treat, and said that he wished to lose no time in fixing the date of her wedding for 10 December of the following year. Greatly to the surprise of Govon, her father's envoy, Dangeau urged him to apply for Marly[1] on that birthday visit and, to his even greater surprise, he was invited; for foreigners, especially ambassadors, were hardly ever included, the King usually saying that Marly was for his friends, not for affairs of State. As soon as they arrived, the King took him to see the gardens, though there was nothing in bloom, and talked of the beauty of the plan, and the mechanism behind the fountains and cascades. Adelaide was with them the whole time, and Govon wrote to Victor Amadeus that 'the King showed her everything, admiring her aloud, like a doting parent, encouraging her to hop, skip, and jump and, over and over again, telling me how charmed he was by her sweet nature; how she was exactly made for him'. 'So talking,' continued Govon, 'we came to the *carrousel*,[2] with its little wooden carriages, and we stayed there watching nigh on three quarters of an hour. The Princess then asked the King if I might join in the fun . . . and he consented.'

Later on, when Govon was talking to Mme de Maintenon, the King joined them, saying once again that the Princess was absolutely his ideal, that she had lately had the toothache, but was better now; she had called the fuss about it ridiculous, vowing that she knew far better how to manage her health than her doctor—her

---

[1] People were not given invitations for Marly; they applied. 'Marly, Sire?' they would say, and were included, or refused.

[2] The mountain railway worked by water-power from the Marly machine.

doctor who had just received 500 golden louis as a reward for curing her!

What with school, toilettes, riding, music lessons, and her daily time with the King, Adelaide had a full programme. She had little leisure to spare for writing home to her parents, and none in which to become better acquainted with her fiancé, except in those fortnightly visits under the eyes of their chaperones. These occasions do not appear to have been inspiring, for the best that Govon could say of them was that 'from the very beginning, the young couple had conversed amicably, and had seemed sad when the time came to part'. It was not always so dull, however, for soon, to the music of Adelaide's orchestra, they began to practise the bransle, and other processional and round dances, with which they would open the balls, at their wedding; and, once a month, when the little princes joined them, there were drawing-room games with Mme de Maintenon and the ladies.

Little outwardly had changed in the life of the Duc de Bourgogne. Still under the governorship of the Duc de Beauvilliers, he spent long hours in the schoolroom and at prayer, and afterwards exhausted himself with violent exercise. More and more, since Fénelon's removal to Cambrai, he was missing his tutor's companionship. Fénelon continued to direct his education from afar, sending formidable lists of books, both sacred and profane, to Fleury the under-tutor, and once a year, for a space of three months, returning to Versailles. During the intervals, long letters were exchanged, often several times a week. But it was not the same, and Louis keenly felt his loss.

There was worse to come. Two years had passed since Fénelon's promotion to the See of Cambrai; it is strange to think that during all that time, when he was acting as tutor to the Duc de Bourgogne, he should still have been strongly influenced by the Quietist doctrines of Mme Guyon, and that even while he was writing *Télémaque* for the prince's instruction, he was preaching those theories of pure love and mystical union that had wrought such havoc among the schoolgirls of Saint-Cyr. No harm need have come of this, had he not, at the time of her arrest, sprung to her defence with a book entitled *L'Explication des Maximes des Saints*, which created a public scandal by its deviations from orthodoxy. The King, deeply shocked, went straight to Mme de Maintenon, exclaiming, 'What is to be done, Madame? What will become of my grandchildren? In what hands have we placed them?' She, feeling none too secure, because of her own involvement with Mme Guyon, offered no defence; and that was the end of Fénelon.

On 3 August 1697, just four months before the wedding, the King summoned the Duc de Bourgogne to his study, and spent a very long time trying to 'detach' him from the tutor he loved so much. It was of no avail; Louis fell weeping on to his knees, begging to be allowed to justify his master by submitting to an examination of doctrine; but the King remained firm. 'My boy,' he said, 'I cannot do what you ask. This is a matter that concerns the defence of the Faith, of which the Bishop of Meaux [Bossuet] knows more than you or I'; and that same evening the Court learned of Fénelon's banishment to his diocese. It was a life-sentence. The King never forgave him; and he was not permitted to return even for his pupil's wedding.

Louis was heartbroken, but sincerely believing, as he was fond of repeating, that the King was an emanation of the Divine will, he forced himself to make the break complete; and, until four years had past, did not even write to Fénelon. Yet a deep attachment remained, as was seen, years later, when, passing through Cambrai on his way to join the army, he was allowed to greet, but not converse with, Fénelon in the open market place.

Meanwhile, he remained the sole charge of the devout Duc de Beauvilliers, to whom, rather than to Fénelon, may have been due the exaggerated piety that made it so hard for Louis to square his religious convictions with life at the Court. Under Beauvilliers's influence he was encouraged to consult his conscience, and his confessor, at every step, and over the most trivial details. None the less, to the Duc de Beauvilliers must go the credit for planning a course of study that was a complete novelty in the education of an heir to the throne. At the beginning of the new year (1697), a list of questions, for the instruction of M. le Duc de Bourgogne, was dispatched to the law officers and commissaries of the various provinces, requiring them to give a detailed account of conditions in their sub-divisions. Enclosed were clear directions for answering, with orders to reply within not more than three months. It was said to have been the prince's own idea to send the list also to intendants and tax-gatherers; but Beauvilliers almost certainly supplied the impetus. As head of the finance council, he would have known better than anyone the true state of affairs, the extreme poverty, indeed starvation, of the peasants, the unfair system of taxation, the rapacity of the tax-farmers. He knew also, from personal experience, the danger of being ruled by a monarch who was unaware of the plight of his subjects.

The project made a deep impression, and was welcomed by all men of goodwill who worried over the state of the country. One such, the Comte de Boulainvilliers, wrote as follows: 'Word had already reached me, buried deep in the country, of the rare gifts of M. le Duc de Bourgogne ... but when I learned that, at his personal request, all the intendants in the kingdom were ordered to send him an exact report of their divisions, and that he himself had framed the questions ... I must confess that my heart leapt with hope for the future.'[1]

So it continued throughout the year, with Louis entirely occupied by his studies, his religious exercises, his hunting and military training, and Adelaide with her school and her amusements. To everyone's continued amazement, the King became increasingly devoted to her. She visibly remained his darling, his 'one joy', whose company he sought at all times, and without whom he never seemed completely happy. As for Mme de Maintenon, her fondness for Adelaide was rapidly turning to a deep attachment, of an intensity which that cold woman had possibly never before experienced. What had served, above all, to win both their hearts was the change, unprompted, in Adelaide's manner, from her confident, merry teasing of them in private, and her public manner, shy, serious, discreet, full of reverence towards the King, shyly formal, with a pretty mixture of love and respect for Mme de Maintenon.

It was a long and bitter winter. The canal, at Versailles, was three times frozen over before it finally thawed, and Adelaide had for most of the time a cold which kept her in bed; but the King and Monseigneur came to visit her, and she spent the whole of one evening playing proverbs. She was well again by the end of that week, and was able to go sledging and sliding on the ice; and soon it was warm enough to go hunting with the King. He felt that she had settled down and that they could confidently prepare for her wedding. Recalling Tessé to his duties as her master of horse, he wrote, 'The Princess is so easy with me now, and so comfortable with her ladies, that she has absolutely no further need for her Piedmontese maid,

[1] Henri, Comte de Boulainvilliers (1658–1722), geologist and economist. Saint-Simon thought 'his scholarship vast, his humility becoming'—but disapproved of his interest in astrology, especially after he correctly predicted, to Mme de Saint-Simon, the date of the King's death.

whom I will send home when the weather improves.' This was Mme Marquet, about whom there had been so much controversy in the previous year. She had been asking to return to her family, and when an opportunity presented itself in April, with Govon's departure, she travelled under his protection. Mme Marquet, or Marquette, as the ladies called her, had been a complete success. She had never interfered or made trouble and everyone had liked her. Adelaide cried when they said goodbye, and made her a present of all the clothes she had brought from Savoy,[1] and Mme de Caylus records that she shed tears for many days afterwards. Some observers, on the other hand, reported that she did not mind the parting, in fact appeared to be quite heartless; Sourches, however, was of the opinion that 'she showed great courage, and quickly dried her eyes for fear of troubling the King'. As for Marquette, she returned to Turin very well pleased, with a present of a thousand golden louis from the King, a silver dinner-service from Mme de Maintenon, and Adelaide's last gift—her miniature framed in diamonds.

As Adelaide settled down, secure in the King's devotion, and amid a chorus of praise from her private world, she could not, perhaps, avoid becoming spoilt. Her manner in public remained beyond reproach—even the hypercritical Duc de Saint-Simon could not fault her; but, in private, with her young friend Françoise d'Aubigné, she drove the Duchesse du Lude and some of the older ladies to a frenzy of annoyance. They giggled and screamed with laughter, and in the carriages, when the King was not present, were never still for a moment, standing on the seats, and scrambling, like monkeys, over people's laps. Mme du Lude asked Dangeau to speak to her once again about the giggling; but she had to suppress her rage, at meal-times, when Adelaide ate with her fingers, and encouraged Françoise to stick her hands into the sauce, and taste everything. One feels inclined to think that when Adelaide wrote assuring Mme Royale that the Duchesse du Lude loved her, she may, at that early period, have been stretching the truth.

One day, she and Françoise went altogether too far, and actually brought down upon themselves a rebuke from the King. They were giggling together at his dinner about the ugliness of one of the attendant officers, and they spoke too loud. Whereupon the King

---

[1] Adelaide did not have very much of her own to give away, but her trousseau from Savoy (which she had probably grown out of) would have been a valuable present, remembering the cloth of gold and silver, the gold lace, and embroidery.

intervened in an icy voice. 'I am surprised that you should think this officer ugly. To me he is the handsomest man in my kingdom, as he is certainly the bravest.'

Madame, who had brought up three little girls with rough kindness[1] and had succeeded with them all, did not view the future with optimism. 'She is not allowed to enjoy herself with anyone except the King and Mme de Maintenon. I expect that the plays they are doing at Saint-Cyr for her benefit will give her such a distaste for others that she will not be able to endure them when she grows up. When she is alone with the King and Mme de Maintenon they let her do whatever she pleases and behave as the fancy takes her. Time will tell what that kind of education is worth.'[2]

Madame, however, disapproved of most people and most things in France, including the training of the King's grandsons. 'They are very badly brought up. They eat alone, go out alone together, and never appear in public. When there is *appartement*,[3] they arrive just as the band is striking up, and leave as soon as it stops. The eldest has a sharp way of speaking; the second hardly utters, and when he does say something, he stammers; only the youngest is always cheerful and seems pleased when anyone speaks to him. He is quite merry and at ease, and does not stand stiff as a ramrod when addressed, as do his elder brothers.' She had no better to say of Monseigneur, their father: 'proud, self-willed and bad tempered,' she told her aunt.' Those who serve him will have their work cut out.' She saw a great deal of what was going on; but, as Saint-Simon relates, 'She was a German to the last drop of her blood', and thought that everything and everybody was far better ordered in her native country.

As the spring advanced and the weather improved, Adelaide spent more and more time out of doors, playing with her ladies in the *Ménagerie*, exploring the *Labyrinthe*[4] (the maze), at Versailles,

---

[1] Her two step-daughters, Duchess Anne the mother of Adelaide; Marie Louise, who became Queen of Spain, married to Charles II, and her own daughter Elisabeth Charlotte (b. 1678) who married the Duke of Lorraine in 1697.

[2] Letter to the Duchess of Hanover, 17 January 1697.

[3] *Appartement*, the evening receptions held three times a week in the state rooms at Versailles. There was music, card-playing, billiards, and conversation, not to mention delicious refreshments, with the pyramids of hothouse fruit from the King's garden, which set a fashion in all the smart houses. Mme de Sévigné says that they got so high that the tops of the doorways had to be raised.

[4] A delightful, informal part of the garden, much sought after for love-

which she especially loved because there were fountains at every turn, portraying one or other of Lafontaine's fables. There were long summer evenings with water picnics on the canal: Adelaide, the Duchesse du Lude, Dangeau, and of course the inevitable Françoise, gliding in a gondola, with a boat following, containing her orchestra, playing harmonious music from violins and hautboys, and other vessels full of ladies and gentlemen of the Court, in their best clothes.

Parties of pleasure Adelaide enjoyed, but her real love was for sport, and especially hunting, either on horseback or with the King in his pony-cart. When hunting went out of season, she took to fishing in the royal fishponds. It became a perfect craze all through that summer of 1697, and Dangeau tells of baskets of 'monstrous fine carp', dispatched, immediately after capture, for the King's supper at Marly, Louis XIV thought her too funny for words, especially when, arriving for the spring visit to Fontainebleau, she ran straight from the carriage to the carp-basin, with footmen flying after her with rod and bait. Dangeau says that he went straight up to one of the balconies to watch her, laughing so much at her antics that he nearly split his sides.

One expedition gave intense pleasure, when Mme de Maintenon took her to Paris, with Mme du Lude and Mme de Mailly on the front seat of the coach, and Mmes de Nogaret and Dangeau by the doors. One may imagine them to have been a merry party, for Mme de Maintenon enjoyed a laugh, and Saint-Simon says that the other ladies were delightful company, and that the three younger ones could be exquisitely funny. They entered Paris by the Porte Saint-Honoré, and crossed the Pont Neuf to visit the convent of Port-Royal, where the nuns gave them a delicious collation. They then did a little sightseeing by way of the Luxembourg, the quays, and Les Invalides, the military hospital which the King had founded in 1670. Adelaide went a second time and enjoyed that visit even more than the first, because the object was shopping. One of the merchants they visited gave them a collation at his shop, where she bought silks and velvets for her trousseau, and she also bought presents of jewellery for her ladies from the other booths.

Preparations for her wedding were already in train; people were talking of very little else, and the King was busy selling a vast number of appointments in her future establishment. Some posts he did

making. The engravings show the fountains to have been charming. It was all destroyed by Louis XV.

not sell, for example those of the Church officials. He personally
appointed her four almoners, and more than two hundred and fifty
other nominations he gave to members of her old household, and
to servants of the late Dauphine. The rest fetched huge sums;
indeed, the King had good hopes of raising more than two million
livres by their sale, which would go some way, at least, towards the
expenses of the wedding.

In April, to Adelaide's great joy, Tessé returned, and began in
earnest the business of buying horses and carriages to furnish her
stables. His letters are full of detailed instructions to coach-builders
and horse-breeders. 'Twenty dapple-greys with white tails, and
eight beautiful blacks, at a very reasonable price, arriving from the
north of Holland; another dozen from Naples, and seven more from
North Italy'. Tessé sent them all to the stables of the Duc du Maine
to be brought to good condition, and then wrote a conciliatory
letter to the King, who was not fond of being asked for money:
'Your Majesty who, unlike most monarchs, is kind enough to consider the details essential for his better service, will readily understand that to buy horses in haste and put them straight to work
from grass, would mean importuning Your Majesty, eight months
later, to make good unavoidable losses. They must be allowed time
to fatten.' Meanwhile, Tessé paid for their upkeep himself, and he
ended his letter with a plea for 'something on account, until such
time as it pleases Your Majesty to command the repayment of the
whole sum'.

It had been announced that there would be two Court balls after
the wedding, opening with a bransle, led by the young couple. Even
the King was becoming excited, and, at his supper, one evening,
rashly expressed a hope that a very great number of ladies and
gentlemen of rank would dance in them, and that their attire and
jewels would be truly magnificent. Saint-Simon says that his words
provided an excuse for the Court to go perfectly mad. The thought
of rejoicing after so many years of dreary dullness so infected them
that, one and all, 'they heeded neither rank nor purse, in their
spending on dress and jewellery'. Soon there was no more silk to
be bought in Paris, at any price, and tailors and goldsmiths were
nowhere to be found. Madame la Duchesse went so far as to send
her archers[1] to kidnap the dressmakers working for the Duchesse de
Rohan; but the King, when he heard of it, was very angry and

[1] The Archers were a corps of 'security men', who formed the private bodyguard of the princes of the blood.

forced her to return them. At that point, says Saint-Simon, he began to rue his unconsidered words, and several times was heard to say that he failed to understand men being such fools as to allow their wives to ruin them by ordering new dresses. It was too late. All the world was talking of clothes and dancing, and the most staid couples were launching out into all manner of finery. Even the Chevreuses and Beauvilliers bought new clothes for the balls, and the Saint-Simons admitted to spending twenty thousand livres. Adding up after the celebrations, the jewellers and silk-merchants calculated that, all in all, they had sold five millions' worth. It had been so long since the King had wished for gaiety, and few had been able to resist temptation.

Meanwhile, the weather had changed and become so bad that even the King stayed indoors. Adelaide and Louis met every afternoon in the Salle des Glaces to practise their steps with a dancing master. They were beginning to enjoy each other's company, and were allowed to be a little less formal, under the ever-watchful eyes of their dragon, Mme du Lude. One day, during the autumn, they had a grand rehearsal, with chairs for the royal onlookers arranged as they would be on the night itself; and went through all the ceremonial of bowing and curtseying, as though the King, the exiled King and Queen of England, and all the rest of the royal family had been present. Adelaide was in her element; she loved to be praised, and she adored dancing, it was one of the things she did best. 'She moved,' said Saint-Simon, 'with an unconscious grace, like a goddess walking upon clouds.' There was something in the way she danced that was simple and full of joy, an innocent, child-like quality that charmed the Court, and filled visitors with admiration.

She was looking forward immensely to her wedding; to reaching the status of a married woman (as she told her grandmother), and, as she imagined, to gaining her freedom. She was deep in all the exciting preparations when, only a fortnight before the great day, the sad news reached her that Duchess Anne's new baby, Victor Amadeus's almost despaired-of son and heir, had died a few hours after his birth. Mme de Maintenon, who was on a visit to Meudon, returned quickly to Versailles to comfort her. She found the little girl deeply upset, crying bitterly for her parents and the little court in far-away Savoy. Adelaide's letters, at this time, show that she had never ceased to love and miss them.

Louis, too, was saddened, and had begun a letter of condolence;

but found himself obstructed for want of a proper form of address. There had been a tiff, at the time of Duchess Anne's marriage, thirteen years earlier, when Monsieur had had the imprudence to address a letter to Victor Amadeus, '*À Monsieur le Duc de Savoie*, my son-in-law'. The duke had taken this as an assumption of superiority, and had immediately cut off all correspondence. When Louis wished to send a letter, the whole team of diplomats, at Turin, was set to find a mode that would be offensive to neither side. The solution they produced was that while Louis, in private letters, should add '*mon beau-père*', Victor Amadeus should write only '*À Monsieur le Duc de Bourgogne*'. This, however, solved nothing for the fortnight before the wedding. There was no time to discover a fresh mode of address, and the letter could not be sent.

Adelaide's tears were soon dried. She was, after all, little more than a child, just approaching her twelfth birthday, and it was not in her nature to brood. The King had advanced her wedding-day from the 10th to the 7th,[1] and had given her a most magnificent set of diamonds. Mme de Maintenon's wedding present was a very pretty casket of jewels, with Louis's portrait in a small box, at the bottom, and something else as well, very characteristic of her dealings with the young, a booklet, inscribed in her own hand, containing 'advice to a bride before marriage'. She had a perfect mania for offering advice, on every conceivable subject, but she may well have thought that Adelaide, who seemed to regard marriage as a first step towards a life of unlimited pleasure, needed to be reminded of its more serious side.

Mme de Maintenon herself did not think much of that institution, Her first marriage to the crippled Scarron[2] had been dreadful to her, and her second, though it gave her the power she loved, was anything but pleasurable. She accordingly did her best to subdue any romantic notions in the heads of her charges, at Saint-Cyr. 'When they marry,' she wrote to the dames, 'they will soon discover that it is no laughing matter. You should accustom them to talking of it very seriously, even sadly, for I truly believe that even in the

---

[1] The *Mercure* thought this a marvellous tribute to the King's integrity. 'No prince,' it announced, in its fifty-page article on the wedding, 'ever kept his word with more exactitude. His Majesty promised to marry M. le Duc de Bourgogne to Mme la Princesse de Savoie when she was twelve years old; her twelfth birthday was on December 5th, and the marriage was celebrated only two days later.'

[2] The poet Paul Scarron was deformed by arthritis into the shape of the letter Z.

best marriages, one meets greater tribulation than in any other state
of life. It is hard to say how far a husband may go in requiring
obedience.' 'There are very few good husbands,' she told the
yellow class, the girls between fourteen and seventeen. 'I have not
known more than two, and if I said no more than one, I should not
exaggerate.'

Her advice to Adelaide was arranged under three headings:
'Regarding God'; 'Regarding Your Honoured Husband'; Regarding
the World'. As might be expected, it was full of that practical piety
and sanctified good sense, which the King so much admired. It
would appear to have offered excellent advice, if a trifle lugubrious,
for a girl in Adelaide's position. Here is an extract from the chapter
'Regarding Your Honoured Husband'.

'Let M. le Duc de Bourgogne be your closest friend and confi-
dant; take his advice; give him your own. Make of yourselves one
person, according to God's ordinance.

'You love joy, repose, pleasure; believe me I have tried them all.
There is no joy or repose save in the service of God. Do not expect
perfect happiness, it does not exist on earth. Do not expect as much
affection as you bear for him. Men are usually less affectionate
than women.

'You will be unhappy if you are over-critical of his friendships.
Pray God that you be not jealous.

'Never seek to recover his love by complaints, miseries, or
reproaches. The only way is by gentleness and patience; but I hope
that M. le Duc de Bourgogne will never subject you to such ordeals.

'Speak, write, and act as though before a thousand witnesses;
for sooner or later all becomes known. Care for your servants, lead
them to God. Give them a fortune, but not a great one; do not
appease their vanity or avarice; try to make them moderate in their
desires.

'Have compassion on the unfortunate; God has placed you in
your high position to do good. The power to serve others and make
them happy is the true compensation for the fatigues, discomforts
and constraints of your position.'[1]

This little notebook was found in Adelaide's jewel-box after her
death, and the King ordered it to be kept as a valuable inheritance
for her descendants; but history does not relate whether it appeared

[1] Mme de Maintenon, as a governess, was not behind her times, for similar
advice was given, in lessons known as '*Morale pour les jeunes filles de 17 ans*',
in some of the finishing schools of Paris, a few years after the First World War.

much read, or quite unthumbed. However that may have been, we know that she valued the old lady's counsels, and turned to her in nearly every difficulty. She was, in many ways, astonishingly shrewd for her age, and very ready to be advised. In the course of her marriage, she was not obliged to bear all the trials predicted by Mme de Maintenon, for her husband, who had fallen in love with her at first sight, remained passionately in love until her death, and she therefore had no cause for jealousy. As for her, the mild dislike which she appears to have felt for him persisted for the first few years, then gradually turned to affection, if never to love, and to a deep concern for his honour, for which she fought with all her strength.

Their wedding day fell on a Saturday. At eleven o'clock, the princes and princesses of the royal blood, and the greatest ladies of the Court, ablaze with diamonds, began to collect in Adelaide's bedroom. At half-past, excited and visibly nervous, Louis arrived, accompanied by the Duc de Beauvilliers. He wore a coat of black velvet, embroidered all over with gold thread, with very delicate and beautiful workmanship, and large diamond buttons. Over this came a black velvet mantle, lined with cloth of silver, similarly gold-embroidered. Beneath, he wore a white satin doublet and hose, with wide lace-covered garters. There were bunches of bright ribbons on his shoes, and he carried a hat with a huge plume of white ostrich feathers.

Adelaide's dress was of shimmering cloth of silver, embroidered with silver thread, while, on her head, a splendid coronet of pearls, diamonds, and rubies crowned her pretty chestnut-coloured hair, still dressed in the simple fashion considered most becoming to very young girls. The King had himself chosen the dress and jewels. His taste in ladies' dress was known to be excellent, and he had had a great deal of experience.

While the bride finished her *toilette*, her bridegroom sat beside her, and they conversed. At noon, news came that the King had finished working with his ministers, and was ready to start for the chapel. The procession began to form, and Adelaide left her room, holding Louis's hand. Immediately behind her walked Dangeau and Tessé, lifting the sides of the weighty silver train (eight metres long by the King's command), the end of which was borne, not by a page, but by a stalwart officer of the guard. No wonder she needed support, for besides the load of the train and the silver dress, she wore an underskirt of silver ribbon, richly decorated with rubies and diamonds, and under that, several layers of petticoat, though, in consideiation for her frailty, the King had ordered there to be a reduction of the usual number. None the less, she often stumbled beneath the weight of it, and several times Tessé had to put out his arm to prevent her from falling; this, however, required discretion, for etiquette forbade his appearing to walk on a level with the bridegroom.

The King, who followed next, behind the train-bearer, appeared in startling splendour. The plain brown coat he habitually wore had been discarded in favour of cloth of gold, embroidered in what Madame describes as 'hair-colour', at the waist. With the old coat, he had, for once, cast off his expression of gravity, and a brilliant smile lit up his face, making it radiant. Monseigneur, also, was in cloth of gold, covered with gold embroidery. As for Monsieur, Madame says that 'his black velvet coat was embroidered all over in gold, and he wore all his biggest diamonds'. She towered over him, grandeur itself but miserably uncomfortable: 'My dress and petticoat were so monstrously heavy that I could scarcely stand upright. I can never forget the exhaustion I was forced to endure. There was such a crush that I waited at each door a quarter of an hour before I could pass through. My dress was of gold, covered with raised flowers of black chenil, and my jewels were pearls and diamonds.' Behind her came the three princesses; the beautiful Princesse de Conti in a skirt and underdress of gold-embroidered green velvet, with a parure of pearls, diamonds and rubies; the Duchesse de Chartres in gold brocade embroidered in silver, and Mme la Duchesse in flame-coloured velvet, silver-embroidered, and bestrewn with diamonds. Those were all the costumes which Madame could remember, when writing to her aunt, except that the Duc d'Anjou wore gold brocade, worked with silver, and the Duc de Berry, black velvet embroidered with little gold flowers.[1]

It was a procession of strong, brilliant colours, with, over all, and everywhere, the icy sheen and sparkle of diamonds cut flat, in the manner of the period. The royal party, moving at a slow and dignified pace, descended the grand staircase to the chapel, passing, smiling, through the ranks of curtseying and bowing courtiers. It was a tremendous occasion; the beginning of a new era when, so the young thought, beauty, pleasure, and the pursuit of fashion

[1] In its enormously lengthy article, the *Mercure de France* describes many more of the coats and dresses; but Madame's letter seems to bring them to life. The picture of the wedding by Antoine Dieu was painted many years later.

would make Versailles once more, the most brilliant Court in Christendom.

At the chapel, there was first a service of betrothal, the arrangements for which amply satisfied the proud heart of Madame. 'The King, Monseigneur, Monsieur and I stood in a semicircle around the bridal pair. When the moment came to say "yes", 'the bride curtseyed four times; the bridegroom twice only—he had only to ask for the consent of his father and grandfather; she had to ask for Monsieur's and mine also, as her grandparents.' The marriage service followed, performed by Cardinal de Coislin, the grand almoner. Louis placed the ring upon Adelaide's finger, and presented her, according to the custom, with a bag containing thirteen gold pieces. The procession then re-formed, returning in the same order to the new Duchess's apartments, to sit down to the wedding breakfast. Only the King and Queen of England, the royal family, and the princes and princesses of the blood had the right to be seated, and the Duc de Saint-Simon was therefore furious at seeing chairs for the King's bastards. He nearly boiled over when he perceived that the ancient Duchesse de Verneuil, widow of a bastard of Henri IV, had been disinterred for the occasion. He said it was like scratching the bottom of a rusty barrel.

It appears to have been quite a lively party, or perhaps the wine was good and freely circulated, for Madame relates that her pet, the little Duc de Berry, managed to whisper to her, 'I have been watching my brother ogling his little wife. I can do that, if I want to, I have known for a long time past how to do it. You look at them hard, out of the corner of your eye,' 'and he put on such a comical face, mimicking his brother, that I could not help laughing'.

After the feast, they all went off for a siesta, or, as the *Mercure* put it, 'they each were given leave to rest a few hours'. Adelaide took refuge with Mme de Maintenon, and for a little while was able to lay aside her heavy wedding-dress. But not for long; punctually, at seven o'clock, they reassembled in the great gallery. In his official report, Nisleo Erizzo, the Venetian ambassador, describes the scene. 'France,' he wrote, 'has never witnessed a greater nor a more joyous spectacle than the wedding of the Duc de Bourgogne. Exactly a week ago today, there took place, among banquets, firework displays, illuminations, and balls in the various theatres, as well as in private houses, a scene of most unusual delight . . .

'Into the great gallery of Versailles, bright with crystal chandeliers that threw their sparkling beams on to the ladies' dresses and the thickly embroidered gold and silver coats of the gentlemen, strewn all over with precious stones, came the King, holding by the hand the Queen of England, leading her, with her husband beside her, to the windows that overlook the garden, where there burst forth, over the fountains, the most magnificent firework display that the world has ever seen.' (What the ambassador's enthusiasm did not allow him to see was that it was a cold December night, and that most of the fireworks were spoiled by the rain.

The royal party, just as before, went in to supper, at which Erizzo, though he did not sit with them, reported that the food was exquisite. When this was over, Adelaide, Queen Mary, the princesses, the highest-ranking foreign ladies, and the ladies of her household repaired to her bedroom for the ceremony of her public bedding with the Duc de Bourgogne. This custom was a most important feature of noble marriages, particularly so in the case of Louis and Adelaide (though theirs, for the time being, was in form only), because it brought promise of the legitimate continuance of the royal line, for all the world to see.

A few days earlier, a vast bed had been set up, with a splendid coverlet of gold-embroidered green velvet, that attracted the admiration of all beholders. People also exclaimed in wonder at the beauty of the dressing table and its appurtenances, the marvellous artistry of the candlesticks, trays, and jewelled boxes. After a while the grand master of ceremonies went to fetch Cardinal de Coislin to bless the nuptial bed. Adelaide knelt down to pray, and the ladies of lesser rank departed. She then undressed, received her nightgown from Queen Mary's hands, gave her cap and garters to her cousin Mademoiselle d'Orléans, and climbed into bed.

The chorus of admiration was meanwhile resounding in the room next door, where Louis's dressing table was on display, and he was getting into his nightshirt, handed him by King James. Then, when word came that Adelaide was ready, cap in hand and his hair tied with a bow of flame-coloured ribbon, he entered the bedroom with his retinue, and got into bed beside her. Erizzo takes up the story. 'Thus placed side by side in the great bed, they were gazed upon by the crowd of lords and ladies, until the King, with his own hand, drew the curtains upon them, saying to the Piedmontese envoy as he did so, "You may inform M. de Savoie that you have seen his daughter and my grandson bedded together". His Most Christian Majesty and His Britannic Majesty then retired, with the other guests, leaving only the Dauphin, who with loving encouragements urged his son to embrace his bride. The pious Duc de Beauvilliers and the Duchesse du Lude thereupon violently objected, recalling that the King had given explicit orders to the contrary[1]; but, for once, the Duc de Bourgogne preferred to obey his father. He turned to the Princess, who flung herself into his arms, with signs of the greatest pleasure imaginable. Yet, once the embrace was over, they did not come together again until the two years required for them to reach maturity had safely passed.'

The long day came to its end, and Louis and Adelaide went to their own beds, he wisely putting on warmer clothes in the antechamber, because the château was bitterly cold. Next day was the start of an entire week of festivities and rejoicings. Adelaide held her first court, which Saint-Simon says was a magnificent sight because of the prodigious number of titled ladies seated in the *cercle* on tabourets, the rows of other ladies standing at their backs, with the gentlemen behind them; all wearing the richest and most beautiful silks imaginable. If Adelaide was tired, her energy was unflagging, for she did not forget her friends at Saint-Cyr but, putting on her wedding-dress again, for their benefit, went off to show herself to them. They received her with songs of joy on the front steps, and bore her off to the chapel to hear a Te Deum, with verses chanted in her honour, based on the choruses in *Esther*, but a very long way after Racine. On the two days immediately after the wedding, Louis and Adelaide supped quietly with Mme de Maintenon. Then came the two Court balls, to which everyone had been looking forward.

No one enjoyed these more than the Venetian ambassador, who was quite transported by the beauty of the scene. 'The first days were spent,' he wrote in his dispatch to the Doge, 'in all manner of entertainments in the State apartments; but by far the most splendid were the two masked balls in Court dress. The great gallery, lit by more than five thousand candles reflected in the mirrors,[2] and the clusters of diamonds in the ladies' hair, and on their dresses,

[1] The Duc de Beauvilliers and Mme du Lude stood by their charges at either side of the bedhead. When the King had drawn the curtains, their bodies remained outside, but they kept their heads poked through, so as to prevent any improprieties, for the King had said that he did not wish the Duc de Bourgogne to kiss so much as his bride's little finger, until the marriage was consummated.

[2] Three lines of crystal candelabra, each set with eight candles; thirty-two many-branched candelabra on gilded pedestals; eight huge pyramids, draped in gold-fringed crimson velvet, each holding 150 candles in silver candlesticks. The band, violins and hautboys, was established in a raised gallery.

made it appear even brighter than had it been in full sunlight. All of a sudden, the Duc de Bourgogne appeared, wearing a coat star-spangled with precious stones, and gave the signal for the opening bransle.

'Watching that dance, so full of beauty and noble grace, eye and mind found delights such as the Blessed can scarcely dream of in Paradise. The princes and nobles were clad in gala attire; the Princess and her ladies, in dresses of a richness never seen before, wore their hair, partly falling in ringlets, partly covered by a net of diamonds. The least costly of the dresses is estimated at twelve thousand francs,[1] the most expensive at thirty thousand, and that is not accounting for the jewels, which were priceless and innumerable.

'At that hour, when the glory and grandeur of France was made manifest, one saw how poor, how despicable are the imitations of other nations. The King's presence enhanced, yet at the same time curbed the gaiety, evoking such silence and order that one might have supposed oneself to be at a meeting of reverent senators, rather than in a ballroom.

'After the dancing came supper, served by a hundred footmen, who rearranged the gallery so quickly and skilfully, that, in a moment, it became like a garden of flowers, fruits, and sweetmeats.

'Amid so much rejoicing, one could see tears in the eyes of the King and Queen of England, unhappy spectators of this magnificent ball which tomorrow will be repeated, with new and equally costly apparel. After this, an opera will be given at the Trianon theatre,[2] followed by spectacles, balls and fêtes, continuing every day until Christmas. But while, in France, they thus celebrate the marriage of the Duc de Bourgogne, in London, King William makes his triumphal entry.'

There is no doubt that the Court balls were extraordinarily magnificent. Others besides the Venetian ambassador were stunned by their beauty. Adelaide's new dresses were glorious: shimmering

---

[1] It is impossible to give any equivalent for the value of the money. A silver franc equalled a livre, and before 1914 was worth approximately 10d. Perhaps it might give some idea, though obviously inaccurate, to imagine the livre as roughly equal to the pound sterling before inflation.

[2] The opera was *Apollon et Issé*, with a libretto by Houdart de La Motte, and music by the King's favourite composer Destouches. It was not thought to be very good. The Princesse de Conti had acted as producer, by the King's special request, and had employed an artist named Bérain to design the scenery and costumes.

cloth of gold for the first ball, with clusters of pearls and diamonds in her hair, in which shone the finest stones in the crown jewels; for the second ball, she wore black velvet strewn all over with diamonds, her ringlets braided with pearls and rubies, while the remainder of her hair was covered so thickly with diamonds 'that it would be no exaggeration to say that it hurt one's eyes to look at her'.[1]

The *Mercure Galant* surpassed itself in descriptions of the gentlemen; Monseigneur's coat of gold brocade with silver facings, and sleeves of exquisitely beautiful lace, excited particular admiration. There had, however, been one major blot on the first evening's perfection;[2] far too many people were invited, with the result that, when the King retired for supper, there was such a fight for seats and refreshments that it seemed almost like a riot. Poor little Monsieur, in all his finery of black velvet with flame-coloured ribbons, and a diamond to every square inch, was knocked down and trodden on. The King, himself, barely escaped being jostled, as he left, and many persons of high rank were crushed and hurt in the confusion. The second ball was far better behaved.

Adelaide, as usual in her public appearances, seems to have conducted herself perfectly throughout—or nearly perfectly, for there had been some criticism. Sticklers for etiquette had been heard complaining that she had allowed herself to enjoy the dancing too much, her face being wreathed in smiles, instead of wearing that expression of bland dignity, considered suitable for ladies of royal birth. She had also been too much entertained by her first opera; had laughed aloud, and had asked so many questions that the King and Mme de Maintenon decided (perhaps with relief), that she was over-excited, and that an end should be put to the festivities until after Christmas.

Thus Adelaide passed her apprenticeship with flying colours. Gone were the days of the little Princess of Savoy. She was now a

---

[1] Her other dresses sound very pretty: a black velvet jacket with a skirt of cloth of gold, for Père Bourdalou's hell-fire Sunday sermon, flame-coloured velvet embroidered with gold for her first court, and, for the state visit of the nine-year-old 'Prince of Wales', or 'Old Pretender', rose-pink satin with the diamonds of the crown jewels on her neck, arms and hair.

[2] Another blot on the Versailles balls was the candle-grease. The windows were left open, by the King's command, and the chandeliers, gently swaying in the draught showered down melted wax onto the heads and dresses of the dancers. It is not too much to say that the guests went home literally caked in grease.

married woman, a royal duchess, a public personage in her own right, and the first lady in all France. The measure of her success is an intimate letter from Mme de Maintenon to Duchess Anne, written a few months before the wedding:

'The Princess fills me with astonishment, for I have never known anything so remarkable as her intelligence. It does not show itself by bright remarks or witty repartee, or by such feats of memory as clever children display. She speaks so little that she says nothing out of place. She hears without appearing to listen, often when she seems entirely engrossed in play. She never strives to look clever. She fears to cause displeasure, but never labours to please. She hates flattery; she listens patiently to advice and afterwards is grateful, and she never fails to put it to good use. I have never known it to be useless. One tries to find a fault in her, and becomes alarmed at the faintest shadow. Her women found her a trifle impatient during her toilette. I spoke to her, and the defect vanished; she has extraordinary self-control.

'All in all, Madame, you cannot have known what a treasure you possessed, for her shyness concealed it. Our gentleness has made her a little bolder; but one sees how easy it would be to frighten her. She is the King's darling . . . He delights in her merriment and her absolute discretion. She always knows when to stop. She grows better looking every day; her face is rounder now, and they dress her hair beautifully. Her complexion is pink and white; she has grown a little taller, and her figure is perfect. They give her fresh underlinen every week,[1] but she is cleaner and neater, by far, than the majority of children, and scarcely needs clean clothes. I do not object to her wearing court-dress, provided it does not impede her walking. She dances extremely well, and no one was ever more graceful . . .

'This is how she is at present; but who knows what the future may hold? She lives surrounded by a small group of respectable women, who speak to her with one voice. No one spoils her; on the contrary, everything is directed towards her training. It will not always be so, for traps are set for princes as well as for ordinary mortals, and the more praise she receives today, the more envy will be stored up against her. I trust God will protect her. She fears

---

[1] '*On lui donne des corps tous les huits jours*', referring to the body, or foundation of her dresses, on which was hung the outside layer, with all its folds and trimmings.

Him; she loves Him; she has a deep respect for religion. Her education so far has been excellent; it is astonishing how much she has learnt. At present we are teaching her something of mythology and Roman history; but only so that she may become familiar with matters that continually appear in general conversation.[1]

'I think myself only too happy to be able to give Your Royal Highness such a pleasing report, at the same time assuring you of my most profound respect.'

1 July 1697.

Whatever uneasiness Mme de Maintenon may have felt regarding Adelaide's life at the Court, she seems to have taken it for granted that she would be in love with her husband. The King, who saw only what he wished to see, believed that it was so already. 'The marriage goes better and better,' he remarked to the Piedmontese ambassador, just six weeks after the wedding. 'The young couple are now in love, and their love will increase when they are put together.'[2] Louis was indeed over head and ears in love; but there is reason to suppose that, so far as Adelaide had time to think of him at all, it was with dislike rather than otherwise, and that she found some of his habits boring, and others repellent. That observant Venetian, Nisleo Erizzo, had noticed something. Describing Louis as 'a studious prince, anxious for information on every conceivable subject', and Adelaide as 'endowed by nature with lively intelligence but a paucity of beauty', he continues, 'It is to be hoped that the years may unite the minds of these two young persons, which, until now, have been as much apart as their bodies.'

The years did bring about that happy union, but only in the face of disaster, when Louis learned to appreciate Adelaide's strength and to rely on her loyal support, and Adelaide to be fond of him, if not to love him. The tragedy was that this should have happened so near the end of their short lives.

---

[1] The stories of the operas, and many of the comedies of the period, as well as the costumes at the masked balls, were based on the myths of Greece and Rome.

[2] Reported by the Marchese da Ferreiro, in a letter to the Duke of Savoy, 28 January 1698. The marriage was consummated two years later.

8

Mme la Duchesse de Bourgogne

IF ADELAIDE had imagined that marriage and being addressed
as Mme la Duchesse de Bourgogne meant freedom to live a
grown-up life, she was never more mistaken. Lessons continued at Saint-Cyr and with her writing-master, though her spelling did not much improve, and the Duchesse du Lude still slept in
her bedroom. Louis, too, shared a room with his governor, in spite
of having reached his majority, on his fifteenth birthday. He was
immersed in his studies, his sports, and his military training, the
pity of which was that while he was taught history, and the 'art of
war', he learned nothing of tactics or of commanding an army in
the field.

There was, however, some relaxation of the rules which had kept
the young couple apart. They were allowed to meet every day, and
even to talk privately to one another, though watched over by their
respective keepers from the far end of the room. Three times a
week they dined in private with Mme de Maintenon, cosy parties
which all three of them enjoyed, for the gold plate and serving men
were banished, and Adelaide made them laugh by insisting on handing the plates and pouring out the wine in a most comical fashion,
mimicking the gestures of the major-domo with his white wand,
who attended on Louis when he dined in public.

Louis, indeed, was already much in love. He adored Adelaide's
light touch and her sense of fun; moreover, despite his moral
austerity, he was beginning to find chastity a burden, and was
eagerly looking forward to having her as his wife in more than
name. Adelaide, on her side, was ready for anything, even for a plan
which they concocted together, with the regrettable assistance of
Mme Quentin,[1] by which Louis was stowed one night in the ward-

---

[1] Mme Quentin was Adelaide's confidential maid; the wife of Louis XIV's
barber, who had been the go-between in the King's affairs with his mistresses.
The King had ennobled him in 1693; but his wife was in no way strait-laced.

robe until Mme du Lude was comfortably snoring, when he crept out, silent as a mouse, and into Adelaide's bed. But the dragon awoke with a start, and in a moment the villainy was discovered, Louis evicted, and next morning a furious Mme du Lude was first in the line to see the King. Louis was summoned; 'I hear, Sir,' said his grandfather, 'that last night something occurred that might have proved injurious to your health. See that it does not occur again.' As Louis retired, embarrassed, perhaps penitent, he may have reflected on the unfairness of it all, since his grandfather at the same age had not been so frustrated.[1]

As for Adelaide, if one amusement failed, others offered, and she settled down happily enough to the duties of her new rank, and to pleasures more suitable for her age. The chief difference in her life, after her formal marriage, was her participation in the official life of the Court. As the wife of the heir presumptive, she ranked above Madame and the other princesses. She held court, received presentations in public audience, and welcomed and bade farewell to ambassadors and other distinguished visitors. She was only a beginner at such functions and, as Mme de Maintenon had foreseen, people tried to take advantage. The first such incident was a repetition of the mishap on Adelaide's first arrival. It occurred at the presentation of Mme Heemskerke who, as the Dutch ambassadress, merited a kiss from Adelaide. That was straightforward enough, but, when the wily lady offered her daughter's cheek as well, Adelaide hesitated, and the Duchesse du Lude gravely shook her head. At that moment, however, Sainctot,[2] the head of protocol, pushed the girl forward, saying, 'Kiss, Madame! It is her right', and Adelaide, unconvinced, but afraid of being rude, applied her lips. Immediately, in the surrounding circle, there were murmurs, and when Sainctot tried to consolidate the claim in the drawing-room of Madame, that lady haughtily resisted. It was of no use for him to plead that Adelaide had so far unbent. Madame replied in a loud voice, 'That was a stupid error which you prompted her to make I shall not consent'. There was a scandal, and the girl went unkissed from Meudon.

There followed a far more serious affair, when the Princesse d'Harcourt, a most unpleasant person,[3] a member of the House of

---

[1] A lady of his mother's household had been enlisted to teach him how to love.

[2] Nicolas Sainctot was a commoner who had purchased this appointment, in 1695, in exchange for a lower one inherited from his father.

[3] Harcourt, Marie Françoise de Brancas, Princesse d' (d. 1715).

Lorraine, with all that family's determination by fair means or foul to take precedence over the French duchesses, made a dreadful scene at the first court over which Adelaide presided. Adelaide, though she realised the rudeness, was too young to set her down, and the Duchesse du Lude, in her nervousness, was so anxious for popularity that she submitted to everything.

It all happened at a reception for Lord Jersey, the English ambassador. Saint-Simon describes the scene. 'The ladies arrived from various directions before the great doors were thrown open. The duchesses who were there earliest entered first, followed by the Princesse d'Harcourt and the other Lorraine princesses. The Duchesse de Rohan took the highest stool on the right-hand side. A moment later when the duchesses were all seated, and great numbers of ladies, titled and untitled, were still arriving, the Princesse d'Harcourt crept up behind her and bade her move across to the left-hand side. Mme de Rohan replied that she was quite comfortable where she was; whereupon the princess, a tall, powerful woman, without more ado put her two arms at the duchess's waist, twisted her round by force, and sat down in her place. Mme de Rohan, completely flabbergasted, half-convinced that she was dreaming, merely curtsied to Mme la Duchesse de Bourgogne and went over to the other side, still only dimly realising what had been done to her. The remaining ladies were most monstrously shocked and alarmed, but the Duchesse du Lude dared not say a word, still less so Mme la Duchesse de Bourgogne who, young as she was, fully understood the lack of respect.'

When the King heard what had happened, he said he thought that the Princesse d'Harcourt had been extremely impertinent, and twice vowed that he would be pleased to bring the Lorraines to order. He had, according to Saint-Simon, 'a somewhat lively scene' about her with Mme de Maintenon, her protectress, and only with the greatest reluctance was persuaded to allow her to accompany him, next day, to Marly.

Although Adelaide may have been disappointed to find that the married state brought her a good deal more work, and very little more freedom, Mme de Maintenon, who still supervised her time-table, gradually allowed certain rules to be relaxed. It was not, however, until 1698 that she first went to the theatre. Until then there had been a strict ban on public plays and operas, and people were not allowed even to mention them in her presence, for fear of her sulking, or appealing to the King. It was in November that the great day arrived, when Adelaide, with Louis and his younger brothers, saw her very first play, Molière's comedy, *Le Bourgeois Gentilhomme*. 'The Duc de Bourgogne completely lost his grave expression,' wrote Madame, 'and laughed till the tears came into his eyes. The Duc d'Anjou was so enchanted that he sat with his mouth open, as though in a trance, gazing at the stage; and the Duc de Berry burst into such fits of laughter that he nearly fell off his chair. The Duchesse de Bourgogne had more self-control. She behaved beautifully at the beginning; smiling gently, and laughing very little; but from time to time she stood up on her chair so as to gain a better view. She, too, in her own fashion, was very much amused.'

It was Monseigneur who first took Adelaide to the opera, an amusing piece, *Le Carnaval de Venise*, with words by Regnard, and music by Campra; but Dangeau, who of course mentions the occasion, says nothing of her enjoying herself, so perhaps she was a little bored. A few weeks later she saw her first serious play, Racine's *Bajazet*, and after that the King gave her permission to visit the theatre whenever she cared to go.

If music had no strong appeal for Adelaide, nothing gave her greater pleasure than an invitation to a ball. She adored dancing (she knew that she danced well) and the masques which had become the rage since the great fancy-dress balls after the wedding, were her delight. Designing her costumes, planning for groups of her friends to go as Siamese or Venetian dancers and rehearsing the steps took up most of her leisure-time. There is an unauthenticated story of how, in the early hours of the morning before Mme de Pontchartrain's ball,[1] she sent a coach-and-six to the Jesuits' house, to wake up her confessor and bring him to her at all speed. He appeared in a terrible state, dreading to hear what mortal sin she had committed to need absolution at that untimely hour. 'No, Father,' she cried, when he appeared, 'Sit down, it's not to confess I need you, but to ask you to draw a Chinese costume for me to wear at the ball tonight.' Useless for the poor priest to plead that when he was in China he had known more of men's clothes than of women's. He had to sit down there and then to sketch the design.

[1] Mme de Pontchartrain, the wife of the Chancellor of France, was socially a nobody, for, though rich and influential, she 'had no birth'. It was an extraordinary honour for her to entertain Adelaide, at her house, and the snobs might not have come; yet she was such a kind, generous woman, and gave such marvellous parties that the best people came flocking.

There were any number of balls, that winter. Mme de Maintenon gave one for Adelaide's thirteenth birthday, when Louis went as Apollo, and Adelaide and her ladies as the nine muses. There was another on 21 January, and still another on the 22nd. On 4 February, the King gave a great ball at Marly, with a masque to follow next day. Dangeau says that he had vast numbers of costumes brought there and allowed anyone who wished to change their disguise; while the *Mercure* reported that groups of dancers were always disappearing to the upstairs rooms, and that some people changed their dress four or five times during the evening . . . 'Nothing was wanting to please the eye, delight the ear, or gratify the taste'.

Even Madame enjoyed herself: 'I must tell you of the masked ball at Marly . . . It began at ten o'clock. At eleven the masks arrived. A lady as broad as a tower entered the ball-room. It was the Duc de Valentinois, M. de Monaco's son, who is immensely tall, wearing a cloak right down to his feet. In the middle of the room it flew open, and out sprang Harlequin, Scaramouche, Punchinello and all the other characters from the Italian comedies. M. de Brionne was Harlequin, my son Punchinello; the Duc de Bourgogne was the Doctor . . . The Dauphin brought another party, all very quaintly dressed, and they changed their disguises three or four times . . . The ball lasted until a quarter to two in the morning. On Friday, all the ladies wore elegant déshabillé; the Duchesse de Bourgogne a beautiful fancy dress, in the gay Spanish fashion, with a tiny little cap . . . At half-past seven or eight o'clock masks with guitars appeared, and danced the opening scene of an opera. It was my son, the Comte d'Ayen, Prince Camille, and La Vallière in ridiculous male attire . . . The Dauphin, M. d'Antin and M. de Brionne came dressed as ladies, in dressing-gowns and shawls, and with towering edifices of blonde hair, much higher than are usually worn. These three gentlemen are almost of the same height. They wore quite small black and red masks with patches, and danced with high kicking steps. D'Antin kicked so hard that he upset M. de Brionne, who fell on his bottom at the feet of the Queen of England. You may imagine what a shout of laughter that caused. Soon after that, my favourite, the Duc de Berry, went and disguised himself as the "Baron de la Crasse"[1] and returned to do a most comical dance all by himself . . .'

But balls and masques were not the only diversions, and by the end of winter they had gone out of fashion. When summer came,

[1] Baron Muck.

the vogue was for water-parties. One evening, the King had seats arranged on the terrace overlooking the water, and stayed there, listening to the music and watching the charming scene, until eight o'clock. He then returned to his supper, and afterwards strolled in the gardens with his courtiers, as late as two o'clock, when he retired to bed. Not so Adelaide, who was by no means ready for sleep. She went back to the water with her ladies and continued to float in her gondola to the music of violins, until long after the sun had risen. At seven o'clock next morning, Mme de Maintenon was due to go to Saint-Cyr, and Adelaide insisted on staying up to see her comfortably settled in her coach, before darting in to give the King his good-morning kiss. Only then would she consent to go to bed, and Dangeau reported that she seemed not in the least fatigued.

Did Mme de Maintenon, with all her experience, not see what a strain was being put on the growing girl's never too robust health? Or did she see but not care, or perhaps dare, to intervene? Nothing in her private letters, or in the records of her conversation at that period, suggests that she was in any way troubled, rather that she was enjoying a kind of rejuvenation in Adelaide's company. 'I have spent the afternoon rowing a boat for the amusement of Mme la Duchesse de Bourgogne,' she told the astonished girls of Saint-Cyr.

Adelaide herself was extremely happy at this time, and, indeed, no wonder. Hers was not the kind of nature to look far ahead, and fear the future; every wish was granted, every plan fulfilled. Her only duty was to please the King; and her whole desire tended that way, for she was beginning to love him. As for Louis XIV, he was finding her more and more necessary to his happiness. The Court, especially the younger generation was in a state of continual astonishment, for tenderness and affection were not the qualities most evident in that monument of selfishness, their King, although at all times they had lain below the surface. Not a day passed without his seeing her. When she was unwell, as sometimes happened, for she was very prone to toothache and inflammation of the gums, he would go early in the morning and pay her a surprise visit. Every afternoon, she walked or drove with him, and if he kept her waiting, she would scratch impatiently upon his door, and he would call to have her let in.

Hunting with him was still her greatest pleasure. To be alone with the King in the new, two-seater carriage, with its team of racing ponies, galloping headlong down the forest rides, free of the trammels of etiquette, filled her with such delight that, one day, she hid from him a very swollen face for fear of missing the hunt—thereby contracting a high temperature. Vanity came into it, no doubt, for she had designed for herself a hunt-uniform, a scarlet velvet skirt, and a jacket to match trimmed with wide bands of gold braid, as we see it in Gobert's picture. A little three-cornered hat went with the outfit, which, according to Sourches, everyone thought marvellously becoming.

The King filled her world, in those years, to the exclusion of her young husband: 'Those who love me, dear grandmamma, will rejoice as I do in the King's kindness. He gives me every day fresh marks of his affection, and I have reason to believe that they will increase. At any rate, I shall do my best to deserve them.' She was well content with her life: 'They tell you the truth, dear grandmamma, when they say that I am happy, I could almost say I have too many pleasures, for they take up all my time.' Yet she remembered her family in Savoy with, perhaps, more than a touch of home-sickness, for in another letter of that winter of 1698, she says, 'It is kind of you to say, dear grandmamma, that you are pleased with me, because I am not at all pleased with my conduct towards you; it seems to me that I do not write to you as often as I should. Will you ever believe me when I say I have no time? Yet that is the exact truth, for my days are completely filled. But no amount of duties or pleasures will ever make me forget how much I owe to you, for all the love which you have always shown me.' Louis Adelaide never mentions, save for one stiff reference, at the New Year: '10 January 1699. I am not sufficiently intimate with M. le Duc de Bourgogne to do the honours for him; but I am very glad that you liked his letter. I wish mine could express all the good wishes I send you for this year, and for many others to come, and how much I want you to love me always.'

But she could not always be hunting or dancing; and there was a day when she drove in state to Paris to show herself to the people. It was 18 August 1698, and a public holiday. Under the escort of her dear Tessé, in her beautiful eight-horse coach, with grooms and footmen wearing her personal livery, surrounded by a merry band of young ladies (but of course under the eye of Mme du Lude), and with several coaches following, she made straight for the fair and the shops, in the Rue Saint-Denis, where she descended from her coach to walk among the people. It was a great occasion, and, knowing Adelaide and her love for clothes, one may well suppose that she had taken particular pains with her appearance, for the *Mercure* proceeds to say that 'everyone exclaimed in admiration of her grace and charm, and especially of her jewels, which were extraordinarily beautiful. She wore a coat of a pale grey-blue, the colour of flax, all frilled and flounced, trimmed everywhere with silver lace, and strewn with diamonds and emeralds. Her hair also was wreathed in precious stones, and her ribbons were bestrewn with them'.

At the fair, she went first to see the tightrope dancers, then to a puppet-show, and she paid most handsomely. Next, she visited the finest booths in the market, and bought many things, especially from a china-shop and a jeweller's, where her visit was expected, and a delicious collation had been prepared. At other shops she made purchases of little gold bottles and needle-cases, and other such dainty trifles. At half-past six, she stepped back into her coach, and after driving twice round the Place Royale, returned, at half-past ten, to Versailles, where she distributed the trinkets she had bought among her ladies. 'What is more,' added the *Mercure*, 'she left a very great sum for the poor of Paris.'

Thus everyone had a good time, and a present, for it was typical of Adelaide in her exuberant joy in living to wish to share her happiness with those around her. Yet there were lapses, regrettably becoming more frequent, and certain people for whom she was developing a positive aversion.[1] The Princesse d'Harcourt was one of these; another was the Duchesse du Lude herself. Yet it is hard to see why the latter, for Mme du Lude was inoffensive, charming, beautiful, with perfect manners, and had been her sure guide and friend through the terrifying maze of court etiquette. Mme Dunoyers, one of Adelaide's ladies, thought that the duchess irritated her with her perpetual fussing, her complaints about draughts and the gout, and her everlasting vigilance. Be that as it may, Adelaide was unmerciful to her, making it a practice to slip out of bed and escape into the gardens at sunrise, becoming 'lost' in the *bosquets* or the labyrinth, deaf to all appeals from the sleepy, alarmed, indignant old lady, calling for her to come back to bed.

Much worse, Adelaide could be unkind, even rude, as on the terrible occasion when she behaved with all the roughness of a guttersnipe. Mme du Lude had been importuning her, perhaps

---

[1] Saint-Simon says that, 'although normally inclined to help, content, excuse, and be kind to everyone, she was sometimes driven to take violent dislikes, as, for instance, against the odious Jérôme Pontchartrain, the Chancellor's son, whom she referred to as 'your one-eyed monster', when speaking to the King.

beyond endurance, to be especially gracious and polite to a cousin of hers, the newly appointed Bishop of Metz; but, to everyone's horror, the Princess, when he entered, burst loudly into song: 'Get y'boots cleaned, Monsieur l'Abbé', the refrain of a popular ditty, referring to country bumpkins being given seminary training, to polish them for polite Society.[1] When reproached afterwards, all Adelaide would say was that no one could have a better welcome than with a song.

Such outbursts do happen with lively, bouncing girls when they can no longer bear the nagging of surrounding grown-ups. They are like corked-down champagne bottles, liable to explode if shaken. Adelaide was no exception. She constantly disconcerted the careful plans laid down for her through her high spirits. But the pressures upon her were very great, demanding almost superhuman patience, endurance, and self-control, and for most of the time she gave of her best. Saint-Simon, after her death, said: 'The constraints of court etiquette, often amounting to torture, of which she bore the entire burden, seemed as nothing to her. Kindness came easily to her; it was part of her nature.'

Yet something clearly had to be done, for her lapses were becoming habitual. The difficulty was that Adelaide's ladies, who protected her so carefully that no word of them reached the King's ears, could not bring themselves to blame her; and Mme de Maintenon would do nothing, preferring to leave all reproaches to Dangeau, a perfect courtier who knew better than to risk unpopularity. In the end, it was Madame who intervened, by the devious method which she sometimes employed when she wished to make her opinions known —in other words, by the post.

Madame knew very well that her letters were opened, and sometimes shown to the King, when the matter concerned him, or his family. She therefore wrote to her aunt in October 1698, 'They are absolutely ruining the Duchesse de Bourgogne; on journeys she is never still for an instant, but scrambles on to people's laps, and jumps about like a monkey. Yet all they talk about is her charm. Sometimes the fancy takes her to go out at five in the morning, and no one does anything but praise her. Any other child would be whipped. They will be sorry, one day, to have so let her go her own way.' Soon afterwards she was writing, 'My God! they do bring

---

[1] *Décrotter.* Saint-Simon speaks of Dubois (later the great Cardinal Dubois) being made an abbé, in other words being sent to a seminary, to scrape the mud off his boots before being made the Duc de Chartres' tutor.

her up badly. I am quite sorry for the poor child. She sings and dances at her dinner, standing up in her chair; making the most frightful faces, and tearing the chickens and partridges with her fingers. She could not have worse manners; but the people watching her all exclaim, "Isn't she sweet? Isn't she clever?" She is impertinent to Monsieur; but the only effect is to make him think he is in favour. They say that she is even more free with the King . . . but everything is permitted to her; everything about her admired.'

Whatever the cause may have been, Adelaide pulled herself together in the following year, as Madame was the first to admit: 'The Duchesse de Bourgogne has become much steadier in the past months,' she wrote in December 1699, 'she no longer behaves childishly, but acts like a grown-up person. I do not know if one of my letters, in which I drew attention to her bad behaviour, was opened and read; but one thing is certain, she now conducts herself quite differently at table, eats decorously and quietly, and no longer jumps about, or sticks her fingers into the dishes, as she was wont to do. In short, she is a reformed character. My letter did some good, and I am pleased to see that they thought me right.'[1]

Yet, although that particular fault was corrected, nothing else was done to further Adelaide's education, strengthen her character, or give her an object in life other than the pursuit of those empty pleasures that filled her days. So long as she was reverent in Church, and to her confessor, amused the King, and appeared generally happy, Mme de Maintenon rather surprisingly appears to have been quite content.

The fact is that Mme de Maintenon was in something of a panic. Tired out, aching all over with rheumatism, brought on, she was convinced, by the draughtiness of her room at Versailles, and the wide-open windows with which the King persistently tormented her, she was in a mood of most unusual depression; far too much afflicted with her own troubles to worry very much about other people. Madame, who watched her with the eye of a hawk, wrote, 'She often

---

[1] Three years later, after Monsieur's death, Madame was caught in her own trap. She had been found writing of Mme de Maintenon, to her German relations, as the 'old rag-bag', 'old hag', 'old spider', etc. Mme de Maintenon paid a call on her, in all apparent innocence; but, when Madame rashly inquired why the King was being so cold towards her, Mme de Maintenon drew from her pocket those very letters with their terms of abuse. As she read them aloud, Madame very nearly expired. Apology, in abject terms, was her only course, and Mme de Maintenon forgave her with the repose of the truly well-bred, which, in Madame's opinion, she was not.

weeps bitterly and speaks of death, though I suspect this is only to see how people will react'. Had it been the twentieth, instead of the seventeenth century, people would have been predicting a nervous breakdown.

Mme de Maintenon had good reason to fear. The spring of 1698 was the time of the winding up of the '*Affaire Fénelon*', as it had come to be known. The King was deeply disturbed, and extremely angry, and she, though his wife, was none too confident of her own security,[1] for Fénelon had been her close friend and protégé, and she knew that the King did not hold her entirely blameless. Worst of all, they were saying that Fénelon's real crime was not against religion, but political, a desire to reform the government of France, which, to Louis XIV, was black treachery, indeed profanity, an attack upon the divine ordinances of God's lieutenant. Madame had the whole story neatly parcelled up in her mind: 'Monsieur de Cambrai used Mme Guyon to mask his own towering ambition. It was a gamble to gain power over the King and the Court. They had been plotting to seduce Mme de Maintenon because she rules the King, and they had succeeded. Religion was the last thing they were mindful of; but, when Mme de Maintenon realised that their plans were known and feared lest the King discover how she had misled him, she immediately turned about and left Mme Guyon and all that party in the lurch. I must say that I was surprised to see how soon she abandoned her good friend the Archbishop of Cambrai. They used so often to dine together, and she never gave a concert, or a party, without his being present' (20 July 1698).

That, of course, was not the whole of it; but Mme de Maintenon certainly did desert Fénelon and her old friends at this time, with remarkable speed, cutting herself off from the Chevreuses and Beauvilliers, even attempting to discredit the excellent Duc de Beauvilliers himself.[2] 'I have spoken to the King,' she confided to her

---

[1] They had indeed been married, and there were witnesses; but Mme de Maintenon had never succeeded in having the marriage announced, though, at least twice, she had been within an ace of success. She may thus have thought divorce or annulment not an impossibility. Perhaps she did not give the King credit for loving her as much as he did.

[2] Saint-Simon, who saw what she was about, urged Beauvilliers to speak to the King. 'He answered that from all he had heard there was no doubt of his being in grave danger; but he had never solicited advancement; those posts which he held God had given him, and would remove them from him when He so willed. . . . Thus thinking he had but to wait submissively for God's will to be done, careful only to do nothing likely to trouble his conscience at the hour of his death. . . He

crony the Archbishop of Paris,[1] urging him to dismiss the men who surround the Princes, 'and I ended by saying that I could not forgive the Duc de Beauvilliers for receiving the friends of Mme Guyon, knowing them still to be so. The King seemed disposed to speak frankly to him. If he has not done so by tomorrow, it will be strong proof of that minister's strong influence.' Her intervention was of no avail, for the King continued to repose the same perfect trust in Beauvilliers as he had done before.

She also interviewed Louis, probably at the King's request. 'M. le Duc de Bourgogne' she wrote, 'came to me this morning, and I kept him in talk of the maxims of M. de Cambrai. He says they are wrong, though at first sight plausible. I do not know, however, if he was being sincere. As for myself, I always speak from the heart; God does the rest.' Louis remained stubbornly faithful to Fénelon. He would obey the King in all things, but his heart was his own, and part of it he had given to his old friend and tutor.

Poor Mme de Maintenon, it was a bad time for her. No wonder she had little to spare for Adelaide. More and more often, and for longer periods, she sought refuge in her bed at Saint-Cyr, 'the only, place where I can hide and be comfortable.' There she spent her days occupied with the school, increasingly involved in Church affairs and intrigues,[2] writing a stream of letters, full of misery and complaints of the King, to the Archbishop. 'I can do nothing of any practical value; for no one tells me anything. If I could do any good I should not mind so much this life of slavery.' She rarely described her position as slavery; but her need for compassion was very great.

Adelaide was concerned about her health, and one weekend, when the old lady had gone with the King to Marly, news came that she was in bed with a fever, and immediately, Adelaide sent a message to say that she wished to come without delay, to take care of her, to which the King gladly consented, for he also was much concerned,

embraced me,' continues Saint-Simon, 'with much affection, and I left him so deeply penetrated by these Christian, lofty, and most rare sentiments that I have never forgotten his words.

[1] Louis Antoine de Noailles (1651–1729), Archbishop of Paris 1695, later cardinal. He was one of Mme de Maintenon's oldest friends. She had moved heaven and earth to gain his nomination to the See of Paris, and thenceforth treated him as a supernumerary confessor, the repository for her most secret problems. Saint-Simon thought him a saint, the very opposite of his nephew the Duc de Noailles, and says that she could not have found a better guide.

[2] Saint-Simon says that Mme de Maintenon thought of herself as the 'Mother of the Church', and was very active in influencing the distribution of benefices.

remembering that, in earlier days, she had made herself seriously ill over the affair of Mme Guyon.[1] It was thus a relief to everyone when a papal bull arrived, condemning Fénelon's book and doctrine. The King did not wait a moment to set her mind at rest; but sent her a note from his council, 'So this affair is at last over and done with. I hope there will be no further unpleasant consequences for anyone. No more now; I will reserve the rest for this evening'. It was his way of telling her that any lapses on her part were forgiven.

Such unpleasant consequences as there had been fell, strangely enough on underlings, and not the principals. No worse happened to Fénelon. Beauvilliers, as we have seen, remained in office and favour, and Fleury, perhaps because the King had appointed him, was not dismissed. Those who suffered were Fénelon's nephew an assitant tutor; a reader his protégé, and two virtuous and inoffensive *gentilshommes de la manche*, for whose appointment Beauvilliers had been responsible.

The Affaire Fénelon was not, however, Mme de Maintenon's sole affliction, in that spring of 1698. There had been great vexation surrounding the marriage of her niece Françoise to the young Comte d'Ayen, son and heir of the Duc de Noailles. The match itself could scarcely have been more gratifying, for had not the bride's aunt been who she was, the Noailles would have thought the connection with penniless d'Aubignés and Scarrons totally abhorrent. Mme de Maintenon's influence, coupled with the King's dowry of a million francs, and all the jewellery which she had hitherto refused to accept from him, persuaded them to regard it very differently.

The problem for Mme de Maintenon was not that, but the bride's father, her brother Charles. A thorough bad lot, profligate, gambler, haunter of brothels, he had for many years been an embarrassment, and had lately become impossible. She had persuaded him to live in Paris, far from the Court, at a home for old gentlemen, and under the eye of a strict chaplain; but now and then he escaped to Versailles and, in his cups, would be heard making dreadful jokes about 'm'brother-in-law', accompanied by ribald laughter. The very thought of him at the wedding was shame enough. In the end, she simply decided not to send him an invitation. His wife, her sister-in-law, was allowed to come for, though

[1] On that occasion, the King, urged on by her confessor, had come to her bedside, and had said to her, smiling, 'Are you going to die of this business, Madame?' and she had smiled back through her tears and decided to survive. But it had been touch and go; and their marriage had been in danger.

regrettably commonplace, she could be trusted to eat and drink, and not otherwise open her mouth. Moreover, the Court had become accustomed to seeing her, on the occasions when she had received a summons, creeping away from the august apartments, more often than not in tears.

While Mme de Maintenon thus drained the cup of her misery, the King was in the highest spirits. His good health recovered, blissfully happy in Adelaide's companionship, he was ready for the next adventure, a review of his troops, army manoeuvres, and a mock-battle, on a tremendous scale, to be witnessed by the entire Court and, above all, by foreigners. Saint-Simon says that Louis XIV's intention was to astonish Europe, in peacetime, with a display of his power, which was generally believed to have been exhausted by a long war; also to give himself, and Mme de Maintenon, a treat—a magnificent spectacle, in honour of the Duc de Bourgogne.

Certainly the King found immense satisfaction in demonstrating his glory to the outside world; certainly his devotion to Mme de Maintenon had increased since his forgiveness of her; but as for wishing to please her by dragging her after him, in considerable discomfort, to military manoeuvres, that appears perhaps more doubtful. He may simply have required her company. The lady herself was anything but pleased. 'It seems to me,' she wrote to the Archbishop of Paris, 'that a charity bazaar would better become me than going to camp with a twelve-year-old princess. But they [meaning the King] want everything their own way.'

The decision was made in May 1698, when the King published his intention of holding, at Compiègne, in early September, a great review of his troops—a camp, as it was then called. It was not the first camp to be held in his reign—there had been three others, but those had been smaller affairs, not, like this one, a display of every wartime military operation. The King informed young Louis that he was to be in command. It was Louis XIV's farewell to his army, the handing over of active command to the younger generation, headed by his grandson the Duc de Bourgogne. Monseigneur, the King had given up as hopeless. He did not even offer him a sinecure, but left him to his wolf-hunting.

There were other reasons for such a show of strength which may have influenced the King in his decision. The long-drawn-out war against the League of Augsburg had ended in the previous year, and France, though at first supremely successful, had been forced to make concessions, at the Peace of Ryswick. There was peace in

Europe, but the future threatened. In Spain, Charles II was child-less and in poor health, and the question of the succession was looming. Both France and Austria had claims to the inheritance, and a family quarrel between Hapsburgs and Bourbons appeared inevitable, in which, if France should seem like winning, neither England nor Holland would be likely to stay neutral. Whatever the future might bring, no harm would come of reminding the Allies of the might and glory of French arms.

A lesser consideration, but still of great weight with the King, was the desire to distract the Duc de Bourgogne from his excessive piety, and his unhappiness over the absence of Fénelon, and to show him to the army as the heir presumptive. A question of finance came into it for, in earlier days, the King's presence with the army had cost millions, with his train of mistresses, their fol-lowers and servants, their accommodation, feasting, and protection. Princes of the royal blood, not so encumbered, and with retinues of very modest proportions, would effect a huge economy in wartime.

Louis, when he heard the news of his command, threw himself into training with all the zest he had shown at the age of seven. The passionate, masterful, impetuous boy that he had been in his early teens returned with a vengeance. One day, riding with an escort in the park of Versailles, the spirit suddenly moved him to clap spurs to his horse and, shouting, 'Those who love me, follow', set off in a mad career along the road to Paris. Only one survivor, an ordi-nary trooper, still remained with him when he reached Cours-la-Reine, with its parade of smart ladies in their gilded and painted coaches. There, after one look at the world of fashion, he turned his horse, and galloped back to Versailles, at the same breakneck speed. Sourches mentions this exploit without comment.

On another day, one of the hottest in June, he insisted on walking his horse all the way from Versailles to Maison and back again, so as to accustom himself to leading an army on the march. He was on the threshold of manhood, and had begun to take decisions for himself, and for his wife also. Dangeau mentions in his Journal some signs of the prince's strict piety, on which he makes no judg-ment. For instance, a play was given at Fontainebleau one Sunday evening, at which the Duc and Duchesse de Bourgogne did not appear. 'They never go to the play on Sunday', is all that Dangeau says; but, for him, it was saying a great deal. One wonders whether Adelaide absented herself unwillingly.

She had had, herself, a splendid piece of news from home, when

Duchess Anne at long last produced a son and heir.[1] She wept for joy, and immediately wrote to Madame Royale. 'You must be in the seventh heaven, dearest grandmamma, now that you have a grandson. Your joy increases mine for, loving you as I do, I cannot but share all your feelings.'[2]

As for the King; he was becoming more and more excited making plans for the great review, which he took under his personal direction. Sixty thousand men, a very large army in those days, assembled at Compiègne, in the early days of August. It consisted of fifty battalions each of 700 men, fifty-two squadrons of cavalry, with fifty horsemen apiece, forty cannon, six mortars, and eight pontoon bridges. An experienced officer, the Maréchal-Duc de Boufflers, was actually to command, but all the honours were to go to the young Duc de Bourgogne, who would wear the commander-in-chief's white sash, and take the King's commands in person. Ten A.D.C.s were to be attached to his staff, and six generals appointed to assist the maréchal.

The King, in his own hand, wrote 'A Memorandum of all the subjects in which H.M. desires M. le Duc de Bourgogne to be instructed', especially in the supply of food and forage, and the organisation of ambulance units. There was to be 'a skirmish, a cannonade, a division of the army into two parts, a battle with all arms engaged, the fording of a river and a crossing in boats; a grand display was to follow, with the siege, assault, and taking of a fortress, and finally a retreat by columns, without confusion or disorder'. To the study of this programme the young commander set his whole mind, with the utmost industry, and almost alarming enthusiasm.

The 'camp' was not by any means intended as a purely military affair. It was also the King's public farewell to his soldiers, for which he needed an audience. He therefore expressed a strong desire to see a great assemblage of courtiers, and no more was needed to provoke a stampede; especially since, instead of making nominations, he loosed his hold, and issued a general invitation, 'which,' Saint-Simon says, 'was not entirely pleasing to the ladies, each one

---

[1] Philippe, Prince of Piedmont, who died in 1715, when he was barely sixteen.

[2] Adelaide almost certainly wrote at the same time to Duchess Anne, whom she mentions in letter after letter, describing those she had received and her answers. The correspondence seems unhappily to have been destroyed, possibly during the siege of Turin, in 1706.

of whom, would have preferred to be named'. Nonetheless, so eager were they to avail themselves of the general permission that they fell over one another in their efforts to obtain transport and accommodation, ignoring certain rules of etiquette about which, at ordinary times, they were excessively particular. 'Anything served,' continued Saint-Simon, 'provided they got there,' and dukes, including the memoirist himself, consented to share their billets, and did not complain.

Adelaide invited four of her young friends, and one day, when all five appeared together in one coach, someone totted up their ages, and found that the total sum did not exceed seventy years. For the journey to the camp, however, she and Louis travelled with the King. Mme de Maintenon, grumbling, went in her own slow, comfortable carriage, doing her embroidery, or, perhaps, her interminable knitting for the poor.

It was on 1 September that they all set out, the King's coach crammed with Monseigneur, the Bourgognes, the Princesse de Conti, Madame la Duchesse, and the inevitable Duchesse du Lude. As soon as they arrived, the Duc de Bourgogne went off to put on his field-boots, and returned, wearing the white sash, to take the King's commands. It was his first act of generalship. He then went to the lines, where he retailed the King's orders, with, according to Sourches, 'astonishing grace', to the Maréchal de Boufflers and the generals. During the entire month that the camp lasted, he lived a soldier's life. It had, at first, been planned for him to keep open board while he was with the army, but the sight of the luxury and profusion of the table kept by the maréchal made the King think twice, and it was arranged for Louis to eat with him instead,which was far less expensive.

Dangeau and Sourches, as well as the *Mercure* and the *Amsterdam Gazette*, gave every detail of the manoeuvres and of Louis's exploits: how he was on horseback all day long, the first to mount in the morning, the last to dismount when night fell; how he crossed a river at night by a pontoon bridge, during a storm, and was nearly thrown by his terrified horse; how well he looked when saluting the King at the head of his troops; how, at the attack on the fortress of Compiègne, he cut the first trench,[1] lectured the engineers

[1] Mlle d'Aumale says that the following day was a Church holiday, and that the King took the men from their work on the trenches, for fear lest they should have no time to go to mass. He said that what he did from pure necessity or for his pleasure should cause no one to fail in their religious duties.

on siege warfare, and sent for beer to encourage the pioneers; how
he rallied his men, and led them forward with 'so proud a bearing'
that the enemy were driven in panic from their defences. Everyone
remarked on his zeal in the mock-attack, and the pleasure that he
derived from it. It was a joy to see that, behind the timorous, scholarly,
over-pious young man, there still remained something of the
ardent, passionate, imperious boy that he once had been.

While Louis was leading the attack upon the fortress, the great
set-piece of the display, a drama was taking place upon the ramparts, where the King, attended by a crowd of onlookers, stood
watching. Saint-Simon relates what happened.

'On 13 September, the day appointed for the assault, the King,
followed by all the ladies, and in the loveliest weather imaginable,
went out on to the ramparts, where crowds of courtiers were assembled and all the distinguished foreigners . . . I was in the semi-
circle no more than three paces away from His Majesty, with no one
in front of me. It was a superb sight, that great army and the crowds
of spectators on foot and on horseback keeping at a proper distance
so as not to obstruct the way . . . There was, however, one other
spectacle which struck me so forcibly that, forty years hence, I shall
see it as vividly as I do today . . . There sat Mme de Maintenon,
facing the troops in her sedan chair, behind its three glass windows.
On the front shaft, on the left-hand side, sat Mme la Duchesse de
Bourgogne, and behind her, in a semi-circle, all the other royal
ladies. The King had placed himself, standing, by the right-hand
window of the chair . . . His hat was off most of the time, and every
now and then he bent down to speak to Mme de Maintenon through
the glass, explaining to her what she saw, and the reason for each
manoeuvre. Each time he did so, she had the courtesy to lower the
window three or four inches, but never so much as halfway, for I
particularly noticed, and I must confess to being far more interested
in this scene than in the troop-movements. Occasionally, she opened
the window herself to ask the King a question; but it was nearly
always he who bent down to speak to her, without waiting for her to
address him first; and sometimes, when she paid no attention, he
rapped on the glass to make her open. He spoke to no one else, save
to give orders, in a few words and very seldom, and occasionally to
answer Mme la Duchesse de Bourgogne, who made efforts to
persuade him to talk to her . . .

'Examining the faces of the onlookers, I perceived that they
expressed ill-concealed nervous and embarrassed astonishment, and

that those who stood behind her chair gazed far more attentively at her than at the troops ... Just before the surrender, it seemed as though Mme de Maintenon asked permission to withdraw, for the King himself cried out, "Bearers for Madame!", and they carried her away ... People could not get over the spectacle they had witnessed, even those down on the plain below, even the troops, were inquiring about the sedan-chair into which the King was continually bending. It became necessary to silence the officers discreetly, and to stop the soldiers from asking questions. All Europe heard of the incident, which was as much talked of as the camp itself, with all its pomp and glory.'[1]

The manoeuvres ended with a mock-battle between the two divisions of the army: one side commanded by General de Rosen, an old soldier, risen from the ranks; the other side by Louis, with Maréchal de Boufflers to prompt him. The final act had of course to be a victory for Louis, and the defeat of Rosen; but, contrary to all expectations, the old soldier fought on, furiously refusing either to retreat or surrender, turning a deaf ear to a stream of orders. The King saw what was happening with considerable amusement; 'Rosen does not care to be beaten', he said; but since Louis, perforce, had to win, he sent such peremptory commands that Rosen sulkily consented to retire.

That was the last act, and the ladies thankfully returned to Versailles, for they had been most uncomfortably lodged, and had not been permitted either to dine with the King or eat at his expense.[2] Nor had they seen much of Adelaide, who had been doing her duty, visiting hospitals, dining at the maréchal's table with the officers, distributing parcels of meat and wine among the soldiers; begging favours for them, visiting the local convents; in fact, carrying out all the functions of a first lady of France, and giving perfect satisfaction to all concerned. She also managed to enjoy herself:

[1] It is possible that Saint-Simon, shocked by Mme de Maintenon's relations with the King, may have exaggerated the effect of the undeniably strange scene. The troops and onlookers far away in the plain below would not have seen very clearly, and presumably the soldiers were busy. In any case, the courtiers were used to the extraordinary position of Mme de Maintenon (she had been there for the past fifteen years), and well knew the King's courtesy to all women.

[2] Saint-Simon reports that many officers and regiments ruined themselves for years to come by offering too liberal hospitality to all-comers, and supplying their soldiers with full dress uniforms, decorated with every kind of embellishment. The King gave the maréchal 100,000 francs, but that 'was a drop in the ocean'.

'I could never have imagined, dear grandmamma, finding myself in the midst of a besieged town, and woken by cannon-fire, as I was this morning. I hope we shall soon emerge safely from this situation. Truly, I am enjoying myself enormously.' She was growing up and learning her trade; Louis, also, had been playing a man's part for the first time, and had distinguished himself. The King was pleased with them both, and with the manoeuvres, which, says Saint-Simon, 'had made all Europe tremble'.

In the new year Louis XIV decided that the moment was approaching to think of the young couple being 'put together', as the expression then was, and to contemplate the gratifying prospect of extending his line to the third generation. Such an intimate happening might, one would have thought, have been kept private; but nothing, in those days, was private in the lives of princes. From their public *levers* to their bedding-down at night they were attended by courtiers; their births, the births of their children, their illnesses, and their deathbeds seem to have been regarded as part of the ceremonial of Court life, no more, no less. In any case, there would have had to be a re-allocation of rooms, at Versailles, a certain amount of reconstructional work, and, of course, redecoration, and such things could not be hidden. Louis could not have gone on sharing an apartment with his brothers; but the King had given away so many 'lodgings' that there was literally nowhere else to put him. In the end, the old Maréchale de la Mothe was moved into a much smaller room;[1] her old apartment was given to Louis, and a dressing-room was built for him over the courtyard, next door.

This work was begun in July 1699, and was finished at the end of October, when the Court was still at Fontainebleau. The King then announced its purpose, and the couple were themselves informed. He no doubt told Louis himself, and Mme de Maintenon spoke to Adelaide. Everyone knew what was happening. 'The King,' reports Baron de Breteuil in his *Mémoires*, 'told us at his *petit coucher*, when speaking of the Duchesse de Bourgogne, that already, in the past four or five days, she had started to cry because of the "alarm to her modesty".' About the duke, opinions differed. The Venetian ambassador wrote that he would have preferred some

---

[1] Although she had many years since retired from being governess to the princes, the King did not want to deprive her of a lodging. He therefore gave her the Duc de Berry's old room, which annoyed her considerably because she no longer had the space to house her daughter.

delay, feeling 'not yet sufficiently mature to be capable of the keenest effects of marital love'. On the other hand, sentimental Mlle d'Aumale says that they were wildly in love, and that just a year after the wedding day they had implored the King so fervently to let them live together, that he had shortened the period of separation which he had at first decreed.

Whether Louis XIV would have been moved by their entreaties to hasten any decision once taken, or to delay it on account of Adelaide's tears or Louis's nervousness, is problematical. However that may have been, his wish was that their new life should begin on the very night when the Court returned to Versailles. Yet he did consider their embarrassment sufficiently to spare them the gaze of too many curious eyes, to the disappointment of Baron de Breteuil, who was preparing a chapter in his *Mémoires*, entitled 'From Evening to Morning: the First Night passed together by Mgr le Duc and Mme la Duchesse de Bourgogne'.

The return was billed for 23 October 1699; and the King, taking with him Adelaide and Louis, did the journey at one stretch behind his swift horses and arrived long before anyone else. As soon as they stepped down from the coach, Adelaide went to Mme de Maintenon's room, and supped with her alone. One may scarcely doubt that a final exhortation was given on the duties of conjugal life, or, judging by Mme de Maintenon's stream of complaints on that subject to her confessor, that they were not made to sound very amusing.[1] At any rate, Adelaide, still two months short of her fourteenth birthday, was seen shedding a few tears as she returned, at ten o'clock, to her own rooms, where the hearty Mme Quentin probably gave her a more cheerful view of love. The Duchesse du Lude had tactfully, perhaps thankfully, gone to bed in her own room, and all the other ladies in attendance had been dismissed.

Louis had supper with the King and then, also at ten o'clock, went to change in his new dressing-room, which was where Baron de Breteuil, the master of ceremonies, went to fetch him. 'His hair,'

[1] Godet des Marais, Bishop of Chartres, was Mme de Maintenon's confessor. 'These distressing occasions,' she wrote, 'are becoming too much for me,' asking whether she might not refuse to submit to the King's twice-daily attentions. His reply was that he also would have preferred to see her in the chaste condition of the brides of Christ; but that it was a holy work to preserve the King from sin, and possibly adultery. Soon, he added, she would be in heaven, and able to follow the Lamb. 'What a martyrdom I endured. While everyone thought me the happiest woman alive, the very opposite was true,' she wrote after the King's death to Mme de Glapion, headmistress of Saint-Cyr.

writes the baron, 'was crisped into tight curls, and the costliness of his dressing-gown and night attire strongly evidenced the bridegroom. He left his apartments looking bold and full of good cheer; and since I had the honour to carry his candlestick, it was I who led him to the threshold of the battlefield . . . All this happened so quickly that the King, who had said that he would go alone, by the back way, to see them in bed, arrived too late, and found the door locked.'

At half-past eight next morning, Louis returned to his own apartments. A crowd, rather more interested than usual, was assembled at his *lever*, and some older courtiers could not forbear to remark that there were rings round his eyes, and that he looked tired. 'You may draw your own conclusions,' commented the baron. Adelaide rose at nine, and immediately drove to Saint-Cyr, where Mme de Maintenon was expecting her. There were no receptions or diversions at the Court that evening, and Louis slept in his own room. So it continued, every other night, until 11 November, when Dangeau notes in his Journal, 'Mgr le Duc de Bourgogne has taken to sleeping every night with Mme la Duchesse de Bourgogne. He says that he will no longer sleep apart from her.' He was seventeen years old.

9

Queen of the Revels

'I T WAS the sole purpose of every man to court her favour, and of every woman to give her joy ... She was the planner and centre of every diversion; all were given for her, and the King enjoyed them only in so far as they gave her pleasure.' Thus wrote Mme de Lafayette of Henrietta, Adelaide's English grandmother. She might equally have been writing of the granddaughter who so closely resembled her.

'The entire Court,' says Saint-Simon, 'was rejuvenated by her youth and high spirits ... She seemed to have the gift of being everywhere at once, and brought animation and gaiety wherever she appeared. Every entertainment was enhanced by her presence, for she was the life and soul of the balls and plays and fêtes, enchanting all by the grace and neatness of her dancing.'

She certainly enjoyed the Carnival of 1700, for there had never been a gayer one. Balls, masquerades, supper-parties followed one on top of another, and she was queen of them all. Free from Mme de Maintenon's apron strings, she flung herself into these pleasures with a zest which the ageing Court had long ceased to feel. Mme de Maintenon, nearly seventy years old, spent her days in bed at Saint-Cyr, writing innumerable letters, giving directions and advice to the clergy and the dames of her school. She saw Adelaide every evening, and intervened when protection was required; but otherwise left her to the care of her circle of ladies. She was probably worried about her, for she says in one of her letters, 'Our princess makes enormous efforts to find amusement; but only succeeds in making herself giddy from exhaustion'. Yet, she would never have risked angering the King by spoiling his pleasure, or making Adelaide sulky by frustrating her.

Mme de Sévigné's old friend Coulanges[1] spoke disapprovingly

[1] Philippe Emmanuel de Coulanges (1663–1716) wrote a great number of letters to her, and to her daughter Mme de Grignan, as well as publishing a collection of songs and verses.

of the life she was leading. 'The King wishes Mme la Duchesse de Bourgogne to do from morning to night just as the fancy takes her. It is enough for him if she enjoys herself. Her life is all excursions to Marly or Meudon, or drives to Paris and back for balls, operas, and masques, with the courtiers at daggers drawn to win her favour. Those ladies who take part in these diversions need to have their purses well-lined, for the expense is quadrupled. The materials they use for the masques cost anything from a hundred to a hundred and fifty francs an ell,[1] and when people find themselves obliged to wear the same dress twice, the gossips say that they only go to Paris for the second-hand clothes shops.'

The *Mercure* has interminable descriptions of balls and costumes, especially of Adelaide's appearances. We hear of her as Flora, surrounded by a bevy of nymphs; as a milkmaid, an old peasant-woman, or magnificently attired as a sorceress, a sultana, a Spanish dancer. In one of the masques she played the part of the bride, at a village wedding, in another she was the Queen of Clubs with Louis as the King, in a quadrille of playing-cards.

On her fourteenth birthday the King finally gave her the present for which she had been longing, the Versailles menagerie, to be hers alone from that time onwards, and he ordered Mansart his architect to reconstruct and restock it just as she wished, with no interference from anyone, not even from himself. Yet he could not bear to be left quite out of it all, for we find him writing to Mansart about the fountains, 'Let there be children everywhere'. Adelaide was supremely happy. 'They are hard at work on my menagerie,' she wrote to Madame Royale, in the following June. 'Just see, dear grandmamma, how wonderful it is going to be.[2] I shall not be able to see it myself until we return from Fontainebleau. Truly the King is marvellously good to me. I do love him very much.' In every letter she speaks of the King's kindness; of her adoring husband she says nothing warm or tender; nothing, indeed, beyond an occasional bare mention.

Adelaide would have been odiously ungrateful had she not loved the King, who was straining his wits to find new ways of pleasing her. Sourches says that he 'had for her all the love and kindness imaginable'; but like many other courtiers, especially those who had not known Louis XIV in his younger, more attractive years, he found so much devotion puzzling, and wondered whether Adelaide

---

[1] About a yard and a quarter.   [2] She must have enclosed a plan.

responded. Saint-Simon was in no doubt. He says that she never forgot the least little thing that might please Mme de Maintenon and, through her, the King . . .' Her personal wishes, her pleasures, even her health she sacrificed for them, and thus became intimate with them in a way that none of his own children had found possible.

The fashion for balls and masquerades persisted all through the autumn and winter of 1700; but people cannot dance forever, and after Lent came the annual visit to Fontainebleau, where there was acting and music nearly every evening. At first they played comedies, including some of Scarron's comic operas, which led Madame to write, 'My reflections last night were that if Mme la Duchesse de Bourgogne had asked the author's name, and had learned that he was her uncle, she would have been very much surprised. None the less since she calls Mme de Maintenon her aunt, Scarron must certainly have been her uncle, seeing that he was that woman's husband.'

Mme de Maintenon was not amused by the comedies. The King enjoyed himself altogether too much in her opinion, singing in the choruses; once even taking part, dressed in a white domino. She thought it bad for his soul, and wished they would revive certain religious plays, like those Racine had written for Saint-Cyr. Accordingly, they did Duché's *Jonathas*,[1] directed by the famous actor Baron,[2] with Adelaide in one of the smaller parts. This was followed by *Absalon*, also by Duché,[3] but no masterpiece. The King, however, was deeply moved and dissolved into tears. As for Madame, she says that she 'cried like a lunatic because although the subject was the death of *Absalon*, they had changed one or two things to make it more pathetic. They pretended, for instance, that he returned wounded to die before the King, in the presence of his wife and child. The Comtesse d'Ayen played Absalon's wife, and the Duchesse de Bourgogne his daughter . . . Mme la Duchesse de Bourgogne is better in serious plays than in comedies.'

Since no one praised Adelaide's acting, one may assume that she was not very good. She, however, was convinced that she had talent, and when they revived Racine's *Athalie*, in 1702, there was trouble. Her old schoolfriend Françoise, now married to the Comte d'Ayen,

---

[1] Dangeau called it a 'pious comedy', others 'a religious tragedy'.
[2] Michel Boy, called Baron (1653–1729), was the son of two players in Molière's troop of comedians.
[3] Joseph-François Duché de Vancy (1668–1704). Mme de Maintenon thought highly of him, arranged for him to inherit Racine's pension, and commissioned him to write religious plays for Saint-Cyr.

had the principal rôle; Adelaide demanded it; Françoise's husband took offence, and Mme de Maintenon, who had gone to considerable trouble over the revival, was forced to intervene. 'Here is *Athalie* once more breaking down,' she wrote to him. 'Ill fortune dogs me in all that I do, and all those whom I protect and care for. Mme la Duchesse de Bourgogne says it will be a failure; that the play is dull; that Racine was sorry he ever wrote it; that I am the only one who likes it; and many other things that forced me to conclude she was discontented with her part. She wished to play Josabeth, which she cannot do as well as the Comtesse d'Ayen. As soon as she had the part her views changed. Now she is perfectly happy and thinks *Athalie* a marvel. Let us proceed, since we agreed to do the play; but truly it is not agreeable to share pleasures with the great.'

Dangeau passes over the performance in silence. The *Mercure's* notice is cool. 'Mme la Duchesse de Bourgogne played Josabeth with all imaginable grace and intelligence. Though her rank hindered her from showing the audacity of an ordinary actress, she showed enough to indicate that she had mastered the part . . . Her costumes were magnificent.'

Athalie marked the end of serious acting for Adelaide. There were no plays the following year, either because religious dramas had ceased to amuse, or because of Mme de Maintenon's withdrawal. The old lady had exerted herself to produce the plays for the princess and her friends, on the model of the old days of Saint-Cyr. If there were to be quarrels she was done with them, and she finished, as follows, the above-quoted letter to the Comte d'Ayen. 'You take too much trouble to please them; it is not worth while. You also try to do these things too well, too richly, with too much regard for the great ones. If they return to acting next year, it must be done quite differently. Goodnight, dear nephew; what a bore everything becomes!'

Madame thought that the King, also, was bored with the theatre. 'It is a tragedy for the poor comedians that the King no longer sees their plays. Comedies were not thought sinful when he used to attend them; far from it, indeed, since the bishops all went every day. There was a row of seats kept especially for them and it was always full; M. de Meaux went regularly. Now that the King has ceased to go, plays are considered sinful.' Sinful or not, Adelaide had had enough of them. She had developed a new craze, less trouble than acting, but far more dangerous, and to her, as to most other people at the Court, totally absorbing. The King was partly to blame, for he had taken her one evening to Meudon, when the Princesse de Conti was playing lansquenet, and had encouraged her to take a hand, standing laughing behind her chair, to finance her losses. That had been enough. Gambling soon became a passion, a mania, a temptation which Adelaide was unable to resist.

Mme de Maintenon was worried from the very beginning, for she wrote to the Princesse de Soubise,[1] 'Mme la Duchesse de Bourgogne went yesterday to Meudon. She saw no one, and they made her play cards for high stakes. All that group there are most embarrassing.' By 'that group there' she meant the Princesse de Conti, Monseigneur himself, and his low-born mistress Mlle Chouin, on whose account he received very few visitors; which did not prevent him from giving card-parties for his daughter-in-law, and encouraging her to drink and gamble.[2]

Cards were the rage, everyone was mad to win money, and there was, regrettably, a good deal of cheating. People played for three, four, even six hours at a stretch, often for huge stakes. There were many tragedies; yet it is only fair to say that, under Mme de Maintenon's strict surveillance of the King's pleasures, there was little else to do, at Versailles, in the winter evenings. Madame, who played only the steadier games, wrote, in 1702, of 'the tragic happenings for which card-playing, especially at lansquenet, is responsible. Only last winter,' she continued, 'four officers committed suicide. They would have done much better to amuse themselves with innocent German games, and confine themselves to drinking milk. They would not then have been reduced to shooting themselves.' La Fare[3] speaks, in his memoirs, of the deterioration in the tone of the Court, during the last years of the seventeenth century. 'Nothing

---

[1] Anne de Rohan-Chabot (1648–1709), second wife of François de Rohan-Montbazon, thus later becoming Princesse de Soubise. Saint-Simon thinks that her brilliant 'and highly rewarding career' was due to her beauty and ambition' and 'the uses to which she put both'. He suggests that she had once been the King's mistress. At any rate, she remained his privileged friend, and that also of Mme de Maintenon. Letters 'flew to and fro between them', usually intrigues for favour or ambition.

[2] This group became known as 'the Meudon parvulo', composed of people who were determined to become powerful during the next reign, believing that Monseigneur would soon succeed to the throne, and be wax in their hands. For that reason they were enemies of the Duc de Bourgogne who, they feared, had a will of his own.

[3] Charles Auguste de La Fare (1644–1712) also wrote a collection of songs and romantic comedies that were very popular.

is now to be seen but gaming, confusion, and bad manners. When Mme la Duchesse de Bourgogne entered Society, she found it hard not to succumb to the fashionable vices of which drunkenness and lansquenet are the most ruinous.'[1]

Madame might feel concern; La Fare and others of his generation be saddened; but the King remained unperturbed. Ruined courtiers depended wholly upon his bounty, a state of which he highly approved; moreover, he thought it becoming for princes to lose heavily at cards, and never minded paying Monseigneur's huge debts. He even assured Louis, who had gambled wildly at first, but latterly had cured himself, that he expected him to lose great sums. Adelaide, however, went altogether too far. Her losses were so great and so constant that both he and Mme de Maintenon were shocked. At first, he had paid kindly enough, promising not to tell Louis, only advising her to be more careful. At last he objected; but Adelaide, applying to her aunt, begged their pardons so sweetly and so humbly in her letters, and so coaxingly by word of mouth, that they always forgave her.

In the May of 1702, she was writing as follows: 'Friday midnight. I am in despair because I am so often guilty of follies that cause you to reproach me. I am firmly resolved to take no more part in the gambling that serves only to ruin my reputation and lessen your love, which is of all things most precious to me. I am overwhelmed by your kindness in sending me the money to pay my debts. I hope with God's help to cure my weakness and become more worthy of your affection.'

After so penitent a letter, so firm a promise, one might have expected at least some improvement, but there was none; for Dangeau mentions her playing cards almost every day, at Versailles, in all the great houses, and even in her bedroom with her ladies, when, as frequently happened, she was unwell and confined to bed. To be fair to her, Adelaide was still very young, not yet seventeen

---

[1] Dangeau was the only person that we hear of consistently making money from cards. Mme de Sévigné was deeply impressed by him, one evening, when the King had embarrassed her by an invitation to play at his table, and Dangeau kindly asked her to be his partner. 'I have been watching Dangeau play,' she wrote, 'and am astonished at how stupid we all are, compared with him. He thinks of nothing but the business in hand, and wins when everyone else is losing. . . . Thus he makes 200,000 francs in a week, and 100,000 écus in a month, all of which he enters in his book.' He played from three to six p.m. every day, regularly, and was never suspected of cheating, as were so many others, often quite openly.

in the autumn of 1702, and the great and the rich vied with one
another to put temptation in her way. She was pleasant to play with,
for she paid her debts promptly and with a smile, though she
hugely enjoyed winning. But she was exhausting herself by burning
her candle at both ends as, not once a week, but night after night,
she danced and played cards until the sun was up. She seems to have
shunned her bed, and all idea of rest.

One day, for example, Monsieur le Duc gave a fête for her at his
house at Saint-Maur.[1] It began early in the evening with a merry-
go-round and wooden horses, on which they tilted at rings for costly
and beautiful prizes. 'Mme la Duchesse de Bourgogne,' says Dangeau, 'enjoyed herself exceedingly.' They then proceeded to go
indoors for active games, and these were followed by a concert,
with Mlle Couperin singing songs from the old operas, to her
father's accompaniment.[2] Next came supper, cards and dancing,
until five in the morning, when Adelaide went home, after a lottery,
in which everyone had a prize-winning ticket.

Adelaide, indeed, started for home, but on her way across Paris
the fancy took her to visit the market at Les Halles, to see the fruit
and vegetables arriving from the country, and there then seemed
just time enough to hear mass, at Saint-Eustache,[3] before returning
to give the King his good-morning kiss when he woke, and sit on
his bed to tell him all that had happened. On most such mornings,
she would wait until she had tucked Mme de Maintenon up in her
coach, and seen her comfortably off to Saint-Cyr, before at last
consenting to go to bed, where she sometimes stayed until four or
five in the afternoon.

In the hot summer months, long nights of connubial bliss with
Louis seem not to have figured very high in Adelaide's estimate of

[1] Monsieur le Duc (le Duc de Bourbon-Condé), so-called, was the husband
of the King's legitimated daughter Madame la Duchesse, who was by far the
most malicious of the bastards—not beautiful like the Princesse de Conti, but
pretty, witty, and intelligent. Even Madame (who hated the bastards) said of
her, 'She mocks at everything so comically that one cannot help laughing. . . .
She has never, in all her life, lost her temper, not even for a moment.' Their
estate, at Saint-Maur, was not far from Sceaux, only a short way from Paris.

[2] Louise Couperin (1674–1748) was one of the members of the King's
orchestra. Her father, François Couperin (1668–1733) the famous organist and
composer, especially for the clavichord, was master of the organ at the King's
chapel of Versailles.

[3] This would excuse her from attending midday mass, at Versailles, when
she would be still in bed.

pleasures.[1] At Marly, after serenading the King outside his window
with hautboys and trumpets, and keeping him up long after his
usual bedtime, she would often run down to the river (she rarely
walked, except in procession), followed by an eager band of courtiers. A row of pretty tents had been pitched for her by the bank,
and there she would spend most of the night, bathing, dancing,
playing cards. It was a dangerous situation for, although in the daytime her ladies guarded her, it was not so during the summer
nights, when the moon lit up the gardens. At such times, like her
English grandmother, she was surrounded by gallants old and young,
burning to please her, chattering, laughing, daring almost to flirt with
her when, as more often happened than not, she was a little tipsy.

Her daytime pleasures were innocence itself, and the best of all,
to her, was her Ménagerie, where she could cast off the burden of
Court etiquette, of which Saint-Simon says, she 'suffered all the
torture'. With her ladies she felt free, treating them with a kindness
and friendly intimacy[2] very shocking to the eyes of Madame. 'No
one knows her place any more ... The Duchesse de Bourgogne,
when she walks in the gardens, gives an arm to one of her ladies
while the rest walk alongside [instead of two paces behind]. One
does not perceive her rank.'[3]

Mansart had arranged for her a small suite of rooms at the centre
of the Ménagerie, equipped with a kitchen and pantries, and there
she relived the happy hours of childhood, at the Vigna della
Madama, baking cakes, making dresses, feeding and tending the
baby animals, playing games less harmful than lansquenet, perhaps
even her old favourite, blindman's buff, or going for donkey-rides.

So, year after year, her life was spent in an endless pursuit of
entertainment, without serious thought or any moral purpose.
Inevitably her health and character suffered. Her letters to Madame
Royale are full of complaints. 'I am very neglectful of you, my dear
grandmamma, not to have wished you a happy new year; but I have

---

[1] 'I do not think that she was much attracted to the person of her husband,
or responded to his passion with any ardour.' Saint-Simon.

Saint-Simon says that, in those early years, she was surrounded by ancient
gallants, whose romantic inclinations were no whit reduced because decrepitude
prevented their enjoyment.

[2] Adelaide was essentially kind, and not afraid of showing it. In modern times
her behaviour would seem natural enough; but not so in her period, and people
were deeply moved.

[3] Saint-Simon, though he loved her for her kindness, thought that she was
too easy-going by far, and that her friendliness encouraged 'certain usurpations'.

been very much troubled by swollen gums and migraines.'[1] Dan-geau also speaks of her migraines, though he might have called them bilious attacks; for Mme de Maintenon mentions 'attacks of indiges-tion, not justly attributable to any weakness of her stomach (in other words due to greed and too much drinking)'. Adelaide also had frequent 'bouts of fever', the prevailing ill, for which she dosed herself freely with quinine, of which not all the doctors approved.

In the summer of 1701, she had fallen dangerously ill, Saint-Simon says, 'from bathing imprudently and immediately afterwards eating too much fruit. She became delirious, and Fagon[2] bled her twice from the foot, in order to clear her head; that proving ineffec-tual, he began to fear for her life, and treated her with emetics'. Thereafter, her condition improved; consciousness returned, and she sent for her confessor, being convinced that she was about to die. To him, she gave evidence of a seriousness and piety that touched and edified the entire Court; so much so indeed that Mme de Maintenon was moved to hope that good might come out of evil, if only she could be brought to realise that her disorderly life was the main cause of her illness.

The old lady, who had nursed her with a devotion which even her enemy Saint-Simon admired, was now herself laid low for a few days with a high temperature. When she returned to Adelaide, she took advantage of a long convalescence to organise quiet card-parties among the household ladies. Non-playing ladies stood watching, or sat, according to their rank,[3] and Mme de Maintenon had an armchair by the bedside, which Saint-Simon considered highly improper, because far above her station.

Mme de Maintenon's parties were never dull, the entertainments at Saint-Cyr speak for that, and Adelaide probably enjoyed her convalescence. 'She was easily amused,' says Saint-Simon, 'and, though she preferred gambling, was as happy and as cheerful spending an afternoon reading and sewing with her "serious ladies", as she called the older members of her household.' Nonetheless, when the time came for her to re-enter the world, she was enchanted,

---

[1] Adelaide's teeth were black and rotten, and she had frequent abscesses and very bad toothache, for which she secretly took snuff and chewed tobacco, which did little good.

[2] Guy Crescent Fagon, the King's first physician.

[3] All except Mme d'Heudicourt who 'was allowed a little low seat, almost at floor-level, and quite near the King, because she could not stand for long on her old legs'.

and (alas! for Mme de Maintenon's hopes) before long had reverted
to lansquenet, and all the old excesses.

The situation had changed, however, though perhaps Adelaide
did not know it at that time. The King, Mme de Maintenon, and
Louis had been driven nearly out of their minds with worry during
her illness, and when, after her recovery, she still refused to care for
her health, a shade of exasperation tinged their doting love. Louis
especially, had suffered, and his fussing had set her against him.
Mme de Maintenon, in a letter,[1] describes what happened: 'Mme
la Duchesse de Bourgogne is unwell; they are prescribing all manner
of remedies that require greater self-restraint than she can muster.
Her husband is furious, there is no other word to describe his
passion. I do not believe that we have witnessed anything more disagreeable either for her, who is the cause, or for the onlookers . .
There are still no signs of her being with child. The remedies mentioned prevent their living together, which is partly the cause of
the rages of which I speak.' Poor love-sick Louis, rage was not now
his usual state; his mood was normally one of tender melancholy, as
we shall see by the letters he wrote, from the army, to Mme de
Montgon, his old friend and ally.[2]

The non-appearance of an heir in the third generation was also
making the King impatient, notwithstanding that Adelaide was not
yet seventeen. There had certainly been frequent miscarriages
brought on, at very early stages, by her imprudence, and though
precautions were taken, they had had no effect.[3] Adelaide's old
friend Tessé, now back in Turin,[4] was moved, or perhaps per-

[1] To Philip V of Spain. In the previous year, the death of Charles II, and his
bequest of the crown to Louis XIV's grandson the Duc d'Anjou, had meant
the departure of the young prince to Madrid. He was homesick and lonely
and Louis and Mme de Maintenon wrote to him very often.

[2] The Marquise de Montgon (1668–1707) was the daughter of the Marquis
d'Heudicourt, and Belle de Pons his wife, an old friend of Mme de Maintenon.
Saint-Simon did not care for her, perhaps because she was Mme de Maintenon's protégée, and had been educated by her. He says 'she was plain, with
sparkling wit, graceful, amiable, as pleasant and amusing as possible, but
correspondingly malicious'.

[3] For instance, her coach was not allowed to travel over cobbles or the horses
to go out of a walk. The journey to Fontainebleau was done by river, from
Corbeil onwards.

[4] He was arranging the marriage of Marie Louise Gabrielle, Adelaide's
twelve-year-old sister, to Philip V of Spain. 'It was a great honour for her
father to have as sons-in-law the two most powerful sovereigns in Europe,' and
the King hoped by this to cement his alliance with Savoy.

uaded by Duchess Anne, to write to her on that subject, when he
orwarded a present from the Princesse de Vaudémont of a charming
toup for Holy Water, containing a baby carved from white coral:
I devoutly believe that she sends it so that the coral baby may re-
waken you, every evening and morning, to the thought that you
we one to us, and that no other thought, not of your lovely figure,
or of anything else, compared with that is of the slightest import-
nce. I am your old servant, whom you sometimes deign to call
ld fool; I shall not mind that, provided you will direct Mme
Quentin to inform me, after M. le Duc de Bourgogne's return,
irst that it may be, then that it is.'

Tessé's appeal did not have the desired effect. Adelaide, though
erfectly willing to find herself the mother of an heir, could not
ersuade herself to protect the embryo. Miscarriages followed one
nother at such short intervals, that the courtiers, growing tired of
peculation, followed by disappointment, began to murmur, and
ot too unkind verses went the rounds:

> 'Unaware of what the gossips say,
> She shyly tells the doctor all;
> In his ear whispering low,
> The oft-repeated question,
> Am I? or Am I not?'

She very often was, but never for long, since she was incapable
f self-control, and beyond the control of others. Every night she
anced and gambled and, in the daytime, spent every spare moment
t the tables. She even organised a card-table at her Paris dress-
naker's,[1] playing for lengths of beautiful material. What most
orried Mme de Maintenon, was that she was keeping bad company
ith the fast, rich, rakish set, particularly the Parvulo of Meudon,
hose members were not her friends, though she was probably
till unaware of their enmity. There was not much that Mme de
Maintenon could do; Adelaide, though still devoted to her,[2] would
eed no advice, and for a long time the old lady was obliged to limit
er efforts to keeping the worst from the King. She feared an
xplosion, when he would thunder, and Adelaide toss her head, or

[1] Mme Lebrion, in the Rue de la Vieille Monnaie.
[2] Mme de Maintenon wrote, after a day spent in bed, 'Our dear princess
ined with me, and gave me all the tender care of a good daughter for a much-
ved mother'.

sulk, which could easily mean the end of a perfect relationship, for the one thing that Louis XIV would not suffer was a cross face, or a person with a grievance. Eventually (and they waited a very long time), the patience of both the King and Mme de Maintenon ran out. They decided that a stand must be made; that Adelaide's life must be brought to order, and she, herself, receive a reprimand. The following letter will show how Mme de Maintenon set about the matter, and is a good example of her methods, and of the supreme tact and 'sanctified commonsense', for which the King so loved and depended on her. She was writing to Mme de Dangeau, on whose gentleness and charm she always relied, when Adelaide required bracing:

'This Saturday evening, at a quarter to five (16 July, 1707)

'The Princesse de Vaudémont, Madame, was the merest pre-text. It was in order to speak to Mme la Duchesse de Bourgogne that I asked you to postpone until tomorrow your journey to Paris. Last night, the King informed me that he had been sur-prised to see card-playing at Bretesche,[1] which goes to show that the Princess is deceiving me. She had told me that Madame la Duchesse had invited herself to a meal there, but I now perceive that it was all pre-arranged. The King says that she had invited Madame la Duchesse to go there, and that M. le Comte de Lorges[2] was one of the first to arrive. I said it was only natural for Madame la Duchesse to go to her brother's house; but that, regarding the card-playing, I was more vexed than anyone. The King said, "Was it not enough for one day to have a dinner-party, a riding-party, a hunt, and a supper-party?", and added after some reflection, "I had better tell those gentlemen that they do not please me when they gamble with the Duchesse de Bour-gogne". I said that lansquenet had always distressed me, for fear lest she inadvertently do something to spoil her good name, or put herself on the wrong footing. We then spoke of other matters; but the King returned to the subject, saying, "Should I not be well advised to have these gentlemen spoken to?" I said I thought that that might be harmful to Mme la Duchesse de

[1] La Bretesche, a little village between Versailles and Marly, where Mon-seigneur had a hunting-box, and where the hounds often met.
[2] The Comte de Lorges, later Duc de Durfort, later still Duc de Lorges, was Saint-Simon's young brother-in-law, a 'powdered and gilded sprig of fashion', a rake of whom the writer disapproved, despite his noble birth.

1 The Duchesse de Bourgogne, by Jean-Baptiste Santerre

2 Bust of the Duchesse de Bourgogne in the King's bedroom at Versailles, by Coysevox

3 The Duc de Bourgogne, by Rigaud

4 Mme de Maintenon and her niece Françoise d'Aubigné, by Ferdinand Elle

5 Louis XIV, by Sir Godfrey Kneller

6 Madame, by Rigaud

7 The marriage of the Duc de Bourgogne and Princess Marie-Adélaïde of Savoy in 1697, by Antoine Dieu

Mausolée pour la Cérémonie
Prince Louis de Bourbon, Duc de
decédé le 18 février 1712 et de très
Marie Adelaude de Savoye

8 The mourning catafalque for the Duc and Duchesse de Bourgogne

Bourgogne, and that it would be best to speak to her personally, and in private. He said he would do so this very day. It is to warn her of this, Madame, that I am begging you to stay.

'We have arrived, sooner than I expected at the divergence I have always dreaded. The King will think he angers her by stopping her lansquenet, and will be colder in his manner. She will certainly be vexed, and more distant with him. I too shall be vexed and shall revert to the formal respect which I owe her rank. But I am not yet so indifferent to public opinion as to let it be thought that I approve such conduct ... Madame la Duchesse will condole with Mme la Duchesse de Bourgogne, which will remind me of the traps her mother Mme de Montespan used to set for the Queen and Mme de La Vallière, in order to make the King admire their own good conduct ... If, Madame, you would come to Saint-Cyr after speaking to the Princess, I should be overjoyed to see you; but I doubt whether, after such a melancholy conversation, you will be in any state to appear.

'Should you find it possible to approach Mme la Duchesse de Bourgogne, you will perhaps give her my letter, so that she may prepare herself to answer the King. You may then be able to speak to her at greater length this evening. Only imagine, dear Madame, what a night I have passed. Let us pray for our Princess, who is drowning herself in a coffee-cup storm.'

This letter shows better than anything the life which Adelaide was leading; the dangers towards which she was heading, and the change in her relationship to Mme de Maintenon. All that lady could do, at this period, was to stand aside, give good advice as an old friend, and preserve the bond of love between Adelaide and the King. When more drastic measures were required, she moved in the mysterious, round-about ways that were typical of most of her dealings. It was a thousand pities that Adelaide and her young husband (who was also in difficulties) could not support or influence one another. They had much to give. Her lightness, gentleness, and charm might have made more tolerable his life at Court; his good principles might have helped her to govern herself. Unfortunately, while he was desperately in love with Adelaide's charm, he failed most lamentably in charming her, as the courtiers began to notice. Madame, writing to her aunt, summed up the situation, as she saw it, with considerable neatness: 'Those people who were astonished

by the misery of M. le Duc de Bourgogne during his wife's serious
illness [1701], were not perhaps aware that he is very much in love
with her, but not she with him. I believe that once she has given
him a prince or two, she will not be sorry if the good man departs
for celestial regions.'

Man and Wife

IN THE first years of his marriage, Louis, desperately in love with Adelaide, had joined in her wild pursuit of pleasure. He would scarcely have been human had he not wished to share in everything she did, and he took to dancing, drinking and gambling, with all the passion that he had shown for games and military training when he was a boy.

During the famous carnival of 1700, when he was eighteen years old, he was leading very much the same life as Adelaide, dancing in the same masques, playing the bridegroom to her bride in the village wedding, and the King of Clubs to her Queen in the playing-card ballet. For a time he was as much amused by the theatricals, but Dangeau says that he preferred the concerts. He particularly loved the opera, and went often to the Paris opera house with his father Monseigneur, who was a regular supporter. Louis, himself, had a pleasant voice, and began seriously to think of training it, taking lessons from the best chorister of the King's chapel. He found in singing a satisfactory way of allying piety with pleasure, for Madame writes that he composed religious words to the best tunes from the operas, so that he could sing them all day without offending his conscience. As a result of much hard work, he was able to assume a rôle in Lully's opera *Alceste*, when it was given at Versailles, along with the other members of the royal family taking part.

Joining in the life of the Court increased his popularity, and the Princesse de Conti, hoping, perhaps, to win his love, as she had won his father's, spent huge sums in transforming her gallery into a private theatre for his benefit, not only decorated with beautiful paintings, but equipped with movable sets of scenery that, alone, cost her a small fortune. Louis's passion, however, was for gambling. It became an obsession, and he an addict, far worse than Adelaide. Morning, noon and night he sat down to cards, at Versailles, at

Marly, in the drawing-rooms of the Princesse de Conti (where Monseigneur, when not decimating the wolf-population spent most of his waking hours), with Adelaide in her apartments, thus sanctioning her own bad habit of gambling with her ladies. Saint-Simon says that he was a bad player because he could not govern his temper; but that he had a perfect passion for cards, and the higher the stakes the more he enjoyed himself. 'People dreaded playing with him because he could be dangerous when losing, which, from pride and a hatred of meeting defeat, even when caused by bad cards, he could not endure.' At first, he played brelan, but before long Dangeau mentions a game of lansquenet, at which M. le Duc de Bourgogne made a fortune, and another, when, unable to meet his debts, he was obliged to seek the King's help, which was immediately forthcoming. 'The King,' records Dangeau, 'gave him much more than was needed, saying that the prince must always come straight to him, and with entire confidence, for he must be free from all anxiety. Money, said the King, would never be lacking. "It is of no importance if people like us lose at cards".' This incident occurred in 1700, but it may be seen from Dangeau's journal that although Louis had found it temporarily embarrassing, it did nothing to moderate his play. This period of dissipation (Louis's form of wild oat sowing), lasted about two years, after which the voice of conscience made itself heard, first to restrain him, then to make him its slave.

Meanwhile, though he was charmed by Adelaide, his companionship did not charm her. His table-manners, the drowning of flies, and puddling them in salad oil revolted her; nor was his physical appearance calculated to stir her heart. Where they seem to have found most enjoyment together was in playing practical jokes, sometimes very cruel ones, a pastime in which other royal persons, in other centuries, have found pleasure and relief. Their favourite target was the altogether odious Princesse d'Harcourt, who had been so unkind to Adelaide on the occasion of her first Court. She certainly merited little consideration from them, but not all the punishment they meted out. 'Pretty enough in her first youth, in middle age she had become a coarse and vulgar creature, with a skin like putty, and tow-coloured hair in permanent disarray, like all the rest of her crumpled and filthy attire. Quarrelsome and mischief-making, she behaved like a harpy, with disgusting habits both at meals and at cards, when she cheated quite openly, even at the Princess's table, pocketing money that was not hers, and saying that should she be in error, she would give any excess to the poor, "since we are all liable to make mistakes".[1] Adelaide and Louis detested her, and never ceased from baiting her.

One night they sent twenty drummers of the Swiss guard into her bedroom, beating their kettledrums; and once, when it snowed, at Marly, they waited until she was in bed and asleep, and then entered to pull back her curtains and pelt her with snowballs. 'There she was,' continues the memoirist, 'waking up with a bound, all furious, screaming her head off, gasping for breath and wriggling like an eel to find some means of escape. They nonetheless continued to bombard her for more than half an hour, screaming with laughter, until her bed was awash with ice-cold water, and the floor flooded.' 'She might well have croaked,' says Saint-Simon slangily.[2]

To be fair, Adelaide and Louis were not the only ones to mock the Princesse d'Harcourt, who was universally feared, hated, and despised. Even Mme de Maintenon condescended to take part in some of the jokes.[3] But there was not the same excuse for Adelaide to torment the old Duchesse du Lude. Yet she made her life something of a misery. Mme du Noyers, at any rate, thought so, though defending Adelaide, on the grounds that Mme du Lude's fussiness and excessive vigilance had 'somewhat spoiled her charm for the Princess'.

Adelaide's mother, on the other hand, saw no excuse for her daughter's misconduct. She was deeply disturbed by the reports, and had begun to think that her ready acceptance of Mme de Maintenon as governess had been a grave mistake. Duchess Anne had swallowed that lady's lack of birth,[4] believing that the impeccable

---

[1] Saint-Simon says that she warranted description to show what the court was willing to put up with.

[2] Another time, they set fire-crackers all along the path to her pavilion, at Marly, and timed them to explode around her chair, as she passed, while her bearers, forewarned, ran off in all directions.

[3] Mme de Maintenon thought it very funny when the Maréchale de Villeroy induced the Princesse d'Harcourt to play cards one Sunday evening, saying that Mme de Maintenon would never notice her absence. The great lady entered suddenly upon them; whereat the princess immediately swooned, crying 'God help me, I am ruined!', while Mme de Maintenon, turning majestically to her, with a most benign smile, said, 'You surely do not mean to go to chapel in that condition, Madame?'

[4] The French considered people not of noble birth never to have been born (*manque de naissance*). Mme de Maintenon's father, Constant d'Aubigné, had indeed inherited from his father the barony of Surimeau; but it was of very small account. It made her a lady, but not a member of the nobility.

rank and breeding of the Duchesse du Lude would make up for any deficiency on that score. It now appeared, however, that Adelaide had thrown off all control and was fast going to the bad. Père Léonard, her confessor, records that, at the beginning of 1700, Mme la Duchesse de Savoie wrote complaining of the bad education her daughter was receiving at the Court of France, of which everyone, not excepting her husband, disapproved. 'She shows no respect for the people at the Court, but is forever poking fun at them and mocking them. All her endeavours are turned to pleasing Mme de Maintenon.' It is interesting to find Madame's scorching criticisms echoed by Adelaide's mother; and there, conceivably, may lie the reason why so few letters from Adelaide to Duchess Anne remain. Many may, indeed, have been destroyed, and others lost during the siege of Turin in 1706; but it is at least possible that the child, who so longed for her absent family's love and approbation, preferred to write to her less censorious grandmother.

'Not excepting her husband,' Duchess Anne had written, for, while Louis thoroughly enjoyed jokes at other people's expense, he would not stand them for a moment when he was made their butt, and he was excessively stiff with his wife's ladies who, it must be admitted, were most of them eager to catch his eye. With them, he was never at ease. Saint-Simon says that he came among them from his study like a novice at recreation, eager for almost puerile games, but sheltering behind his rank at the least familiarity. Madame recounts that, when one of them innocently remarked on the beauty of his eyes, he took to squinting at her most horribly whenever he looked in her direction. Once, the Comtesse d'Estrées tried to kiss him, when she had caught him, playing blind man's buff. He had turned his face away; but, finding it impossible to escape, had seized a pin and rammed it so hard into her head that she had been confined to bed for several days. The courtiers said he had gone farther even than Joseph, who fled without his coat but never hit or scratched anyone. 'Such prudery is inconceivable!' exclaimed Madame; or, as another courtier put it, 'the propriety of the most virtuous ladies is as nothing to the modesty of the Duc de Bourgogne'.

The fact of the matter was that he was terrified of Adelaide's ladies. He saw himself in grave danger, against which he continually had to arm himself, for he was not blind to their charms. He compared them to the island nymphs in *Télémaque*, whose songs lured the son of Ulysses to a carnal love that was mortal sin. Fénelon had taught him that the only sinless love would be for his wife; and for Adelaide he reserved all his tenderness, and all his passion.

Thus, when she decided to play a somewhat improper joke at his expense, it altogether miscarried, as she might well have foreseen. Madame describes it. 'You no doubt have heard,' she wrote, 'how excessively prudish the Duc de Bourgogne is, even to the extent of looking at no woman other than his wife. One night, to tease him, she told Mme de La Vrillière[1] to lie down in her bed, and make a great play of feeling sleepy, herself. The duke was enchanted to find his wife eager to go to bed, and to go before him, and he quickly undressed in order to join her. Entering their bedroom, he asked, "Where is Madame?" "Here I am," cried she, as though from within the bed, whereupon he dropped his dressing-gown and jumped in. He had hardly done so before she appeared, looking very angry. "How is this possible?" she said. "You pretend to be so pious, and I find you between the sheets with one of the prettiest girls in France!" "What do you mean?" he said. "Well, look who lies beside you," she replied. Immediately he flung the lady out, giving her no time to dress or put on her slippers because he had set about beating her in good earnest with his own. At last she escaped barefoot. He could not catch her again, though he tried; but he shouted all manner of abuse after her, of which "shameless hussy" was the least offensive. They tried to make him listen to reason, but it was a very long time before he calmed down.'

Louis never learned from Adelaide the art of inspiring respect. 'With her household,' Saint-Simon says, 'her desire to be loved moved her to show a care and consideration that won all hearts. Lively, gentle, approachable, open-hearted within wise limits, compassionate, fearful of causing pain, with becoming dignity to all who came near her, she was their joy, inspiring disinterested affection in even the most self-seeking people. That certainly required intelligence; but intelligence alone would not have sufficed, and it was a thousand pities that M. le Duc de Bourgogne (so intelligent himself) could not appreciate his wife's talents, and incline himself to imitate her grace.' Saint-Simon thought that when the girls took liberties which he should not have allowed, 'a little attention given to reminding them of their place by a cold glance or, when they went too far, an appearance of vexation, though always polite, with a little show of somewhat prolonged silence and gravity towards the

---

[1] She was Mme de Mailly's daughter, twenty years old and, although not exactly pretty, 'as sweet as a cherub, and just as charming'.

worst offenders, would soon have brought them all to order, with a more far-reaching effect than perhaps may be imagined.'

It was Adelaide's serious illness and recovery, in the spring of 1701, that awakened Louis's conscience and brought him suddenly to a possibly excessive sense of sin and of time wasted. That, at any rate, is what he wrote to the Duc de Beauvilliers, who was at Bourbon, taking the waters.

Marly, 11 April, 1701.

'God has shown me many mercies, my dear duke, as you yourself have witnessed. Yesterday he accorded me yet another for which I never cease to thank him. I was within an hour of losing Mme la Duchesse de Bourgogne. Only imagine the blow that would have been to me. A fever, beginning on Sunday the 7th, put her at death's door by the morning of Wednesday the 10th, and without the emetics that were immediately given her, she could not have lasted out the day. Her head had for some time been confused; she was in a state of lethargy, and would soon have suffered a rush of blood to the brain.

'I was in the depths of despair. I prayed to God. Before him I confessed my sins, with loathing, for I was firmly convinced that He had chosen that way to punish me. I entreated Him to lay all the blame on me, to spare that poor innocent and, if she had sinned, to let mine be the guilt. He took pity on me and, thank God, Mme la Duchesse de Bourgogne is now quite out of danger . . . There is almost no fever now. I never cease from thanking God for his mercy, for he clearly intended to punish me; but he has withheld His anger and taken pity on me.'

From that time onwards, Louis progressively drew away from the life of the Court, taking no further part in the ordinary diversions, except when etiquette required his presence. His first step was to give up dancing which, presumably, was not a great sacrifice since State balls were out of fashion and, by general request, had not been held in the early spring of that year. Moreover, he was a bad dancer, for his hump made him stiff and awkward, and he could not bear his deformity to be noticed.[1] Dangeau, in 1702, mentions his having given up dancing, saying that it was a great misfortune that he was not more graceful; but that there were other

---

[1] Saint-Simon says that his legs and thighs were equal in length, but he limped because the hump on his shoulder made him lean to that side instead of standing upright. The same was true of him on horseback, when he gave the appearance of leaning sideways.

more desirable qualities, 'and these the prince hopes to acquire, in order to make up for what he lacks'. 'One sees every day, Dangeau added, 'that his mind is set on nobler and more admirable acquirements.'

Gambling was far harder for Louis to renounce. He never did so entirely, but he learned to control his play, first refusing to play cards in Lent, and never afterwards returning to lansquenet, the game at which fortunes were most often lost or won. It was not scruples about the money lost that persuaded him to stop, but horror at the realisation of his joy in winning. According to Père Martineau, 'he conquered his addiction with the thought that the love of gambling is, at root, no more than a sordid lust after money, and thus unworthy in a prince who should strive only for noble things'. A remarkable tribute to Louis's strength of character is that, for the sake of the Court, he was able later to return to card-playing; but that he played always for ready money, limiting his losses to the sum he brought to the table, and obliging the other players to do the same. Mme d'Aumale recounts that if Adelaide lacked a player at her table, or he thought that the company appeared dull, he would sometimes play even lansquenet; but on those occasions the stakes were very low indeed. This was a deliberate policy, a way of gathering people around him; it also provided him with a means of showing courtesy to those whom he knew to be badly off, by inviting them to play at his table.

There were other excesses which Louis learned to control, for instance a propensity to eat and drink a great deal more than was good for him. Like all the Bourbons he had a colossal appetite, and he was often drunk; although, unlike his brother the Duc de Berry, he never reached the state of permanent tipsiness. Père Martineau mentions his liking for too much good food and wine, but excuses him, saying that it was largely because conversation flowed more easily amid the pleasures of the table. There is no doubt, however, that he was often drunk, for some verses written soon after his marriage say that, while 'at the table of Louis le Dauphin they fear the fumes of alcohol, with M. le Duc de Bourgogne it is a crime not to be fuddled'. But in this also he learned to restrain himself.

Louis wished that Adelaide could be induced to take a more serious view of life. It was not that he objected to her living for pleasure, but, like Mme de Maintenon, he would have liked to see her more deeply imbued with the fear of God. He consented to accompany her to the balls and pleasure parties given for her amusement, always provided that the date did not coincide with a Sunday or a saint's day. Then he was adamant in his refusal. On one occasion, Saint-Simon thought he went altogether too far, when he persisted in going against the King's wishes. The Court was at Marly, for Twelfth Night and, on the day of the Epiphany, there was to be a ball. Louis refused even to appear, and let this be known so long beforehand that the King remonstrated with him, jestingly at first, then sharply, and finally with extreme seriousness, for he was much vexed by his grandson's attitude of disapproval. Mme la Duchesse de Bourgogne and her ladies, even M. de Beauvilliers tried to move him, but all in vain. He would only repeat that the King was master, and that he did not venture to blame him; but, the Epiphany being a triple feast, he would not himself profane it. It was useless to urge that, if he spent the morning and afternoon in church and long hours in between at prayer in his study, he might do well to devote the evening to his duties as a subject and a son. 'Truly,' added Saint-Simon, 'his budding religious fervour was making him behave like any novice. He owed that service—not even so much—that gracious concession to the King, his grandfather, in order not to anger him by such marked antagonism. It was not a great matter, but fundamentally it had vital importance, for it exposed him to all the consequences of opposing the King, and to the rancour of a Court that idolised their master.'

Equally bad for Louis's popularity was the boredom he displayed, not only at balls but also at the theatre. One evening the King said to him that he appeared to take very little pleasure in the plays. 'I have the pleasure of accompanying Your Majesty,' replied Louis. 'As to that,' said the King tartly, 'you are free to do as you please,' after which Louis went less and less often. As Dangeau recounted, 'There were cards at Monseigneur's until it was time for the comedy. M. le Duc de Bourgogne never now attends, which makes people think that he has quite given up the theatre.' Worse than that, Louis tried to discourage the courtiers from going, to the great annoyance of the other princes. Writing from his flagship, at Toulon, to the Duc de Gramont, the Comte de Toulouse observed,[1] 'I see that the Duc de Bourgogne is going back to his old life.[2] What you tell me

---

[1] The Comte de Toulouse, Louis Alexandre de Bourbon (1678–1737), was the youngest of the King's sons by Mme de Montespan. He was an admiral in the French navy.

[2] The Duc de Bourgogne and the Duc de Berry had been absent for several months. They had accompanied the Duc d'Anjou to the Spanish frontier, on

about the comedies is really too bad. It would be far better if he tried to enjoy them, instead of keeping other people away. But that he will never do.' Mme de Maintenon, on the other hand, was inclined to share Louis's views. Comedies, she thought, did no one any good. It would be an excellent idea if plays were restricted to religious subjects.

Poor Adelaide! It was a hard time for her. She did so love fun, and the pleasant, easy-going relationship which she had built up among the ladies of her household; and there was her husband with his constant reminders of duty, abstinence, and the need for restraint. 'Only imagine,' she said to Mme de Mailly, 'the man I married lives on a stricter plan than any other Frenchman. What is the good of inheriting from Henri IV, if all it means is abject slavery?' To which Louis replied, calling her Draco, his pet name for her (After Draco the Athenian tyrant, whose laws were said to have been written in blood):

> 'Draco, what sweet servitude,
> to be the slave of duty and of you.'

However much he may have deplored her frivolity, he never could resist her charm. It was his tragedy to know that she did not return his love or share his aspirations, and the knowledge made him increasingly wretched. As for Adelaide, who might have echoed Mme de Lafayette in saying, 'My husband adores me, and I am fond of him', she set herself to build a tolerable life with him on terms of affectionate, teasing companionship. Austerities and religious fervour had no appeal to her, and she seems to have concluded that a good-humoured acceptance of his fads was the best solution. One evening, seated on her *chaise-percée* among her best loved ladies, the time when, according to Saint-Simon, she talked most freely, she suddenly exclaimed, 'I hope I die before M. le Duc de Bourgogne, so as to be able to see what happens to him. I am sure he will want to marry a nun, probably one of the Grey Sisters'.[1]

It is hard, despite all the letters, memoirs, and journals of the period, to discover exactly how Louis and Adelaide appeared to the people who saw them together every day. One writer says, 'Mme la Duchesse de Bourgogne continually opposes her husband. They

his accession to the throne of Spain, and, returning, had made a kind of royal progress, through provincial France.

[1] The nursing sisters of Saint Vincent and Saint Paul.

agree on nothing; yet their hearts are as one. I do not suppose there has ever been a married couple with such different characters who loved one another so dearly.' That, however, was not the view of everybody. Madame, for one, thought the complete reverse. One thing seems certain; Adelaide still had the strong sense of duty, the same touching desire to please and oblige that had melted the hearts of those who served her when she first came to France. A letter which she wrote to Mme de Maintenon about this time shows that she did her best, though perhaps she was exaggerating. 'I am not content only to do what M. le Duc de Bourgogne desires, I try to enter into his views, and that is no easy matter for me. Only think, dear aunt, he sometimes presents me with them in three degrees, the good, the better, the perfect, just like M. de Cambrai, and then leaves me to decide. I should often vastly prefer to opt for neutrality; but, somehow, I cannot tell why, I always make the choice he wishes, even against my inclinations.'

Louis was now living the most extraordinary life for a prince of his quality. When not hunting, the only distraction he still allowed himself, he shut himself away in his study, spending long hours in prayer and alarming even his friends by the length of his sessions with Père Martineau his confessor.[1]

Now that he saw in Adelaide a hostage for his own reformation, he regarded his failings with an altogether disproportionate loathing. He feared temptation everywhere, and felt safe only with his wife or in solitude. When he emerged from his study to join her, he was like a schoolboy let out to play, releasing his pent-up energies in childish games which she also enjoyed.

He had always been devout; but the fervour with which he now turned to religious observances was as violent as anything he had previously expended on his pleasures. Saint-Simon, anxiously watching him, said that he showed all the immoderation, fear, and lack of discernment that usually accompany a new conversion. He would not, for example, accept that mass said quickly in the chapels of Marly or Fontainebleau was sufficient recognition of the holiness

---

[1] People did not fear Père Martineau. What disturbed them was the thought that, in the next reign, Church and State might become inseparable, and public affairs a matter for the king's conscience, as had happened so disastrously in Spain, in the reigns of Philip II and the later kings. Père Martineau himself was worried because he feared that Louis's exaggerated scruples were preventing him from acting on his own initiative. He always asked for advice, and not from one person only, with the result that he reached no decisions. Such fears were realised when Louis had command of an army.

of Sunday; but insisted on returning all the way to Versailles for vespers or benediction in the parish church; and publicly, every fortnight, sometimes every week, he took communion, dressed up in the robe, garter and bands of the Order of the Holy Spirit, so as to be seen to reverence the Sacrament.

With Père Martineau's help, he had drawn up a list of ever-increasing austerities and mortifications that included the sacrifice of the personal possessions he most valued; for example, a pair of silver wine-coolers, which he greatly admired and had specially ordered for his own table. Saint-Simon tells how pleased he had been with them, how he liked to drink his wine cool and had found them convenient and of excellent craftsmanship. Then suddenly, repenting of extravagance and his love of them, he had had them melted down, to become 'food for the poor'.

People at the Court were alarmed by the violence of the change. Madame, that keen observer, wrote to her aunt; 'There are many fanatics here. I am sure that when M. le Duc de Bourgogne comes to the throne, bigotry will gain the upper hand. It is unheard of for a man of his age to be so devout. He takes communion every Sunday and every saint's day, and fasts so much that he is a pitiful sight. Already he has become as thin as a rail.' Even Mme de Maintenon thought Louis went too far in piety, 'M. le Duc de Bourgogne is still devout, in love, and full of scruples; but,' she added, 'he daily becomes more reasonable.' This letter is dated 1706, and seems to infer that she had hitherto been thinking him rather the reverse.

One thing is certain, at this period the Sun King's heir and grandson was no ornament to his grandfather's Court. His monkish look, his intolerance, his refusal to share in the usual diversions, were making him still less approachable. Saint-Simon says that 'he made everyone feel ill at ease by his air of disapproval, and that his insistence on literal accuracy (a relic of his schoolroom days) stopped all conversation. Moreover, he appeared always distracted, always impatient to be gone, like a man who feels that his time is being wasted.'

Many people, including Adelaide, believed that Fénelon was responsible for the change, and was encouraging Louis in his austerities. They were much mistaken, for there had been no communication between them in the four years since the archbishop's exile, in 1697. The prince had kept his promise not to write, and Fénelon's only channel to him had been through the Duc de Beau-villiers. It was not until 1701, in his misery and self-reproach at the time of Adelaide's illness, that Louis had returned to Fénelon, with a desperate appeal for help, sending his letter by a circuitous route, in order to avoid the censorship.

Fénelon was much moved. His answers, for this was the beginning of a correspondence, all make an appeal for moderation: 'Do not spend long hours in prayer; but pray a little every morning, at some quiet moment'—'God does not require of all Christians austerities like those practised by the hermits of ancient times . . . He does not ordinarily demand great deeds of heroism, the sacrifice of wealth honestly acquired, or the relinquishment of the privileges of rank. He leaves princes in their grandeur and abases them with the same hand that made them great.'

In another letter, he gave the following advice. 'Study human nature continually; learn to use men, but do not let them use you . . . The Kingdom of God does not require scrupulous obedience to the outward forms of religion. It lies for everyone in the nobler virtues, as befits such person's rank. A prince must not serve God after the fashion of a hermit or a private individual. Saint-Louis was a saint, but he was, at the same time, a great king.'

Fénelon wrote in similar terms to the Duc de Beauvilliers; but although his words had their effect, it was not in the character of that excellent man, seven of whose daughters were in convents by their own wish, to be easily convinced that any amount of piety could be excessive. Madame, at any rate, thought him an impediment. 'He is a good and an upright man,' she wrote, 'but too devout to be a wise governor for our princes. He has not taught them how to live, or allowed them to mix in Society, and the result is that they are nervous and at a loss for words.' Yet Beauvilliers was deeply disturbed, for he went so far as to ask Saint-Simon, whom he knew to be devoted to Louis, to write a memorandum, setting out frankly his view of the Duc de Bourgogne's character. To write frankly in criticism of the King's grandson and heir presumptive was a dangerous undertaking, and at first he refused. Later he changed his mind, on condition that the prince should never be allowed to see what he had written. The result was an essay, so far-sighted, so appreciative of Louis's virtues, so frank on his faults and weaknesses, so much the echo of Fénelon's appeal for moderation in all things, that Beauvilliers was impressed, and marked Saint-Simon down as a man fit to be a friend and counsellor for the heir in years to come.

Although the courtiers talked of a sudden change in the Duc de

Bourgogne, that was an illusion. Louis had not changed. He was still as impetuous, passionate, incapable of governing his temper as he had been in his boyhood, when he broke the clocks that interfered with his pleasures. Fear of God and of the King, most of all, fear of himself, lest he yield to temptation and lose the grace of God, had not changed his character; it had simply turned his passions in a new direction, making him just as immoderate in his piety as he had been in his pleasures. It was a thousand pities that one result of his great efforts to perfect himself should have been to drive him still further away from Adelaide. In the difficult years that followed, he did slowly learn to govern himself and to be more tolerant, but the intervening period was a most unhappy time for him.

II

The Spanish Succession

WHEN ADELAIDE went to France as the bride of M. le Duc de Bourgogne, her friend Tessé had remained in Savoy. It was not where he wished to be—far otherwise. Thoroughly bored with the provincialism of the poverty-stricken court, and the shiftiness of Victor Amadeus, its prince, he had become genuinely attached to the little princess, and had hoped to accompany her to Versailles, and take up his duties there as her master of horse. He had appealed for permission to do so; but had received a reply to the effect that the King had better use for him where he was, keeping a watchful eye on Adelaide's father, and holding him, at this critical time for the peace of Europe, loyal to his newly-signed alliance with France. That loyalty was already in doubt, for the Austrian envoy, Count Mansfeld, still remained at the court of Turin, a welcome guest, which made it impossible to forget that in a former alliance the prince had not hesitated to change sides, when he wrongly supposed that France's enemies were winning.

Tessé had been marvellously successful in conducting the laborious negotiations that ended with Adelaide's marriage and a treaty that promised permanent alliance, and safe passage across the Alps for French armies entering Italy. He had also appeared to be liked and trusted by both Victor Amadeus and his Duchess, which was no small achievement. Soon after Adelaide's departure, however, he awoke with dismay to the fact that his popularity had waned. Difficulties arose whenever he tried to see the prince; and invitations to his supper-parties, once so sought after, were no longer in demand, the courtiers seemingly having been warned that to be seen in his company was no way to please their ruler. Worse even than that was Victor Amadeus's remark that although he liked Tessé as well as he could ever like a Frenchman, future French ambassadors should not count on a close relationship. Since Tessé's chief function was to report to the King on the Duke of Savoy's state of mind and intentions, this loss of communication was a severe blow, and he therefore looked about him for an ally. He found one ready and eager to assist him in the pious Duc de Chevreuse's very different sister, the Countess of Verrua, known as *La dame de Volupté*, who for the past eight years had combined the functions of official mistress to Victor Amadeus and lady-in-waiting to the unfortunate Duchess Anne. Mme de Verrua was heartily sick of both occupations, more especially of the jealousy and caprices of her royal lover, who had kept her in close seclusion since she had been marked by small-pox, two years earlier. What she now desired was to escape to France, under Louis XIV's protection, and she therefore accepted Tessé's suggestion of an alliance, raining upon him a stream of little notes, jotted down whenever she found a moment of privacy. 'You will never guess where I write this,' ran one of them, 'I'm sitting on my *chaise-percée*.' Tessé sent them all to the King, recommending that he should burn them; but, in fact, they were not destroyed. Mme de Verrua was not unduly dismayed by the irregularity of her past life, believing that if the King found her useful he would be inclined to forgive her. 'I am perfectly enchanted, and infinitely grateful,' she wrote, 'at your assurance that the King does not regard me as deserving pity, a miserable candidate for a home of fallen women. Not even my brother Chevreuse, with all Saint-Sulpice behind him, could have saved me from the fate that my husband's callous betrayal, my mother-in-law (worse even than he), and other members of that family, brought down upon me . . . I am distracted with love for the King and, in any event, I am a good Frenchwoman;' and she ended by describing the new mode of life which she now proposed to adopt. 'We are nearly separated, the Duke and I, and you may have seen, at Tuesday's ball, how sulky we both were. He wanted certain basenesses from me which no longer become me, and are now discontinued. I sent him, by mutual consent, to vent his passions elsewhere, and we have arranged all this in the most agreeable manner imaginable. You shall hear the whole story.'

Mme de Verrua did manage to escape from Savoy a few years later, when Victor Amadeus was away from home, and Louis XIV did overlook her past—he could hardly have done otherwise, in view of his own vagaries. What Mme de Maintenon thought is not recorded. The Countess's diligence and her wish to please were evident; but all she could supply Tessé with was gossip, amusing no doubt, but not what the King most urgently needed to know—the prince's secret mind and intentions should war break out in Europe, over the succession to the Spanish throne. The childless Charles II, King of Spain, was expected to die at any moment. That, in itself, was nothing new, for his imminent death had been prophesied for the past thirty-five years, ever since, as a sickly boy of five, his governess had had to lift him by his sash at his first public *lever*, in order to take the weight from his rickety legs. In 1697, however, there appeared to be no doubt of his imminent death, and no successor was apparent.

Louis XIV, the Emperor, and a little Bavarian prince of four years old had claims to the huge Spanish empire, with its rich possessions in the Americas, in Italy, the Catholic Netherlands, and Morocco. Neither the King nor the Emperor contemplated claiming that rich inheritance for their immediate heirs the Grand Dauphin and the Archduke Joseph, for that would certainly have precipitated a war against the combined European powers; but both put in a claim for younger members of their families—King Louis for his grandson the Duc d'Anjou, and the Emperor for his younger son the Archduke Charles. Even so the danger of war appeared very great and, after twenty-five years of almost continual conflict, neither France, Austria, Holland, nor England wished for that. They therefore settled down to a serious attempt to solve the question by negotiation.

In 1698, the Treaty of Loo was signed between Louis XIV and William III (whom he was reluctantly forced to recognise as the rightful King of England), by which the Bavarian princeling was to be given Spain and its colonies, while France and Austria would receive, in compensation, parts of the Spanish possessions in Europe. It was a triumph of diplomacy; but soon afterwards the little prince died (some thought murdered by the Austrians), and all was to do again.

The King, meanwhile, had had good reason for concern regarding the intentions of the Duke of Savoy, who was not the man to see a redistribution of the Spanish possessions without putting forward claims of his own. He, himself, had a distant right to the throne of Spain, through his great-grandmother, Philip II's daughter the Infanta Catherine, who had married Charles Emmanuel I of Savoy. Victor Amadeus was not so vain as to imagine that, important though alliance with the 'keeper of the gates of Italy' undoubtedly was, neither France nor Austria would see sufficient advantage in that to risk a war by making him King of Spain. The fact that he had such a right, however, lent substance to his much more direct and pressing claim for the rich Duchy of Milan, which the House of Savoy had coveted for generations past; and, although Victor Amadeus knew that he might be compelled to see that rich province go to one or other of the great powers bordering on his tiny duchy, it was a matter of vital importance to him to know which of them was most likely to gain it.

He had reason to hope for Milan. When the peace treaty between France and Savoy was concluded, Louis XIV had insisted on a secret agreement, by which the Duke of Savoy bound himself to assist France by driving the Imperials out of Italy; and, as an inducement, the King had signed a clause promising 'with all his might to help His Royal Highness in the matter of the Duchy of Milan, should His Most Catholic Majesty die childless during the present war', and renouncing 'in the event of the death of the aforesaid Most Catholic Majesty all claim, by conquest or otherwise, to the Duchy of Milan'. Louis XIV was, in fact, quit of these engagements because Charles II had not died during the war; but he had given a kind of promise, and the Duke of Savoy had no intention of letting him forget it.

Thus Tessé was having a difficult time. In December 1696, he reported that the Duke had spoken to him of the troubles that might be occasioned by the King of Spain's death, and had not failed to raise the question of Milan. Tessé said that he had made some non-committal answer, and wrote for further instructions, to which the King had replied: I was aware that the smallest sign of the reopening of the Succession would inspire the Duke of Savoy to wish for some profit to himself, and I see that he has already communicated his desire for the Duchy of Milan, for which he requires my help, believing that my own advantage will lead me to prevent the Emperor from adding it to his other possessions. The prince should be persuaded that I, more than anyone, have his real interests at heart, and that this thought touches me more deeply than the reasons he advances. The time, however, has not yet come for measures to be taken. The health of the King of Spain has always been so poor that the slightest mishap makes them fear for his life. His age gives cause to hope that the dreaded tragedy is still far distant, for a tragedy it would be, bringing the danger of war closer than ever before, with each claimant nation armed and ready to uphold its rights by force. You know all that I have done to bring peace to Italy. All my endeavours would prove useless, and foreign armies would at once re-enter it, were it thought that I was taking preparatory measures with the Duke of Savoy for the conquest of Milan. I therefore much approve your reply on that subject, and counsel you to avoid going into details. Simply assure him that if the King of Spain dies he will find me ready to do all that may contribute to his personal advantage.'

This prudent reply, refusing nothing, and making no clear promises, was none the less an assurance that the King had the Duke of Savoy's interests at heart. What is more, it was the second such assurance. Victor Amadeus not unreasonably assumed that he had received a moral promise, and several times called on the King to remember it, until an absolute denial set him, once and for all, on the side of France's enemies.

In the meantime, Louis XIV took steps to hearten the Duke by recalling his envoy Tessé, and sending instead an ambassador of the highest rank, such as were appointed to the courts of the greatest European powers, not to small dukedoms. The Comte de Briord arrived at Turin in April 1697, but it was not until December that he made his state entry and presented his credentials. His instructions, after warning him of the duke's nature—'ambitious, distrustful, double-dealing, jealous of his authority'—bade him temporise should the question of the Spanish succession arise, but at the same time, gently but firmly, to impress upon him the urgent need to regard his personal interests as inseparable from those of the King of France. Tessé reported that Briord's reception was reasonably cordial, but was careful, immediately afterwards, to take him to visit the Comtesse de Verrua, who, Briord wrote, 'appears wholly devoted to Your Majesty's cause'.

The new ambassador discovered that there had been substance in Victor Amadeus's remark that Tessé's successor 'should not count on a close relationship'. Before long he was reporting to the King that the Duke was scarcely ever available; that the courtiers were instructed to avoid him; that His Royal Highness's young nephew was refused permission to go to France for his education, and threatened with a terrible beating if he were ever heard speaking French. Whether or not Louis XIV was influenced by such reports, his next instructions to Briord marked a complete change of policy. 'It now appears to me,' he wrote, 'that a revision of the existing treaty might be the means of preventing the Emperor from conquering the whole of Italy, and at the same time bind the Duke to oppose him for the sake of my advantage. It is in my interests to pursue this policy.'

Yet the circumstances were different. By the old treaty, Victor Amadeus was committed to handing over to France the Savoyard portion of his duchy, containing the Alpine passes. He was no longer in the strong position of an Austrian ally, needing enticements to desert to France, and Briord was ordered to demand from him not only Savoy in exchange for Milan, but the town and domain of Nice as well.

Louis XIV was now concentrating on extending the frontiers of France to its natural boundaries, by absorbing Savoy, Nice, and the semi-independent princedom of Lorraine, at the same time resigning any claim to the Spanish territories in Europe, at the coming partition. He had reconciled himself, for the sake of peace, to renouncing the Spanish throne, and he sent instructions to the Comte de Tallard, his ambassador in London, to submit one of two plans for the redistribution, to William III. By one of these the Duchy of Milan was to be allotted to the Duke of Savoy; by the other, it would go to the Archduke Charles, the Emperor's second son, while by both, needless to say, France would stand to gain a very large proportion of the inheritance.

In London, meanwhile, Tallard was encountering William III's absolute refusal to take Victor Amadeus seriously. 'Oh! as for the Duke of Savoy,' he exclaimed with a sardonic smile, to which Tallard replied that it was not for him to say why his King should favour the prince, but undoubtedly all would be advantaged by having a power capable of obstructing the Emperor's designs, on the farther side of the Alps. But King William, said Tallard, had not forgiven the Duke's desertion in the past war, and he continued to display his resentment and animosity, if only by hints and gestures.

In Savoy, Briord was making it abundantly clear to Victor Amadeus that, although a possible beneficiary, he was to have no part in the bargaining. The Duke was no fool, and he bitterly resented being used as a pawn, to be benefited or rejected as best suited the interests of his ally. No wonder, perhaps, that he began to look elsewhere for friends. Briord's reports, at this period, are full of his letters to foreign princes, particularly to the Emperor, and of the distress of Duchess Anne who, through all the years, had remained a loyal Frenchwoman at heart. 'I hear,' wrote Briord, 'that Mme la Duchesse de Savoie has returned very sad from La Vénérie, and since she has been in the Duke's company throughout the visit, and they appear to be in perfect harmony, I can only attribute her distress to awareness of M. le Duc de Savoie's secret intentions.' The King's reply was an order to watch him closely, especially when he went to take the waters at Saint-Maurice-en-Valais, which was near enough to the Austrian frontier for secret meetings to be practicable.

The Duke now began to display his resentment. 'All the people here,' wrote Briord from Turin, 'are noticing his disquiet, and he has been heard to say that he is apparently condemned to grow cabbages for the remainder of his life, and would gladly give fifteen years of it to take command of an army and help in achieving something glorious.' If this was meant as an assurance to Louis XIV of his readiness to fight the Emperor, it fell on deaf ears, for at that time the King was intent on keeping the peace.

At this point the sudden death of the six-year-old Prince of Bavaria, who for the past months had been the accepted heir to the Spanish throne, entirely changed the situation, and reopened the succession. Louis XIV immediately proffered a new plan, by which, astonishingly enough, Victor Amadeus, because of his descent from the Infanta Catherine, would inherit the Spanish throne and colonies, and all else would go to France. In Turin, joy abounded; the Duke made little pretence of grief at the sad news, and was reported as saying that if it were a question of his being offered the crown, a treaty might very quickly be signed. Briord wrote that 'everyone here, poets, people, and gentry alike, all speak with the same voice, and regard the Prince as the next King of Spain'. But, thinking perhaps that such a solution would never suit King William, the fertile brain of King Louis produced still another, which might conceivably have been acceptable to all concerned. By this, the Archduke Charles would have Spain; the Dauphin, Naples and Sicily, which he would exchange for the princedom of Lorraine, and Milan would go to Victor Amadeus on his surrender of Savoy and Nice. Negotiations began and everyone would have benefited, had not the Duke been tempted to demand more, which made Louis XIV think of making further stipulations for the possession of the all-important fortresses on the passes through the Alps. Eventually they came near an agreement; but it was too late, for a courier speeding from Spain brought the news of Charles II's death; and that courier was followed by another bearing a copy of his will. He had left everything, the whole of his vast possessions, all the riches of Spain and its colonies, all its possessions in Europe, to one or other of Louis XIV's grandsons. There was no mention of Savoy, and none of Austria. The peace of Europe was now in the hands of Louis XIV.

The Spanish Succession

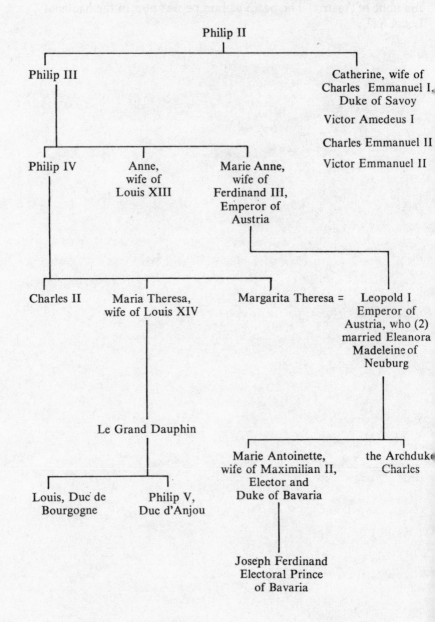

12

The War Begins

THE KING was at Fontainebleau on 9 November, when the
courier from Spain arrived with the momentous news and for
the next seven days the Court was in a turmoil. The decision
to accept or refuse the inheritance for his grandson was the greatest
in the King's long reign. To accept would bring power; it also almost
certainly would mean war. No other topic was discussed; some were
for acceptance, others against; the young saw new possibilities of
adventure and fame; the old feared and were doubtful; all felt
personally involved; but it was for the King alone to decide; the
final word was his and, since he was the most secret man imaginable, no one could tell which way he would go; the courtiers were
kept on tenterhooks until the very last moment. Saint-Simon's
marvellous description of what happened hour by hour in that
eventful week until the decision to accept caused the whole structure
of Court etiquette to be re-organised so as to accommodate two
reigning monarchs, cannot be imitated. What follows here is a bare
record of what he says occurred.

The courier arrived early in the morning and was immediately
taken to the King, who was in council. The King read the will, but
made no comment, merely announcing that the King of Spain had
died; that there would be Court mourning, and a meeting of ministers, at three o'clock, in Mme de Maintenon's room. Monseigneur,
who had returned from hunting, Chancellor Pontchartrain, the
Duc de Beauvilliers, and Torcy were the only ones summoned; but
the news that Mme de Maintenon had been present the entire time
was a revelation to the courtiers, who had never before heard of
her taking an active part in State affairs. Monseigneur, to everyone's
surprise, grew heated during the meeting. Saint-Simon says that he
'appeared a different man', when, after voting for acceptance, he

went scarlet in the face and claimed the inheritance for himself, as being the rightful property of the late Queen, his mother.[1] He then added that he would yield it, for the sake of peace, to his second son the Duc d'Anjou, but would not cede a single inch of Spanish soil to anyone else. The King had listened attentively and had then turned to Mme de Maintenon, saying, 'And you, Madame, what is your advice?' She had made a becoming show of reluctance; but, after being first urged, then commanded to speak, she had uttered a sentence or two in praise of Monseigneur (whom she detested), adding that she favoured acceptance. Opinions among the three ministers were divided. Pontchartrain was in favour; the Duc de Beauvilliers strongly against, foreseeing a disastrous war, in which France would be ruined. Torcy was also against acceptance, but less firmly, than Beauvilliers, and on the following day he changed his mind.

Historians differ on the subject of Mme de Maintenon. Many believe that she was fundamentally opposed to risking a war and, had she not feared to make herself unpopular, would have advised refusal and a return to a Treaty of Partition. There is no certainty. She never spoke again, and her opinions remain, as so often, a complete enigma.

At seven o'clock, the King closed the council, saying only that the decision was so grave he would sleep on it; but since, on the following day, he summoned, first the Spanish ambassador and then the Duc de Bourgogne, it was generally supposed that he had already made up his mind. Three days elapsed before he sent for the Duc d'Anjou, and still the courtiers knew nothing, for, when questioned, the young prince would only say that, 'after the honour done to him, the late King of Spain's memory would ever be precious to him'. He and the Duc de Bourgogne were seventeen and eighteen years old respectively; and already well practised in the art of silence.

There is no record of what Louis thought. Dangeau believed that he knew the King's mind; but was keeping absolutely silent. One wonders if he talked to Adelaide, who was inquisitive by nature, and would almost certainly have questioned him, but probably he kept mum even to her; for once before, when she had teased him to know what happened at the Conseil des Dépêches, of which he was a member, he had replied with one of his little verses:

[1] Queen Marie-Thérèse, the daughter of Philip IV.

'Draco! my heart is thine alone,
For it is mine to give,
Thine too the secrets of my soul,
When they are not the King's.'

She does not seem to have been present when the King had
jokingly asked the Princesses, his daughters, for their advice, to
which they had replied in concert that he should send the Duc
d'Anjou immediately to Spain, basing their opinion on having heard
that this was what the people wanted. Whereupon he had sagely
remarked that he knew many people would blame him, no matter
what he did. She had, nonetheless, been heard to say to the Duchesse
de Sully that the King would be a fool if he did not accept the
crown of Spain for his grandson, and it appears that, in so saying,
she voiced the opinion of the younger set.

On 15 November, they all returned to Versailles, six of them—
the King, the Bourgognes, the Princesse de Conti, Mme la Duchesse,
and the ever-attendant Duchesse du Lude, in the huge travelling
coach. Covering the distance at great speed, and eating their dinner
as they went along, they took only six hours to reach the château,
a remarkably short time, even for the King's fast horses. One
wonders what they could have found to talk about, since the one
great subject on which all their minds were intent was presumably
barred until the King's decision was announced.

Next day, Tuesday, 16 November, the Duc de Bourgogne and
the Duc d'Anjou went by the back way to the King's lever, where a
large crowd had assembled. As soon as the courtiers had been dismissed, the King summoned the Spanish ambassador to his study;
both sides of the door leading into the Salle des Glaces were opened,
and an eager throng crowded around to witness the historic scene,
and hear Louis XIV proclaim the Duc d'Anjou King of Spain. It
was then that the famous words 'There are no longer any Pyrenees'
came from the lips of the Spanish ambassador—not from the King,
to whom Voltaire mistakenly attributed them. It was a glorious, but
sorrowful occasion, for the King, who had been beaming, almost
immediately burst into tears at the thought of the imminent parting.
Many of the onlookers followed suit, while the Duc de Bourgogne
and the Duc d'Anjou embraced one another, the tears running down
their cheeks.[1] The King then went to mass, with the King of Spain

---

[1] The three young princes were sincerely fond of one another. Louis and the
high-spirited little Duc de Berry often quarrelled; but the Duc d'Anjou, who

walking at his right hand, and the rest of the royal family processing behind them. From that moment, until King Philip left for Spain, the rules of etiquette at Versailles were changed in order to do equal honour to two kings at once. The first difficulty occurred in the chapel. All the members of the royal family, in one row, kneeled upon the step of the balustrade in the King's gallery; with a single hassock provided, for King Louis's use. He immediately took it and offered it to the King of Spain, who tactfully refused it, after which it was put on one side, and both kneeled on the carpeted step. After that, two hassocks were provided whenever they attended the same mass, which, Saint-Simon says, happened very often in the days before 1 December, when King Philip departed.

Another thing which the observant eyes of Saint-Simon had noticed, during the proclamation, was the extreme discomfiture of the Austrian ambassador who, by an unlucky chance, had asked for an audience at that precise moment. He had come to announce the birth of a son to the Queen of the Romans,[1] not in the least knowing what was happening, and devoutly wished that he had chosen any other time. Another ambassador to be much embarrassed was the Comte de Vernon, the Duke of Savoy's envoy, who scarcely knew which way to look. No one was observing him, however, for the negotiations with Savoy had been kept so secret that the courtiers were not aware of his embarrassment. His chief concern was the proper attitude to adopt in greeting the new King of Spain, with whom he had been so unexpectedly confronted, and who was triumphantly ascending a throne to which his own master had confidently aspired. He tells how he dealt with the situation, in a letter to Victor Amadeus, written on the following day. 'I did no more than bow very low to the new king, who stood facing His Majesty, and I then immediately, but not too pointedly, continued my conversation with King Louis, who said how much he hoped that Your Royal Highness would rejoice in this happy event that gives promise of abiding peace.'

The answer was an explosion of rage. 'We had always suspected,' wrote Victor Amadeus on the 16th, 'that the offers made by France

was patient and gentle, acted as peace-maker. One of the strange things in the extraordinary character of Louis XIV is that he was a family man, with a great deal of paternal affection, and very kind to his daughters and grandsons, always provided that they did not disturb his comfort or his pleasures.

[1] Wilhelmina Amelia, the Duke of Hanover's daughter. Her husband became Emperor, under the name of Joseph I. This baby only lived until 1711.

were not intended sincerely;' but, apparently still believing that some kind of a treaty might be effected that would bring him the Duchy of Milan in exchange for Nice and Savoy, he asked Vernon to inform him by return of courier what he might legitimately hope to gain from France, 'so that we may take the necessary measures'. He wrote in the same way to Président de La Tour, his ambassador to The Hague, who happened to be in Paris; but the answer, when it came, gave him no encouragement: 'I can only confirm the general opinion that there will be little opposition, and that they will feel themselves perfectly safe. Thus they will alter none of the intentions of the will.' When Victor Amadeus had had time to calm down a little, he resolved to put a good face on adversity, and instructed Vernon to join with the other ambassadors in congratulating the King of Spain.

This was a great relief to Adelaide, who knew and dreaded her father's temper, and the lengths to which it might lead him. She managed to see Vernon, at her *toilette*, after he had left the new king's audience to the ambassadors, and was much comforted when he told her of a personal letter from her father to Louis XIV, which began: 'This latest extension of Your Majesty's glory, by the acquisition of the entire Spanish empire on behalf of Mgr le Duc d'Anjou—my gratification on this subject cannot be too highly estimated, considering, as I do, that blood so august as Your Majesty's is rightly destined to fill the greatest thrones in Europe.' No one could have spoken fairer than that; unless Louis XIV noticed any irony in the reference to 'the entire Spanish empire', which he may not have done because he was, at that moment, bursting with pride. 'I still think that this is all a dream,' he said to the Spanish ambassador, at the first public supper, with the new king sitting on his right hand in an armchair similar to his own, while the Bourgognes and the Duc de Berry were relegated to the end of the table, and sat on folding chairs. This was the beginning, the first of the problems of improvising etiquette to meet the new situation which, according to Dangeau, occupied the minds of the courtiers to the exclusion of all else during the following week, when both kings were in residence.

Louis XIV may not have observed any irony, if such were intended, in Victor Amadeus's letter; but, in any event, he could argue that Charles II's will had changed everything. The inheritance had to be refused or accepted *in toto*, and he had now no authority to dismember an empire that belonged to someone else. Yet the

French ambassador had been very close to Charles II in his last illness, and it was hard to believe that King Louis had not known what was likely to happen, even when he was negotiating with William III. Victor Amadeus may thus have felt fully justified in accusing him of insincerity.

At Versailles, the days before King Philip left France were spent in a sad and stately display of private sorrow and public glorification. The King's paternal instincts, which were very strong, despite his failure with the Grand Dauphin, kept him brimming over with tears, as he lavished upon his grandson a mixture of affection combined with exquisite courtesy and respect. Coming away from evening prayer, on that first day, he led King Philip to the door of the state apartment, newly allotted to his royal use, saying with weighty politeness: 'I trust Your Majesty will sleep well tonight.' The Marquis de Breteuil, who was head of protocol, observed, however, that while both monarchs acted their sovereign rôles in magnificent style, neither of them could quite keep from smiling.

The following days were also taken up with visits of courtesy. The three brothers had hitherto lived together, but, although they were brought up supposedly as equals, the younger two had been very firmly suppressed, in order to let their elder shine. It was not so now. The King of Spain was a foreign monarch visiting the Court, and when he called on the Duc de Bourgogne, Louis received him formally at the outer door, being very careful to stop there, and not go down the three steps that led into Adelaide's apartments, for that would have been contrary to etiquette and lowering to his rank and dignity. No chairs were provided; thus he was spared having to sit on a folding-stool while his brother took an armchair. It was the same when King Philip visited the Duc de Berry and the rest of the family, and when he received their return visits. The only one who refused to cooperate was Adelaide, who sought him out, as usual, in his private study; and he came to her room with no ceremony at all; which considerably upset Breteuil, struggling to maintain the formality required for historic occasions. Worse even than that, she hid in the *ruelle*, under the counterpane, when the president of the Academy came to address her royal brother-in-law lying in bed, and had difficulty in suppressing her laughter at the flowery compliments.

Philip accepted the ceremonial with a gravity which Mme de Maintenon said came easily to him, 'for he had been aware of the possibility since leaving the womb of Madame his mother'; but in the evenings he was able to relax, for the young ones supped with her, and in her quiet room there was music and singing, and they played the old games, even hide and seek. On one of these evenings Philip, rather shyly, gave Adelaide a farewell present, a beautiful pair of diamond ear-rings that had belonged to his mother, as a token of their fondness for one another in the years that had passed. Dangeau says that he feared they were not valuable enough, and asked Mme de Maintenon to persuade Adelaide to receive them kindly.

Meanwhile Louis had sent the Duc de Beauvilliers to ask the King (he dared not ask himself) for permission to accompany King Philip to the Spanish frontier. He need not have feared, Louis XIV was much pleased, and replied saying that he would do even better, for the Duc de Berry might go with him, and, to the boy's delight, without a tutor; and that on the return they should make a tour through Languedoc, Provence and Dauphiné, to complete Louis's education. It was to be a long and leisurely tour, covering about two-thirds of France, and would take them four months. The King said he would personally arrange the details. Arranging details was the work he most enjoyed and on which, in his ministers' view, he wasted far too much time. In this case, it was particularly complicated. The journeys of princes, in those days, always presented many problems of etiquette; but the arrangements for three brothers, one, the younger, a king, appeared almost insoluble. At last, a system was devised. The Duc de Beauvilliers was put in complete charge, with the Maréchal de Noailles as his understudy in case he should fall ill, which seemed highly likely as he was not yet recovered from a persistent fever (accompanied, Saint-Simon says, 'by most distressing diarrhoea'), that necessitated his dosing himself with large quantities of quinine. The King settled the route himself, and personally appointed the military escort—several detachments of household troops, cavalry, musketeers, and twenty-six of his own bodyguard. He decided that the King of Spain should eat alone 'because of the armchair difficulty', and hear mass alone, 'because of the hassocks'. On the road, however, where there were no armchairs, the brothers might picnic together, all in the same coach. At public receptions, no chairs were to be provided; all would stand, thus no problem about seats. They were accompanied by a throng of the handsomest and smartest young courtiers, including the Comte d'Ayen, Mme de Maintenon's nephew, and an orchestra to give them pleasure en route.

The whole idea of making a tour pleased the Duc de Bourgogne enormously. He had continued to work long hours in his study, sending lists of questions to be answered by intendants and provincial governors, and insisting on the most detailed replies. It was already being said that he knew France as well as he knew the park and gardens of Versailles; but he took his future responsibilities very seriously and snatched at this chance of seeing things for himself.

It was on 4 December that they left. On the evening before, there had been a tearful farewell of Adelaide; and, next morning, after mass, and the last ceremonial visits, the royal family climbed into travelling coaches to go to Sceaux, the Duc du Maine's newly purchased country-house, where the last goodbyes were to be said. The road was lined with carriages far out into the country, and when they arrived, soon after mid-day, they found the house full of ladies and courtiers, for the King had (according to the *Mercure*) kindly ordained that everyone who wished should witness the historic occasion, and only the rabble be denied entry. The excited crowd was so great and in such disorder that Adelaide, herself, was for a while engulfed by them.

As for the King, tears were running down his cheeks as he quickly led the King of Spain through the lower rooms to the furthest of them all. A quarter of an hour later, he sent for Monseigneur and the Spanish ambassador to make their farewells, then for the Bourgognes, the Duc de Berry, and Monsieur and Madame, all together. After a short interval the Princes and Princesses of the Blood were allowed in; the doors remained wide open, and the onlookers in the adjoining salon could see the entire royal family weeping bitterly; Monseigneur with his face hidden in the curtains, and the rest uttering loud sobs and cries of distress as they embraced King Philip for the last time. Breteuil recounts that, while all this was taking place, the courtiers and princes in the outer room maintained a stunned silence, 'a very rare thing with French people'.

When the time came for the Princes to leave, the King led the King of Spain back through the drawing-rooms as far as the great entrance (etiquette would allow him no further). There, taking him once more in his arms, he embraced him long and closely, and then let him go; but the final parting was more than he could bear, and stepping out under the portico, he called him back for one last embrace, and then retired to recover his composure while they drove away. Adelaide went quickly after him, alone. She was probably the only person who could comfort him in a grief that was very real while it lasted. Like many of the King's emotions, however, it did not long endure, and she was soon able to persuade him to go with Monsieur and Madame for a drive in an open carriage, after which they all returned to Versailles.

At this point, Louis XIV became aware that, despite all his protestations of peaceful intentions, war had become inevitable, and had, indeed, almost begun, for the Emperor Leopold had an army ready to cross into Italy by the Austrian passes and lay siege to Milan on behalf of the Archduke Charles. The King's first need, therefore, was to regain the friendship and assistance of Victor Amadeus, so as to ensure safe passage across the Alps for French troops, and a fresh treaty of alliance based on something more solid than assurances of goodwill. He accordingly ordered Phélypeaux, his new ambassador at Turin, to start negotiations; but in his monumental selfishness he did not for one moment consider that Victor Amadeus might have a just grievance.[1]

'My brother and nephew,' he wrote, 'I am so well persuaded of your devotion to my interests that I cannot doubt your pleasure at learning of my decision to accept, on behalf of my grandson, the Duc d'Anjou, the succession of the entire empire of Spain, to which his birth, the testament of the late Catholic King and the voice of the Spanish peoples unanimously entitles him . . .' and, in a covering letter to Phélypeaux, 'Tell His Royal Highness that I am persuaded he will rejoice to see a monarchy to which the testament of the late King of Spain may conceivably summon his descendants made safe from any form of partition, and all the various dependencies retained under that same rule which for so long has governed them.'

That, however, was not how Victor Amadeus viewed the situation. The thought of his descendants possibly ascending the throne

[1] If Louis XIV truly desired peace in Europe, he was quite extraordinarily tactless. After accepting the will of Charles II, he should surely have allayed fears of French domination; yet he immediately had letters patent registered in the Parlement, by which Philip V retained his right to the crown of France. He then offered a threat to Holland by replacing with French troops the Spanish garrisons in the fortresses on the Dutch frontier. Not content with that, he infuriated the English by recognising the Old Pretender as the rightful King of England, after James II's death in 1701. Finally, by ignoring his repeated promises to protect the interests of Victor Amadeus, he made an enemy of him, and was thus instrumental in his own betrayal.

The result of Louis XIV's diplomacy was to place France in the disastrous position where she had been in 1690, with a war to fight on two fronts in defence of the Alpine passes, and of the French frontier with Holland.

of Spain was no consolation to him for seeing an empire, from whose dismemberment he had had such high hopes of personal advantage, remaining intact. Full of resentment, he relapsed into silence, and Phélypeaux reported that he had angrily refused to allow that Louis XIV could withdraw from his earlier engagements. 'What!' he had exclaimed. 'Is this all that comes of my hopes of benefiting by his expressed affection, and the honour of becoming his near relation—an honour which I flattered myself I was doing him. Oh! I might have expected this.' Phélypeaux explained his state of mind very clearly to the King. 'M. le Duc de Savoie is brimful of honour, pride, arrogance, and ambition. All these sentiments would have been satisfied by the acquisition of Milan, of which he had believed himself as firmly possessed as of Turin. Nothing can compare with his pain at seeing his hopes dashed, and of all the Spanish succession, nothing remaining to him, beyond the honour of offering his congratulations, and the prospect of a royal marriage for his younger daughter.'

Louis XIV's ambassador had tentatively proposed a match between Adelaide's twelve-year-old sister Marie Louise, Princess of Piedmont, and the new King of Spain. Though Amadeus, on this point as on every other, remained obstinately silent, he at once perceived the advantages to be gained from becoming, eventually, the father of two queens. There was, however, the Emperor to be considered and, just as he had offered Adelaide to the Emperor, at the beginning of the negotiations for her marriage to Louis, so he now offered her sister to the Archduke Charles. By this means he was able to inform the King that 'the King of the Romans had already observed her distinguished appearance', at the same time pointing out that the will of Charles II discountenanced his successor's marriage with a princess of lesser rank than archduchess.

At Versailles, the King and his ministers were growing anxious. A new treaty appeared essential to guarantee safe conduct, food, and shelter for a French army crossing the Alps in mid-winter; but Victor Amadeus would promise nothing and sign nothing, and Phélypeaux was plainly having no success with him; in fact his latest report contained the Duke's sarcastic retort that he 'was glad to think that his country could be of some service, and hoped that his army might be also'. 'He flatters himself,' said Phélypeaux, 'that he will not be pressed to do anything contrary to his character or his interests, or to the honour he feels at being part of your family.' That vague assurance not being enough on which to risk the safety of French troops, the King commanded Tessé, who was at Milan, conferring with the Spanish governor about the reinforcements needed to repel an Austrian attack, to go at once to Turin, and see what he could do.

Tessé did his best with his old friend, but to no avail, and soon he was complaining of the Duke's 'strange, suspicious, irresolute, ill-natured or self-seeking conduct'. 'Enough to try the patience of a saint,' he continued, and he proceeded to accuse both Victor Amadeus and Vernon, his ambassador at Versailles, of having dealings with Vienna, by frequent couriers sent from Turin, and by interviews with Sinzendorf the Austrian ambassador in, among other places, the Paris churches.

Phélypeaux tried once again to extract a written promise regarding the safe conduct of troops; but all he gained was the remark that 'the King is powerful enough to send troops through my country whenever it pleases him. He does not need my consent'. And, in response to the ambassador's demand for some arrangements to be made for feeding the two cavalry regiments waiting to cross the frontier, all that Victor Amadeus would say was that he was not 'a tax-farmer, to bargain with a commissioner over food supplies'.

At this point the King lost patience and sent an angry dispatch, but he also offered a new treaty of alliance, and although Victor Amadeus was displeased by the wording, which he thought humiliating, the very generous sum of money offered for support of the troops, and the title of generalissimo of the combined French and Spanish armies, finally induced him to sign. Yet there was little doubt that his signing was not wholehearted. The King had insisted on the inclusion of a clause to the effect that, peace having been made in Italy, everything should remain in its established order— which removed from Victor Amadeus all hope of Milan, or any other territorial gain. As Phélypeaux continually reminded the King, 'his heart is still set on Milan and the King's promises; if he should be disappointed, a desire for vengeance will lead him to side with the Emperor'.

All this time, poor Adelaide had been desperately worried by the reports that came from Savoy of her father's strange behaviour. The Marquis de Sourches says that, at her public toilette, she jumped for joy, when the news of the new treaty was brought to her. On hearing of this Victor Amadeus felt it was time to explain matters to the Emperor, saying that an advance to the frontier by the imperial army appeared to threaten one of the richest provinces of Italy, and that for the sake of peace he had felt it his duty to yield to Louis XIV's urgent appeals for an alliance. He took the opportunity to explain also about the marriage. It had all come so suddenly, he said, that he had consented, being quite overwhelmed, but politically, of course, it meant very little; and he left it to his ambassador the Marquis du Prié to make his excuses. At this period, the early spring of 1701, neither France nor Savoy had recalled their ambassadors from Vienna, for although the Emperor had declared war on Spain, Savoy was still neutral, and Louis XIV desired to prolong the peace to the last possible moment.

Adelaide was in a painful situation. If war should come and if her father defected, she would be cut off from her family and perhaps regarded in France as an enemy and a suspect. Louis was away on his tour of the provinces, and the members of the Meudon Cabal, seeing that the King was unwell and preoccupied, were allowing their ill-will to become apparent. The three princesses, especially, sneered (when they thought themselves unobserved) at Adelaide's childish antics that so charmed the King.

In fact, she was finding him increasingly hard to amuse. He was worried, not without reason, at the thought of war, and the emptiness of the treasury, and perhaps was suffering from a reaction after the glories and excitement of accepting the Spanish crown. However that may be, he was so much dispirited that Adelaide decided to play a very bold stroke, even at the risk of outraging his modesty. Saint-Simon tells the story of how, one evening before the play, she was chattering to the King and Mme de Maintenon when Nanon, the latter's ancient waiting-woman, entered the room. 'Instantly, arrayed as she was in full court dress, with all her jewels, the princess went and stood with her back to the fire, and leaned on a little screen placed between two tables. Nanon, who seemed to have one hand in her pocket, slipped quietly in behind her and went down upon her knees; whereupon the King, who was nearest to them, asked what they were doing. The princess said, laughing, that she was only doing what he often did before a play, but he persisted. Then she said, 'Must I really tell you; can you not see for yourself? The truth is that I am having a *lavement*.' 'What?' said the King, in an explosion of mirth. 'You are not seriously telling me that you are having an enema at this moment?' 'Indeed I am,' said she. 'But how?' asked the King, and all four of them laughed until their sides shook. And, in very truth, Nanon had brought in the syringe all prepared, hidden beneath her petticoats, and had lifted the princess's skirts while she pretended to warm herself. Then she had inserted the nozzle, the skirts were pulled down, and Nanon had carried away the syringe underneath her own petticoat, so that everything was discreetly concealed. The King and Mme de Maintenon had paid no particular heed, thinking that she was arranging some part of the princess's dress. Thus they were taken completely by surprise, and found the whole episode intensely funny. What is extraordinary is that Mme la Duchesse de Bourgogne used to go to the play still holding the *lavement*, and in no hurry to be quit of it. She said she found it cooling, and that it prevented her from contracting a headache in the stuffy theatre. After they found her out, she continued in the same way; for she knew them through and through and could not help seeing and feeling what Mme de Maintenon and Mlle Choin really were.'

Once the King had countenanced *lavements* there was no restraining the ladies of the Court. *Lavements* became a naughty joke, and a source of much giggling. There was even a picture in one of the gazettes of a very royal lady, dressed as for an outing; her maid holds her shoes, and her little dog is begging. She lies on a day-bed, pointing towards a handsome young footman, who is handing the instrument to another of her maids. Below is a recommendation of the practice before going to a ball, with the caption, 'They call this a delightful amenity'.

The King, who should have been outraged by the indecency, appeared to regard it as no more than an innocent prank, and was hugely tickled by it. He was always charmed by courage in women, and he may have been moved that a little Italian girl should dare to take such a liberty with him, in the supreme confidence that nothing she did could spoil his love. Yet it is puzzling that Mme de Maintenon should have allowed her to take so great a risk, for the effect on the King might have been disastrous. It is possible, however, that the old lady had not discouraged her, hoping to draw down upon her such a reproof as to have checked her once and for all. For she was becoming more and more unmanageable.

Adelaide herself indeed may not have been acting as innocently as the King believed, nor was she always unwilling to make sport of Mme de Maintenon. She, who 'knew them through and through', was well aware that, although the King loved and depended upon his old wife where his soul and good morals were concerned, she bored him at times by her sanctimoniousness, and he was not above enjoying a sly dig at her himself. She had irritated him lately by

complaining, 'for the sake of his soul', when, on wet afternoons, he
sometimes allowed the more amusing of the older ladies among his
friends, the Comtesse de Gramont,[1] for example, to be shown up
to his study, by the back stairs, for a cosy chat. It was purely for
conversation, but the kind of witty talk he loved, and had known in
the *ruelles*, in his younger days. But laughter had been heard
through the closed doors, and Mme de Maintenon could not help
suspecting that, on some occasions, her own name was not kept un-
profaned. It is possible that Adelaide guessed that to see her dis-
comfited might add to the King's amusement.

Yet that in itself was hardly enough to make Adelaide, who was
fundamentally kind, and certainly fond of her 'aunt', humiliate and
embarrass the old lady in this rather cruel way. It is possible that
jealousy entered into it, for Mme de Maintenon had recently
brought another little girl into the family circle, who bade fair also
to become the King's darling. This was Jeannette Pincré, a destitute
orphan, whom she had adopted, intending her for Saint-Cyr.
Jeannette was a very pretty child, who enchanted the King by
appearing not in the least alarmed by him. He petted and played
with her, and when the time came for her to go to school, he would
not hear of it. Thus she continued to live in Mme de Maintenon's
apartment, growing ever prettier and still more amusing, yet so
discreet that she won the affection and esteem of the entire household. Saint-Simon says that 'even Mme la Duchesse de Bourgogne
treated her with respect, and feared her too, thinking that she
carried tales to the King; although, in fact, she never harmed
anyone'. It is probable that Adelaide found, in this child's appearance, sufficient cause for jealousy, at a time when she herself felt
unhappy and insecure.

Mme de Maintenon was not the only one to worry over Adelaide
Tessé, in Milan, was much concerned by the reports, and her mother
Duchess Anne wrote a pathetic letter to the Comte de Vernon, (Victor
Amadeus's ambassador to Versailles), showing how deeply she was
troubled for the future. So long as the King thought Adelaide perfect there was little that could be done, the dangerous time would
come after his death, when she would be totally dependent on her

---

[1] Elizabeth Hamilton, Comtesse de Gramont (1641–1708). Saint-Simon says,
'No one was wittier than she, or pleasanter or more polite. . . . She was always
on excellent terms with the King, who delighted in her wit.' 'Mme de Maintenon,' he continues, 'feared, but could not remove her, for the King was too
much diverted by her company.'

husband, and, if she lost his love, find herself no longer favoured, but alone against her enemies.

Adelaide, however, did not long remain the centre of attention, for by the end of 1701 the War of the Spanish Succession had started in earnest, and the King had become absorbed in the distribution of military commands, and the direction of his armies. For the campaign of 1702, Louis XIV decided to send his strongest army against the Dutch republic, with Boufflers and Tallard in command, in consultation with the Duc de Bourgogne, serving for the first time with the army. Louis was enchanted, despite the fact that the King, unusually parsimonious, allowed him no personal staff, with the result that while the royal bastard, the Comte de Toulouse, was well attended, the heir to the throne left for Flanders with no one but his valet to attend him and announce his visitors. The King, indeed, was far less concerned for his grandson's dignity than with his having to pass through Cambrai on his way to the army. He issued strict orders that the Duc de Bourgogne was not to sleep or even to eat there and, to prevent any private conversation with Fénelon, he forbade him to leave his coach.

When Louis arrived at the posting house, Fénelon was there waiting, and came up to the coach door. There was no private talk because the King's envoy stood between them; but the crowd was touched by the transports of delight that, despite his reserve, overcame the young prince when he saw his old tutor. When the parting came they embraced again and again through the window of the coach, and Louis was able to whisper in the archbishop's ear, without disobeying the King's command. The long, loving glances exchanged between them were noted by the courtiers, and especially by the troops for, notwithstanding his disgrace, veneration for Fénelon was felt increasingly throughout his diocese, and had now permeated the entire army.

The campaign of 1702 was an unfortunate one for France; but for Louis it was something of a triumph. Relieved from the pleasure and pain of Adelaide's teasing, and from the King, who terrified him, he could be more relaxed, and less careful of his dignity. Moreover, since the war and how to wage it was the thought uppermost in every mind, and the topic of every conversation, his intelligence and integrity became apparent, and he was generally considered to show promise. In the autumn he returned to Versailles with a glowing report from the Maréchal de Boufflers, praising him for his keenness and courage, and his cheeriness under fire. Not much more had been required of him, for he was still under tutelage.

Adelaide's daily letters had made him very happy, and the King's approval gave him fresh confidence. He returned to Versailles a day sooner than was expected, and ran up the narrow back stairs to the King's bedroom. It was shortly before midnight, and the courtiers were leaving after the Grand Coucher. Louis stood in the doorway to make a very deep bow, but the King held out his arms, saying, 'Well! Are you not going to give me a kiss?', and embraced him often and most affectionately. He then said, 'Go quickly to Mme la Duchesse de Bourgogne; she will be waiting impatiently to see you'. But Adelaide had not waited. As soon as she learned of Louis's arrival, she had run the entire length of the Salle des Glaces to join him in the King's room, with her clothes all in disarray, for she had been undressing to go to bed. They embraced with great tenderness, and she immediately took him back to her rooms, where her ladies brought them supper. They did not sit over it long, however, for Louis was eager to undress and join her in bed, where, at last, they could be alone.

In the following months, before the campaigning season of 1703 opened, he was happier, and more at ease with Adelaide and her ladies than he had ever been before, less disapproving, falling in with her plans, doing his utmost to please her. This was the time when he composed a great number of ponderous verses in her honour, addressing her by his strange pet-name.

> 'Draco, you would command the universe
> To serve your pleasure and your sense of fun,
> What won't men do for you, and to what height not climb,
> Since I, your husband, write to you in rhyme?'

Verse after verse followed in the same strain, though he did have the grace to finish,

> 'Loved I you less, my verses might be better.'

In the spring, he rejoined the army, full of love for Adelaide, and with so much confidence that he dared to disobey the King's renewed order to have no talk with Fénelon as he passed through Cambrai. Fénelon, as before, was waiting at the posting-house, and walked forward to the side of the coach. Louis, indeed, did not get out, but this time the door was left wide open, and once again the crowd were touched to see the joy of the young prince as they embraced. The place was too public for there to be any conversation, beyond inquiries after health and the condition of the roads;

but spectators observed the loving looks that were exchanged, and the whispering between the embraces.

After this moving encounter, Louis continued his journey to the army's headquarters nominally to take over the command, assisted by the Maréchal de Boufflers. He had eagerly expected to find letters from Adelaide, but none had come, and none arrived for several weeks—then only one dull little note, followed by one more, equally short, and after that, silence.

Louis, out of his mind with worry and disappointment when all appeals proved ineffectual, made the extraordinary decision to use a go-between in corresponding with his wife, choosing for that purpose the Marquise de Montgon, one of her older and most intimate ladies. He could hardly have picked anyone better, for though her intervention met with little success, she was at least loyal and secret, and made no mischief. Saint-Simon, who disliked her on principle, because both she and her mother were protected by Mme de Maintenon, could find no worse to say against her than that 'she was plain, though excessively witty, charming, pleasant, as amusing as possible, and malicious to match'. Malicious she may have been; but she showed no malice in her dealings with Louis and Adelaide. It may even be thought that she tried to put a little stiffening into the love-lorn boy, which might have earned him his wife's respect.

He wrote altogether sixteen letters to Mme de Montgon, that summer, from his headquarters, outside Brisach. The town was besieged; he was nominally in command, and supposedly a keen soldier; yet in none of them is there any mention of the army, only of his passion for Adelaide, with bitter complaints because she did not write. Here are some extracts from this astonishing correspondence:

'Encamped at Sultz, 12 June, 1703.
'I am surprised, Madame, at not hearing from you, and still more so at the tardiness of your royal mistress, who has allowed infinity of time an to elapse without writing more than two letters . . . I am resolved not to weary her with reproaches; yet I become impatient, and last night I was really angry, when the courier again brought no word from her. I wish you could have seen me at supper, looking black as thunder, muttering to myself, with my hat dragged down over my eyes . . . As for that wicked one, of whom I speak, tell her that if she does not write more often I shall break with her, and send her no letters for the remainder of the campaign.

P.S. I fear that such threats are mere idle words, for it is I who would suffer most.'

In his next letter, dated the 17th, he thanks Mme de Montgon for writing to him, but bids her scold Adelaide, from whom he still has not heard. 'I am delighted to learn from you that she is well . . . but speaking often of M. le Duc de Bourgogne, inquiring after his health, and not finding his memory altogether repugnant, does not tally with leaving him twelve days without a word, and I always come back to that because it vexes me so much . . .'

Again, on June 24th:

'Encamped at Schleittal.

'This letter, Madame, must serve as my reply to two from you, which I received at almost the same time. Both drove me crazy with their descriptions of the charms of your royal mistress . . . Tell her that I am charging you to learn from her own lips whether she loves me, and to give me her answer in her own words.'

This brought the neglectful Adelaide up short. Clearly she had to do something in the way of appeasement. Always ready to oblige, and, indeed, to do anything, provided it did not entail letter-writing, she hit on the brilliant idea of dictating, to Mme de Montgon, a letter written in her blood, a commodity readily available, since the doctors were all too frequently bleeding her to relieve her toothache. Mme de Montgon thought that this would be going altogether too far, and that Louis would rightly be disgusted. But not at all, for he received the epistle in transports of delight:

'Encamped at Salmbach, 3 July, 1703.

I cannot wait a moment before sending my reply. Far from being sickened by that adorable blood, I have already kissed it a thousand times, and shall do so a thousand times more before the day is over. I have drawn some of mine to send her, if so be that it is not unworthy of her; and if she says she would shed all for me, I would assuredly keep none back of my own. But we must retain both, and join our hearts as in this little picture, delineated in blood drawn with my knife, this very moment, from a finger of my left hand. This letter is all bespattered with the blood that love constrains me to shed, and I am only too happy to be shedding it for her.'

There then followed a poem in the heroic manner, and directions for Mme de Montgon, on how to present the epistle to Adelaide:

Kneel down before her; kiss both her hands in my name; offer her this blood, which I have shed for her alone. I fear you will think me mad; but how otherwise can I convince that Queen of my great love for her, although she knows it already? Adieu! dear Montgon, unless I should think of some fresh extravagance to add to this letter.'

And, indeed, that same evening, he added a long postscript, still harping on his blood-letting, urging the unfortunate lady to impress on Adelaide the touching nature of this proof of his love, since, having no supply of blood conveniently at hand, he had not hesitated to cut his finger, quite badly, for her sake.

Other letters followed, in the same manner, or begging for a reply from Adelaide, but still none came, until, at the beginning of September, when he was encamped before Brisach. She sent him, not indeed a letter, but her portrait in miniature, perhaps as a peace-offering, for the season was far advanced, and she knew that he would soon be home. This picture Louis received with an outpouring of gratitude, still addressed to Mme de Montgon, in a letter beginning, '*Grâces infinies, grâces extrêmes*', and continuing, 'Tell me, does she ever speak of M. le Duc de Bourgogne, and if so, in what manner?', and so on for several pages.

A few days after this, Brisach having surrendered, Louis made haste to return to Adelaide. He was reported to have 'conducted himself with honourable distinction, behaving throughout with quiet and unassuming courage'. None the less, the King, who would have preferred him to remain with the army until the end of the campaign, was not pleased by the speed with which he left it. Unfortunately for Louis, he did not find Adelaide burning to see him again. Doglike devotion rarely succeeds in winning hearts, especially not the hearts of young women as light and laughter-loving as his wife, who probably did not understand what torment his passion for her had been causing him. She no longer positively disliked him; she even enjoyed his company, when he was not scolding her; but his complaints failed to move her.

In the previous year she had written to him every day, when he was away with the army. In 1703, she had promised to write twice a week, but had not kept her word even to that extent. Writing and composition were still a hard labour; but that was not all; something clearly had happened to make writing to him impossible. The truth was that she had nothing to tell him, for she could not write of what occupied her mind—her father's treachery in breaking the French alliance, which was making her wretched and ashamed. Mme de Maintenon was especially kind and comforting, saying that her heart ached for her; but Adelaide was in something of a panic, for she had heard rumours that she herself might soon be considered an enemy of France and sent back to Savoy in disgrace for having failed to produce the long-awaited heir. Another cause for fear was the thought that her beloved grandmother might come to love her less. Louis, who should have comforted her, was being singularly heartless, saying only that if he were to be sent to the Italian front, she would be hard put to it to decide whether to pray for his triumph or her father's, and that all she could do was to keep them both remembered.

There had been other troubles to sadden and worry her. The sudden and horrible death of Monsieur her grandfather in an apoplectic fit, after a violent quarrel with the King and too much fish for supper, had been a shock and a grief; for Monsieur had always been kind to her, and she was fond of him. It was her first experience of death in the family circle, and it had brought the realisation that the King and Mme de Maintenon would not live for ever, and that when they were gone she would be exposed to the enmity of Monseigneur's clique. She realised moreover that with Madame de Maintenon growing old, the King looked increasingly to her for comfort and encouragement. He was much afflicted by Monsieur's death, and very frequently in tears, indeed, their quarrel may have made him feel partly responsible for his brother's death, although it was Saint-Simon's opinion that what depressed him most was the thought that Monsieur was two years younger than he, and had appeared equally healthy. Adelaide would have liked to have been allowed to mourn for him a little while; but that, to the King, would have been mere selfishness. Versailles must never be an unhappy place, others must never be brought low by personal griefs, and thus, on the very morning after his brother's death, music was heard coming from Mme de Maintenon's room, and the courtiers were astonished to find the King and Adelaide singing duets together from Lully's operas. Later that same morning, he himself was surprised to find her sitting alone in a corner, looking the picture of misery, and when he had discovered from Mme de Maintenon the reason for her sadness, he had tried to distract her by getting her to play a game. Adelaide was learning that the old King depended on her to cheer him day after day with the gaiety and high spirits of the little child, who had given him back his youth, when she first came to his court. She was, however, no longer a child of ten; she did her best; but it had become a burden.

Adelaide's sense of the weight of her responsibilities towards the King was further increased by a letter from Tessé, who was at Turin, performing for her sister Marie Louise functions similar to those that he had performed for her, before she came to France; in other words, preparing Marie Louise to leave her home, arranging her betrothal to young King Philip and her journey to Spain, and, in the process, becoming nearly as fond of the new little queen as he was of Adelaide herself. Tessé wrote that the King, Duchess Anne, and Adelaide herself had drawn his attention to something of which he was already well aware, 'namely that you are very much the youngest and no doubt born to be a consolation to them. You must therefore conserve your health and, although your good will and common sense place you beyond the need for advice, I think you will pardon the liberty I take in thus exhorting you ... to be a comfort to the King by your behaviour, and to Madame your mother by your letters ...'

It was a very serious letter, quite unlike Tessé's usual style, for he generally wrote (as Louis never did) to entertain her with subjects well calculated to interest and amuse a girl still in her teens.

13

Tender Attachments

ANOTHER REASON why Adelaide did not write to Louis during the campaign of 1703 may have been that she was in regular correspondence with her sister in Spain, showing keen, protective interest in her life and her marriage to King Philip. In letters to her mother and grandmother, and to Philip himself, she is always speaking of her younger sister: 'I want to know,' she wrote, 'exactly what she does from morning until night.' She worried over her clothes, her health, her pregnancies, and sent her parcels of dresses and, when the need arose, a nurse and an accoucheur.

Marie Louise Gabrielle, Princess of Piedmont, was by three years younger than her sister, just two years older than Adelaide had been when she, too, had left home to embark on marriage with a stranger, and in a strange country. The two children had been together in the nursery, and had been fond of one another. Adelaide now believed that her experience and her friendship with King Philip made her especially well qualified to caution, encourage, and advise, and she wrote to Tessé, asking for a full description.

Tessé replied, very tactfully, that there was a slight resemblance between the sisters, but that Adelaide was the better looking, that Marie Louise's complexion was good, but her teeth bad; that her lips were not so red as Adelaide's and that she did not possess her sister's 'roving eye'.[1] 'Finally,' he said, 'the Princess is reputed to be kind, easy to serve, and seldom if ever out of humour. My own view is that she is well-adapted to be Queen of Spain, and that the notion does not at all displease her.' Phélypeaux, the French ambassador, took a rather different view, saying, 'She is haughty, proud, full of ambition . . . As far as I could judge in the last three

---

[1] It was said that when Adelaide entered a room, her eyes took in every detail in a fraction of a second, even including those things which she was not supposed to see.

months, without paying too much heed, she sometimes lets it be seen, in private conversation, that it would offend her to be treated with less ceremony than a reigning monarch.'

The truth lay somewhere in between. Marie Louise was a far stronger character than Adelaide, and possessed a violent temper. The Spaniards, who came to love her, called her 'heart of fire'. She had arrived in Spain, in 1701, determined to be the senior partner in her marriage, and to make her young husband a loyal servant of Savoy. Soon after their first encounter she had shocked and surprised him by arguing fiercely with him about politics, and expecting him, in everything, to take her father's side. Yet she was still only a child, thirteen years old, physically immature, and missing her parents and her home far more than Adelaide had done in similar circumstances.

Philip, on the other hand, was almost unnaturally quiet and reserved. He had not been brought up for kingship, but trained to give way in everything to the will of his elder brother, the Duc de Bourgogne. He was, nonetheless, courageous, sensible, capable of making decisions, but so pathetically shy that he became speechless in the company of those whom he did not know well, and was therefore wrongly suspected of being weak and indecisive. It was his father-in-law's firm belief that Marie Louise would come to dominate him, and for that purpose he had given her as thorough a training in statecraft as he had given to Adelaide. The intention was to separate Philip from France, and to make him the obedient supporter of Piedmontese ambitions. Victor Amadeus, however, had overlooked two hindrances to his plan, first, Philip's veneration of his grandfather Louis XIV, and secondly the immaturity of Marie Louise. The young man was profoundly lonely, but more than that, he was, physically and most urgently, in need of a wife, and had therefore been looking forward to her coming with ardent desire. What was his dismay to find on her arrival that, though evidently precocious in all other ways, she was physically undeveloped, and quite unfit for married life. It was two years before she became a woman, and three more before she could bear a child.

Their first meeting had been disastrous. Marie Louise had minded far more than Adelaide the parting with her ladies at the Spanish frontier. She had wept long and bitterly, as Adelaide had not done, feeling homesick and deserted amid so many foreign faces. To make matters worse, there had been a disgraceful scene, that same evening, during which her new Spanish household had

behaved abominably. The King had ridden out to meet her, at
Figueras, not far from Barcelona, and a banquet had been arranged
in his honour, of French and Spanish dishes to be served alternately.
It was a delicate compliment; but the ladies contrived to spoil it, by
spilling the French dishes on the floor, and serving only the Spanish
ones. There was great confusion. Nothing was said during the meal,
but the strain of it was too much for the tired, unhappy little girl,
and afterwards her temper exploded. She refused to join the King,
and angrily demanded to be sent home immediately.

Fortunately for all concerned, comfort was at hand, in the shape
of Princess Orsini, known in France as the Princesse des Ursins,[1]
the great lady whom Louis XIV appointed to be the *camarera-major*,
the duenna[2] who would supervise the education of Marie Louise,
and train her to be Queen, as Mme de Maintenon had trained and
cared for Adelaide. It was an inspired choice, although made with
reluctance, and only because no suitable Spanish lady could be
found. Mme des Ursins had lived in France, and had known and
been sincerely attached to both Duchesses of Savoy, Adelaide's
beloved mother and grandmother. She was extraordinarily charming, eminently capable, and highly intelligent. 'Unequalled in
grace, intelligence and charm,' is what Saint-Simon says of her,
'capable of saying whatsoever she pleased in the manner that she
desired; most secret regarding herself; most loyal to her friends,
delightfully funny, but never vulgar, with an even temper that
allowed her to be mistress of herself at all times.' This famous
lady entirely fulfilled the King's expectations, for she won the
hearts of both Philip and Marie Louise, and remained their all-
powerful friend and adviser, virtually ruling Spain for France, until
the young Queen's death, in 1714.

Already, on the short tearful journey from the frontier to
Figueras, Marie Louise had found her comforting. By the end of
that first unhappy evening, she had allowed herself to be quietened,
though she still refused to go to the King. As for Philip, he was full

---

[1] Anne Marie de La Trémoïlle-Noirmoutiers (1642–1722). She first married
Adrien Blaise de Talleyrand, Prince de Chalais; and then Flavio Orsini, Duc
de Bracciano. At his death, she took the title of Princesse des Ursins. She was
supremely powerful in Spain, from 1704 to 1714. For the dramatic description
of her banishment and adventures at the latter date, see Saint-Simon's *Memoirs*.

[2] The duenna fulfilled the functions of a royal governess. Always a grandee
of Spain, she was usually a widow, and of the highest rank. She lived in the
palace, and never left her pupil's side, presenting persons of quality at audiences,
ordering her clothes, controlling her petty-purse, and going with her everywhere.

of compassion, but deeply disappointed, having, so Saint-Simon tells us, remained 'wholly continent until that moment'. Next day, Mme des Ursins sent him out hunting, and tactfully avoided a recurrence of Marie Louise's angry tears. The ladies were reprimanded; their mistress was punished by the King's coldness, and his decision to spend the evening alone in his study. On the day after that, the little Queen discovered that he was charming. After three days all went well; 'their minds became fully occupied with feasting and revelry', and Mme des Ursins was able to write to Louis XIV, 'I believe, Sire, that I may say with confidence that the Queen's only thought, at present, is to please the King and his subjects'. Marie Louise, writing to her dearest Mamma, exclaimed, 'The King, Our King! becomes every day more charming. I did not like him at all, when he was so serious.'

This was all very fine, wonderful that they should like each other, but it provided no solution to the King's urgent physical problems. Marie Louise could not yet be his real wife; and a wife was for him a necessity. His exorbitantly amorous nature had revealed itself a very short time before he left France; the Pope had been consulted, and a dispensation had been granted, similar to the one enjoyed by Louis XIV in his boyhood, allowing him to be accompanied, on his journey to Spain, by the daughter of his wet-nurse; but she had been sent home on the day of his marriage by proxy. The solution of taking a mistress, so obvious to the Spanish Court, was out of the question. King Philip believed that adultery was sinful, and he would not commit a sin. In his distress, he wrote to his grandfather, and sent the letter by his friend Louville,[1] with instructions to tell all. Louis XIV, as was his usual custom in moral issues, referred the matter to Mme de Maintenon, who consulted prelates. But no further dispensation was forthcoming; a letter to the Pope evoked the unsatisfying reply that the King of Spain must be patient, for time would cure all.

At that point Marie Louise's father lost all hope of ruling Spain through her. His alliance with France had seemed permanent, once he had secured the world's most eligible Frenchmen as husbands for his two daughters; but he did not for a moment believe that Philip would long resist the temptation of keeping a mistress, and he was convinced that Marie Louis's influence would then be negligible. In both assumptions he was proved wrong. Philip stood

[1] Charles Auguste d'Allonville, Marquis de Louville, (1664-1731). He had accompanied Philip to Spain and had become head of his French household.

firm, and Marie Louise, despite her immaturity, won his love and
trust. What is more, the Duke of Savoy would seem to have overlooked the capabilities of the Princesse des Ursins, and her devotion
to France.

Victor Amadeus, deeply suspicious of Louis XIV's intentions,
had begun to doubt his capacity to win the war. On 5 January 1702,
he had therefore approached the other side, and entered into an
alliance with Prince Eugene; which he very prudently kept secret
from Versailles. It was not long, however, before reports of it
reached the Court, for Phélypeaux, with a sharp eye for treachery,
sent word to the King that the Duke of Savoy was returning to his
old trick of having, as Tessé termed it, 'a foot in both boots'.

Louis XIV and Mme de Maintenon could not bring themselves
to believe in such treachery from a near relation; but, in 1703, all
doubts were dispelled, when Victor Amadeus publicly announced
his union with the Grand Alliance, remarking that he preferred the
rough bread of his own country to the soft white loaves of France.

The desertion of the Duke of Savoy was largely the fault of the
King and his tactless diplomacy, for he had continually underestimated the strength and intelligence of his ally, and had disregarded his propensity to change sides. He had deeply hurt the
duke's pride by ignoring his claims during the negotiations for the
Spanish Succession, and had disregarded his personal interests. As
for Victor Amadeus, no doubt he was disloyal; but he was doing
little more than follow the example of other minor princes of his
period, when he sold his services to the highest bidder.

The first rumours of the rupture had been profoundly upsetting
to Adelaide, and when there was no longer any doubt that France
and Savoy were at war, she broke down completely, seeking refuge
in the kind arms of Mme de Maintenon. That lady was, as always, a
comfort and support; but she could not resist telling the ladies of
Saint-Cyr of her hard lot. 'Mme la Duchesse de Bourgogne,' she
wrote, 'is dreadfully unhappy and brings all her troubles to me.
Last night, for example, she appeared just as I was going to bed
half-dead with exhaustion. She flung herself into my arms, and kept
me a long time listening to her woes. It is true she inquired whether
she disturbed me; but despite the liberties she allows me, and
although she has begged me to treat her as a daughter, I cannot
possibly forget her rank, or show her disrespect.' Something else
that Mme de Maintenon could never resist was the opportunity for
a little sermon on the deceits of rank and riches: 'Oh! my dear

daughters,' she continued, 'how happy for you to have left the world! It promises joy and gives none. The King of England[1] played here yesterday with the Duchesse de Bourgogne and her ladies. Our King and the English queen looked on. All was dancing, laughter, and cries of delight; yet nearly all of those present felt a dagger at their hearts. Verily, the world is a mocker, you cannot be sufficiently thankful to God for having removed you from it.'

She also wrote to Mme des Ursins—with whom she had begun a regular correspondence: 'The Duchesse de Bourgogne is extremely attached to her father and deeply resents his treachery. She dearly loves her lady-mother, and takes as keen an interest in the affairs of Spain as in those of France; she also loves the King, and cannot see him looking even a little more serious than usual without bursting into tears.' In another letter to the ladies of Saint-Cyr, she said, 'Although still very young, she has become far too serious. She speaks of State matters as though she were forty years old.'

The King showed unusual tact and kindness in his dealings with Adelaide. He made a pact with her never to mention her father and, according to Saint-Simon, 'took enormous pains to avoid any allusion to him in her presence'. What is more, in order to show the Court that his love for her was in no way diminished, he refused to allow the Carnival festivities in the winter of 1703–1704 to be at all reduced on account of the war. Adelaide was the centre of them all and appeared to delight in them; but she continued to grieve for the breach between her father and the King.

She had yet another reason for disquiet, for she had begun to realise that she had enemies, especially at the court of Monseigneur, and her father's treachery might jeopardise her own future. Vernon, Victor Amadeus's minister at Versailles, wrote of her deep distress.

17 August 1703
'I hear from a trusty source that a few days ago Mme la Duchesse de Bourgogne entered Mme de Maintenon's room, when His Majesty was present, weeping and sobbing so bitterly that they could not make out what she said. At length, somewhat calmed by their kind manner, she managed to say that she had received a mortal blow, someone having told her, concerning the rumours about Your Royal Highness, that His Majesty had decided to

---

[1] The Old Pretender, whom, to the fury of William III and the English people, Louis XIV had recognised as King of England, after James II's death, in 1701.

send her home because she had not produced a son, and so
saying, she had relapsed into desperate sobbing. His Majesty
was as much moved as he was indignant, and immediately gave
orders to discover the offender and see that he was severely
punished.'

'My heart aches,' wrote Mme de Maintenon, 'for the sadness of
our princess since Monsieur de Savoie declared war against the
King; but she somehow contrives not to show her feelings too
plainly.' One consolation was that the King still allowed her to
write regularly to her family. She could hardly bear to think of her
mother and grandmother in danger from the war, and expressed her
feelings very frankly: 'I swear to you, my dearest mother, that the
greatest joy for me would be to see my father return to reason. I do
not understand why he will not treat for peace . . . Is he determined
to let Turin be besieged? They say here that a siege will certainly
be laid before long. Only imagine how I feel about that, having so
great a concern for all that affects you.'

Tessé, who had been posted to Madrid, understood and was
sorry for both homesick little girls, and he had the thought of urging
Adelaide to undertake a regular correspondence with her sister, no
light endeavour, considering the hard labour that writing was to
her. She did, however, undertake it, and maintained it for many
years. Tessé was amused and pleased. 'One of the things that most
pleases the Queen,' he wrote, 'is the regularity with which you
write to her by every post. It goes to confirm my belief that when
you make up your mind to do something, you do it better and more
charmingly than anyone else.'

Tessé was one of the nicest people in the King's service, although
Saint-Simon thought little of him—after admitting that he was
handsome, that his smile was charming, and that he could be very
funny when he wished, he went on to say that 'his mind was far
below the mediocre, if one disregarded his genius as a courtier, and
his familiarity with ladies' jargon'. Tessé was, at any rate, sorry for
the little girls whom he had served, and he did his best to comfort
them by bringing them together.

'I have committed myself to a promise, Madame, on behalf of
your sister the Queen,' he wrote to Adelaide. 'It will set you to
some small expense, and a command to Mme de Mailly; but
nothing costly, outlandish, or richly embroidered is required . . .
This, Madame, is the need.

'The Queen returned from hunting wearing a jacket, hat, and wig. The hat she wears nearly as elegantly as you do yours; she does not absolutely need a new one. But truly, Madame, you would not wish to see your sister, a queen, in a wig, jacket, and skirt, of the kind she was wearing—half French, half Spanish in style. The King said to me, "Confess it frankly, is not the Queen abominably dressed?" I shrugged my shoulders, and then made so bold as to say, "Madame, will Your Majesty not ask my mistress[1] to send you a well-cut riding habit?" "I should indeed be glad of one," she replied. "But I dare not, for I would not be a burden to my sister." "Let me undertake it all," said I (being certain of excellent results). "Very well," said the Queen, "but nothing grand, just a well-cut jacket, with good sleeves, in the simple style which my sister wears when she hunts from a carriage; for I do not, nor will I ever, ride on horseback."[2]

'Thus you will see, Madame, that I have committed you to a task; one for which I trust you will forgive me. To be brief, what we require from you is a jacket and skirt of red, blue, or grey cloth, with a band or two of gold braid, or a few rosettes—but no finery. We also need a wig, for hers is dreadful. All these to be exactly what you would choose for yourself and, if possible, done with such speed that my courier may bring them back with him.'

Adelaide applied herself with enthusiasm to playing the elder sister. Streams of food-parcels went out from Versailles, and when, in 1707, the Prince of the Asturias was born, she provided the most beautiful layette, exquisitely embroidered. The parcels were much appreciated, for an Austrian invasion had driven the Spanish royal family from Madrid, and they were living, in uncomfortable circumstances and considerable hardship. It was Marie Louise's courage and cheerful endurance at that time that won for her the people's love, to such an extent that, when Philip remarried after her death, the crowds still persisted in cheering for 'La Savoyana', although the new queen was a princess of Parma. In many ways Marie Louise was more fortunate than Adelaide because she could love her husband who, unlike Louis, was pleasant and easy to live

[1] Tessé was Adelaide's Master of the Horse.
[2] It was strictly against Spanish etiquette for noble ladies to ride. No man must ever see their legs. The etiquette weighed very hard on Marie Louise who was used to a country life; but the King and Mme des Ursins thought that, to win the affections of the Spaniards, she must conform, and ride in a carriage, or a litter, drawn by white mules.

with; she also very much loved Mme des Ursins, and enjoyed her company. 'I am really extremely happy with her,' she wrote to Duchess Anne. 'She is not at all the dragon that I had expected'; and Adelaide, the recipient of a stream of letters, was able to inform her parents, 'I am delighted to tell you that my sister is now perfectly happy, and that the King is pleased with her. What happened with her women was just childishness, and of no consequence.'

To Adelaide, at Versailles, the affairs of her sister provided a new and lively interest. With Tessé's encouragement, she wrote regularly and often received replies. She was grateful to him for giving her something new to think about, and by pure luck was able to show her gratitude by getting him promoted. It happened in this way. One evening, in Mme de Maintenon's room, she was keeping the King in fits of laughter with the unimaginable liberties she was taking with the papers on his writing-table. He thought her too funny for words, as she rummaged among his letters, reading them aloud in mimicry of the pompous officials, behaving, one would think, like the comic notaries in Mozart's operas, making faces, putting on a squeaky voice, and dancing about the room. Suddenly she came on a list of four generals to be made Marshals of France. She stopped fooling; her eyes filled with tears, and she cried out to the King that he had forgotten her dear Tessé, who would die of the disappointment. She always made a point of expressing her fondness for Tessé, saying that it was because he had negotiated her marriage, and brought her to so much happiness in France, and she knew that it pleased the King to hear her express appreciation. This time, however, he was vexed with her for reading the list, and, either because he had decided not to create new Marshals, or was not disposed to promote Tessé, he said crossly that she need not distress herself, for there were going to be no promotions. And, indeed, none were announced next day; but some days later, when the list appeared, there was a fifth name, Tessé's, added to it.

It was a thousand pities that Adelaide never had the kind of guidance which the Queen of Spain received from the Princesse des Ursins, the training to be a good wife and mother, to know her place in Society, and the duties and responsibilities of being a queen. When Adelaide came to France, she had been eager to begin a new life; they called her *franc du collier* (a willing horse), because of the enthusiasm with which she accepted the dullest public engagements, imagining that they would lead to more important things. They had led to nothing. All that had been required of her, day after day, year after year, was to remain a little girl, amuse the King with baby-talk, and appear to be happy.

Mme de Maintenon, whose only desire was for a quiet life, did not conceive it part of her duty to develop Adelaide's character. She saw in her a golden opportunity to relieve herself of some of the burden of the King's fears, and thus did her best to keep the child happy and prevent her from growing up to become awkward and demanding. But Adelaide was ceasing to be a child. She was light and frivolous by nature; but she had been brought up by her father to discuss and study State affairs; moreover, she was intelligent, deeply interested in the fortunes of her family, in Savoy. In France, she felt excluded. No one, least of all her husband, would talk seriously to her; the war, which so much distressed her, was a topic barred. She had been given no purpose in life, nothing to strive for, except to produce an heir, and to keep the King cheerful. It was not enough; she grew spoiled, bored, and secretly very unhappy. Since pleasures were all that was offered her, it is small wonder that in the years that followed, she became thoroughly dissipated. She danced, and lost fortunes at the card-table, and more often than not was put to bed, drunk. She undermined her health with miscarriages, brought on from lack of rest, for she turned night into day, first at the Opera in Paris, and going afterwards to balls and gambling-parties in the great houses.

Adelaide, as well as Mme de Maintenon, conceived it to be her first duty to please the King, and indeed she had come to love him more than a little. Nonetheless, she made no effort to conceal from the Court that she still loved her father, and rumours were spread by her enemies around Monseigneur, at Meudon, that she was his spy, and regularly sent him secret information, gleaned from the King's writing-table. It seems most unlikely. First of all, the King worked with his ministers, and was the most secret man imaginable. Knowing that Adelaide would rifle his desk, it is hard to believe that he would not have removed anything secret before they left. Secondly, there was the censorship of the posts. Private letters from the royal family were stopped and shown to the King and Mme de Maintenon, as Madame and the Princesse de Conti had discovered to their cost. Michelet, the historian, found the accusation 'hard to believe', and Voltaire's conclusion is that 'it was one of those vulgar rumours that bring news-writers into disrepute, and disgrace the histories'. It was Charles Pinot Duclos, a gossipy and untrustworthy memoirist who long afterwards published the story; but, since he was not born until 1704, he could have had no first-hand information. The same accusation was made against Marie Louise, in Spain, who wrote fiercely to Tessé, 'How is it possible that I should be suspected of communicating with my father to send him information and money? I know that this is being said; but should I be likely to wish to dethrone my husband and myself, for my father's advantage?' There is a story that Louis XIV discovered Adelaide's treachery when he and Mme de Maintenon were going through her letters, after her death, and that he exclaimed jokingly, '*La coquine, elle nous a trahi!*' (The little baggage, she betrayed us). But that, too, seems unlikely. There is no evidence, for they were alone, but Louis XIV was extremely fastidious in his choice of words, and *coquine*, at that time a vulgar expression, would scarcely have come into his vocabulary.

Adelaide did send her family one warning, in the letter already quoted, of the King's decision to besiege Turin; but there was no attempt at secrecy, she sent it by the ordinary post, and the King knew of it.[1] She was very much concerned for their safety, and her letter continued, 'I am in despair at the pass to which my father has reduced himself. Is it possible that he believes we should not make good terms? I do assure you that the King's only desire is to see his kingdom and that of his grandson at peace once more. It appears to me that my father should wish the same for himself, and when I consider that he is the master, I am continually astonished that he does not act. I fear, my dearest mother, that you will think me foolish to be so outspoken, but I can no longer contain myself. Despite all my father has done he is still my father, and I love him very dearly. Therefore, dearest mother, forgive me if I write freely; it is my urgent desire that our interests should be the same that forces me to speak as I do. Love me always, and do not be angry with me. You will understand my good intentions and the motive that drives me to write. I enclose a letter from my sister, you will perceive that she feels as much disturbed as myself over what is happening.'[1]

Victor Amadeus paid no attention to the pleas of his unhappy

[1] In the end, Turin was not besieged. The ladies of the Court retired to a country house at Cuneo, and Victor Amadeus, with his courtiers and most of his cavalry, began a rapid flight, zig zagging backwards and forwards over the entirety of Piedmont. By so doing, he gained valuable time, and Prince Eugene was able to come to his rescue. A battle at Turin was fought, on 7 September 1705, in which the French were defeated and driven out of Savoy.

daughters, which caused Mme de Maintenon to write to the Princesse des Ursins, 'Monsieur le Duc de Savoie is a mighty prince. He leaves it to the bourgeoisie to take pity on their daughters; but you will agree with me, Madame, that his own children deserve better treatment.'

Adelaide had something else on her mind to worry her, for in the winter and spring of 1704 she was again pregnant, and looking forward without pleasure to the months ahead, since the King, determined to have no more miscarriages, had laid down strict orders—no balls, no riding, no journeys to Paris; but early nights, and the last four months to be spent mostly in bed. She found life wearisome, was frightened, and deeply depressed. Here is the Duchesse du Lude, writing to Duchess Anne. 'For the past three days, Madame, we have been much alarmed by the condition of Mme la Duchesse de Bourgogne. She has been in pain, and has retired to bed. They find that the baby has turned and is very low; but they say that this is not a bad thing. She greatly fears giving birth, it causes her to have the vapours and puts her into a pitiable state. You may well believe, Madame, that I also deserve pity for having to see her in such dread of labour. The baby moves and is strong and, judging by her feeling him so often and so vigorously, is in good health.' This baby, Adelaide's eldest son, was born on Wednesday, 25 July 1704, after causing his mother three hours of agonising pain. The King stood at her bedside throughout her labour, and Mme de Maintenon was by her pillow. Louis, overcome by emotion, and too agitated to stay with her, awaited the news in his study. Monseigneur and other members of the royal family stood in a distant corner of the bedroom.

When all was over, the new heir, immediately given the title of Duc de Bretagne, was received by the royal governess, the old Maréchale de La Mothe, kneeling. The ribbon of the Order of the Saint-Esprit was placed round his neck, and he was taken by her to be kissed by his father, who then once more retired to the chapel where, alone and incognito, he had spent most of the previous night in prayer. The arrival of this precious baby, the King's great-grandson and heir, was an enormous joy to Louis XIV, who saw his line secured down to the third generation. The Court and Paris went wild in their demonstrations of loyalty and rejoicing. The King gave a magnificent fête at Marly, and himself chose presents to be sent to Adelaide at Versailles, where she was still convalescent and confined to her apartments. The offerings took the form of tributes from all twelve of the guest-pavilions. From the first came Flora, in person, bearing flowers and verses; Pomona and Cupid, dispatched from the second and third, brought baskets of fruit and sweetmeats, with liqueurs and ices of every imaginable colour and delicious flavour. From the fourth and fifth came other goddesses laden with ribbons and scarves, and all manner of beautiful fans, studded with rubies, diamonds and emeralds.

The sixth pavilion sent a spinning wheel and a Chinese lacquer table with two hundred pounds' worth of silk upon it, ready for spinning because she loved to spin. From the seventh came curiosities from India; from the ninth a telescope to view the stars; from the tenth, an extremely lovely dinner service, wrought in silver; from the eleventh a similar one fashioned in gold, and from the twelfth a richly framed portrait of Adelaide herself with the baby in her lap.

Madame, who sent this description of the presents to her aunt the electress, was temporarily out of favour. She said that with so many festivities in progress around her, she felt as though she were in Limbo, hearing the sound of rejoicing in Heaven, yet not allowed to participate.

'Yet,' says Saint-Simon, 'there was every opportunity to repent of so much money ill-spent in rejoicings, considering the straits that we were then in, and that the pretext for them lasted less than a year.'[1] The birth of Adelaide's son did indeed herald a whole chain of disasters; two months later came the catastrophic defeat of the French army, at Blenheim, to be followed by Ramillies, Oudenarde, and Malplaquet.

In her letters to her family, Adelaide never mentioned the defeats; she loyally followed the King's policy of presenting to the world the continued splendours and pleasures of Versailles, and his refusal to allow that any trouble or adversity existed for France. She was, in any event, writing very few letters, except to Marie Louise, and the first mention of her little son seems to have been on 2 September.

'I am ashamed, dear grandmother,[2] at having been so long without writing, but there were many hindrances . . . I cannot refrain

---

[1] The precious baby did not long survive. It died suddenly in convulsions, on 12 April 1705.

[2] Adelaide had ceased to write 'dear grandmamma', 'dear Mamma'. She had explained to her mother that such familiarity did not suit her rank.

from telling you of my son, who is in excellent health. He would not be ill-looking if he did not have jaundice; but I hope that when we return from Fontainebleau he will have recovered.'

Six months later, she wrote again, wishing that her grandmother could see him, because she would be pleased with him; but she gave no details. Adelaide herself saw very little of the baby, brought up, as he was, in his own establishment, at the other end of the palace. It was the custom to separate royal mothers from their babies, on the principle that their children belonged to France and not to them, and that it would not do for there to be too much fondness between them. It had been very different in Adelaide's babyhood, in Savoy, where Duchess Anne had herself supervised the children's nurseries in her own home. However, in spite of everything, Adelaide did love him, and when he died the following spring, she was prostrated with grief, and confined to her bed until the beginning of August. A fortnight after the tragedy, she wrote to Madame Royale, ' I can wait no longer, dear grandmother, to seek comfort from you in my misfortune. I am sure that you feel for me, for I know the love which you have always borne me. If one did not take all the ills of this life as being sent by God, I do not know what would become of one. I think He means to draw me to Him by wearing me down with sorrows of every kind. My health has greatly suffered; but that is the least of them . . . I have received one letter from you, dear grandmother, which has given me much comfort. These tokens of your love are a great consolation, of which I have much need in my present condition.'

Louis also was grieved and disappointed. In a letter to his brother King Philip, dated 26 April 1704, he expressed his sorrow; comforting himself with pious reflections and faith in the perfect life that was to come. 'It was to have been hoped, dear brother, not only for myself but for the State, that this misfortune would not have happened, but we must blindly submit to the will of God. God knows better than we do what is best for us. Life and death are in his hands, and He has placed my son where I ardently desire, one day, to be . . . I am surely right in so believing, as I reflect upon my son's happiness in reaching Heaven without having encountered the fearful dangers by which we are surrounded.'

It was a very long letter; but he did not mention Adelaide. A few days later, he wrote again, giving news of her, and of a new medicine which the doctors had prescribed. 'I think they will soon repeat the dose, and then give her a bath, after which she will be drinking the waters of Forges,[1] so as to dispose her to repair as speedily as possible the loss which we have suffered.' But nature or Adelaide decided otherwise, and the loss was not made up until 1707, when the second Duc de Bretagne was born;[2] but he made his appearance at a time so disastrous for France that the King forbade all public rejoicings.

From this time onwards, Adelaide's health began to deteriorate. She mentioned it every time she wrote to her mother or grand-mother, and plainly showed that she was worried about it. 'God be thanked, I am at last free of the toothache, dear mother, after having suffered from a swollen face for the past week, and a slight fever each evening. It has been too cold for them to do anything about it; for which I am profoundly thankful, since they were set on bleeding me, with the assurance that if they did not do so, my tooth-ache would continue. Yet I am now quite free of it, without having been bled and, provided it does not return, I am well content.'[3]

Louis, who, at such a time, might have been expected to comfort her, or, at least, to be showing her his gentler, more attractive side, was at his least amiable. The anonymous writer of *Les Nouveaux Caractères de la Famille Royale* describes him as solemn, gloomy, atrabilious, with a violent temper often displayed at the wrong moment. Sunk in a piety which even Mme de Maintenon described as uncouth, he took less and less share in the activities of the Court, and infuriated the King with his sanctimonious disapproval. He also displayed an 'angry passion' for his wife, making himself 'a nuisance to everyone, and perhaps to her also'.

Everyone, even including the pious Duc de Beauvilliers, was worried about him, and Fénelon, from Cambrai, sent a letter, possibly intending it to be shown to him at a suitable moment. It was full of wise advice, urging Louis to relax the outward displays of piety, to which he was so much addicted and, above all, to be gentler and kinder to his wife. 'I believe,' he wrote, 'that M. le Duc de

---

[1] Forges-les-Eaux was a spa, in Normandy, much patronised by the nobility for the tonic effect of the waters.

[2] Born 8 January 1707, he died in 1712. A third son, entitled the Duc d'Anjou, was born 15 February 1710, and lived to become Louis XV.

[3] Although Adelaide wrote more often to her grandmother than to Duchess Anne, it must not be thought that she did not dearly love her mother. In a letter of this period, she says, 'Forgive me, dearest mother, that I write so badly, but I am always in a hurry. You must believe that I would far rather write to you, and amuse you for a while. Farewell, dearest mother, I kiss you with all my heart, dear mother, with all my heart'.

Bourgogne should not oppose Mme la Duchesse de Bourgogne. He should let her doctors decide in what manner she should observe Lent ... If he wishes to inspire her with a love for religion, he should make it appear sweet and gentle and, avoiding all that is irksome, allow her to realise for herself the value and pleasantness of virtue, simple and unadorned. In all the things that do not entail serious moral laxity, he should appear cheerful and easy. In short, he should comply with her wishes and be patient.'

Had Louis accepted Fénelon's advice he might have been a great deal happier; but it had no effect on him. In the disastrous years of the Duke of Marlborough's succession of victories over the French armies—Blenheim in 1704, Ramillies in 1706—he made a show of abstaining from all the Court amusements, shutting himself up for entire days in his study, closeted with his confessor or, in solitude, reading physics and astronomy, to the great distress of his well-wishers. It irked him that, after his two good campaigns, the King should leave him without a command. He felt ashamed to see other young men go to the war while he was left without employment, and thus, in his rare descents upon the courtiers, he looked black as thunder and most disdainfully superior.

It is something of a mystery why the King, who had given Louis high praise for the reputation he had won in the earlier campaigns, should have let him stay at home, unoccupied. It may be that Louis's excessive piety, and his attempt to run an army like a monastery, was having a bad effect on the troops,[1] or that the King wished him to increase the size of his family before again absenting himself. However that may have been, the result was that Louis, bored, humiliated, obsessed by religious practices and the finer points of Church discipline, made himself thoroughly unpopular with the courtiers, nagged at Adelaide who could do nothing to please him, and angered the King by his discouragement of every attempt to maintain the glories and pleasures of Versailles.

The Court, to all appearances, and by the King's command, was as magnificently festive as ever, in 1704, and Adelaide was at the very centre of its brilliance. That was her public face, for, as Mme de Maintenon wrote to the Dames of Saint-Cyr, 'She is more distressed about the war than is fitting for someone of her age'.[2] In

---

[1] The punishment for desertion in the face of the enemy was a great deal less severe than for looting in order to break a fast.

[2] Adelaide was eighteen years old throughout nearly all of 1704. Although born in 1695, her birthday came at the extreme end of the year, on 5 December.

another letter she called Adelaide 'very serious-minded', an adjective one could scarcely imagine being applied to the frivolous little princess of former years. She understood and loyally supported the King in his determination to keep untarnished the image of Versailles, yet, according to Mlle d'Aumale, her considerable intelligence made her 'conscious, as the King was not, that the time for feasting was past'. In private, she let her heart speak. 'I recollect,' continued Mlle d'Aumale, 'that on the day after the arrival of the Maréchal de Villeroy's courier,[1] someone proposed a card-party, to which Mme la Duchesse de Bourgogne answered very sharply, "With whom would you wish me to play? With ladies who may have lost their husbands and fathers, perhaps even their sons in the battle? What are you thinking of? How can I be indifferent when the whole country suffers?" '

It was this capacity for sympathy that made Adelaide so much loved by those who knew her best. She was so different in her freshness and simplicity from the other royal princesses, who thought of themselves as set apart and above the rest of humanity— from Madame, for example, who remembered her rank even on her deathbed, saying to a lady who bent to kiss her hand, 'You may kiss me on the cheek now. Where I go, all will be equal'. Madame, incidentally, disapproved strongly of Adelaide's sociability, complaining that when she went walking, she would have a lady on one arm, and others abreast of her, instead of making them walk in a respectable manner, three paces behind. Saint-Simon mentions that although Adelaide gave her love too readily, and retracted it just as soon, she was so kind hearted that she could not bear to cause people the smallest hurt.' He also said that they loved her because of her loyalty, for she never betrayed secrets or made mischief. 'In that,' he added, 'she was like a deep well, truly protecting the interests of others.' Her charm was clearly very great; her sweet smile and friendly ways won her the loyalty of by far the greater number of the courtiers. She was indeed fortunate in that respect for, when she was free of the guardianship of Mme de Maintenon, she chose her intimates badly, 'more for their looks than their characters', and let them lead her into excesses that, had

---

[1] Bringing the news of the defeat at Blenheim, where the Maréchal de Tallard's entire army was either killed or captured. There was no list of casualties, the Court was left for six whole days, knowing that a battle had been lost, but ignorant of all the details.

it not been for the conspiracy of silence, would have brought her into serious trouble.

She had, at this time, much need of their loyalty and protection. When Louis was serving with the army, in 1703, and receiving no letters from her, her roving eye (as Tessé called it) had settled upon a young nobleman whom she was used to seeing at their court. This was the Marquis de Nangis, just twenty-one, and a newly promoted brigadier of infantry. Even the carping Saint-Simon, who thought him a great bore in later years when he became a Marshal, grew lyrical about him in his youth—'the flower of the flock, trained in courtship by his mother and grandmother who were past-mistresses in the art, moving in the highest Society, and a favourite of the most sought-after ladies, winning them by a discretion that was far beyond his years'.

Nangis was evidently an Adonis, with a handsome face; a perfect figure, and a reputation for gallantry in the campaigns of 1701 and 1702, which his female admirers at the Court had vastly magnified. He was serving in Flanders in 1703, and returned several times on leave, the distance not being very great. In June, just at the time when Louis took over the command, Nangis had fallen ill, and had returned to the Court for a long convalescence, and it was then that a romance developed, which may have been one of the reasons for the long silence that caused Louis so much suffering.

It would appear that the first approaches came from Adelaide, probably no more than languishing glances, and that Nangis, moved and flattered, was not slow to respond. At the same time, it was hideously embarrassing for him since he was not heart-free, being deep in a love affair with Mme de La Vrillière[1]—as pretty and as amorous as Cupid himself; but not the kind to endure a rival, not even one of Adelaide's lofty rank.

Nangis was, in very truth, on the horns of a dilemma, for on the one hand he loved his mistress, but feared an outburst of fury that would ruin them both; on the other hand, to show reluctance towards a princess as powerful as Adelaide would ruin him just as surely.

The outsider who saw most of what was happening was the Duc de Saint-Simon. He was fascinated; buzzing in and out of the houses of great ladies who thought they knew everything, gossiping with Adelaide's household who, so he said, trusted him and 'told him all', and sitting up late every night discussing the latest moves

[1] Mme de La Vrillière was Mme de Mailly's daughter.

and their portents with his wife who was Adelaide's friend. His memoirs are, in fact, the only source of information, since other memoirists and letter-writers kept an almost impenetrable silence, either from loyalty to Adelaide, or from fear of becoming involved. Indeed, so carefully did the courtiers (including Saint-Simon) guard the secret that, incredible to relate, no word of the affair reached the King's ears, moreover, Louis never to his dying day, so much as suspected that his wife's eye had ever strayed from the narrow path of marital fidelity.

At first only the ladies of Adelaide's intimate circle were aware of a budding romance; but she soon betrayed herself by blushing scarlet whenever her eye lit on Nangis. 'I have heard my late mother declare,' said Mme de Louvigny,[1] 'that her household first suspected her partiality for M. de Nangis because she reddened whenever he appeared, and they so well understood the danger of that show of impropriety that they made it their business to see that she did not have cause to blush too often. They kept watch over her.'

This state of affairs lasted a longish time, with Mme de La Vrillière occasionally indulging in shameless fits of jealousy, and the princess showing her distinct coldness which, Saint-Simon says, 'provided a most remarkable and fascinating spectacle'. At length, either because Nangis appeared to need rousing, or because fate so decreed, a rival presented himself, in the shape of the young Marquis de Maulévrier, married to Tessé's daughter, only a few years older than Nangis and, like him, a brigadier in the King's army, highly distinguished for his valour. That, however, was the only likeness between them, for Maulévrier had none of Nangis's elegance and charm. He was the very opposite of handsome, being altogether coarse and vulgar-looking, with a far from pleasing expression. On the other hand, he was a much cleverer man, and had more spirit. He was also ambitious and scheming, with a lack of self-control that brought him at times perilously near to madness. His wife was pretty and silly and, although looking as if butter would not melt in her mouth, spiteful to the last degree. Her position as a member of the princess's household, and his own as the son-in-law of Tessé, made it easy for Maulévrier to approach Adelaide,

[1] Mme de Louvigny (1703–1765) was of the Order of Saint-Louis, at Saint-Cyr, and her mother had also been one of the dames. She also said, according to the Maréchal de Noailles, that Nangis often went to the Ménagerie with the Duchesse de Bourgogne, to make cheese and indulge in day-dreaming'. 'No other evidence mentions this.

and very soon he fell, or pretended to fall, in love. He risked a love-letter, by the hand of Mme Quentin who may or may not have been led to believe that it came from Tessé. Adelaide was rash enough to reply, also under cover of Tessé's name. 'So much was known to her household,' says Saint-Simon, 'I shall not add how much else was believed.'

What people believed, and what reason they had for suspecting the worst, is impossible to know. Was Adelaide simply flirting? or was she caught in a trap of her own setting? And did her heart, awakened by Nangis, fall also to Maulévrier? It seems unlikely that she fell in love with both at the same moment, and the young men watched each other jealously. In any event, Adelaide was so closely guarded, not only by her ladies (who might conceivably have abetted her) but by the Swiss guard, who day and night perambulated the gardens of Versailles and Marly, and reported all movements to the King in person. The general opinion among the courtiers was that the affairs went no further than strolls in the more lonely parts of the garden and surreptitious letter-writing.

So little has come to light of Adelaide's affair with Nangis that one can still only guess how far it went. Mme de Caylus, who watched every move and reported it to Mme de Maintenon, did not think that it went very far. 'Let us believe in flightiness and indiscretion, rather than in wrong-doing, of which there is no proof, and of which one would like to think her innocent'. One thing only is certain, that somewhere between 1703 and 1706, Adelaide fell in love, or nearly in love, or at least felt the prick of Cupid's darts.

One person who knew the situation and the danger which Adelaide was courting was Mme de Maintenon who, at length decided to intervene. When the time came for Maulévrier to return to the army, Adelaide openly paid several calls on his wife, to condole on his departure. On one or two such occasions Mme de Maintenon accompanied her, and it was noticed that on their return the princess's eyes were red, which caused much laughing speculation as to whether her tears were not for Nangis. However that may have been, the visits aroused in him such jealousy that Mme de La Vrillière's temper rose to boiling point.

Mme de Maintenon thereupon decided that the time had come to make an end. One day when they were alone, and Adelaide was playing her favourite game of ferreting among the papers on her writing-table, she asked her more seriously than usual to leave her letters alone. Adelaide laughed and paid no heed, until her eye was caught by a folded letter with her own name on it, and the signature of Mme d'Espinay[1]—ill-disposed towards her, and one of the members of the Meudon cabal. Reading the very first line made Adelaide blush and falter, which appeared not to displease Mme de Maintenon. 'What have you discovered, pet?' she said. 'What is the matter?' And when Adelaide did not answer she rose and came to stand beside her, and was shown the signature. 'Well!' said she, 'so I have a letter from Mme d'Espinay! When people are inquisitive they sometimes learn more than they bargain for.' Then in an altogether graver tone, 'Read the whole letter, Madame, and if you are wise, profit by it,' and she compelled Adelaide to read therein an account of her life in the past four or five days, word by word, place by place, hour by hour, as accurate and as detailed as though the writer, who was seldom in her company, had never let her out of her sight.

There was much of Nangis in the letter, and descriptions of intrigue and imprudence, which made Adelaide feel quite faint and suffused her face with blushes. Mme de Maintenon then gave her a severe talking-to, pointing out that all her doings were known at the Court, and warning her of the possible consequences. 'No doubt,' said Saint-Simon, 'that she added much more, impressing upon the princess that she spoke with full knowledge, and was employing Mme d'Espinay and others to deliver frequent and detailed reports.' Adelaide beat a hasty retreat to her privy, calling, in an outburst of tears and rage, for Mme de Nogaret, her 'nanny', her 'well of silence'. Mme de Nogaret listened patiently and gave such advice as she deemed beneficial, warning, more especially, that to show any less amiability towards Mme d'Espinay would mean certain disaster. It was a hard lesson, but Adelaide, who loved and trusted Mme de Nogaret (as well she might), put it so well into practice that no one ever suspected her enlightenment.

During all this time, Maulévrier, driven mad by love or ambition, had been devising a plan for holding private conversations with Adelaide. According to Saint-Simon, he pretended, for more than a year, to lose his voice, so as to approach her closely and whisper in her ear, without arousing suspicion. Sometimes, to his ordinary remarks, she replied out loud, but to others, she gave short answers,

[1] Elisabeth de Lorraine-Lillebonne, Princesse d'Espinay (1664–1748). It is noteworthy that Mme de Maintenon did not trust any of the ladies in Adelaide's circle to report unfavourably on her. When she wanted a spy, Mme de Maintenon used this hard, cold, discreet person, who was Adelaide's enemy.

which no one but he could hear. The truth is that Maulévrier was really very ill with tuberculosis, but was using his illness to make a pretext for intimacy, and the result was that, throughout the whole of 1704, Adelaide found herself the object of a dangerous dispute between him and Nangis. There was, indeed, nearly a tragedy, when Maulévrier mistook Mme de La Vrillière's fury as clear evidence of Nangis's success, and thus, between rage and jealousy, was driven to the point of madness.

One day, after mass, he offered Adelaide his hand, to lead her back to her apartments, and took the occasion to abuse Nangis, threatening to report him to the King, and almost crushing her fingers in his anger. Then, to make matters worse, he began to attack Nangis publicly, claiming that he had been insulted, and demanding satisfaction. One may imagine Adelaide's terror, the effect upon Mme de La Vrillière and her temper, and, above all, the agony of Nangis. He managed not to panic or quarrel with Maulévrier; but he saw his whole future at the mercy of a raving lunatic, and resolved to say nothing and to appear as rarely as possible at the Court.

For six long weeks, Adelaide lived in terror; but nothing more happened. Someone informed Tessé, who persuaded his son-in-law to follow him to Spain, promising him advancement as well as astronomical rewards. He also enlisted the help of Fagon, who gave it as his professional opinion that, if Maulévrier did not seek a warmer climate for his lost voice, the approaching winter would certainly kill him. Such was the story that was given out, and Tessé made all possible speed to remove his son-in-law from the Court and the country, to avoid awkward questions about so ill a man being fit to travel. This occured in the autumn of 1705.

Louis, who had been at Versailles all this time, had noticed nothing. On 6 November 1704, he wrote to King Philip, highly recommending Maulévrier: 'I have promised to give him a letter for you, when he goes to join the Maréchal de Tessé. It will greatly please me if you will treat him kindly, and give him tokens of your esteem, if, as I do not doubt, he comes to deserve them . . . He goes to Spain to avoid idleness, and to do as much as his health will allow. I believe that the little I have said, telling you of my good will, and the interest I take in him, will be sufficient recommendation. He is particularly devoted to my service, as is his wife to that of Mme la Duchesse de Bourgogne.'

Thus Maulévrier, when he reached Madrid, was greeted with

open arms, and behaved there with just as little consideration. He won the confidence of the King and Queen, and was received as a friend; but he abused their trust, by falling, or pretending to fall, as much in love with the queen as he had with Adelaide. Mme de Caylus regarded him as mad, and believed that he truly cared for neither. She says that he wrote to the queen, and that she sent him answers rolled up inside dice-cubes. By the following May he had outstayed his welcome, and Tessé was obliged to ask for his recall, using once more the pretext of his delicate health, for which the Spanish summer would be too hot.

Maulévrier, bearing a letter from the King of Spain, highly praising his courage at the siege of Gibraltar, made a round-about journey home, arriving at Versailles only in the autumn of 1705. He had much to report of the Spanish Court and of Mme des Ursins, and was therefore closeted alone with Mme de Maintenon for tête-à-tête conversations, some of them lasting three hours. His private audiences with the King and Queen of Spain gave him an excuse for being alone with Louis and Adelaide, each separately, and on those occasions Saint-Simon says that Adelaide indulged him, and that he claimed all from her. Yet he found the situation entirely changed, for a new rival, the Abbé, later Cardinal, Melchior de Polignac, had appeared. He was forty-four years old, extremely handsome, the member of an ancient and noble family, whose descent, so they said, could be traced to the god Apollo—hence the name. Saint-Simon despised him, referring to him as 'that most obsequious and servile of courtiers', whose famous remark, 'Sire, the rain at Marly is never wet!' (when told to put his hat on, during a shower), he repeats with loathing no less than eight times in his memoirs.

Yet not even Saint-Simon could deny Polignac his qualities: 'a tall man, very well-built, a beautiful countenance, witty and gracious, and with especially seductive manners. Learned in every subject, he was manly, original, persuasive, loving to set the most obscure ideas within the range of ordinary minds.'

He seems to have been an attractive and sought-after figure at the Court, a friend even of Louis, who had a curious propensity for liking Adelaide's admirers. (On the other hand, he may have felt especially drawn to Polignac, who could converse with him on physics and astronomy, and the other topics that so much interested him). As for Adelaide, who met him constantly in her husband's drawing-room, how could she resist this charmer, of whom Mme de Sévigné had said, 'He is the most agreeable man in the world. He knows everything, will talk on any subject, and has all the gentleness, brilliance, and tact that is most admirable in conversation'. Far above Nangis or Maulévrier in intellect, he talked seriously to her as Louis never did, and she was clever enough to respond, and to delight in his company. Despite the twenty-six-year difference in their ages she became entirely captivated.

'Polignac's ambition was aroused,' says Saint-Simon. 'He sought an attachment, and established one. Soon he was braving the Swiss, on fine nights, in the gardens, at Marly.[1] Nangis's star grew dim; as for Maulévrier, though he had been out of the running since his return, he once again seethed with rage.'

'Out of the running' Maulévrier might be, but rejection he could not endure, and he was further infuriated by his wife's making advances to Nangis, who responded to them in order to hide his real love for Adelaide. This was too much for Maulévrier, who dreaded his wife's malice, and was torn between violently conflicting emotions and the ravages of his illness. In the end, he went mad. He gave vent to outbursts of most dangerous abuse, was seldom seen at the Court, and lived mostly in Paris. There he took to walking alone at night, behind the Carthusian monastery, in the Rue de Vaugirard, whistling from time to time. Occasionally, a royal footman was seen to emerge from a dark corner, to give him a letter, or letters were thrown from an upper window; and, once, he was seen to stop by a milestone to pick up a box, which was afterwards found to contain papers.[2] Before long he was showing such clear signs of madness that he was confined to his house; his wife and several devoted friends kept watch over him, but, at about eight o'clock on the morning of Good Friday, 1706, he eluded them, and throwing himself from an upper window died on the cobblestones below.

Adelaide was given the news at Tenebrae, in the presence of the King and all the Court. She outwardly controlled herself; but, in private, she wept most bitterly, and for three days her eyes were red. She nonetheless attempted to recover her letters, and Mme Quentin with a deputation of her ladies visited Mme de Maulévrier. It

[1] Dangeau says, however, that the Abbé de Polignac was not invited to Marly before 1710. He would therefore have had to climb over the wall, at night, a dangerous proceeding for a man of his age, and especially for one in Holy orders.

[2] He wrote letters both to Mme de Maintenon and to Adelaide, but to the latter always under cover of Mme Quentin's name. Saint-Simon was shown several such letters, one from Mme Quentin, seeking to pacify him.

seems that they were not well received, and that the letters were not returned, for never afterwards was she on good terms with Adelaide. These visits were given out to be ones of condolence; but no one believed it. For several days thereafter, Adelaide appeared distressed, while Mme de Maintenon looked cross and nervous, quite unlike her usual self. They were closeted together for long sessions, after which the princess emerged in tears. Thus it was strongly suspected that Mme de Maintenon had learned a great deal more than she had known earlier, and it was even rumoured that Maulévrier had revenged himself by giving her certain indiscreet letters. Meanwhile Louis, feeling anxious about his wife's evident unhappiness, 'seemed on the verge of learning more than would have been good for him. But they say that love is blind, and he was ready enough to accept the explanations offered. Eventually the gossip ceased, or at least diminished, and Adelaide gradually became more cheerful.'

Her determination to keep her spirits high was made all the harder by one of the consequences of Maulévrier's death, the disappearance of Polignac. His great friend Torcy, the minister for the posts, becoming alarmed by his growing reputation for gallantry, had gained for him an appointment as auditor of the Rota, attached to the papal court. Polignac, who chose to regard this promotion as dishonourable exile, delayed his departure as long as possible, until, in October 1706, he was compelled to go. It was remarked that when Adelaide wished him goodbye she did so in a manner very different from her usual, and few believed in the headache that kept her all that day extended upon a couch in Mme de Maintenon's room with the windows tightly closed, and bitter tears when evening came. This, incidentally, was the first occasion that public opinion turned against her. Madame, walking in the gardens a few days later, found two verses as rude as they were apposite, scrawled upon a balustrade and some pediments, and she was neither discreet nor kindly enough to hold her tongue. But Adelaide was much loved, and the verses had little effect because people everywhere united to suppress them.

So ended, in a flood of tears, the series of love affairs (or perhaps only tender attachments) to which Adelaide had very imprudently abandoned herself. For Nangis, all ended happily. He recovered his health, returned to the army, and continued to distinguish himself in every campaign. At the Court, he remained popular and highly esteemed; but never again was he in any way involved with the princess. As for Adelaide, Maulévrier's suicide and Polignac's departure brought her abruptly to maturity. As she herself had realised, her carefree youth had passed; the years that followed proved a time in which her grown-up character was to be tested.

14

Calamity at Oudenarde

IT IS hard to imagine why Louis XIV should have kept Louis unemployed in the four years between 1703 and 1708. It may be that he had been disillusioned by his grandson's headlong return before the end of his last campaign; he may have perceived that, while Louis enjoyed soldiering, he took little interest in strategy, and did not wish him to lose the good reputation won in the earlier campaigns. Perhaps he hoped that time would cure Louis's weaknesses, especially the indecision, lack of initiative, and unwillingness to take risks, for which he had been criticised. It may also have been that, since the war had gone very badly for France in the intervening years, he wished to spare his grandson the ignominy of defeats which he dould do nothing to prevent.

If the year 1704 had been rendered disastrous by the defeat at Blenheim, 1706 had seen the humiliation of Villeroy's defeat at Ramillies. In Spain, Tessé had failed to take Barcelona from the Austrians, and Philip V, hard pressed by the Archduke Charles, had been forced to abandon his capital, and for a time appeared in grave danger of losing his throne. In Piedmont alone there had been a victory, when Vendôme defeated Victor Amadeus, at Calcinato; but, after Vendôme's recall to Flanders, the siege of Turin had ended in disaster, and the French army was temporarily driven out of Italy.

1707 began badly enough, for Victor Amadeus actually invaded the south of France, in the direction of Nice, and laid siege to Toulon. The French general opposing him was Tessé, better by far in diplomacy than in war, and with a reputation severely shaken by his failure at Barcelona. In France, the cost of the war, with entire armies destroyed, and defeats in almost every campaign, was exhausting the country's resources, and bringing about a financial crisis. In spite of the King's determination to let nothing dim the glory of Versailles, some economies appeared necessary. He did not cancel the balls at Marly, but when Adelaide's second baby arrived, on 8 January, he forbade 'the excessive sums spent in rejoicings for the birth of the first Duc de Bretagne'. He also directed the masters of the horse and the wardrobe to curtail all unnecessary expense, and gave similar orders to Mansart, for the works and buildings. His chief economy was to dock completely the New Year presents to his family and the royal princes. Although, in the last few years, they had already been considerably reduced, they had cost the treasury the enormous sum of thirty-five thousand gold louis. The blow fell hardest upon Mme de Montespan who, ever since her retirement, had been used to receiving twelve thousand gold louis annually; but, unlike the others, she had appeared quite unruffled, merely saying that she minded only for the poor 'and indeed,' says Saint-Simon, 'she was accustomed to giving alms very lavishly'.

In the spring and summer the news was better. Berwick, at Almanga, won a great victory, which restored the position of King Philip. On the Italian frontier, Victor Amadeus's army was in full retreat. It had been much weakened by disease and desertions, and after a battle lost to Tessé, outside Toulon, the duke had decided to raise the siege and return home. One reason for his army's discouragement was said to have been the news of Louis XIV's decision to send the Duc de Bourgogne to command on that front. The prince's conduct in the 1703 campaign had won him a reputation with the Piedmontese, and the appointment certainly had a disheartening effect on them; but contemporary historians may have exaggerated in saying that the thought of his coming 'struck terror into the army of the Duke of Savoy'.

It was 13 August when the King had announced, after his supper, that the Duc de Bourgogne would take command of the army 'now assembling to drive the Duke of Savoy out of Provence', and that the Duc de Berry would accompany him, but without a command. It was said that people were astounded by the news, for it appeared exceedingly strange to send a prince to fight his own father-in-law; but, although the courtiers might sympathise with his embarrassment, Louis himself felt none. He was not at all disturbed by Vendôme's victory; indeed, had written to him during his triumphal march to Turin, 'You are presented with a brutal task. I hope and believe that my father-in-law will listen to reason, and that you will not need to be harsh . . . You will contrive, Monsieur, to show him that his best course is to trust the King, who wishes only to be sure of him, and not at all to injure him. I have long expected what is now happening.' Adelaide, on the other hand, was deeply distressed, horrified at the thought of her husband and her father meeting in battle and preparing to kill or maim one another. She wept a great deal, but said little, for Louis only laughed. Mercifully for her, she did not have to bear that trouble long, for the news of her father's retreat came only a few days after Louis's appointment, and there was thus no need for his departure. He was disappointed, but having offered him a command in 1707 the King was morally bound to use him in the following year, and he could at last see the end of his idle, boring life at the Court.

Meanwhile, good news brought an excuse for festivities. The King gave a magnificent party for Twelfth Night, four tables, richly set for sixteen and seventeen guests, with a Twelfth-cake on each. Adelaide was at the King's table, and Louis took the head of another. It was all very merry; they cheered loudly, whenever the Bean-Queens drank,[1] and were especially hearty at the Duc de Berry's table. The ball that followed lasted until half-past three in the morning, and was the first of many—at least ten at Versailles, and several at Marly, not to mention Monseigneur's supper-parties at Meudon, before taking Adelaide to the opera in Paris, and the private theatricals got up by the Duchesse du Maine at Clagny.

Blenheim, Ramillies, and Turin were all forgotten. The general feeling was that the coming year would see the end of France's troubles. As Saint-Simon said, 'The year 1708 opened with rejoicing, festivities and parties of pleasure,' but he sadly added, 'It did not long continue in that way'. Yet the spring began cheerfully enough with preparations for the new campaigns. There was the usual shuffling of commanders; Villars, much to his annoyance, was moved from the Rhine army to replace Tessé in Dauphiné. (It was something of a disgrace, for rumour had it that he had too freely interpreted the King's invitation to 'fatten his calves'.) Berwick took over on the Rhine, and the Duc d'Orléans received the army in Spain as his first command. Vendôme remained in Flanders. He had held the line, and although he had not won an important victory, he had obeyed the King's orders to husband his resources and prepare his army for the decisive battle expected in the coming season.

Throughout the winter, the Court buzzed with rumours that the

---

[1] Each twelfth-cake had a bean, or a little china figure, hidden in it, and the one to whom it fell became King or Queen of the table.

Duc de Bourgogne would take nominal command of the Flanders army, but the official announcement was not made until 30 April. On the afternoon of the 30th, says Sourches, when the King returned from stag-hunting, he went to the Duchesse de Bourgogne's apartment, to inform her that her husband would be leaving on 14 May, accompanied by his brother the Duc de Berry, to command in Flanders, where he would have the Duc de Vendôme to assist him; and Dangeau noted that the two princes were extraordinarily pleased by the King's decision. 'You will readily understand how glad I feel,' wrote Louis to King Philip. 'My brother de Berry is as pleased as I am; but the King has forbidden him to show anything, and he controls himself astonishingly well. It is a great pleasure, after a lapse of four whole years, to be in some sort returned to the service, and not to have to stay idle at Versailles, Marly, and Fontainebleau.'

The prospect of leaving the Court may have come at an especially good time for Louis, and helped to console him for a disappointment when, earlier that year, Adelaide had aroused the King's anger by suffering a miscarriage. It was by no means the first mishap, nor would it be the last; but it was thought to have been caused by heedlessness and neglect of her duty. There had been a scene with the King. To modern ears, perhaps, it does not sound so very terrible—more bark than bite, in fact; but Saint-Simon makes of it one of his best stories, blowing the whole incident up into a drama of such shocking proportions and significance that it cannot be ignored.

This, according to Saint-Simon, is what happened. On the Saturday after Easter, the King was at Marly, feeding his carp in the fishpond, after mass. He was in a bad temper, there having been efforts to dissuade him from this excursion, on account of Adelaide's being pregnant and unfit to travel; and objections, though he seldom heeded them, always put him in a bad temper. The Duchesse du Lude suddenly appeared, hurrying towards the group of courtiers, and the King went forward to speak with her privately. It was not for long; the duchess returned to the château, and the King to the carp, without uttering a word. Everyone guessed what had happened, but no one dared to speak. At last the King turned round and, addressing no one in particular, said angrily, 'The Duchesse de Bourgogne has miscarried'—no more. There were exclamations from some, from others, a repetition of his words, and M. de La Rochefoucauld said out loud that it was a thousand pities, for this was not the first time, and she might well bear no more children. 'And what do I care?' angrily exclaimed the King. 'She has one son already, has she not? And if he should die, is not the Duc de Berry of age to marry and have children? Why should I care who succeeds me, are they not all my grandchildren?' Then, in a burst of impatient rage, 'Thank God she has miscarried, since it was bound to happen. Now, perhaps, my excursions and all the other things I want to do will not be obstructed by doctors and midwives. At last I shall be able to come and go as I please, and they will leave me in peace.' Saint-Simon says that 'a silence during which you might have heard an ant walking' followed this explosion. People scarcely dared to breathe, and even the workmen and gardeners stood still.

After a good quarter of an hour, the King leaned over the balustrade and began speaking of one of the carp. None of the courtiers replied, and thereafter he addressed his remarks to the gardeners, to whom he did not ordinarily speak. Soon after that, he departed, but it was not until he was out of earshot that the courtiers looked at one another and were, for a moment, united in feeling both shocked and sorry. Then they shrugged their shoulders. Saint-Simon carefully noted their individual reactions, congratulating himself, meanwhile, 'for having long known that the King loved and considered only himself, and was the prime object of his own existence'. One might imagine that Louis XIV's colossal selfishness was by this time known to all. (He had been used to his mistresses accompanying him on journeys, whether ill, pregnant, indisposed, or just risen from childbed.) As Mme de Maintenon said, 'He had been King for forty years, and during all that time, no one had dared to contradict or oppose him, or done otherwise than pander to his smallest whims. It should also be said that he had sacrificed his pleasures more for Adelaide than for any other, and that she had been exasperating and inconsiderate enough to try any man's temper. The old King loved her; she cheered and amused him; he could not bear to be without her; yet time and again (by her own neglect, it was supposed) she suffered miscarriages that kept her away from him for weeks on end, either in bed, or confined to her rooms. It was her duty to produce living children, no matter what the cost, so as to fortify the succession, a debt she owed France in exchange for rank and privilege; but it was Mme de Maintenon's conviction that, having presented her husband with an heir, she was unwilling to gratify him further, and the old lady wrote to Mme des Ursins, 'Mme la Duchesse de Bourgogne does not sufficiently understand her true interests'.

Certainly the King had shown very little concern for her; but Louis was not much better, for, a few days afterwards, he wrote to Philip V: 'My joy [at having a command] would have been perfect, had it not been for a mishap to Mme la Duchesse de Bourgogne, whom too much walking has caused to miscarry at six weeks, almost before we knew that she was pregnant. We comfort ourselves with the hope that it will not be long before she becomes so again, and that they will then look after her better.'

It is noteworthy that in the many intimate letters which Louis wrote to his brother, describing his delight at being once more employed, he never mentions Vendôme, the famous general, who was nominally to serve under him. Such a silence would seem to show that the thought did not immediately inspire him, and considering Vendôme's avowed free-thinking, his debauchery and filthy personal habits, it would be a wonder if Louis from the outset had not been repelled by the idea of a partnership.

As for Vendôme, it would be hard to imagine any man less likely to accommodate himself to Louis's hesitancy and need for constant reassurance. It had probably been the King's own idea to put them together. He considered Vendôme to be his best general and believed that the defects of the one would be corrected by the other's virtues. He may even have expected Louis to be won over by the brilliance and cheerful heroism that had made Vendôme the idol of the army. Strangely enough, the King was as blind to his weaknesses and debauchery as Saint-Simon was to his outstanding merits as a leader.

Louis Joseph, Duc de Vendôme, fifty-three years old in 1707, was the bastard great-grandson of Henri IV and Gabrielle d'Estrées, an ancestry that goes far to explain the King's indulgence to conduct which he would never have tolerated in a member of the royal family. There is also the possibility that, considering his own past history, he may not have wished to appear strait-laced regarding Vendôme's lapses. But there was a difference. In his youth, Louis XIV had been free with women, yet he had never been debauched, and he had a genuine horror of all kinds of perversion. Vendôme, on the other hand, was so freely and frankly perverted that his name on the broadsheets was almost invariably rhymed with *Sodome*. Yet, according to Saint-Simon, the King uttered no reproaches, and when Vendôme was forced to return early from Spain to undergo the mercury cure for syphilis, and spoke of it almost boastfully, the courtiers were ordered to welcome him as though he were in no way changed, even though he had become toothless and noseless, resembling nothing so much as a dirty, diseased old woman.

Quite as strange as his tolerance of Vendôme's debauchery was the King's acceptance of his blatant impiety, for ordinarily he was extremely strict regarding church attendance, and kept notes of those people who were in any way lax or irreverent. Yet he only smiled when Vendôme replied to a gentle reprimand for missing the Lenten sermon by saying that no one should be expected to listen to a man talking exactly as he pleased, without the possibility of contradicting him. But irreverence apart, Vendôme's general filthiness might have been expected to disgust the King, who was extremely clean in his own person, and most fastidious where others were concerned. It was one of Mme de Maintenon's greatest charms for him that she smelt delicious, and wore fresh, unspotted dress and linen. Vendôme's clothes were foul with food stains, and his personal habits scarcely bore description, although Saint-Simon reveals them at great length, including his custom of giving audience to his officers while seated on his *chaise-percée*.

He had nonetheless many of the qualities of a great soldier; but his abilities were marred by his indolence and self-indulgence, for he frequently hazarded the success of a campaign by refusing to leave comfortable quarters before noon. The army called it 'the coolness of M. de Vendôme', and loved him for his determination never to be hurried or to require his troops to march before dinner or after nightfall. In battle, he enjoyed hand-to-hand fighting among the common soldiers, and relied upon his staff for information; but since he seldom believed what they reported he was very liable to be taken by surprise.

It was his pride to wear a white feather in his hat, in imitation of his great ancestor Henri IV. The comparison was noted, and Mme des Ursins, writing to Mme de Maintenon after the battle of Cassano, reported that 'many people imagined that they were seeing the ghost of the hero of Ivry as they watched M. de Vendôme rallying his troops in his own inimitable fashion, showing them an example of valour which they most admirably imitated'.

Vendôme had one quality, supreme in the King's eyes. He had never yet been defeated. That alone, at a time when French armies were losing battles on every front, was enough to guarantee him blind trust and favour. When he was recalled from Italy to command the

Flanders army in 1707, the Court went mad with joy. Saint-Simon describes his arrival at Marly. 'All the stable-boys and chair-men, in fact the entire staff of outdoor servants surrounded his coach. He had scarcely reached his room before a flood of visitors appeared. The Princes of the Blood, hitherto so jealous of the favour shown him in the service, were the first to pay their respects, Ministers came flocking, and so many courtiers that the drawing-rooms were emptied of all but ladies.

'The King and Monseigneur sent for him at once, and when he had changed his coat, he was almost borne into the presence. The King came forward to greet him, and Monseigneur had the music stopped so as to hear better what he said . . . He was the hero of the hour; poems were addressed to him with La Fontaine contributing one (not of his best) in praise of "the darling of the army and the Court".' Such adulation would turn most people's heads, and Vendôme was no exception. He left Marly to go to his country house at Anet, and was pursued. Versailles became like a desert, and that village the height of fashion, with not a room to be had anywhere in the neighbourhood for love or money. The King himself shared in the hero-worship. Usually he took offence if his courtiers neglected him; but he highly approved of being abandoned for Anet, and continually inquired whether people had been there, or when they intended to go. He seemed to think that Vendôme, exhausted in his service, had gone there for rest and quiet, in order to plan the coming campaign.

To plan or do other serious work was, however, the last thing contemplated by Vendôme. In a week or two he went to Clichy to be entertained at the great house of Crozat the millionaire banker, and had the temerity to dismiss two generals, sent to him by the King to discuss the campaign. He told them that he was at Clichy for amusement, not to talk business, for which there would be ample time at army headquarters. That did not endear him to his officers, nor did his demand, though still only a lieutenant-general, to have authority over all Marshals of France. Even this was accorded him; but when the warrant arrived, he sent it back, because it failed to include the royal princes. It irked him to be nominally under the command of the inexperienced Duc de Bourgogne. He had no doubt of course that he would have superiority; what is more, he had asked for the association, for his bastard the Chevalier de Belle-rive had told Saint-Simon that Vendôme's aunt the Duchesse de Bouillon had said to him, 'You desired the princes, and you will be sorry. You will find that whatever you decide with the Duc de Bourgogne in the morning, will be reversed by him at his *petit-coucher*.' That may or may not have been true; but it is hard to understand why Vendôme should have requested a partnership the result of which, at best, would mean a sharing of his glory.

The ministers, like their royal master, were all in favour of the combination. Fénelon, however, was of the opposite opinion; writing to the Duc de Beauvilliers, he said, 'I should not wish to put either the King of Spain or the Duc de Bourgogne with M. de Vendôme. Apart from his being too dangerous in religious matters, he is of a hard, stubborn and headstrong temperament.' One other person, equally devoted to Louis, was as certain as Fénelon that the association would prove disastrous. That person was Saint-Simon, who frankly told Beauvilliers of his forebodings, walking round the horse-pond, at the far end of the gardens at Maily, where they would not be overheard. He saw certain disaster, and prophesied the very worst. 'The stronger character will overcome the weaker, and the stronger will prove to be M. de Vendôme. He knows no restraint, and his vices in those licentious surroundings will make M. le Duc de Bourgogne's piety appear contemptible. His age and experience will prevail over youth, his boldness put indecision to shame, and his sanction of debauchery make a young man's censure intolerable. The army, so proud of Vendôme's glory, and knowing the weaknesses of M. le Duc de Bourgogne, will quickly abandon the latter and follow him whose reputation froze all the ink in Italy when he commanded there.'[1] At this point, knowing that it was too late to make a change, Beauvilliers began to lose his temper. He spoke of the need for the presence of the heir to give the army much needed encouragement, at a time when morale was low. He praised the excellent qualities shown by the prince in his earlier campaigns, adding that his reputation and authority were wanted to keep discipline, since, under Vendôme, slackness and debauchery would inevitably exceed all bounds. 'Only the prince,' he said, 'can rouse M. de Vendôme from his lethargy and force him to take those precautions the neglect of which has brought us so often near to defeat. Only he can brace the generals, recall junior officers to their duty, and restore the order and discipline that has so conspicuously been lacking since M. de Vendôme took over the command.'

Saint-Simon questioned every one of Beauvilliers's arguments,

[1] During Vendôme's Italian campaign, only Puységur had dared to report that his victories had been grossly inflated.

and still foresaw nothing but disaster. The fact that Dangeau, in his Journal, restricted himself to a bare statement of the appointments, making no comment on the great event, seems to show that he did not, at any rate, view the future as optimistically as Beauvilliers. Meanwhile the Duke of Marlborough, writing to Godolphin, was greatly cheered. 'It is my idea that the Duc de Bourgogne and the other French princes will prove to be more of a burden and embarrassment to M. de Vendôme, and no benefit to him whatsoever.'

Between 30 April and 14 May, the day appointed for his departure, Louis was kept busy inspecting the horses and carriages and the other equipment that he was to take to Flanders. He gladly welcomed the Marquis de Puységur,[1] in former days a member of his household, who had been recalled from the Flanders army to advise him. The choice of Puységur was an excellent one. He was devoted to Louis, had been for a considerable time in Flanders, and was a capable general with long experience of the terrain on which they would be operating. It was a thousand pities that Louis's other two official advisers, the Marquis d'O and the Comte de Gamaches were not of the same kind.

They had been the personal choice of Mme de Maintenon and Adelaide in the previous year. Saint-Simon deplored them both, most of all d'O, who, in truth, would appear to have been entirely self-protective, seeking only to avoid responsibility and bring his prince home alive, and in every dilemma counselling inaction, so as to incur no blame, whatever happened. His charm for Mme de Maintenon was his grave bearing and public display of piety, attending every service at the Versailles chapel, and often to be seen there at private prayer. Gamaches was let off more lightly: 'a decent, honest man who knew how to manage his drink and very little else.' Most of all, Saint-Simon blames the King. 'Any private gentleman,' he says, 'would have seen to it that his son was better supported.'

Another officer from whom Louis might legitimately have expected advice and help was the Maréchal de Matignon, third in the line of the high command in Flanders; but he proved no better than a broken reed. His promotion had come suddenly, only a month earlier, the reason being, or so it was said, that he would be the only

[1] Jacques François de Chastenay, Marquis de Puységur (1655–1743), a friend of the King's boyhood. He was said to have obtained the Order of the Saint-Esprit by reminding Louis XIV that he had promised it him when they were children.

Marshal of France willing to take orders from Vendôme. The other marshals and the generals who had themselves been expecting promotion were furious. They spoke of the bâton being dishonoured, and very bitter things were said when seven or eight of them gathered together in the Marly drawing-rooms.

On the afternoon before Louis left, he had bidden farewell with an affectionate embrace to each of Adelaide's ladies. With Adelaide the parting was exceedingly tender. Dangeau says no more than that, but the *Mercure* devoted to it a long paragraph: 'I shall say nothing of the farewells between the prince and Mme la Duchesse de Bourgogne; love has mysteries that belong to love alone. Suffice it to report that the emotion shown by the princess after the departure of her august spouse impressed the entire Court with the grief she was suffering, and the love that she bore him.' Louis, on the other hand, appears to have suffered less, for the *Mercure* continued, 'It is hard to describe the joy which departure imprinted on his countenance. For a long time past he has been longing to make the journey. One might almost say that he left on wings for the place where glory awaits him.'

The direct road to the frontier lay through Cambrai and, this time, the King did not forbid a conversation with Fénelon. They met at the inn where Louis dined, and where the archbishop and all the other notabilities of Cambrai had assembled to greet him. It was a very public occasion; but the bystanders were deeply moved when the young prince took his old tutor in his arms and embraced him tenderly and many times, saying out loud that he could never forget all that he owed to him. The ardour with which he gazed into Fénelon's eyes and the eloquence of his glance achieved precisely what the King had wished to prevent, and thereafter the archbishop's palace at Cambrai was crowded with distinguished visitors, arriving on one pretext or another to win his approval or ensure his future protection.

Louis, continuing his journey to his headquarters at Valenciennes, found his command 'complete, healthy, splendidly equipped, and in excellent spirits'. He wrote to his brother on 29 May, 'Here the army is in splendid condition and ready for anything. M. de Vendôme is as eager as I am to find the opportunity to fight a battle. I hope, dear brother, that when the right moment comes we may be able to restore to your authority part of the territory which you lost two years ago.' He was obviously full of ambition and longing for glory; and so, one would have supposed, was Vendôme. He had never before commanded so large an army, nor one of such high quality, containing, as it did, the cream of the French regiments—the famous *maison du roi* (the King's household troops), the gendarmerie, the carabineers, the guards regiments, headed by some of the most famous and experienced officers of the previous campaigns. As Saint-Simon describes, 'it was complete, active, with morale extremely high. Moreover, no force was ever so well supplied, served by a prodigious train of artillery and food waggons.' All was in perfect order save, unhappily, for a certain confusion in the chain of command. In principle, the commander-in-chief was bound to have been the Duc de Bourgogne. As heir to the throne he could be under no one's orders; yet, in fact, it was Vendôme who ruled supreme by reason of his fame and greater experience. Moreover the King had particularly recommended Louis to follow his advice, 'should he be persistent', and had given Vendôme a letter to show to Louis, in which he had written, 'the prince will wish, both from personal inclination and a desire to contribute to the success of the campaign, to overlook difficulties that may appear greater to him than to yourself, and will consent to abide by your advice, being persuaded that you will not compromise his honour or his life'.

At first all went very well. Louis visited Vendôme at his headquarters, carefully filled his glass with water, and said, 'Monsieur de Vendôme let us drink to success in this campaign'. Vendôme rose most respectfully to his feet, raising his own glass to touch the base of the prince's glass; whereat Louis exclaimed, 'Let us have no ceremony, for we all regard you as the father and leader of our armies.'

A few days later, Louis wrote to Chamillart the war minister, 'You know how gently M. de Vendôme needs to be handled. If one approaches him tactfully, one may persuade him to change even those opinions on which he is most headstrong.' On the same day, Vendôme was writing, 'I perceive in Mgr le Duc de Bourgogne an intelligence and amiability that will, I believe, stand every test'.

Yet they did nothing to activate the campaign. Marlborough was at Brussels, with his army encamped not many leagues away from the French. Everyone at Versailles, and in England also, expected a great battle. 'I agree with you,' wrote Godolphin to Marlborough, 'that there will soon be the opportunity for action, not only because the French will take advantage of their superiority in numbers, but because of the impetuous nature of the young prince [Louis], who is full of ambition and eager to acquire a reputation.' But Vendôme, comfortable in his quarters, showed no inclination to move. He said there was no urgency, and although none of the other generals agreed with him, he stuck to that opinion with such an air of superior knowledge that they yielded. Puységur, at least, clearly foresaw disaster, and sent a long letter to the Duc de Beauvilliers, who repeated the substance of it to Saint-Simon.

Marlborough, meanwhile, waited uneasily for Prince Eugene to join him. As so often before a battle, he was unwell and full of the gravest misgivings, seeing himself greatly outnumbered; and he sent urgent messages for the prince to come to him with all speed. This would have been the moment for Vendôme to attack, and so he would have done had he been inspired by one of those flashes of genius that had won him so many victories in the past. On this occasion, he appears to have given way to the indolence that some-times overcame him, and he would not leave his comforts. He per-sisted in saying that there was no need for haste; and nothing that Louis or the other generals could say convinced him of the danger of further delay. In the end he waited too long. Marlborough stole a march on him and, taking him by surprise, inflicted on him at Oudenarde, on 11 July, a most catastrophic defeat.

During the interval, Vendôme proposed several plans, including a most daring one to capture Brussels. Louis thought it too great a risk; the King was therefore applied to and he refused his consent, which put Vendôme in a thoroughly bad temper. The whole of June was thus wasted and, on the 29th, Louis wrote to King Philip, 'we have been here very peacefully since the beginning of the month . . . We are free to move right or left as best pleases us, always in advance of the enemy, who wait to learn what we propose to do . . . Let us hope that the campaign will continue in the same way, and that with God's help we may come to a good and favourable peace.'

Louis himself had not been idle during the weeks of inactivity, for the *Mercure* describes him riding out at daybreak each morning to visit the outposts of his command and inspect their supplies of food and ammunition. According to the writer, he made himself the idol of the troops by his concern for their well-being, notwithstand-ing that he had re-imposed the strict discipline of his first campaigns. He had also checked the laxity of the junior officers, making them send away their private carriages, and setting them the example by travelling always on horseback. As regards religious observances, he remained as zealous as at Versailles, praying frequently in public and 'edifying the entire army by his piety'. On 7 July, which was Corpus Christi, he organised a long procession, in which he followed on foot, very different from Marlborough, who spent the day riding out with his generals and five hundred of his cavalry to reconnoitre the banks and crossings of the river Dyle.

At the beginning of July, Louis achieved a considerable triumph by sending a force to capture Ghent and Bruges in a surprise attack. The enterprise was well prepared and completely successful, and the good news reached Louis XIV at Fontainebleau on the night of 8 July. At eight o'clock next day the King came himself to waken Adelaide, so as to be the first to bring her the joyful tidings, whereupon, says Saint-Simon, the whole Court went wild with delight. Two days later there was a picnic in celebration, in a clearing of the forest, near the Moret road. The King drove there with Adelaide in his coach at six o'clock in the evening, and Mme de Maintenon accompanied them. Three other coaches followed with Adelaide's ladies. Supper was served, and altogether it was a most joyful occasion; but although they did not know it, at that very moment the battle of Oudenarde was being fought.

Even before the fighting started there had been disagreements and interminable argument between Louis and Vendôme. Vendôme wished to take advantage of the capture of Ghent and Bruges by using his entire army to besiege Oudenarde and its strong fortress. Louis considered that this would take too long, and the matter was sent back to Fontainebleau for the King's decision, which caused even longer delay. Fresh disputes arose with accusations (not unfounded) exchanged by the generals, some blaming Vendôme for his slowness, others Louis for indecision and excessive caution. Saint-Simon, with the King at Fontainebleau, lay all the blame on Vendôme; military historians on the spot were not so positive; the English reports tended to praise Vendôme and severely censured Louis.

The facts were that on the night of 10 July Marlborough moved his army with almost incredible speed, and that Biron, commanding the French advance guard, was astounded, on the morning of the 11th, to find himself facing the major part of the Allied armies. Three aides-de-camp were sent one after the other to warn Vendôme. They found him dismounted, picnicking by the roadside. At first he refused to believe them; but at last he rose from table and, mounting his horse, exclaimed that, 'the devil must have lent the enemy wings, for otherwise such speed was impossible'. He returned the first aide-de-camp, with orders for Biron to attack, promising to come to his support, and sent forward some of the best troops in the French army. He then instructed the princes to follow quietly with the main body, and immediately set off at full gallop to Biron's aid.

On arrival, Vendôme threw himself into the attack on Marlborough's right wing, expecting to be supported on his left by the Duc de Bourgogne; but that support never came. No plans had been made before the action, no precise orders given, and thus, according to Vendôme's own account, fifty battalions and eighty squadrons of cavalry remained idle on a hilltop, taking no part in the battle. In an explanatory letter to the King, he said that he had sent clear instructions to the Duc de Bourgogne; but that the prince had allowed himself to be deflected by cowardly advisers—not, however, without compunction, for Vendôme added that he had been heard to cry out, 'What will M. de Vendôme say when he hears that instead of charging, I have entrenched myself?'

It is not by any means certain that clear commands were either sent or received, for after that first instruction to 'follow quietly with the main body', Vendôme had been fighting like a tiger in the thick of the battle, 'his sword ever in his hand in the place of greatest danger, inspiring the troops with shouts and gestures, providing a spectacle of the most brilliant heroism'. But heroism, however inspiring, is not generalship. What was missing was the settled plan which Vendôme had never found time to make, and by which a succession of prearranged orders would have gone out to each branch of the huge army. In the heat of the fighting, Vendôme found himself incapable of devising any alternative. All he could do was to send forward, one after another, against the far better situated enemy, breathless detachments of troops that had joined him after a long and hurried march. To make matters worse, they had almost no artillery, for Saint-Hilaire,[1] the general in command, states in his memoirs that he received no orders whatsoever, and on his own responsibility sent forward ten guns, without which the army would have been destitute.

Utter confusion ensued, as the various detachments reached the enemy lines and came under fire. 'Nearly every man,' says Saint-

---

[1] Armand de Mormès de Saint-Hilaire (1651–1740). Lieutenant-general, 1704, in command of the artillery of the Flanders army, 1708.

Simon, 'was separated from his troop. Cavalry, infantry, and dragoons were mixed higgledy-piggledy; not a battalion, not a squadron managed to keep together, all became entangled and embroiled with one another. When night fell, an immense amount of terrain had been lost, and half the army had not yet reached the battle-front.'

At nine o'clock, when the light was almost gone, Vendôme and the Duc de Bourgogne met on the disordered field to hold a council of despair. Vendôme, furious with himself for his gross miscalculation, behaved with scantest courtesy. M. le Duc de Bourgogne tried to speak; but was told rudely to hold his tongue, Vendôme saying aloud in front of everyone, 'Your Highness should remember that you are with the army only on condition of obeying me.' The enormity of these words, amounting to high treason, spoken at a time when all were conscious of the fearful cost of obedience to Vendôme's stubborn indolence, caused his hearers to shake with anger. The young prince to whom they were addressed had then to win a battle even harder than the one which the enemy was inflicting on him. He perceived that there was no middle way between the final extreme of ordering Vendôme's arrest and complete silence, and was sufficiently master of himself to choose the latter. It was a decision that was not generally admired.

Vendôme then proceeded to hold forth on the state of the battle, contending that nothing had yet been lost; that half the army was not yet engaged; that they should turn their thoughts to continuing next morning. Only one very young officer shared that opinion, Matignon, the most experienced of the generals and Puységur also, thought otherwise, and their reasoning left no room for doubt. When one officer after another arrived from the battle-field reporting total disorder, Vendôme, almost mad with rage, burst out, 'Oh! Well, I see that since you all desire it we must retire, more especially,' he continued, looking hard at the Duc de Bourgogne, 'since you, Monseigneur have had that wish for a long time past.' 'Those words, whose hidden meaning could not fail to be understood, were uttered just as I say, and so delivered that none of his hearers could mistake their significance.'

M. le Duc de Bourgogne remained, as on the first occasion, perfectly silent, and all the rest followed his example, frozen in various degrees of horrified astonishment, until at length Puységur inquired how the retreat was to be conducted. They then all spoke at once but Vendôme, either from anger or uncertainty, remained speechless. At last he said that they must march to Ghent, but without explaining how or making any comment . . .[1] The disorderly meeting then broke up, and the princes with a small retinue accompanying them set off on horseback along the road to Ghent. Vendôme issued no orders, called for no reports, and was not seen again that night. The generals returned to their posts, or as near to them as was possible, and it was not Louis or Vendôme, but the third in command, the Maréchal de Matignon, who sent the order to retire to every part of the army. It was by then nearly midnight; the sound of desultory firing could still be heard coming from various directions; but at last, as the orders reached them, the troops began their retreat, and silence fell over the battlefield. No further orders were given, detachments withdrew as best they could and in great confusion. Louis rode on towards Ghent, refusing the post-chaise which had been sent after him. His advisers had wished him to leave the army on the pretext of gathering reinforcements; but he preferred to stay at its head and, passing through Ghent, rode on to Lowendegem,[2] where he set up his headquarters with the army encamped nearby.

Vendôme reached Ghent between seven and eight o'clock on the morning after the battle, as the army passed through the city. There he gave vent to his feelings of disgust, in one of those exhibitions of what Voltaire called his 'cynical filthiness' to which his staff had become accustomed. After standing for a moment with a remnant of his staff, to watch the soldiers go by, he then, close before their faces, let down his breeches and planted his stools. Having done that, he hurried to his quarters and flung himself into bed, refusing any reports, and remaining there sleeping for thirty hours on end, recovering from the effects of his exhaustion. Only later did he learn that the main body of the army was encamped just ten miles distant, at Lowendegem.

That the retreat was not a total disaster was due, not to its organis-

---

[1] This is Saint-Simon's account, and is accurate in all the essentials; but Saint-Simon was too great a writer not to have exaggerated here and there so as to make the story live. Thus it is noteworthy that, in the letters the Duc de Bourgogne wrote to Mme de Maintenon and his brother Philip, he does not mention Vendôme's insulting speeches, though he complains of him bitterly in most other ways. Bellerive, Vendôme's bastard, says that he was in a violent passion. Saint-Hilaire, of whom Saint-Simon recounts that he was a good gunner, but monumentally dull, says only that 'a great deal was said, which it is useless to repeat'.

[2] A little town not far from Ghent, situated near the western bank of the Ghent–Bruges Canal.

ation, for there was none, but to the gallantry and quick-thinking of certain individuals. The *maison du roi*, the cream of the army, was nearly captured because, receiving no orders, their officers had held a council, during which the Dutch surrounded them. It was only by the gallantry of a very junior brigadier-general that they were saved. Pointing out that if they delayed any longer they would be hemmed in, he cried, 'Follow me', and led them in a charge through the lines of the Dutch cavalry and infantry, thus bringing them safely into Ghent, under cover of the darkness. Saint-Hilaire with the artillery, though he too had been left without orders, managed against fearful odds to save the guns. But it was Nangis, Adelaide's old flame, who was the real hero of the retreat, for next day, in broad daylight, he succeeded in rescuing the cavalry of the left wing, a hundred squadrons who had been left forgotten. Gathering stragglers together to form a rearguard, he brought them fighting all the way, together with a large body of grenadiers, also forgotten, safe into camp at Lowengedem. Unhappily many other portions of the army were cut off from any chance of retreat and were taken prisoner. Indeed, the number of prisoners was a measure of the catastrophe, for although the deaths on either side were roughly equal, the Allies lost 4,000 as prisoners as against 7,000 French, many hundreds of whom were young officers, whose families at the Court anxiously awaited news.

15

Enemies at Home

NEWS OF the disaster reached Versailles on 14 July, just three days after that joyful picnic celebrating the capture of Ghent and Bruges. Between noon and one o'clock, as the King emerged from a meeting of the Finance Council, a messenger from the Duc de Bourgogne arrived, 'bearing with him,' says Dangeau, 'the sad tidings of a great battle in Flanders, wherein we did not have the advantage'. 'That same evening,' he added later, 'a second messenger appeared; but he brought none of the details that might have enabled us to know what had happened. All that we have learned is that there has been a disaster.' The Court was stunned by the news of a defeat and, in a moment, the great hopes for the campaign and almost hysterical jubilation changed to dismay and apprehension, as people waited anxiously for further news.

Mme de Maintenon, writing to her crony the Princesse des Ursins, voiced what most people were feeling. 'You already know, Madame, that our happiness has not lasted long. The capture of Ghent had put us in an excellent situation. No more was needed than to hold fast for the remainder of the campaign. It was for the enemy to move, and they were desperate.[1] M. de Vendôme, who believes according to his wishes, insisted on fighting a battle; he lost it, and we are in a far worse plight than before, as much by our losses as by our fear of the consequences and the enemy's apparent superiority ... The King supports this latest mischance with full submission to the will of God, and displays his usual courage and equanimity. As for me, poor unhappy me, you may well believe, Madame, that I am much afflicted. My sad heart rose somewhat at the capture of Ghent, it now sinks more deeply than

---

[1] The fall of Ghent and Bruges was a severe blow to the Allies. Ghent, as Berwick said, 'was the key to all the rivers and waterways of Flanders', Bruges, only slightly less important, guarded the direct line of communications with England. Marlborough was deeply depressed by the news.

ever, on account of my fears for the rest of the campaign.' She foresaw that bitter quarrels would soon divide the courtiers and the
nation, for she ended her letter, 'It is impossible that there should
not be enmity between M. le Duc de Bourgogne and M. de Vendôme because of their different opinions, and many people will com-
bine to increase it by malicious talk.'

The malicious talk was not heard for some time, because the
friends of the Duc de Bourgogne and Vendôme were at first re-
strained by a complete absence of news. The King said nothing,
and since he stopped and read all the private letters brought by the
first couriers, and forwarded precious few of them, there was
nothing with which to supplement the official silence.[1] Even had
silence not been the King's usual practice, it may well have been
forced upon him on this occasion, seeing that the two commanders
of the defeated army had left him without information. Neither of
them sent him the detailed report that was customary after a battle.
The Duc de Bourgogne limited himself to one brief letter, describing only the disastrous result. To Adelaide, however, he wrote more
frankly, and at greater length, stating that the defeat had been due
to Vendôme's excess of confidence, and his persistence (against all
advice) in delaying the advance for at least two days too long,
adding that should such a thing ever recur, he would immediately
leave the service, unless prevented by the King's absolute command,
for he 'could make no sense of the battle or of the retreat', and felt
so disgusted that he would say no more.

Vendôme sent two letters, which arrived together. They were
almost equally short, but full of complaints. In one of them he
said, 'I shall give Your Majesty no details, merely have the honour
to inform you that the enemy would not have been successful, had
we not freely given them the victory by our retreat. We had gained
some ground; lost neither guns, baggage, nor flags, and we had
captured one flag, a standard, and a pair of kettle-drums. That,
Sire, is the truth; and I am heart-broken because, for a whole hour,
I believed the battle won, and had I been supported, as it was my
right to be, our victory would have been complete.'

A third courier brought a very long dispatch from the Duc de

---

[1] People knew nothing, and were desperate for news. Madame to the Duchess
of Hanover, 1 August 1708: 'I knew that a battle had been fought and lost, but
I did not know where. I know now, but am ignorant of the details because we
are not allowed to discuss it, and the men who were in the fighting may not
write of it.'

Bourgogne, written from start to finish in his own hand, and yet another from Vendôme, full of excuses for offering no details. The rest were private letters, all of which the King read, some of them three times over. This courier arrived after the King's supper, when the princesses and their ladies were present, and thus the King was seen to read the letters, though he said very little. There was another letter for Adelaide, with a note from the Duc de Berry, to the effect that M. de Vendôme had been very unfortunate, and that everyone was blaming him. When she returned to her apartment, she was heard to exclaim that M. le Duc de Bourgogne appeared to have had monstrously stupid people around him; but she said no more than that.

The King, during all this, acted with moderation and restraint. He neither supported nor blamed his grandson, or the general to whom he had given his trust; but did his best to pacify them both. To Louis, he wrote, 'I am extremely sorry that the first occasion on which you have figured has not had a more successful issue. Do not be discouraged. You should rather try to hearten the officers and troops with words of good cheer. It is at times like these that men of high rank need to encourage their inferiors . . . There will be other times when you will feel obliged to put on a good face. Do nothing without careful consideration. Neglect no practicable means of learning the enemy's movements.'

On the same day, the King wrote to Vendôme, saying only that there appeared not to have been the close accord desirable between him and the Duc de Bourgogne in order to avoid a situation whose consequences could not be otherwise than disastrous or, at the very least, highly doubtful. He was, however, careful to add, 'I am sending word to the Duc de Bourgogne that, to prevent any such embarrassments in the future, he should consult with you as to the next move. I recommend him to show you all the respect that is your due because of the manner in which you constantly expose yourself to danger. Most of all, I desire him to have in you all the confidence deserved by your zeal for the glory of my armies, for his own glory, and for that of the nation. Finally, I commend you to him for your long service at the head of my armies which, under your command, were never defeated.'

Vendôme, however, was very far from being pacified. Even before receiving that letter, he had sent another, full of recrimination, addressing the King as no other man would have dared. 'Mes-seigneurs les Princes,' he wrote, 'are a fearful burden on an army.

When night fell they were within a hair's breadth of capture. I still tremble when I think of it. I do not know what Your Majesty plans; but it appears to me that the movements required during the remainder of the campaign do not in any way require their presence.' The King's letter irritated him to such a degree that, on the 19th, he let fly in a violent attack on the Duc de Bourgogne's conduct during the battle. He did not name him directly, not even Vendôme dared do that, but levelled his accusations against Puységur, whom the King recognised as being the prince's chief adviser, holding him responsible for Louis's lethargy, and his decision not to make the supporting charge, and quoting him as saying, as he gave the order to entrench, 'What is M. de Vendôme going to say about this?' 'I could never have believed,' the letter ended, 'that fifty battalions and nearly a hundred and twenty squadrons of out finest troops would have been content to spend six hours watching us do battle, for all the world as though they were seated in a box at an opera. M. le Duc de Bourgogne will bear me out, for he admits he was wrong not to have followed his first instincts, and to have taken such bad advice. If things go as I hope, the glory will all be his; but should they miscarry, I shall ask Your Majesty not to lay all the blame on me, since you must concede that my decisions are not always accepted.'

Louis himself remained very quiet, but he did not suffer Vendôme's assault without an effort to defend himself, and wrote to the three people on whose support he could rely, namely Adelaide, Mme de Maintenon, and the Duc de Beauvilliers. The letter to Adelaide no longer exists; but to Mme de Maintenon, after excusing himself for an appearance of lacking in charity, and praising Vendôme's heroism, he enumerated all the latter's errors, both before and during the battle, and continued, 'In fact, Madame, neither in the direction of a campaign nor in battle does he act as a general should, and the King is gravely mistaken in having so high an opinion of him. I am not the only one to say this; the entire army says the same. He has never gained the confidence of the officers, and has lost that of the rank and file. He does nothing, as it were, but sleep and eat, for truly his health no longer supports fatigue, and he is thus unable to fulfil his necessary duties. Consider also his extraordinary conviction that the enemy will act as he desires and that, since he has never been defeated, he cannot be vanquished in the future (something which, after the events of the day before yesterday, he can no longer claim). Pray reflect, Madame, whether

the interests of the State are well served in such hands.' Louis concluded by asking the King to grant him, not only the right to
advise, until then his only prerogative (as Vendôme had so rudely
reminded him), but also 'the casting vote, in concert with the
Marshals of France, and other able and experienced officers'. Then,
fearing lest he had said too much, he humbly took stock of his own
failures, accusing himself of too much impetuosity on some occasions, and of indecision on others, 'for I must admit to having all
the weaknesses of a Frenchman. Yet the worst of all would be to
lose courage, and it is at the worst moments that one most needs it.
Let us hope that God does not abandon us entirely, and that the
future may not be as bad as we fear'.

In his letter to the Duc de Beauvilliers, Louis was even more
humble. 'Our spirits are very low; our situation critical; we are in
great difficulties and much mortified. I trust that when God has
sufficiently punished us, he will not quite abandon us, but will
bring us to a happy issue from this time of affliction . . .' 'Pray to
God,' he concluded, 'more than ever before, that he may grant me
wisdom and courage, whatever may befall, and that he may teach me
increasingly to recognise my own weakness and unworthiness,
which I think prosperity had somewhat concealed from me; for I
did not then have perfect faith in God. Should He still find a use
for me, it would be an act of pure mercy, for I have not been as
faithful as, after His recent goodness, I had promised to be.'

Had things gone as the King intended, and Mme de Maintenon,
Adelaide, and Monseigneur been the only ones to know what had
happened, the trouble between Louis and Vendôme might have
become stale news, by the time the details were made public. But
that did not suit Vendôme's ideas. Still furiously angry, and not a
little alarmed for his own safety, he determined to publish his version of the defeat, discrediting the prince, and relying on the strong
support of the Meudon Cabal, the King's bastards and the other
minor royalties who surrounded Monseigneur. Vendôme was the
hero of that group, and they rallied to him, using every opportunity
to blacken Louis's character, with an eye to the next reign,
when they hoped to be the paramount influence at Monseigneur's
accession.

Hesitantly at first, dropping a word here and there in commis-
seration with Vendôme for his lack of support, and with veiled hints
that Louis's insistence on retreat had cost France the victory, they
proceeded on a campaign of vilification. There was little protest,

not because the Bourgognes had no friends, but because the bewildered Court knew almost nothing, and many feared to antagonise the powerful group at Meudon. The Cabal, thus encouraged, went beyond all bounds, sending their followers to spread rumours in the gaming-rooms and playhouses, until broadsheets were printed and rude songs heard in the streets.[1] Some of the worst were said to be written by Mme la Duchesse, the cleverest and most spiteful of the King's daughters.

What finally brought the scandal into the open, and aroused a raging controversy, was the printing of two letters, which had previously been passed from hand to hand, in order to prepare the ground. The first was from the secretary of Vendôme's friend Crozat; the second from his own confidential secretary the Abbé, later Cardinal, Alberoni[2] was an out and out laudation of Vendôme, who was stated to have been capable of winning a hundred Oudenardes, had it not been for the Duc de Bourgogne's advisers (the prince was not named, though clearly enough indicated). When the *Gazette d'Amsterdam*, much read abroad, published the first of these letters, and went uncontradicted, the scandal spread like wildfire across France and many of the European capitals. The vast majority, at home and abroad, took Vendôme's side, and soon it was positively dangerous to speak for Louis because of the powerful personages calling for his disgrace, and making his defenders feel that in the future they would be called to account.

Nonetheless, strong support was on the way. The Duc de Beauvilliers, remembering their conversation in the Marly gardens, called horror-stricken upon Saint-Simon, to apologise. They were joined by the Duc de Chevreuse, and spent many hours endeavouring to find a way of opening the King's eyes, and calming the furore. Their first decision was to see that Adelaide knew all, through the good offices of Mme de Nogaret. Adelaide, however, had not waited

[1] Madame to the Duchess of Hanover, 23 December 1708: 'Some new ballads have come, sent by I know not whom. In one of them, M. d'O. is represented flying, like Punchinello, from the marionette theatre. It is all a matter of fashion, in France, and nowadays it is fashionable to be a coward, to run away and be defeated, just as it was once the mode to defeat the enemy and put him to flight.'

[2] Jules Alberoni, born 19 May 1664, near Piacenza, in Italy, was first attached to Vendôme's staff as an agent of the Duke of Parma. Saint-Simon says that he wormed himself into Vendôme's confidence by making most delicious cheese soup, and pandering to his filthy habits. He is reported to have exclaimed, 'Oh! angelic bottom!', when Vendôme turned from his chaise-percée.

to be informed, but had sent Mme de Nogaret to them on her own account, asking them how she stood with the King and Mme de Maintenon, and what she might or might not do to be safe in that direction. She was not as sure of her influence on the King as in the past, for more than once, when she had urged him to support his grandson, he had rounded on her with what might almost have been called a public snub although, invariably, he had later done what she asked.

Now twenty-two years old, she had been roughly shaken out of her worthless existence. The trials of the past few years had brought her suddenly to maturity. Mme de Maintenon said that she 'was agonised by events and that although she said nothing there were always tears in her eyes'. In June, when the Court had gone to Fontainebleau, she had not seemed to miss the customary pleasures, but had settled down to serious occupations. Writing to the Princesse des Ursins, Mme de Maintenon said, 'Do not be alarmed, our princess will never be a scholar or a wit. It amuses her to listen to learned talk, but she does not pursue her studies very far . . . I think that a slight acquaintance with the arts and sciences is as good a distraction as card-playing all day.' Adelaide, however, did learn enough to write a letter in Latin to Louis, and she took lessons in philosophy, which Mme de Maintenon viewed lightly—'That will not last long,' she said.

It certainly did not survive the attack on her husband, for she took his side and did battle for him with a vehemence that surprised even Mme de Maintenon, who thought she knew her so well. 'At this unhappy time,' she wrote, 'she shows all the sentiments of the good Frenchwoman, I have always believed her to be. But I must admit that I never realised how much she cared for M. le Duc de Bourgogne. Her fondness for him includes the finer feelings, and she minds profoundly that his first battle should have been a defeat. She would like him to have exposed himself to danger, like an ordinary soldier, and to have returned without a scratch. She feels his distress, and shares the anxiety that the present situation necessarily causes him. She would like him to fight and win, and fears for him at the same time. She misses nothing; she is even worse than I am.'

In another letter, she said: 'There is no more happiness for our dear princess . . . philosophy no longer distracts her; her mind is all in State affairs. Flanders, the interests of Spain, her father, occupy her exclusively, with a sensibility almost inconceivable in one so

young. I have never known a heart like hers. She is adored by those
who come near to her; but is most unhappy in being capable of the
sentiments which I see she has in her husband's cause. I said to her
the other day, that, despite his intelligence and great love for her,
he will never understand such refined feelings.'

It was not easy for Adelaide to do battle. She was gentle by nature
and rather shy, and had devoted herself, until then, to studying the
King's moods and pleasing him in every possible way. Now, however, she had a purpose in life—to conquer Vendôme—and she
rode out fearlessly to bring back his head on her saddle-bow. She
took on a different character, badgering the King incessantly to do
justice to her husband; vociferous in her complaints, uttering shrill
cries, bursting into angry speeches against Vendôme; railing even
against Chamillart, who had sinned by writing to Louis, urging
him to make peace with the monster. It was at such times that the
King turned on her with a public rebuke.

One of her first successes was to win over Mme de Maintenon, in
spite of all the Duc du Maine's endeavours to keep her on the side
of Vendôme and the Cabal, and she persuaded the old lady to speak
to the King on Louis's behalf, which no one else would have dared
to do at that moment. What is more, Mme de Maintenon summoned
the Duc de Beauvilliers for an interview, although, since the trouble
over Fénelon, they had not been on speaking terms.

The King's first reaction to Mme de Maintenon's description of
the abominable letters, and the rumours being circulated, was to
lose his temper; but later, at the council, he furiously demanded to
have them read aloud, including a particularly bad one from Vendôme's cousin the Comte d'Evreux. At first he seemed to defend
Vendôme, but rapidly changed his mind, ordering Chamillart to
send strong letters to him and to the others, including d'Evreux,
commanding them to be silent.

At his headquarters, at Lowendeghem, Louis was suffering from
a bad attack of remorse; writing to Mme de Maintenon and Beauvilliers accusing himself of having been uncharitable, and receiving
from Beauvilliers quiet, temperate replies that seemed to echo his
own sentiments. The subject of the correspondence was virtue and
the difficulty of living a Christian life. The prince's tone was
humble, unambitious, quite selfless, with a resignation to the will of
God that appeared to many people like fatalism or indifference. In
none of the letters is there any sign of interest in the campaign, or
of plans for victory.

In Fénelon, however, Louis had a correspondent of a very different spirit from his own, who urged upon him a more manly approach; greater confidence in his ability to make his own decisions and not always to send to the King for orders; less concern for trivial lapses in discipline in an attempt to rule the army like a monastery and, above all, shorter sessions with his confessor, who should not be allowed to advise on military matters. But Fénelon, far from Paris and the Court, did not at first know the full extent of the attack, nor dared he speak freely, for his letters were opened. It was not until September that he found a safe messenger in Chevreuse's son, the Vidame d'Amiens, by whom he was able to write regularly, and receive private letters from Louis.

It is unfortunate that Beauvilliers's letters to the prince should not have survived, and still more so that those of Mme de Maintenon and Adelaide, together with his answers, have also disappeared. Somewhat to Louis's surprise, Adelaide was writing to him regularly and with quite unusual fondness: 'Nothing shows me better the affection which you have always said she felt for me,' he wrote to Mme de Maintenon and, in a letter he sent her immediately after Oudenarde, he says, 'Now I come to what you say of Mme la Duchesse de Bourgogne. I realise more and more her affection for me, and you may be sure that it does not diminish my love for her. Your description of her is so vivid that I am deeply touched. I only wish she had a more fortunate husband; but she could not have one who loves her more dearly; and she knows that very well. I am delighted, Madame, to hear that you continue to be pleased with her.'

Encouraged by the King's annoyance with Adelaide, the Cabal ventured to send Louis a letter, suggesting that it was in his best interests to be reconciled with Vendôme, which Louis, full of remorse and terrified of the King's anger, was not unwilling to do. At this point, however, the Duchesse de Bouillon, Evreux's mother and the aunt of Vendôme, took fright at the danger of attacking the heir, and counselled prudence; whereupon the Comte d'Evreux visited Louis at his headquarters, was welcomed, and promptly forgiven. Thereafter, to the disgust of the army, and the horrified astonishment of Versailles, the prince appeared to single him out for particular favour, as though anxious to make him forget the King's reprimand. To Louis, perhaps, this was an act of Christian charity, a turning of the other cheek, but to men who held honour sacred it seemed despicable, and many of those who had hitherto supported him thought it safer to say nothing, and to be seen more often at Vendôme's headquarters.

Louis was worried and miserable. Saint-Simon says that his face no longer had that cheerful, open expression that made him attractive to those who saw him face to face. Chamillart's letter, and the news of the King's vexation with Adelaide, both depressed and embittered him, and drove him still further into himself. Following Chamillart's advice, he began to make overtures to Vendôme, who visited him, very proud and condescending, and even had the insolence to bring Alberoni in his retinue. When Louis accepted that presentation and even deigned to speak to the slanderer, his humility had a very bad effect upon the troops who, says Saint-Simon, 'seeing only the exterior, began to blame him, to use no stronger word'.

But Vendôme, despite his bold front, had become almost as much worried as Louis, because word had reached him of the activities of the Duchesse de Bourgogne and Mme de Maintenon, who were furious with Chamillart, among others, and at all times within range of the King's ear. Much upset, he had the temerity to mention to the prince his concern at the princess's outspoken criticism. He made no excuses, nor did he apologise, merely begged Louis to take the matter up with her, since he was hesitant to write himself. It was a clever gesture for, without appearing to make any move, he offered Adelaide, through her long-suffering husband, the opportunity of a reconciliation which she would find it hard to refuse, and at the same time pleased the King by making humble advances to his grandson's wife.

It seems almost incredible that Louis's pride should have allowed him to swallow that insult; but he wrote to Mme de Maintenon asking her to use her authority to remind Adelaide of her Christian duty. 'It has come to the ears of M. de Vendôme,' he wrote, 'that Mme la Duchesse de Bourgogne has publicly let fly against him, and he is greatly distressed. Pray speak to her, Madame, so that she may take extra care lest her love for me lead her to provoke, or even to offend, other people. Her affection, though it delights me, would not be welcome to me in such circumstances.'

'That letter,' says Saint-Simon, who presumably heard of it from Mme de Nogaret, 'received the answer it deserved.' In Adelaide's reply, she begged her husband to believe that she could never like or respect Vendôme again, and told him that she failed to understand why her name should have been mentioned. Lastly, she said that 'nothing would ever persuade her to forget Vendôme's conduct, and that he was a man for whom she would always feel the greatest loathing and contempt'.

Sad to say, neither Louis's Christian humility nor Adelaide's proud defiance had the smallest effect upon the Cabal, whose attacks found only too much justification in worse military defeats, and further errors on the part of the Duc de Bourgogne, whom Vendôme, sulking in his comfortable lodgings at Ghent, had left in sole command. It was a curious situation, for the French army, safely based on Lowendeghem, behind the line of the canal from Ghent to Bruges, had its back turned to Holland an enemy country, and faced towards France. The Anglo-Dutch army, on the other hand, with Marlborough in command, was encamped around Oudenarde, its back to France, and had every opportunity to turn and attack the line of strong fortresses, Ypres, Lille, and Tournai, that protected the French frontier. Berwick, shadowing Prince Eugene's army, near Mons, saw the terrible danger, and urged Vendôme to march with all speed to attack Marlborough's supply columns, and so prevent a siege of Lille. The King also saw the danger. He had been fighting wars in distant parts of Europe for the past forty years; but the war had now come to the very gateway of France itself and soon even Paris might be threatened. He was old, tired, and discouraged by disasters; when the full account of the events at Oudenarde reached him he was near to breaking point; but he fortified himself for one more battle to save Lille, a masterpiece of fortification, the capital of French Flanders, the second greatest city of France.

At the army's headquarters, neither Louis nor Vendôme appear to have understood the danger. Vendôme, after several days spent in sleeping off the effects of Oudenarde, had relapsed, as usual, into a false sense of security. He persisted in believing that the enemy were planning nothing of major importance, and that there was nothing to fear beyond an attack on the army, in its strong position between Ghent and Bruges. 'We shall strengthen the fortifications along the canal,' he wrote to the King, 'for, in all likelihood, the enemy has no other aim than to drive us out of here.' In another letter he wrote, 'We have nothing to fear beyond attacks in the direction of Cambrai and Arras, which the Maréchal de Berwick is capable of dealing with unaided. It is simply a question of standing firm until he has crossed the Scheldt.' He had managed to persuade the other generals to agree with him; Matignon, it hardly needs saying, saw no difficulty. 'The enemy's intention,' he wrote to Chamillart, 'is to make us abandon Ghent and Bruges, but I hope that we take no false steps.' Even d'Artagnan,[1] a capable general whom the King himself had appointed to advise Louis, thought the same, for on the same day he was writing, 'I believe that the enemy is in a situation far worse than ours.'

Louis was not so sure, but he took no action. Day after day couriers came from Berwick, pointing out the danger, reporting the movements of Prince Eugene's army (which he alone was not strong enough to oppose), and asking for orders. No orders came; he could get no clear opinion from either Vendôme or Louis, and he wrote to Chamillart, in protest: 'I must tell you that I live in terrible anxiety because, if a decision is not quickly taken, the result may be awkward in the extreme.' Chamillart was no hero, nor was he a professional soldier. All that he did was to urge Louis and Vendôme to forget their quarrel and work together in the service of France. His words had no effect, Vendôme continued his flood of complaints, Louis wavered and hesitated, writing to Beauvilliers and Chamillart of his mistakes at Oudenarde, of his unfairness to Vendôme, of the poor return he had made for God's infinite mercies. His attitude may have been virtuous; it was certainly not warlike, for it is perfectly clear that whatever else was filling the mind of the twenty-five-year-old prince, it was not the problems of his military command.

In fact, the life he was leading with the army differed very little from his life at Versailles. He spent long hours in church, or with his books, and far too long with his confessor. He bought an English telescope and nightly studied the stars, and nearly every afternoon he was on the tennis-courts, playing shuttlecock. When he did go among his troops, he persisted in taking Père Martineau with him, giving the impression that he cared more that the men should confess before going into battle than that they should win a victory. The drinking songs showed him no mercy. Immediately after the defeat, they laid all the blame on him, and praised Vendôme to the skies:

[1] Pierre de Montesquiou d'Artagnan was made a Marshal of France in 1709. Saint-Simon did not think much of him, saying that the King liked him because he provided gossip about all his friends, through the 'back offices'; which was why the King attached him to Louis, in 1703, 'wishing,' said Chamillart, 'to know everything that he does when he is with the army'. D'Artagnan was the nephew of Dumas's hero in *The Three Musketeers*.

'Our timid, pious Louisot,
With his confessor Martinot,
Is no more than an idiot.
But our big, fat blondy,
Courageous and poxy,
With his bold marauders,
Goes his own way,
And don't wait for orders.'

There were, of course, other, more atrocious versions, scarifying poor Louis, and showing Vendôme rising like a phoenix from the ashes. After the latter's temporary retirement and Louis's evident indifference to the outcome of the campaign, some songs were aimed at both:

' They hazard neither limb nor life,
Nor yet their honour in the strife,
One plays with shuttlecocks all day,
The other roosts on his *chaise-percée.*'

Yet something must be said in Louis's defence. Only twenty-five years old and without experience; with advisers whose only idea was to bring him home alive, and avoid fighting; with Berwick pressing for immediate action, and Vendôme refusing to move, it is perhaps little wonder that he desperately turned for help, almost for instructions, to every trusted friend, writing to Beauvilliers, Chamillart, Fénelon, Mme de Maintenon, the King himself, of whom he was, quite literally, terrified. All that he got from Beauvilliers were sermons, from Chamillart exhortations to trust Vendôme, from Fénelon nothing to the purpose,[1] from Mme de Maintenon, who thought his best encouragement would be the support of his wife, mainly news of Adelaide's loyalty. It was the old King who best understood the fundamental, tragic weakness in his grandson's character—a total inability to take the initiative,[2] caused by a tyrannical conscience, and excessive regard for religious scruples. 'I am obliged to tell you,' he wrote to Louis, on 23 July, 'that, although in general I approve of prudence and caution, there are moments when one is obliged to take risks, as I am resolved to do now if, as

[1] It was not until September that Fénelon found a safe means of sending his letters.

[2] An inheritance, perhaps, from his mother the poor Dauphine, and from the apathetic Monseigneur.

appears very likely, our enemies decide to besiege Lille. There is no time to lose in setting in motion the arrangements for your march to form a junction with M. le Maréchal de Berwick . . . No other town but Lille could constrain me to try by every means to prevent its falling to the enemy. It is for you, after well considering what I have said, to take the final, swift decision.'

One might have imagined that Berwick's almost daily warnings of Marlborough's movements, and the urgency and number of the King's dispatches would have spurred Louis to action. On 30 July, Louis XIV wrote to both commanders. To his grandson, he said, 'I have already told you that I am determined to relieve Lille or Tournai, should they be besieged. The enemy is using extraordinary diligence, and will go beyond our expectations if they find nothing to impede or prevent them.' To Vendôme, he wrote, 'The train of siege artillery, which they have withdrawn from Maastricht, must by now be at Brussels. It would be highly advantageous to attack the escorting troops with a stronger force, and one could take no more serviceable action.' But nothing shook Vendôme from his blind obstinacy, or Louis from his qualms. It was not disagreement with Vendôme that kept him immobile, for they were in perfect harmony: 'It appears to me,' he wrote to the King, 'that M. de Vendôme and I are acting in ever closer accord, on every subject; and I hope it may always continue like this.' But the only result was complete inaction, and Berwick fumed because, daily expecting orders to join forces with the Duc de Bourgogne, he dared do nothing independently.

On 11 August, the siege of Lille began, for Vendôme had never been more mistaken than in concluding that Marlborough would attack on the Ghent to Bruges canal. Marlborough had not contemplated such an action. His first idea had been to march into the very heart of France, through the gap between the fortresses of Lille and Tournai; but Prince Eugene had dissuaded him, on the grounds that it was too great a risk, without protection for his supply-columns and line of retreat. Marlborough had given way, and both commanders had turned to the siege of Lille, with Prince Eugene's army investing the fortress, and Marlborough's still encamped midway between Lille and Oudenarde, waiting to see where the French would attack.

The French did not attack. On 29 August, the armies of the Duc de Bourgogne and Berwick at last effected their junction, at a place named Mons-en-Peule, twenty kilometres to the south of Lille. The short-lived harmony between Louis and Vendôme came to an abrupt end, when Berwick categorically refused to take orders from Vendôme, and was appointed as Louis's adviser in opposition. On 5 September, all three of them spent the day reconnoitring the enemy's dispositions, and all the night in argument, for they violently disagreed. Vendôme wished to attack; Berwick thought the risk too great; Louis wavered, and referred to the King for orders and advice. The answer came promptly, 'attack at once, even at the risk of misfortunes inseparable from failure; they would be less dishonourable to yourself and to the army than to be mere spectators at the capture of Lille'. On the 8th, Chamillart was dispatched to Flanders, with orders to compel Louis to obey. When he first arrived, he was in favour of an attack; but having seen the position for himself he sided with Berwick, and the armies retired to Tournai.

The Court, at this time, was at Fontainebleau, a good deal later in the season than in other years, because Monseigneur could not be torn from his wolf-hunting. He seemed quite unperturbed by events in Flanders, and bored everyone with minute by minute descriptions of each day's adventures. 'Lord! Monseigneur,' said the Princesse de Conti, 'what a memory you have! Sad that it is only for such trifles!' His court remained the centre of hostility against the Duc de Bourgogne, and the serene way in which he listened to the criticism of his son was an encouragement to Vendôme's friends. The Cabal had kept very quiet since the King's angry letters to Alberoni and the Comte d'Evreux; but they soon had cause to become once again vociferous.

When the King returned to Versailles, there was consternation verging on panic, at the news of the retreat from Lille; but a courier from the Duc de Bourgogne, arriving later that day, brought news of the junction with Berwick, and the impending march of the combined armies to the relief. Saint-Simon wonderfully describes the state of the courtiers: 'everyone lived in the expectation of a decisive battle; everyone was tempted to hope for one; it would have seemed like treachery to wish otherwise. People spoke quite openly of their fears and hopes, and even the ladies discussed strategy.' 'Poor Prince Eugene!' sighed Mme d'O, whose husband was in Flanders, with Louis. 'His reputation will be destroyed by this foolhardy siege. Enemy though he is, one cannot help grieving at the disgrace of so great a commander.' But not everyone was so optimistic, and many were afraid.[1] 'Fear,' said Saint-Simon, 'was

---

[1] Mme de Maintenon, shivering from the draught, in her curtained chair, lost confidence. 'I have so often seen towns captured and recaptured that

seen in every face, and to a shocking extent in people's words. The sound of a trotting horse set everyone running they knew not where, and Chamillart's apartment was so crowded with lackeys that they overflowed into the street. Everyone wanted to know the moment a courier arrived, and that dreadful state of anxiety lasted nearly a month, until the uncertainty was ended.'

Life, at Versailles, seemed to come to a standstill. There were no plays or card-parties, for the King had written to the bishops requesting public prayers, and forty-hour services were held in all the churches. Adelaide, as may well be imagined, was consumed by anxiety; she spent long hours praying in the chapel before the Holy Sacrament, when she should have been in bed and asleep, and exhausted her ladies with these nightly vigils.

Mme de Maintenon watched the destruction of her health with loving concern. 'I think as you do,' she wrote in one of her frequent letters to the Princesse des Ursins, 'regarding M. le Duc de Bourgogne, and I agree that it would be wisest to tell him only half of what his wife is suffering. She is now fasting for his sake, and you will readily admit, Madame, that this is the last thing one might have expected of her affection for him. Amid all her different worries, she no longer has any life of her own. I do not at all know what she writes to the Queen, her sister, but I do assure you that your affairs are very close to her heart. She trembles for our predicament. She constantly studies the King's face, and is in despair when she perceives any sadness. She thinks that the Dauphin is not sufficiently disturbed. She talks of nothing but these things that occupy her mind. She tries to find distraction, but continually fails. Her heart flutters whenever a courier arrives. She fears both for her husband's life, and for his reputation; she would like him to court danger; she cannot bear to hear the least criticism of him, and would be deeply grieved were he in any way to vex the King. Truly, Madame, she is at present one of the unhappiest people in the world; and it is I who urge her to be calm and confident.'

A fortnight later she wrote again, this time from Saint-Cyr: 'The truth is, Madame, that I am becoming deeply concerned at what everyone else so much admires in the conduct of Mme la Duchesse de Bourgogne. I love to hear her praised, but the strain is more than

nothing seems secure to me.' She should not have expressed her doubts to Mme des Ursins; but her love of facing the bitter truth made her clearsighted. 'If they take Lille,' she cried, 'they will be in France.' It was the cry of a frightened old woman.

her health can stand; it is not her death that I dread; I cannot regard death as a misfortune for those who suffer; but I fear for her health, because of a swelling on one of her sides, which may well become enlarged in so long a period of unhappiness. The tears that she sheds have brought on inflammation of the gums, to which she is only too prone, and she is bereft of sleep. She fears for France; she fears for Spain; she fears for the Duc de Berry; but above all, she fears for M. le Duc de Bourgogne, lest he allow himself to be over-persuaded by the advice of those around him.' A few days later, she wrote again, 'Three-quarters of the people here share my opinion that Mme la Duchesse de Bourgogne's conduct is truly admirable, and would be highly commendable in an old queen-dowager. She spends her days, either in the chapel, or else writing letters to the army'—and, as Saint-Simon relates, a large part of every night, in vigil before the altar.

What a change in Adelaide! Who could recognise the frivolous young girl who, five years earlier, was too much absorbed by amorous intrigues to correspond with her husband in all the months of his absence?

The King was not particularly concerned about her. Coming on her, one evening, looking sad and depressed, in Mme de Main-tenon's room, he appeared surprised and asked her what was wrong, then tried to cheer her by talking of his relief and satis-faction at the news of the armies being at last united. 'And the princes your grandsons?' she retorted. 'I am anxious about them, of course,' he said, 'but I expect that all will be well.' 'I also am anxious,' she sharply replied, 'which is why I am low and out of spirits.'

Loyal to his principles, Louis XIV remained, at least in appearance imperturbably calm. Yet it was noticed that, when a deputation from the Paris merchants came to address him, at the swearing-in of a new provost, his manner had never been gentler or more gracious. He used the words 'gratitude to my good city', and, in speaking, his expression had softened, a sign of emotion which he would never have allowed himself in earlier days. He was visibly moved, but he continued the routine of his daily life with clockwork regularity, holding long meetings of his councils in the morning, until mass, and working late, after supper, with Chamillart, or another of his ministers. At two o'clock, every afternoon, he went hunting. If a courier arrived before he left, he would tell the main points of the news to the courtiers as his boots were put on, enjoining them to repeat his words exactly. If one came after his departure, the bags were left unopened until his return, no matter how feverishly those with loved ones in the army longed for news. 'The suspense nearly killed us,' said Saint-Simon.

Hunting was the recreation the King most enjoyed. Driving alone in his pony-carriage, he was away from observation, and he lengthened these hours of solitude in the woods, returning, Mme de Maintenon said, 'quite exhausted by the wind and sun'. He discouraged gloomy faces around him, and consumed his bean soup, at supper, with all the proper ceremonies. His chief concern seemed to be the quality of his special bread, in which flecks of barley, rice, straw, and bran were clearly visible. He never appeared depressed. 'Lille must be defended,' was all that he would say; but in those evening sessions, when he and Mme de Maintenon were alone together behind locked doors, he told all his worries, and wept (he cried very easily) upon her bosom. He was, indeed, desperately tired, but he was not defeated. The defence of Lille was a matter of personal pride; for Lille had been his own conquest, the achievement of his victorious youth, the key to France itself. He was disappointed in his armies, his generals, and his children. The Duc de Bourgogne had indeed shown zeal for his service, and Christian virtue, but zeal was no more than good intentions, and virtue wins no military victories.

One sign of the King's fatigue, which the Court remarked on, was that, on 1 September, his monthly purge, by Fagon's advice, was discontinued, 'on account of the disturbing news from Flanders'.[1] It was thought advisable to 'wait until the conclusion of this grave question, so that he may be purged more at leisure.'

The example set by the King of moderation and restraint availed nothing against the venom of the Cabal which, headed by Madame la Duchesse, exploded in abuse of Louis and Adelaide, and fulsome praise of Vendôme. All the talk was of the latter being the only general eager to attack the enemy. All Vendôme's idleness, his missed opportunities, his negligence were forgotten, and Louis was accounted the cause of every failure. It was he, they said, who had refused to attack at Oudenarde, he alone who had insisted on a shameful retreat when the battle was almost won. Far worse even than that, his physical courage was called into question, and his

---

[1] When it was discovered that the King had gone against Fagon's orders by taking physic on 10 September, the courtiers had their first intimation that the campaign in Flanders was not coming to an end as soon as had been expected.

unfortunate dependence on his confessor made the basis of a rumour that he hated war and would be glad to see Lille captured, partly because it would mean the end of the campaign, and partly because someone had put it into his head that the fortress was an unjustified conquest.[1]

In the disturbed atmosphere of Versailles, still without news from Flanders, rumours, once planted, struck root and spread like wild-fire, especially since the King himself appeared not wholly to disbelieve them. He did not go so far as to speak against his grandson, but he let slip certain remarks to his bastards and his valets that were only too well attuned to what the Cabal were saying. He refused, moreover, to hear a word spoken against Vendôme, and publicly rebuked the Prince de Conti for speaking ill of him.

Mme de Maintenon, meanwhile, was strong in her defence of Louis, and a loving support of Adelaide, who was heard to say, one evening, 'Dear Aunt, my heart is bursting, I am afraid of being a trouble, but I do so much want to weep with you'. It is not easy to find reasons for Mme de Maintenon's unusually firm stand. It may have been her love of Adelaide; or perhaps a sense of injustice; or possibly, as Saint-Simon thought, because she was outraged at discovering that, for the first time, other people had influence with the King. Be that as it may, she did her utmost to defend Louis; not that she approved of his conduct, for she very well knew how clearly the King had made his wishes known and how obstinate the prince had been in disregarding them. Her own excuse appears in a letter to the Princesse des Ursins:

'The King alone is unfaltering in his desire to relieve Lille and so protect the honour of France. M. le Duc de Bourgogne does not share that opinion, because he is among those generals who oppose it. M. de Berwick is their leader. M. de Vendôme is the only one of them who wishes to attack and carry by storm all the entrenchments. The rest maintain that the King's army would be destroyed in such an assault. They have lost confidence in M. de Vendôme since the defeat at Oudenarde. Mme la Duchesse de Bourgogne fears that her husband is being led astray by bad advice; yet how can he oppose M. le Maréchal de Berwick,[2] a capable soldier, with long experience, whom the King himself has appointed to be his

---

[1] This was casting suspicion, quite unfounded, on Fénelon.

[2] It is hard to understand why Berwick should have given the prince such bad advice. One suggestion is that he loathed and distrusted Vendôme, and thus automatically refused all proposals coming from him.

adviser?' 'What can our prince do?' she continues in another letter, 'having so little experience himself, and facing such difficult problems, except rely on the man who enjoys the trust of his grandfather, the King. How can he take it upon himself to decide that the advice offered is faint-hearted, and that he should opt instead for M. de Vendôme, against whom three-quarters of the army are bursting with indignation.'

These were strong words, but hardly a vindication, for whatever virtues Louis possessed, his inertia clearly showed that he lacked the moral courage, initiative and, above all, the sense of military honour that were considered the special attributes of a prince. Established at his headquarters, near Tournai, and ill-advised by Berwick, he kept the entire French army inactive, except for an unsuccessful attempt to stop an enemy convoy of five hundred waggons, loaded with all the supplies needed for a very long siege. It was altogether a shameful incident, for the advance guard of French infantry broke, and disappeared into the woods, rather than face the fire of the escort.

After that reverse, Louis lost all heart for the campaign. Nothing, he believed, could now save Lille, and he wrote to the King to that effect. Berwick also wrote, stating that the wisest plan would be to leave Lille to its fate, and return with a fresh army, in the following spring, to besiege and retake it. Vendôme on the other hand was supremely confident. No further convoys would be allowed to pass, he wrote, on 30 September; but little harm had been done, 'for I cannot believe that five hundred waggons are sufficient to capture Lille'. He, at the same time, proposed wildly optimistic plans to capture Ostend and the Channel ports and thus cut off Marlborough's retreat. The King replied to Berwick that he did not share his views. 'I assure you that it will be far easier to save the town under present conditions than to lay siege to it in enemy hands.' He tended to support Vendôme, who at least proposed action, and wrote strong words to Louis, urging him for his honour's sake, not to remain idle; but to do all possible to prevent more convoys from reaching the enemy.

His words had no effect on Louis; but the fall of Lille, on 23 October, after a heroic defence, ended all argument. The terms of surrender were sent to the prince for his signature, and arrived at his headquarters on the following day. Louis was playing his favourite game of shuttlecock, and refused to stop, or even interrupt the match. It is true that he had already heard the news, but he should not have kept the officer from the beleaguered fortress waiting a full hour before seeing him. The army learned of it and were shocked and disgusted, and the Cabal was thus provided with fresh ammunition for their malice.

It was not only the fall of Lille that gave substance to their abuse, for Louis's entire life, at that period, was apparently idle and ineffectual. He seldom appeared on horseback, being unwilling to face the troops and their displeasure. He did not enjoy the society of senior officers on his staff, and spent his days writing letters, studying anatomy and mathematics, playing tennis or billiards with his brother, or indulging in those repellent games which Saint-Simon says so much disgusted his wife—the killing of flies and frogs at mealtimes and dreamily grinding grape-pips to powder. In spite of all the criticism, he continued to see his confessor far too often and for too long; but his main preoccupation, at this time, seems to have been the question of whether he was sinning by having his headquarters at a nunnery, the Abbaye de Saulsoy, and he wrote frequently to Fénelon asking advice, and promising to go elsewhere, if so instructed.

There then followed a series of most admirable letters from Fénelon, full of affection and praise for Louis's devotion to religion, but gradually trying to make him understand how his indecision and lack of confidence were destroying the great hopes which people had had for him. He then, with many apologies for lacking due discretion, took Louis quite harshly to task: 'People are saying that while you are pious to the extent of asceticism in small things, you yet allow yourself to appear noticeably tipsy on many occasions. They complain that your confessor is too often closeted with you, and interferes in discussions on military matters; they say that you have corresponded with rash men unworthy of your confidence.' Then came most excellent advice. 'Though God has given you many talents, you are in danger of making irreparable mistakes by your hesitancy, if you give yourself over to a weak and over-scrupulous piety. Listen to people of long experience, and then make up your own mind. It is less dangerous to make a wrong move than to make no move at all or to move too late.' As regards the question of the Abbaye de Saulsoy, Fénelon at first praised Louis for his sensitive concern, then passed the matter off by saying that such things frequently happened during campaigns, and should not be regarded too seriously.

The prince's replies to his old friend, for whom he had so deep and loyal an affection, are disarmingly humble and sincere. Proud as Louis was, he might well have been offended by Fénelon's frank criticism, and his apparent willingness to believe all the accusations; but there is no sign of resentment in the letters. After saying that he was far less devout than Fénelon supposed, and that he saw in himself 'nothing but failure, lapses, omissions, and negligence of the most essential religious duties', he admits to being intemperate, over-scrupulous, proud, arrogant, and contemptuous of the human race; also to an attitude towards individuals, life, and the world in general, that was devoid of the love of God, or love of his neighbour, as himself. He than set about to defend himself in much the same way as Mme de Maintenon had excused him in her letter to the Princesse des Ursins. He never abused Vendôme; saying only that the latter's sudden and ill-considered plans had destroyed all confidence in him; but that on several occasions he, himself, had acquiesced in them, when he should have made a firm decision—a weakness for which he might well be held at fault.

After this, he explained to Fénelon, at great length, the orders he had given, at Oudenarde, and the reasons why he had not moved to relieve Lille, and ended his letter: 'I expect there will be much discussion. I accept censure for mistakes where I have been to blame, and disregard the rest; I honestly forgive those who wish and do me ill, and shall pray for them all the days of my life. These are my sentiments, dear Archbishop, and despite my failures and mistakes, my absolute determination is to live with God. Pray for me without ceasing, that He may complete what He has begun in me and destroy all that comes from original sin and my own wickedness.'

In these letters to Fénelon, Louis shows generosity, even a kind of nobility among the grave weaknesses that spoil his character; but where is the fire and resolution, the power to command men, and the sense of military honour which the people looked for in their future king? He does not seem to have had the makings of a great king; on the other hand, he only too clearly showed the probability that he would become a bigot.

During the last weeks of the campaign 'the army at Saulsoy, near Tournai,' said Saint-Simon, 'was in a state of complete torpor that overcame even M. le Duc de Bourgogne'. Vendôme, on the other hand, was as full as ever of reckless confidence. 'It is a pity,' he wrote to Chamillart, 'that the town of Lille should have capitulated, and I am mortally sorry for it ... But if we can manage to stay where we are for some time longer, I will answer for it that the enemy will

be more impeded than ourselves.' He was full of plans to attack
Marlborough's army, to all of which Berwick objected, thinking
them too dangerous. Louis supported Berwick in the quarrels that
ensued, but he does not seem to have been worried or made unhappy by them, for he wrote to Chamillart (whom the King sent
to Flanders between 1 and 9 November, to settle future plans),
suggesting that there should be a great ball, at Tournai, in honour
of Adelaide. 'We have oboeists in the army, who play, perhaps, even
better than those at Marly, and without this ball I cannot hope to
see her dance this winter, being persuaded, as I said to you, that I
shall spend the greater part of it on the banks of the river Scheldt.'

There was no ball, Berwick was sent to command the army in
Germany, which was very near to being disgraced, and Vendôme
was given permission to put his plan of an attack on Marlborough
into action. Marlborough, however, forestalled him, by suddenly
leaving Lille and advancing at tremendous speed across the French
lines and the Scheldt to relieve Brussels, which was besieged. This
was something that Vendôme had said could never happen, but
which Louis had always seen as a serious danger.

Vendôme sent warning of Marlborough's plan to Louis, urging
him to march with the entire army, on the following day, in order to
intercept him. The courier arrived late at night, when Louis was
undressing to go to bed. His staff disagreed in their advice. Some
wished him to march then and there; others to keep his clothes on,
so as to be ready to leave at dawn; others again advised him to do
as Vendôme suggested—retire to bed, and leave on the next day. It
was this advice that Louis followed; but, when he rose, he learned
that the enemy were already across the Scheldt, and that the time
for action had passed. As a matter of fact, even had he taken the
first course, and gone at once as he should have done, he would still
have been too late to stop Marlborough. Nonetheless, his fallen
reputation was not helped, and he did something even worse in that
respect for, having eaten an excellent dinner, and not having to
march, he went off quite publicly to play tennis. It is easy to
imagine what use the Cabal made of that lapse, and how songs of
the most vicious and malevolent kind were heard in the army, Paris,
and the Court, 'drowning,' as Saint-Simon says, 'the magnitude of
M. de Vendôme's errors in the uproar created over M. le Duc de
Bourgogne's unseemly conduct'.

It was the final disgrace; the French army was split in two and,
all Vendôme's plans now being impracticable, the only course

remaining was to bring the army home. The King wrote to Vendôme, 'It would have been more fitting for my army to have been disbanded in a reputable fashion, instead of retreating as though they had been routed.' But that was his only comment. To Louis he said, 'It was to be desired that you should have had more satisfaction in a campaign, during which I am persuaded that you did your best, on every occasion.'

There was, however, still trouble with Vendôme, who wished to postpone the break-up of the army, in order, one of the generals said, 'to risk the killing or wounding of fifteen thousand men', in one last glorious enterprise. Louis rightly thwarted that idea, and also prevented him from obtaining his wish to remain in Flanders, in sole command of the troops left to defend Ghent and Bruges. It was plain enough that Vendôme, angry and aggrieved by failure, would be most unlikely to return without some dangerous adventure, regardless of the risk. This brought, from the King, a peremptory order for him to come home, and Louis, relieved of that worry, at least, was able to make arrangements for his own return.

16

The Return

LOUIS RETURNED to Versailles to find his personal situation even worse than he had feared. Saint-Simon, his staunchest and most outspoken supporter, out of favour with the King, had retired to the country, leaving the defence to Beauvilliers, whom he termed 'unnecessarily faint hearted', and to Chevreuse who appeared to believe that princely dignity was best maintained by silence, and that, given time, all the fuss would blow over. It was thus left to Adelaide to struggle gallantly on, loyally supported by Mme de Maintenon, whose distress may be seen in a pathetic letter she wrote to the Princesse des Ursins:

'You will have learned by the general post that our army has acted true to its form, by successfully avoiding the enemy throughout the summer, and now permitting them to cross the Scheldt unopposed. This conduct is so outrageous that one would hang oneself, did one not see in it an act of God, to try the pride of kings, and humble that of the French nation . . . I am grief-stricken, Madame, by the present state of affairs, and by the condition of Mme la Duchesse de Bourgogne. She sheds a great many tears; but they are tears of courage and true love, and there is not, in them, the smallest hint of weakening. She sees an outburst of hostility against her husband which is truly incomprehensible. They blame him for all our misfortunes; yet he never made the decisions. I have already had the honour to inform you that he trusted the Maréchal de Berwick's advice by the King's command. There has been no quarrel between our prince and M. de Vendôme since they have been alone; but it was not M. le Duc de Bourgogne's fault that the Scheldt was crossed. They warned M. de Vendôme that the Duke of Marlborough was already on the move, but he said it was a lie, and when at last he marched against him, he found that it was too late.'

For the Cabal it was a moment of triumph, and the campaign reached new heights of slander and vilification. Mme la Duchesse was the author of several verses, some of them frankly vulgar; one of them branching out into a new line of attack. It had become customary to call him a coward; she now added a thirst for vengeance to his other vices:

> 'They say that the Burgundian
> Has lost the honour that becomes a man.
> Beware lest he turn round on you,
> For he's a coward and bigot too,
> You'll find in him no pity.'

But it was not in Louis's nature to be vindictive. Only a few months earlier, he had greeted the unspeakable Alberoni with graciousness, and was reproached for his eagerness to forgive the Comte d'Evreux. His friends, who knew him best, feared that he might not defend himself, to the King, and that Christian charity would prevent his speaking the truth about Vendôme. Fénelon clearly saw that danger. He wrote to Louis that 'nothing becomes you better than your disposition to forgive everything, and even to profit from adverse criticism'; but he added that this should not be carried to the extreme of failing to justify his actions by condemning those of other people, and he gave a plan for the difficult days ahead when the prince returned to Versailles, and for his all-important first interview with the King. Louis, Fénelon said, should begin by admitting humbly and sincerely, all his faults and mistakes, but, that accomplished, should speak freely of Vendôme, listing his weaknesses—'Laziness, negligence, rashness, and obstinacy. Seeing nothing for himself, listening to no advice, deciding everything without regard for risks; without foresight, deliberation, or plans, and with no other resource in moments of crisis than impetuous courage; having no respect for men of capability and experience, and existing in a perpetual lethargy of mind and body.' He ended with a clear warning: 'If you speak out strongly and nobly, you will gain the King's respect. If, on the other hand, you appear nervous and ineffectual, the whole world, which has been waiting for this moment, will conclude that there is nothing to be hoped from you, and that you are not concerned to re-establish your good name, not even at the Court.'

Beauvilliers and Chevreuse fully shared Fénelon's opinion; so also did Saint-Simon. Everything seemed to them to depend on that first encounter with the King; and they were anxious to see Louis and instruct him before it could take place. Unfortunately Court etiquette made that impossible, for, on his arrival at Versailles, it required him to see no one, not even his wife, before making his report. They were thus obliged to fall back on Adelaide, who had been desired by Louis to drive out several miles from the château to meet him on the road. Adelaide wanted that also; but in the end it was considered too dangerous, and she was advised to say nothing, but to start out as on her ordinary drive, and let the meeting happen, as though by pure chance. In the end, she decided not to go, and Saint-Simon made a different plan, by which the prince would arrive at two in the morning; spend the night with his wife; see M. de Beauvilliers, perhaps also Mme de Maintenon in the small hours, and go to the King at a time when no one would be present, except for a few valets.

Louis either did not get that message, or decided otherwise, for he arrived at seven in the evening of Monday, 11 December, just an hour before the King's supper. He came in by one of the back entrances; Beauvilliers met him at the door of his coach, and Saint-Simon, who happened to be looking out of a window, left Mme de Roucy, on whom he was calling, and ran with all speed to the head of the staircase. He saw the prince come up, cheerful and smiling, chatting gaily to a small group of courtiers following him. He did not appear in the least apprehensive, but his friends were not able to speak to him alone. He did, however, warmly embrace Saint-Simon, and breathed into his ear that he had heard what that nobleman had said and done on his behalf. There was not time for more; they had to watch him go uninstructed to meet the King, not knowing what kind of reception he would have from that disappointed and terrifying old monarch. They need not have been afraid, for they might have known that Louis XIV's reverence for the blood of his royal ancestors would have prevented him from humiliating his grandson.

It was the hour when he was invariably to be found, working in Mme de Maintenon's bedroom with one or other of his ministers. Monday was the turn of Saint-Simon's close friend Ponchartrain the Chancellor, who thus saw all and told Saint-Simon exactly what happened. Mme de Maintenon was sitting rapt in thought, in her 'nook' of crimson damask, designed to protect her from draughts, and concealing from her visitors the precise grandeur of the armchair in which she sat in the King's presence. The King sat on the other side of the fire, his back to the wall, and in front of him a table for the minister's portfolio, with a folding chair for him to sit on. When they heard the bustle that heralded the prince's arrival, the King concealed his agitation, though he several times changed countenance. Adelaide, in Mme de Maintenon's great drawing-room, appeared to be trembling, and ran backwards and forwards, wondering by which door the prince would enter. Mme de Maintenon herself seemed to be in a trance.

Suddenly the doors were flung open, Louis appeared, and presented himself to the King who, now completely master of himself, came forward a couple of steps, and kissed him affectionately. Then, after talk of the journey and the roads, he turned him towards Adelaide, saying with a smile, 'Have you nothing to say to her?' 'The Prince,' says Saint-Simon, 'looked for a moment in her direction, answering the King with deep respect, but as though he dared not move or turn away. He then greeted Mme de Maintenon, who did very handsomely by him. There was further talk, all standing, of journeys, roads, and lodgings, after which the King dismissed him, saying that it was not fair to keep him any longer from the pleasure of his wife's company, and adding that there would be time for other meetings.'

This first and most dreaded encounter thus passed without disgrace, but there was still Louis's father to be greeted. Monseigneur had not troubled to be present at his son's arrival. He had gone instead to the play and, returning just before the King's supper, waited for him grumpily, in Mme de Maintenon's drawing-room. The Maréchale d'Estrées, a silly woman who kept no guard upon her tongue, asked him how he could bear to stay so calm and not go after his son to embrace him, to which he answered coldly that it was not for him to search for the Duc de Bourgogne, whose duty it was to come to him. When the prince eventually appeared, Monseigneur's embrace was kind enough, but not by any means as affectionate as the King's had been.

Halfway through the King's supper, the Duc de Berry arrived and received a welcome rather better than that accorded to the Duc de Bourgogne. The young prince had done well in the army and had made himself popular, and the King wished to show some difference. Adelaide, who was very fond of him, asked him to supper in her private room; but Saint-Simon relates, that 'M. le Duc de Bourgogne's conjugal ardour cut that festivity rather short'.

So ended that first perilous evening, which passed off a good deal better than Louis's friends had dared to hope. Saint-Simon, however, was not reassured; he thought that the prince was unsuitably confident after his disastrous campaign, and he had learned that the entire Court was blaming him for his ill-timed cheerfulness. He said as much to Beauvilliers; they decided to issue a warning, and waited in suspense for the next interview. It came three days later, on Thursday 14th, when Louis and the King were closeted together for more than three hours, in Mme de Maintenon's room. His friends had been afraid that, despite all their advice, piety might restrain him on the subject of Vendôme; but they had underestimated Adelaide's influence; fortified by her brave spirit, he had dared to speak out, and had not spared him. As he came from his audience, he scribbled a note to Beauvilliers. 'I am well pleased,' he said, 'and have reason to believe that the King is satisfied with me. I thought that I should tell you this, so as to give you a good night's rest. He did not seem to be against making further use of me. I dare to think that I am sure of re-employment, should I desire it; and that I most heartily do.'

It was going to be far more difficult to appease Monseigneur, but the indomitable Adelaide set out with Mme de Maintenon to prepare the way. They went together to visit Mlle Choin, Monseigneur's unofficial wife, and charmed her into speaking to him; indeed, she went farther, by being present during the whole of the long conversation that he had with Louis just two days after his audience with the King. That same evening, Monseigneur gave a dinner-party at Meudon in honour of the Bourgognes, and thus the appearances, at least, were preserved.

Vendôme arrived on the morning of Saturday the 16th, and made his bow as the King went from his study to dine. The Cabal, who had been disappointed by the kind reception of Louis, were greatly heartened by the glad look with which the King greeted Vendôme—'a beaming smile', said Saint-Simon. He clearly wanted to hold the balance and show no displeasure to either. But Vendôme had hoped for something better, and although he was granted an audience, it lasted only an hour, and Mme de Maintenon was present the entire time. He then went off to Meudon, where he was sure of a welcome from Monseigneur, who kept him a long time in conversation; but it was merely gossip and small talk; he did not mention the campaign. At this point, Vendôme made a major error, for he tried to compromise Monseigneur, by extracting from him a promise to visit him at Anet. To his surprise, Monseigneur looked profoundly embarrassed, and would say nothing definite;[1] whereupon Vendôme left in a huff. Saint-Simon saw him that evening, climbing the staircase of the new wing, on the way to call on his friend the Duc du Maine. He was in darkness, without servants or torchbearers; but Saint-Simon was pleased to see, by the light of his own torches, that he looked extremely worried.

Vendôme later called on Louis, who received him kindly, as was his nature; but it says much for the prince's generosity that he should have done so since by then he had learned of the evil reports, spread by Vendôme's friends. The one person whom Vendôme dared not confront was Adelaide. He did not set foot in her apartments, even to pay the obligatory courtesy-visit to the first lady of France, for he feared that she would send him packing. It was an impossible situation, and after a week at Meudon and Versailles he departed to Anet, where he thought he would be submerged under a wave of courtiers, as had happened in 1706. He suffered a great disappointment, for the courtiers he invited spoke of the fatigues of the journey (which in earlier years had seemed no longer than to Marly), and fabricated excuses, or sent none, but failed to honour the engagement. The King had said a word; or rather, had said nothing, but had allowed it to be understood that Vendôme, if not in disgrace, was out of favour, and that it would not be a good way to pay one's court to be known to visit Anet. Thus the grass grew in the courtyard, because no guests trod it down, and the place became a desert. If Louis had lost to Vendôme in Flanders, Adelaide was victorious at Versailles.

Her victory, however, did nothing to raise Louis in public esteem. Vendôme was still popular—the great general, undefeated in Italy, and thwarted of victory in Flanders, who appeared likely, because of the antagonism of the Duchesse de Bourgogne, to be taken from his command. The lampoons were directed at her, for the first time:

> 'Princess, you are welcome to dance,
> And share all the pleasures of France,
> For you cause us no harm by your joy.
> But when Vendôme you attack,
> Your husband to back,
> You work in your father's employ.'

In earlier days, the King's word would have been enough to change public opinion; but he was old, and although at the Court

[1] No doubt the King had had a word with him.

he was still feared and obeyed, at Meudon and in Paris people looked forward to a new reign, when Monseigneur and his clique would come to power.

Vendôme was bored; alone at Anet he grew restless, and went off to stay with his millionaire friend Crozat, planning a return to favour by way of Marly and Meudon, where his friends were gathered. He was bold enough to ask for Marly, and the King, according to the Marquise d'Huxelles 'received the request most graciously; but,' she adds, 'he has been forbidden even to mention the campaign, a favour granted to Mme la Duchesse de Bourgogne who bears a grudge against him'. The first time he went to Marly was on 6 February 1709, and he was there again on the 15th. Saint-Simon says that 'this small remainder of privilege somewhat consoled him, for it seemed to show that, despite the efforts of his enemies, the King and Monseigneur were not displeased with him'. He there 'resumed all the arrogance of his days of glory, his haughty bearing, his loud voice, and his habit of monopolising every conversation. To see him there, although sparsely surrounded, one might have thought him master of the salon, and with Monseigneur, and even with the King, when he dared be so bold, he had all the air of a favourite'.

Louis's piety obliged him to endure the presence of Vendôme; but his staff were sorely tried. Adelaide, growing more and more indignant, kept silent, and waited for a chance to destroy the monster. She had succeeded in ousting him from Versailles, where she had refused to speak to him; but her ability to banish him from Marly and Meudon was by no means certain, for the King still retained for him much of his old affection, and the efforts of the Cabal seemed to have more effect than Mme de Maintenon's gentle pressure. Louis, in all this, was no help to her; indeed, in his readiness to forgive the past, he had publicly received visits from Vendôme, the very person whom the Cabal were using to tear his character to shreds. He had taken up his old life, shut away in his study, or in church, and seemed proudly uninterested in events at the Court.

Adelaide's opportunity came on the King's first excursion to Marly, after Easter, when Vendôme, talking too loud, and making himself intolerably conspicuous, had either forgotten the King's ban on discussing the past campaign, or had stung the princess to fury by his mere presence. Brelan was the card-game then in fashion. Monseigneur, making up a table for her, needed a fifth person to take a hand, and seeing Vendôme at the other end of the room, had sent for him. 'Thereupon, Mme la Duchesse de Bourgogne said quietly, but very distinctly, that M. de Vendôme's presence at Marly was sufficiently painful to her, without having to play cards with him, and that she begged to be excused. Monseigneur, who until that moment had not given the matter a thought, could not disapprove; he looked around and chose someone else. Vendôme, however, persisted in approaching them, and received the humiliation of a snub straight in his face, before the whole company.' 'You may imagine,' continued Saint-Simon, 'to what extent that proud man was stung by the affront . . . He turned on his heel, and retired as soon as possible to his bedroom, where he could fume in private, and unconstrained.'

When Adelaide had time to reflect, she was greatly heartened by such an easy success; yet she feared the King's displeasure for, despite the affectionate terms on which they lived, she was naturally shy and gentle, and very easily disconcerted. She nonetheless decided to press on, and that same evening went to tell all to Mme de Maintenon, saying that Vendôme's presence at Marly was more than she could bear. It was a sign of the King's continued friendship and, after all that had happened in Flanders, it was acutely painful to her to see his royal affection divided, apparently equally, between his grandson and M. de Vendôme. Mme de Maintenon was very much of the same opinion. She spoke to the King that night, and he, desiring the return of peace and quiet, caring too much for Adelaide to let her be hurt, and abominating people with grudges, sent his head-valet next day to tell Vendôme not to ask again for Marly, because it pained Mme la Duchesse de Bourgogne to see him, and it was unfair to embarrass her. His sudden departure caused a rumour that he had been turned out of Marly; but that was not so, he was allowed to come one more time to keep up appearances; but never after that.

With Marly closed to him, there still remained Meudon, and there he was on firmer ground. The King had said nothing of forbidding him Meudon, and Vendôme was there for every excursion, boasting aloud of his friendship with Monseigneur, and parading himself before Adelaide, as though eager to prove that there, at least, her wishes did not prevail. There was nothing she could do but bear his insolence patiently and bide her time. Her moment came two months later, when the King and Mme de Maintenon went to dine, but not to sleep, at Meudon, and she accompanied them. Vendôme had the temerity to be one of the first to approach the door of their coach, when they stepped down, which so much vexed her that she showed him less than her usual civility, turning her back upon him after the merest sketch of a curtsey. Vendôme, instead of absenting himself, had the folly to stay near her and, after dinner, came to her table, as though to take her hand. He received the same treatment to an even more marked degree, which cut him to the quick, and put him so much out of countenance that he retired furiously to his bedroom, and remained there until late next day. He paid dearly for that indiscretion, for Adelaide spent the rest of that evening making Monseigneur aware of his lack of consideration, and, after returning to Versailles, complained openly to Mme de Maintenon and the King, pointing out that Vendôme was making his home at Meudon purely in order to spite her, and to make up for being deprived of Marly.

Next day, when Vendôme complained to Monseigneur of persecution by the princess, he was given so cold an answer that he retired, his eyes wet with tears. The day after saw the end of the affair. He was playing cards in one of the private rooms, when d'Antin arrived from Versailles. He went to Vendôme's table, asking with an air of such deep gravity when the hand would be finished that Vendôme inquired the reason for it. D'Antin said that he had delivered the message entrusted to him. 'But,' said Vendôme, much surprised, 'I gave you no message.' 'Excuse me, Sir,' replied d'Antin. 'Have you forgotten that I must give you an answer?' At that Vendôme left the game and accompanied him into Monseigneur's dark little privy, where he learned, tête-à-tête with d'Antin, that the King had ordered Monseigneur never again to take him to Meudon, for the same reason that he had ceased to be invited to Marly—the displeasure caused by his presence to Mme la Duchesse de Bourgogne. Vendôme was seized with a perfect transport of rage, spitting out every insult he could call to mind. He remained at Meudon, until the end of that excursion, and on the day of Monseigneur's departure fled back to Anet alone. He was now bereft of all support, save what consolation he could find with his valets and his vices. It was disgrace indeed, for he was also informed that his services in the army were no longer required, and that his pay would cease.

Vendôme's friends seethed with rage; all the more so since it was plain to every eye that it was Adelaide who had brought him low. One has only to hear Saint-Simon's shout of triumph. 'One saw that huge monster blown over by the breath of a brave young princess, who received well-deserved acclaim. Those who loved her were charmed to see the stuff of which she was made, and those who were against her and her husband, shook with fright. That high and mighty Cabal, so closely united in their determination to rule after the King's death, those captains, both male and female, so venturesome, so insolent, to whom success brought the promise of greater power, now fell prostrate, overcome by terror. It was a pleasure to watch their low cunning, as they attached themselves to such of their opponents as they judged to be most powerful, and whom, in their arrogance they had lately hated and despised. Best of all was to observe the embarrassment, the doubt, nay, the fear with which they cringed before the young princess, lingering miserably in the vicinity of Mgr le Duc de Bourgogne, and of those who were closest to him, and to his friends showing all kinds of servile compliance.'

No one gained more than Mme de Maintenon by Vendôme's collapse. Apart from the joy of crushing the man who was making Adelaide unhappy, there was the relief of seeing her own influence once more become paramount with the King, for no one doubted that she had been the principal agent of Vendôme's disgrace.

In the following year, Philip V, remembering Vendôme's victories, asked the King to send him to command the Spanish armies, and actually asked Louis to support his request. That prince had taken no part in the battle fought so bravely against Vendôme by his wife. 'Deep in prayer, and in his studies,' said Saint-Simon, 'he scarcely knew of earthly happenings, and was thus very ready to do what his brother asked. "I am much flattered," he wrote, "by your good opinion. It seems to me, God be praised! that I shall always value the public good above private interests, and as for anything approaching hatred or resentment, I must shun it, and do so as a Christian duty. Perhaps you will think this only vanity, but I speak as I believe. Therefore, dearest brother, be sure that if there is any support that I can give for what you ask, I shall apply myself to it with all my heart." '

When the King decided to allow Vendôme to take up the Spanish command, Louis thought that he should tell his brother something of the man's true nature. 'Although you already know him, I think it would be wise for me to say a word, which I do protest is free from malice, for God knows how I have been regarding him, blaming him for nothing that appeared to originate in others, and freely recognising his attachment and respect for the King, Monseigneur, and the rest of the royal family. It is M. de Vendôme's nature to take the wish for the fact. All that he wishes he believes to be true; what he fears, he thinks will never happen. He clings to his opinions, and once an idea enters his head, nothing will dispossess him of it. He is arrogant and quick to anger, even with his best friends. Moreover, he is lazy, for which I believe that his past illnesses are partly responsible . . . He has all the courage imaginable, perhaps too much, exposing himself to danger more even than ordinary soldiers. He has the best intentions in the world, and a kind heart, there, in a few words, dear brother, is a true portrait of M. de Vendôme, in which I have essayed only to show him as he is, for God be thanked, I have no disposition to speak ill of anyone unnecessarily.'

While Adelaide was struggling with Vendôme, France had been suffering the most terrible winter within living memory. On Twelfth Night the glass had begun to fall, and within a few days the temperature had reached 21 degrees centigrade below zero. By the fourth day, the Seine and all the other rivers were frozen and—what had never been seen before—the sea froze hard enough to bear transport all along the shore. To make matters worse, it had thawed altogether for seven or eight days, and then had as suddenly refrozen. The second bout did not last so long as the first, but all the crops and even the fruit trees were destroyed; the seeds died in the ground; vegetable gardens were ruined; no walnuts or olives survived, and scarcely any of the vines.

We have known winters as cold in the present century, but there was this difference. In the old houses of the rich at that period, with their huge rooms and tall windows, there were no means of keeping warm, except for the wood fires which did little to raise the general temperature. At Versailles people suffered greatly. Saint-Simon tells how bottles of eau-de-Cologne broke in the cupboards of rooms that had fires and were surrounded by chimney-flues; and of how, one evening when he was supping with the Duc de Villeroy, in his little bedroom, splinters of ice fell into their glasses, from the decanters on the chimney-piece, though they had been brought there straight from his tiny kitchen, where a huge fire was burning.

Madame describes the bitter cold in one of her letters, telling of the King's supper, when the huge fire burned people's faces, but did nothing towards warming the rest of them. She speaks of the ink freezing on the Marquise d'Huxelles's pen, as she wrote, and of how one of the counsellors of the Metz Parlement found the bodies of two poor boys frozen to death by his cellar door, when he went to examine his champagne bottles.

If the rich suffered, the poor, as may be imagined, were infinitely worse off. The King had firewood distributed to the poor of Paris, but that availed little, and there were many deaths. 'People are dying like flies,' said Madame, reporting that twenty-four thousand had died in Paris between 5 January and 2 February. Vast numbers fell ill with chest complaints, and very many succumbed, including the old Maréchale de La Mothe, who had looked after Monseigneur and Louis, when they were babies, and Mme de Maintenon's crony, Mme d'Heudicourt. The absences caused by illness or mourning were so numerous that when the King went to Marly, in February, Versailles was left with a bigger population of sick or otherwise incapacitated than had ever before been recorded. In Paris, the Opera and gaming-houses were closed, and so was the Parlement. Most of the labourers were unemployable, and herds of deer died in the open fields.

But the sufferings from the intense cold were as nothing to those caused by the famine that followed. It was soon realised that there would be no harvest at all. The rumour spread; everyone hoarded last year's grain, and the price of bread soared. The more prudent resowed their cornfields with barley, and they were the lucky ones, for it saved their lives. Speculation rapidly made matters worse, and according to Madame and Saint-Simon some of the highest in the land were involved. 'The old ragbag,' said Madame, meaning Mme de Maintenon, 'has been buying corn cheaply and selling it at a high price ... When she saw that the harvest had failed, she bought up all the corn remaining in the markets. She has made a vast amount of money, but people are dying of hunger.' Saint-Simon reported, furthermore, that 'the gentlemen of the Finance Department have seized, through their agents in the markets, all the corn in France, and are selling it at their own price, to the King's advantage, not forgetting their own.'

Mme de Maintenon may have been wrongly suspected. Her pathetic letters to the Princesse des Ursins show her unhappiness at the suffering, and her belief that it was a punishment sent by God, to humble the pride of France. 'How can you say, Madame,' she wrote despairingly, 'that God is not against us when He sends us such a winter as has not been seen for the past hundred and five or six years? ... The poor are dying and we are helpless to save them because our land no longer produces food.' Boislille, annotating the Memoirs of Saint-Simon, strongly defends the financiers, saying that they were following Desmaretz the minister's prudent instructions to buy corn where it was cheapest, in order to feed the provinces where it was being sold at an exorbitant price. Nonetheless, there was speculation by those known as *les blatiers*, the corn-chandlers, who 'profited by the people's destitution, and turned their indigence into a barbarous source of wealth'. Public opinion did not confine its anger to corn-merchants and financiers. There were murmured threats of rebellion in Paris; d'Argenson, the head of police, was set on in his carriage, and Monseigneur was several times held up on his way to the Opera by mobs composed largely of women screaming for bread. He had only escaped by throwing money to them, and promising miracles. The King heard the rioting through the windows of the château de Versailles, for the people went shouting in the streets, exhorting the poor to be patient no longer, since nothing worse could befall them than their imminent death from starvation. The speeches were frequent and insolent, with loud and bitter attacks on the government and the King's person. Mme de Maintenon herself was not spared, when a sacrilegious version of the Lord's Prayer was printed.

> 'Our Father that art at Versailles,
> Thy name's no longer hallowed,
> Thy kingdom is no longer great
> Nor is thy will done on the earth or the sea.
> Give us this day our daily bread, for we cannot buy it.
> Forgive the enemies who have defeated us,
> But not the generals who let them win.
> Fall not to the temptations of the Maintenon,
> And deliver us from Chamillart. Amen.'

Other verses were plainly insulting, with an ominous forecast of the events that came with the Revolution.

> 'The Grandpapa's a braggart,
> The son's an idiot,
> The grandson has a cowardly heart,
> Oh! what a gallant lot.
> I pity you poor Frenchmen,
> Beneath their rule, Oh God!
> Do now as did the Englishmen,
> A wink to you is like a nod.'

The King was deeply disturbed. Maréchal, his first surgeon, had the courage to tell him what was being said and done, and warned him of the frightful conclusions to which even the steadiest sections of the population were being driven; but, although he was moved by compassion and not angry, he did not act. Unlike his usual self, he allowed himself to show signs of the appalling strain that he was undergoing, and to Maréchal's anxious questions he admitted that he felt 'very low indeed'. 'He contains himself,' wrote Mme de Maintenon, 'he keeps his thoughts to himself; but he does not believe that peace is as near as our generals could wish.' He pursued the ordinary course of his life; his only respite being his solitary drives in the forests. 'Your love for him would be vastly increased, Madame,' wrote Mme de Maintenon to the Princesse des Ursins, 'if you could see with what courage and fortitude he endures the misfortunes that strike him from more than one direction.'

The Princesse des Ursins ruminated over these descriptions of the King's state of mind and, for the sake of Spain, took comfort from them. Louis XIV might, indeed, be inclined to seek a peace. But the seeking of a peace is a great distance from the signing of one. Her desire was to see King Philip found a French dynasty in Spain; but he might die, or be forced by defeat to abdicate, and she therefore thought it imperative for the baby Prince of the Asturias to receive the oath of loyalty from the grandees and the nation. 'It has never before been done with an infant of twenty months,' said Mme des Ursins, but the ceremony would impress our enemies with the wishes of the Spanish people, and the grandees, once they had sworn, could not go back on their word. Moreover, though Louis XIV might be forced by the Allies to abandon Spain, he could not hand the country over, like one of his own provinces. When Mme des Ursins carried the precious baby to church, on that April day in 1709, she saw 'the great majority of the grandees file past him and go down on one knee to take the oath, while the baby, sucking at the breast of his wet-nurse, extended his hand to be kissed in the manner of a great prince'. Thereafter, should Philip die or abdicate, he would leave a successor, and to make matters doubly secure the Queen was again pregnant. 'It will be another boy,' she said. 'He will be born on St Philip's day, and we will name him Philip.' The Spanish people were wildly excited, drinking wine at the fountains in the public squares, and throwing jasmine and pomegranate flowers in the path of the queen. 'On that sunny April day,' wrote

Mme des Ursins, 'the very wind seemed to stir up the people and to be crying out "unto us a child is born".'

The princess had fulfilled the task for which Louis XIV had sent her to Spain. Perhaps she had gone too far, for what she had done, Louis XIV could never undo, even were he to be so minded. He had dispatched to Spain a shadow of himself, a mere boy, and the boy had grown into a king. Despite his faults and his taciturnity, Philip had shown himself to be scrupulously honest. What Spaniards most desired of their kings was that they should be loyal Spaniards, and Philip had made himself a Spaniard through and through. As for his twenty-year-old queen, Adelaide's sister, she had won the love of the entire nation for the way in which she had wholeheartedly adopted Spain as her country, willingly sharing its pride and poverty. Never once had she been known to accept gifts of jewellery from the king; indeed, her wedding presents were in pawn, and the money had gone to feed and clothe the army. She enjoyed no pleasures; not even the lovely gardens of their country house at Aranjuez were visited. No fêtes were held in her honour, and the only times she appeared in public were at royal christenings, or the services of *Te Deum* and *Parce Domine*, for victories or defeats. The French ambassador, the Marquis d'Amelot, wrote in a report that she exemplified what it meant to be a true Queen of Spain, and that anyone who told the King otherwise was a liar.

A very short time after the swearing of the oath of loyalty, Mme des Ursins learned without much surprise that a French envoy, a judge, and M. Rouillé, a president of the Parlement of Paris, were at The Hague, bearing a peace-offer. Louis XIV had consulted no one, not even King Philip or the princess; all the information received in Spain came from rumours to the effect that the King was ready to accept the Austrian archduke as King of Spain, and claimed for his grandson in exchange the tiny kingdoms of Naples and Sicily. 'We have suffered a series of disasters,' wrote Mme de Maintenon, 'from which France can recover only after a long period of peace, and now famine, the latest and worst of our misfortunes, has us in its grip. I must allow that in all my fears for the future I never foresaw our being reduced to desiring the abdication of the King and Queen of Spain. No words, Madame, can express my sorrow at the thought.' 'It would be a shameful peace,' wrote Mme des Ursins. 'An atrocious peace,' echoed Mme de Maintenon. But at Versailles the courtiers were murmuring that there could be no other way, if the King, who knew all, deemed it a necessity.

Meanwhile, in France, everything visibly deteriorated. The nation was exhausted, as was the treasury; the troops, unpaid and discouraged by bad leadership, had no more will to fight; the generals and ministers had proved themselves incompetent; promotion went by favour or intrigue; crimes were not punished; there were no official inquiries, and no councils to prepare for the next campaign. It appeared equally impossible to make either war or peace, and such was the desperate situation when first Rouillé, then Torcy, were sent to The Hague to advance the negotiations, despite the huge sacrifices demanded of the King.

There seemed to be no money left in France, and the people wondered where it had gone, for the food shops were empty, and no one was any longer paid for their work. Prices reached such fantastic heights that even the cheapest markets were beyond the reach of the poor, and cattle died because their owners had no money to buy food for them. Yet new taxes were added, and many of those who, in former years, had assisted the poor now found themselves reduced to a bare subsistence. The sight of so much destitution aroused a zeal for charity, and great sums were given in alms, but many people were ruined by a revaluation of the currency, which brought the millionaire banker Samuel Bernard to sudden bankruptcy, and disaster to the merchants of Lyons.

Louis was deeply moved by the hunger and suffering that he saw around Versailles, the sight of people dying by the roadside from cold and starvation, the bands of women roaming the streets and crying out for bread. There was little that he could do to organise relief, for he had no power or office; but he conscientiously attended every meeting of the councils on which the King had placed him, and listened with evident distress to the reports. 'The Duc de Bourgogne,' recounts the Abbé Proyart, 'asked for detailed information regarding the condition of the people, notwithstanding that, more often than not, there was nothing he could do beyond suffer the misery of being unable to assist them. At one meeting, it was observed that the Prince had burst into tears, and several of the ministers wept with him.' He played his part in the charitable schemes organised by the bishops, to which most people gave generously. The almsgiving was, indeed, on a grand scale, but not all of it voluntary, for, over and above the ordinary taxes, a new tax, entitled *Taxe contributive et Réparation faite sur les Propriétaires des Maisons bourgeoises et habitants de la Ville de Versailles*, was levied for the benefit of the poor. In the list, every householder figured,

including the King for 4,220 livres, Monseigneur for 2,110 livres
the Duc de Bourgogne for 397, and so on. Seven officers were
appointed to manage the fund and the distribution of bread. Every
poor person received a card with a seal upon it; when it was presented at the various centres, bread was given, and the card was
snipped with scissors. The whole affair was very well organised, and
the poor of Versailles and the neighbourhood were fed and supplied
with firewood for six and a half months.

Such obligatory contributions were, however, not enough for
Louis, who told the Curé of Versailles that if he did not give him
the name of every person in urgent need, he would have to answer
to God if they perished. Of his allowance, from the King, of twelve
thousand livres, it was found, after his death, that he had given
eleven thousand in charity. No one realised, at the time, that he kept
almost nothing back for his own spending, for he never spoke of it;
and thus earned something of a reputation for miserliness. There
was one occasion, for instance, when he was shown some silver ink-
stands. They were all the rage, and he did not possess one. He
examined them and greatly admired one of them for its style and
workmanship; but when he heard the price he refused to buy it.
The courtiers asked him if he had not cared for it. 'On the contrary,'
said he, 'it pleases me enormously—but the poor!' Thereupon Mme
de Maintenon intervened, saying, 'Truly, Monsieur, your poor
would be excessively mean to grudge you an inkstand after all you
have done for them,' and she forced it on him, saying that she would
give it him if he did not buy it for himself.

In the summer of 1709, he gave the Curé of Versailles all his
jewellery, to be sold for charity. He would have liked Adelaide to
feel as deeply as he did for the suffering multitudes; but he found
her hard to move. Not that she was heartless, for when a case of
personal distress was brought to her notice, she gave generously
and repeatedly; but she failed to comprehend the horror of the
general situation, which was perhaps not surprising, since she no
longer went hunting, nor, when the Opera was closed, did she see
the streets of Paris. Her life was spent in the park and gardens of
Versailles and Marly, often confined to her room with headaches
and toothache from one abscess after another. Nonetheless, it was
insensitive of her to ask Louis to give her some of the money that he
was raising for charity, in order to pay her debts. He did not refuse
outright; but handed her a list and a pen, telling her to cross out
the causes that appeared less needy than her own. When she saw

that it consisted entirely of the uncomplaining poor, abandoned orphans, and widows of officers ruined in the King's service, 'I must allow,' she said, 'that these people all deserve more pity than myself.' But she could not help adding, 'I cannot imagine, Monsieur, how you managed to unearth so many unfortunates.' Yet the incident made an impression and, as time went on and she became more serious-minded, she came to a better understanding of Louis's concern for the poor of France. She controlled, once and for all, her passion for gambling, and undertook on her own account certain charitable enterprises. Louis was both surprised and delighted when they told him of the large sums that she had given away, and of how, during Lent, she had fed forty people, every day. 'Oh! What are you saying?' he exclaimed. 'I am absolutely delighted, and what pleases me most is that she did it out of kindness, and wants no one to know.' They were gradually becoming friends; Adelaide was beginning to understand and share his interests, and Louis, ever grateful for her spirited defence of him in the previous year, was developing a new respect for her good qualities.

With the warmer weather of early summer, Versailles recovered something of its old cheerfulness. The King would have liked there to be balls and other festivities, for he said to Mme de Maintenon that it would be well not to give foreigners the idea that France was downhearted. It was Adelaide who dissuaded him; she was, said Mme de Maintenon, 'in deep depression', and he did not wish to force her. In spite of all that had happened, she was still in correspondence with her grandmother by the ordinary post, writing letters just as loving as those of her childhood. 'It would not take long to tell you of the pleasures of this carnival. It has been very dull until now, and I do not think it will improve. There cannot be balls, for there are too few to dance. Many ladies are in mourning, others with child, and most of those now of marriageable age have spent their entire lives in convents and have not learned the steps. At present there are, at the Court, only nine ladies able to dance, and they are still half in the schoolroom. I should be the oldest of the ladies, and that quite removes my desire to dance. I do not know what possesses them to believe that women are past dancing by the age of thirty. If that mode persists, I must make the best of what little time remains to me.'

The magnificent supper-parties that had been such a feature of life at the Court were no longer given by the best people, for they could scarcely refrain from following the example set by the King, who had sent his gold and silver table-ware to be melted down to pay the troops, and was regularly to be seen dining off porcelain or silver plate. He had pledged even the crown jewels to secure money, and had made other eye-catching economies that tarnished much of the old brilliance. Life was very dull for the courtiers; most of them were too poor to play cards for high stakes, and although the theatres re-opened at the beginning of April, the Paris mob made the journey unpleasant; they had even stopped a train of three coaches in which Monseigneur was conveying Adelaide and her ladies to the Opera. Monseigneur was popular and no violence was threatened, but rough women gathered shouting round the coach doors, calling for bread, and thrusting up at the windows the musty loaves which were all they had to eat. Monseigneur yet again threw out money, and the crowd dispersed; but thereafter theatricals at Versailles became the mode, with the players bringing their scenery from Paris, at huge expense. *Phèdre* was given, and *Tartuffe*, as well as *Le Misanthrope*, *Britannicus*, and a great number of farces. Adelaide enjoyed them so much that, when she was expecting her third child in the following year, she had her dining-room turned into a theatre, so that she should not have to miss anything. Music was a joy that she could share with the King, and this was her opportunity, for Sourches tells how 'returning from Trianon, he looked in upon her to hear an extremely lovely symphony, composed by Descouteaux,[1] for the German flute, theorbo, harpsichord, and bass-viol'.

In the autumn there were official visitors to be entertained. The Elector of Bavaria arrived towards the end of November 1709, presenting something of a problem for etiquette. He had been France's ally in the war, and had been deprived of his lands by Prince Eugene. He therefore needed to be shown commiseration and respect—yet he came *incognito*. In the end, the King invited him to Marly and himself did the honours, and Adelaide greatly added to his enjoyment by her charm and courtesy. Mme de Maintenon felt proud of her, and quickly wrote to Mme des Ursins, 'Mme la Duchesse de Bourgogne has surpassed herself, and we hear already that the Elector is charmed. As soon as he entered the drawing-room, he recognised her by her delightful appearance, and I was all the more elated because Mme la Princesse de Conti was standing close by. Our princess owes her success to me: she wanted

[1] Philibert Descouteaux, an accordion player and a member of the King's orchestra. A theorbo is a very large bass-lute, with a double neck.

to appear in a shawl, on the excuse of her pregnancy, with a general air of informality that suits her less well than it does other ladies. With much difficulty I persuaded her to dress properly, and even to put on her jewels, and I must confess that the result surprised me. She did not look as though she were five months gone; indeed, her looks were extremely good, for she was in excellent health, rose-pink and white from head to toe. She renewed her old acquaintance with the Elector, who maintained that she could not possibly remember him; but she said that she remembered seeing him in her mother's boudoir, when he was mimicking the Emperor.'

While all this was going on, Louis's mind was set on the coming campaign, in which the King had given him command of the army in Germany, with the Maréchal d'Harcourt to assist him. The latter was in all probability Mme de Maintenon's nomination, for he was the son of the Marquis de Beuvron who, in the days of her widow-hood, had been an intimate friend or possibly, as Saint-Simon suggests, 'something rather more'. Harcourt was not a bad choice for, although lacking in experience, he had proved himself capable of commanding armies and was, moreover, a highly skilled diplo-mat, unlikely to question Louis's personal authority, and ready to support him, as Boufflers had done in the Prince's earlier cam-paigns. Both appointments had been made in the previous February, and Harcourt had at once proceeded to hold daily sessions with Louis, coaching him in the art of war, a subject which had been neglected in the Prince's schoolroom. He then, 'being crafty' (said Saint-Simon, who disliked him), conceived the brilliant idea of proposing that Adelaide should attend their sessions, thus flattering and pleasing them both. Recognising Adelaide's good sense and intelligence, he went still further, reserving important matters for discussion in her presence, asking her opinion, admiring her every word, and praising her to her husband. In this way, he prolonged their meetings, persuading them of his ability, and most respectful devotion. 'The Princess was certainly flattered,' continues Saint-Simon; 'Harcourt was too firm a friend of Mme de Maintenon, and she of him, not to be thought well of, and the princess was apt to appreciate flattery from people of importance.' What is more, for years past she had been hoping that Louis would discuss with her matters of public interest; it was a way of becoming friends, on a footing of greater equality, and of being allowed a share in State affairs.

Their hard work came to nothing. The campaign began very late,

for the peace negotiations at The Hague had dragged on through
the spring into early summer, and it was not until June that Torcy
returned bringing terms so humiliating that Louis XIV, in spite o
the desperate condition of France, could not bring himself to
accept them. They included a demand for the King to guarantee
his grandson's abdication, which the French interpreted as a
promise to drive King Philip out of Spain by force of arms, should
he refuse to comply. But the King of Spain showed no sign of being
willing to abdicate. He was winning small victories against the
Austrians; he believed that 'God, not his grandfather, had placed
him on the throne and was not now deserting him; his people were
showing themselves loyal; he could not abandon them'. 'Death
alone,' wrote Mme des Ursins, 'can deprive him of his throne.'

Louis XIV had burst into tears before his whole council when he
first read the 'hard terms', declaring that he had no other choice
then to agree to everything, He now called, for the first time in his
reign, a full council of war. It was, unfortunately, Sunday, and when
he told the Duc de Bourgogne, he added, somewhat sourly, 'Unless
you prefer to be at Vespers'. The others summoned were Monseigneur, the ministers for finance and war, and Harcourt who,
finding himself for the first time set on a level with the administrators, proceeded to harry them unmercifully. It was then that the
true condition of the troops (unpaid, underfed, and with their
morale at a very low ebb) was publicly revealed. 'I have corn for a
month,' said the Maréchal de Villars, responsible for mustering the
Flanders army, while Chamillart, unable to resist a dig at the
finance minister, besought the King to believe that the situation
was general; that not a single regiment had received their pay, and
that the results would soon become apparent. Harcourt wisely
refused to leave for Germany without the assurance of having
sufficient bread, meat and money to sustain and pay his army of
the Rhine.

To do so emptied the treasury; nothing remained to defray the
huge cost of keeping the royal princes in their accustomed state at
the various headquarters, with their numerous staffs and retinues,
offering lavish hospitality to all-comers. Even Louis, who was
considered parsimonious, had kept a staff of twenty-six officers and
ten civilian secretaries during the Oudenarde campaign, with a
table set with sixteen covers. The expense of similar establishments
for Monseigneur, the Duc de Berry, and the Duc d'Orléans was
clearly prohibitive at this juncture, and the King sadly announced

at his dinner after the council that the princes' baggage-trains were to be dismantled, and their retinues dismissed, for they would not, that year, be campaigning. Louis was wretchedly disappointed, and pleaded very hard to be allowed to go. 'Since money is lacking,' he said, 'I should go with no retinue, live like an ordinary officer and, if necessary, eat the soldiers' rations. No one will complain of austerity if they see that I have only the bare necessities.' But the King would not be moved. He believed that to let his grandson serve, divested of the grandeur belonging to his rank, would be an admission of poverty to the outside world. He thought it unnecessary to give Louis the chance of regaining his reputation and forgetting the mistakes of the previous year.

Mme des Ursins had been relieved by the decision to continue the war, but felt no compassion. 'I have received, Monsieur,' she wrote to Torcy, your letter of 3 June, and had already heard from the ambassador of the conditions which the enemy desired to impose on the King. The terms are so unjust and humiliating that I am not surprised at the King's decision to continue the war. He could face no greater misfortune than to yield to everything demanded as a preliminary, without knowing what might be required of him later. I am persuaded, Monsieur, that the French people are too loyal and too careful of their own welfare not to prefer risking their money and their lives rather than become the slaves of a proud, cruel Alliance, whose main purpose it is to humble their sovereign's pride.'

At the beginning of the campaign of 1709, neither side was eager for action. Louis XIV forbade Villars to fight a battle, instructing him to display the utmost caution, in order to give the army time to recover its strength. Marlborough, Prince Eugene, and the Dutch, confident that France was on the verge of collapse, thought they had only to wait. Marlborough wrote on 4 July, 'All the wheat is dead everywhere that we have seen or heard of. It grieves my heart to see the sad condition of all the poor country people for want of bread, they have not the same countenance they had in other years.' On 11 July, he said, however, 'We shall not find forage for a long campaign, and that is what I fear the French know as well as we . . . The poverty of all the poor people we see is such that one must be a brute not to pity them.'

The surrender of Tournai, on 2 September, seemed to change the character of the campaign. It was as though both the French and the Allies suddenly became filled with the desire to bring the struggle to an end. The King gave Villars permission to court a battle if he thought it advantageous, Villars did so, and on 10 September Marlborough and Eugene attacked him in his strongly entrenched position at Malplaquet. There then ensued the biggest and bloodiest battle of the entire war—a 'very murdering battle', Marlborough called it—in which twenty thousand of the Allied troops and twelve thousand of the flower of the French army were killed. It ended with a victory for the Allies and a defeat for France, whose only gain was a breathing space, since the enemy dispersed their armies after the battle, and did not press home an invasion.

'The Maréchal de Boufflers,' wrote Mme de Maintenon to the Princesse des Ursins, on 14 September, 'has described the battle as glorious and unlucky, for we have lost it despite the courage of our soldiers, not one of whom deserted during the action or the retreat . . . God's will is so clearly apparent that we should be rebellious did we not make peace, and you know, Madame, even better than I, that a king's first duty is to protect his people's well-being.'

That peace, which continued to be so necessary for France, seemed impossible to conclude, for the price of it was always Spain. Louis XIV recalled his troops; he could defend his own country, but no longer support his grandson with military assistance. He needed, he said, all his people: 'In the midst of all the calamities which it has pleased God to inflict upon my kingdom, the war in Spain has become impossible to sustain; it is no longer a question of personal preference. I stand as a father to my subjects, and I must think of their welfare. That is dependent upon peace, which I know that I cannot conclude so long as my grandson remains King of Spain. I am well aware that my reasoning will appear hard to my grandson the king; but it is more painful to me than to him to be obliged to refuse him assistance when I can see that it is sorely needed. I feel for his needs with all the affection of a parent who has always loved him with a particular love. He will feel for me also, if he can grasp the state of my kingdom.'

Mme des Ursins nonetheless managed to persuade him to leave twenty-five battalions in Spain, not to fight, but to act as a guard for the king and his family, should they be forced to retire into France as refugees. Her correspondence with Mme de Maintenon continued, but there was beginning to creep into their letters a note of antagonism. 'No words, Madame,' wrote Mme de Maintenon, 'can express our grief. The King is overwhelmed by it; the Duchesse de Bourgogne weighed down; my own sadness is immeasurable.

Distress unites us all . . . Everyone is deeply sorrowful or at prayer. But there is nothing more that we can do.'

Seeing in the defeat only the will of God, she longed for peace at any price, and viewed with strong disapproval the warlike spirit of Mme des Ursins, at Madrid. The self-imposed mission that had placed her, in the strangest circumstances, so close to the King, required her to impose the Christian virtues in correction of royal selfishness and savage pride. She yearned to see an end to troubles that afflicted the family she loved; wanted them to accept the sacrifices that God demanded, and bitterly resented the fact that she had no political power. Although the King admired her honesty and good sense, he would not listen to her on this subject that profoundly disturbed him, and on which she felt a God-given right to be heard. She therefore fell back on her other source of influence; her power as his wife.

Mme des Ursins, who dared everything, presumed to raise the veil on that dark secret. In answer to a letter in which Mme de Maintenon expressed a wish to see King Philip quickly defeated, she wrote, 'Have you not the same tender love for the King and Queen of Spain as for your other children?', thus reminding the unofficial queen of France that not only was she abbess of Saint-Cyr and mother adoptive of the hundreds of past and present pupils, but the wife of Louis XIV, and step-mother of his royal children and grand-children. It was unheard-of presumption; but it brought her no reprimand from the King, for she was still of great value to him, at Madrid; yet the more freedom he allowed her, the more liberties she took. 'I sometimes feel a little bitter towards you,' Mme de Maintenon gently chided, 'for you no longer seem like a Frenchwoman.' 'I am the best Frenchwoman of you all,' retorted Mme des Ursins.

17

The Marriage of the Duc de Berry

BY THE end of September, although the Austrians were still in Madrid, King Philip's army remained undefeated; but, on the northern frontier of France, Mons had fallen as well as Tournai, and Prince Eugene was threatening to encamp his army below the walls of Paris. One day it was learned that German scouts, penetrating into Marly forest, had kidnapped one of the officers of the Court. He had been released almost immediately afterwards, but it was seen as an alarming foretaste of what the future might bring.

At Versailles, more families mourned their loved-ones killed in battle and there was much anxiety; yet, although the war dragged on, and the state of the country went from bad to worse, social life continued, not as brilliantly as in the old days, but with all the quieter pleasures of the previous year. In February 1710, dismay gave place to rejoicing when Adelaide gave birth to her second surviving son, thus securing the royal line of Louis XIV into the third generation. Her eldest son, the first Duc de Bretagne, had died, in 1705, only a few months after his birth and thus, not unnaturally, the health of her next baby, the second Duc de Bretagne, had been a constant source of concern. 'I know,' she had written to her grandmother, 'that children often withstand illnesses better than grown-up people, but that does not stop me, however sensible I try to be, from worrying dreadfully whenever my son is in the least unwell.'

When she discovered in the spring of 1709, that she was once again pregnant, she took all the precautions required of her, avoiding cobbled streets, riding, staying up late, or becoming overtired. At the beginning of February, as the event approached, there was much excitement, and the King, who thought it his kingly duty to assist at the labour of his daughters and granddaughter-in-law, kept his clothes beside his bed, so as to dress quickly and go to Adelaide as soon as he received the call. It came on Saturday, 15 February when, at seven o'clock in the morning, they told him that she had felt the first pains. She suffered very much, and there was a moment of extreme anxiety, when it looked as though the delivery would be difficult. Mme de Maintenon, writing to her crony in Spain, reported that there had been very bad moments, and that many of the gentlemen had left the bedroom, unable to bear her pain. Fortunately Clément, the famous royal accoucheur, had just arrived back from Spain, where he had been attending Adelaide's sister and, according to the *Mercure*, had acted with such cleverness and speed that all had been well. By eight o'clock in the evening the baby had arrived, 'which,' continued the *Mercure*, 'is enchanting the astrologers, for it has been recognised, from time immemorial that children born in daylight are more fortunate than those born at night'.

The great bell of the Château de Versailles announced the happy event, and in Paris a carillon rang out at the church of La Samaritaine. When the baby's brother had been born, in 1707, the King had forbidden all public rejoicings. In 1710, the times were harder still, yet he banned nothing, and there were festivals in a great many French towns, more especially in Paris, where the magistrates and the merchants organised a grand display of fireworks. The people needed something to cheer them, and relieve the general gloom. The birth of a new prince was regarded as a good omen, a promise that one day the war would end, and peace and prosperity return. Adelaide, too, was much relieved. She dreaded pregnancy; now that she had done her duty, there need be no further demands upon her to go through it again.

The baby was immediately called the Duc d'Anjou, the accepted title for a Dauphin's second son, which King Philip had renounced when he became King of Spain. The blue ribbon of the Order was put round his neck; he was placed in the arms of his kneeling governess, the Duchesse de Ventadour (daughter of the old Maréchale), and borne off by her to his own apartments. He grew up to become Louis XV.

Adelaide was not much dismayed at being parted from him. Considering her own happy childhood in the care of a loving mother, and her fondness for her younger sister, it is strange how little she minded being separated from her babies. Hers was too light a nature to be capable of strong passions, and one is reminded of the surprise she had caused at the time of her arrival in France, by her ready acceptance of the ladies of her new, French household, and her easy parting with the Piedmontese ladies with whom she had been friends for many years. When her eldest son was only a few months old she had written calmly to her grandmother, saying, 'I do not see him often, lest I should become too fond of him', and, in another letter, had said that he was very yellow and not as yet interesting or good-looking, not a becoming baby, or fit for his grandmother to see, even were it possible for her to come to France.

Royal governesses, like Victorian nannies, contrived to keep a jealous hold over their charges, and to resent any interference from mothers. Thus Adelaide had little to say regarding the upbringing of her sons; but she does not seem to have been much dismayed by that. Writing of her three-year-old son, in 1709, she said, 'I went, on the day before yesterday, to see him, at Versailles. I wanted to whip him because he is so extremely naughty and obstinate, which angers me very much, for the greatest pleasure I used to find in him was his sweetness, and the fact that he never cried. Mme de Ventadour, by giving him so much love, spoils him completely.'

On the other hand, at this period, Adelaide's life was so full that she would have had little leisure in which to raise a family. Since her victory over Vendôme she had gained confidence, and was more and more taking her place as the first lady of the Court. But the Cabal, at Meudon, still existed and still actively opposed her. 'The entire Court is buzzing with intrigues,' wrote Madame. 'Monseigneur is completely under the influence of his sister Madame la Duchesse; the Princesse de Conti has become her ally, so as not to lose all power over him. Mme la Duchesse de Bourgogne, who would like to rule the Dauphin as she does the King, is jealous of Madame la Duchesse, and has therefore made a pact of friendship with our Duchesse d'Orléans, in order to thwart her designs. To watch them is as good as a play, and I might well say, in the words of the song, "If we were not dying of hunger, we should kill ourselves with laughter".'

Adelaide was well aware of the intrigues, but was not much disturbed by them, for she felt her power increasing every day and towards the end of 1710 received dazzling evidence of the King's confidence, when he gave into her hands the management of all the expenses of her household and the bestowal of appointments as they fell vacant. He had not shown so much trust in either the Queen or the Dauphine, and when one astonished courtier in his intimate circle had said, 'I suppose, Sire, that she will render an account to you of all that she spends,' he had replied, 'I have sufficient confidence in her to desire her to account for nothing, and I am leaving her the absolute mistress of her household. She would be capable of governing greater and far more difficult affairs.'

Mme de Maintenon's joy was complete. She found it wholly delightful to see her 'dear princess' appreciated at her proper value, and she wrote, bursting with pride to Mme des Ursins: 'Pray, Madame, allow me to unbosom myself for a little while, over Mme la Duchesse de Bourgogne. After having endured so much criticism for the mistakes I made over her education, after being blamed for the freedom with which she gadded about from morning to night; after seeing her generally hated because she said nothing; after seeing her accused of the most shocking deceit in her attachment to the King and the affection with which she honours me, I now find everyone singing her praises, believing her to have a kind heart and a noble spirit; admitting that she is capable of holding a large court in awe of her. I see her now, adored by Mgr le Duc de Bourgogne, dearly loved by the King, who has given the direction of her household into her own hands, saying publicly that she is well able to govern greater things. I am acquainting you of my joy on this account, Madame, being persuaded that you also will be pleased, for you perceived sooner than others the fine qualities of our dear princess.'

Even Madame appreciated the change. 'She has greatly improved and is now living on excellent terms with her husband,' she wrote, in 1711, and continued with a kindlier portrait of Louis himself: 'The good prince is not so much ugly as mis-shapen; he limps and is hump-backed, but his face is not ugly. He has beautiful eyes, full of intelligence, and the rest of his countenance is quite pleasing. His hair is magnificent, as though he wore a full wig . . . One must admit that he is somewhat over-devout, but he hardly ever sermonises.' Louis was indeed very much happier, in his new-found friendship with Adelaide. It was not that she was less merry and pleasant in her daily life; but she was becoming more serious-minded now that she shared to some extent in her husband's interests. She was more stict with herself regarding the proprieties, and the requirements of religion. She went, for example, nearly every day to Saint-Cyr, not, as in the old days, to play games, but to attend the services in the chapel, and she took care to see that her presence caused no disturbance or lack of decorum. There is a record in the *Mémoires* of the Dames of Saint-Cyr of one Saint's day when she graced them with her presence; a large number of the dames and schoolgirls had gathered behind the grille and, in order to see better, they hooked the curtains right back with their fans. 'The Princess,' says the *Mercure*, 'was not amused, she went over herself and with a very set face pulled the curtains together, not only over the smaller gratings, but over the large ones as well; whereupon there was confusion and the sound of a speedy retreat.'

She showed herself equally severe with one of her pages who had attended regularly at those times when the young ladies were visible behind the grille. One of them, Mlle de Buidbarre, an extremely pretty girl, took his fancy, and he managed to convey to her in a secret letter the intensity of his passion. Unfortunately for him, the virtuous young lady was greatly shocked, and reported the matter to the headmistress. He was forbidden to write to her again, or to steal glances through the grille, and there followed a most stinging rebuke from Adelaide herself, who never again took him with her when she went to the school. Had she forgotten her own lapses and the secret notes to Nangis and Maulévrier? Was she now so reformed a character that her roving eye never strayed from her husband?

There was, however, at least one occasion when she seems to have allowed it to wander, and then to settle upon an Adonis, the youthful Duc de Fronsac (son of the Duc et Maréchal de Richelieu, by the second of his three marriages), who first appeared at the Court in January 1711. Mme de Maintenon, an old friend of his father, viewed him with particular interest, and thus described him, in a letter to her nephew the Duc de Noailles. 'He is sixteen, and looks twelve. For one of his slender build, he has the most charming figure imaginable; he is also one of the best dancers; looks well on a horse; plays cards; loves music and is capable of conversation. He is very respectful, very polite, and a most agreeable quiz; when it is required of him he can be serious. Everyone finds him such as I have described.' She says in another letter, 'One longs to pet him, like a pretty little boy, and I was just about to chuck him under the chin, when he asked me to sign his marriage contract.'

The old lady was susceptible to youthful charm, but she quickly changed her opinion of this young sprig, whose father, having no confidence in his ability to stay out of trouble, married him off at that early age to Anne Catherine de Noailles, his step-sister, by the Maréchal's third wife. She was the elder by two years, 'plain, well-shaped, and sensible', said Mme de Maintenon, but evidently not the kind to enrapture the spoilt darling of Adelaide's young ladies, in whose circle his wit and beauty shone especially bright. Adelaide had given him a warm welcome, on Mme de Maintenon's recommendation. She proceeded to find him delightfully amusing, and responded to the extent that, imagining her in love with him, he took liberties which, with any other princess, would have caused his immediate dismissal. Adelaide, however, regarded him like a naughty child, to be scolded, forgiven and petted. So encouraged, he went altogether too far, and provoked a scandal.

Exactly how far he went is not easy to discover; but the account given in the nine-volume edition of his *Private Life*[1] says that during one of Adelaide's morning receptions he managed to conceal himself under her bed, and gave the excuse, when discovered, that he wanted to know what she thought of him.[2] On another occasion, at her *toilette*, he hid behind a screen when the gentlemen left the room, and poked his head out as she was changing her shift. Adelaide jumped back with a cry, whereupon her ladies also perceived him. They swore not to peach on him, but betrayed him nonetheless, not because they wished him any harm, but for fear lest they should find themselves in trouble. When the King was told, he took immediate action, dispatching the young nobleman, with his guitar and his tutor, to cool his heels in the Bastille.

'Bastillization' for noble prisoners, however, was not exactly durance vile. They were the King's guests; ate at the governor's table; had fires in their rooms, and comfortable furniture from the King's warehouses, might visit and receive visitors, and keep servants. The chief disadvantage was that they were forced to stay there, a loss of liberty likely to have weighed heavily on a young man of Fronsac's kind. Moreover, there was no recourse to the law, or possibility of an appeal. They were arrested and released at the King's pleasure which, in Fronsac's case, kept him incarcerated for more than a year.

How much Adelaide had been to blame is uncertain. She had certainly encouraged, and probably had flirted with, him, and her charm, when she wished to use it, was impossible to resist. One thing is sure, her own heart was not involved, for by that time she had become genuinely and devotedly attached to Louis.

[1] *La Vie Privée du Maréchal de Richelieu*, published 1791.
[2] The Duc de Lauzun, many years previously, had hidden under Mme de Montespan's bed for much the same purpose when the King visited her one afternoon. That feat was infinitely more dangerous; but Lauzun was not discovered.

Versailles and Paris gradually recovered some of their old buoyancy and lustre. The end of 1709 marked the lowest ebb in the fortunes of France. Thereafter the miracle in which Mme des Ursins believed, and for which Mme de Maintenon prayed tremulously, began to happen. The war on the northern frontier still dragged on, but the great and glorious Alliance, becoming increasingly disunited, did not invade; the harvest, bad though it was, brought desperately needed relief. By 1711 France had recovered and, in 1713, Louis XIV was able to claim better terms, at the Peace of Utrecht, than would have appeared even remotely possible three years earlier.

In 1710, there occurred what Saint-Simon describes as an 'epoch-making event' that brought the rival factions into such violent collision that their intrigues split the Court in two. This was the marriage of Louis's younger brother, the twenty-four-year-old Duc de Berry, who was showing every sign of needing to settle down with a wife. It would have been best for him to marry a foreign princess; but since France was still at war with Austria and Savoy, no Catholic princess of marriageable age appeared available. The time had passed when the chance of marrying a Prince of France aroused fierce competition in all the European courts. The choice was therefore limited to French princesses, of whom only two were of suitable rank. One was Mademoiselle de Bourbon, the daughter of Adelaide's bitter enemy Madame la Duchesse; the other, known as Mademoiselle, was the daughter of the Duchesse d'Orléans. The mothers of both were the King's bastards; but, circumstances being what they were, no better matches could be found.

The Duc de Berry himself was the sweetest-tempered, the most approachable of the King's grandsons; but his spirit had been broken by an oppressive education, designed to render him incapable of competing with his elder brother. It had made him so nervous that he was panic-stricken in the King's presence, and unfit for even the ordinary duties belonging to his rank. None the less he had made himself popular with the army during the Flanders campaign, and had received an affectionate welcome on his return, from the King and Monseigneur, the latter openly preferring him to Louis whose excessive piety made him feel uncomfortable. The brothers, however, were good friends and, after they came home, the Duc de Berry spent most of his time in Adelaide's drawing-room. Madame, who had made a pet of him when he was a little boy, strongly disapproved. 'For the last few years,' she had written in 1708, 'the Duc de Berry has been entirely taken up with the Duchesse de Bourgogne and her ladies. Since in that circle they have no more notion of good breeding than cows in a cowshed, they treat him like a servant, and he forgets his rank.' In 1710, she said, 'It is not surprising that the Duc de Berry acts like a child. He never talks to anyone of sense. Day and night he is to be found in the Duchesse de Bourgogne's room, waiting on her ladies as though he were a lackey. One of them makes him bring her a table; another her sewing; a third sends him on an errand. He stands about or perches on a tabouret, while the young women loll in armchairs wrapped in shawls or lie full-length on chaises-longues.'

Adelaide was very fond of him and treated him like a younger brother. He was devoted to her and loved the society of her ladies, even though they intimidated him. Saint-Simon relates that he had had the beginnings of several love affairs but 'had not known how to embark on them, conduct them, or bring them to a successful conclusion'. But he was showing unmistakable signs of needing a wife, and it was high time that he was provided with one, for the royal family had begun to fear that he might fall seriously and unsuitably in love and create difficulties.

Had Mademoiselle de Bourbon been chosen, it would have been disastrous for Adelaide; for, although her triumph over Vendôme had forced the Meudon Cabal to modify their tone, the two factions, with Madame la Duchesse and Monseigneur on the one side and Adelaide on the other, were just as hostile as they had ever been. The Duc de Berry's marriage had brought them to a confrontation, for if Madame la Duchesse's daughter were to be successful, the Duc de Berry would inevitably be drawn into the Meudon camp, and how much more dangerous would Madame la Duchesse's power over Monseigneur become if their children married.

Saint-Simon, horrified, decided to interfere. He perceived the whole plot, and the danger of Adelaide becoming estranged from Monseigneur, who had taken a strong aversion, almost a hatred, for Louis, since the last campaign. Saint-Simon's respect for the Duc de Bourgogne and his love for Adelaide were very real; but, as he frankly confessed, 'It was from self-interest of the most active kind' that he passionately desired the Duc d'Orléans's daughter to be successful. Both Madame la Duchesse and Monseigneur were at daggers drawn with the Duc d'Orléans. Saint-Simon saw that they might, without too much difficulty, bring about the disgrace of the entire family, and involve him in their ruin. The duke was already in serious trouble. During the last campaign in Spain, when he had commanded the French army, there were strong rumours, half-believed in France, and not entirely without foundation, that he had conspired with the Allies to dethrone King Philip, and take his place as King of Spain. Louis XIV was not entirely convinced of his innocence and, though he had forgiven him, was not yet reconciled. Worse even than that, his name was anathema to Mme de Maintenon because of an insulting jest which he had uttered, in Spain, at her expense. When he had gone there, he was disgusted by the want of supplies for the troops under his command, and had put it down to petticoat government and a general mishandling of affairs by Mme des Ursins and Mme de Maintenon. Coming one night, angry and frustrated, to supper with his staff, he had raised his glass with a toast to 'our c... captain and her c... lieutenant'. The jest had of course been repeated and had shocked Mme de Maintenon to the core. It was the sort of language to which she was totally unaccustomed; and she never forgave him.

Saint-Simon himself was by no means secure. He was known to be the Duc d'Orléans's intimate friend, and was in semi-disgrace on his own account, the King still not having forgiven him for an ill-advised wager that Lille would fall without any attempt at relief. Nonetheless he proceeded to take charge of the whole affair, marshalling to Orléans's support all the available forces, not only those most concerned, but outsiders as well; the Duchesse de Villeroy, for example, 'whose blunt common sense was often more effective than tact'; and Mme de Levis, the Duc de Chevreuse's daughter, who proved a strong ally, because she hated Madame la Duchesse, liked the Duchesse d'Orléans, and was genuinely devoted to Adelaide.

Strangely enough, the hardest to arouse was the Orléans family itself. The duchess was the first to be stirred, not so much from ambition, for she was extremely lazy, but from an intense desire to see her sister deflated. The duke was more difficult, he was too easy-going, too indolent, to seek a family quarrel and, although Saint-Simon may not have been aware of it at the time, he feared lest revelations of his immoral relationship with Mademoiselle should put him into still worse odour with the King.

As for Adelaide, Saint-Simon says that he 'made most excellent use of her', but it is highly probable that she saw for herself the danger of allowing the Duc de Berry to be drawn into the Meudon faction, and was, in any event, on affectionate terms with the Duchesse d'Orléans. However that may have been, she was very active in the campaign to have Mademoiselle chosen, and made the first move to break down Monseigneur's resistance.

One evening she took the fifteen-year-old Mademoiselle with her when she visited Mme de Maintenon. The King and Monseigneur were already seated there, and she took the opportunity to praise the young girl to her face, saying casually, as she left the room, that she was cut out to be the wife of the Duc de Berry. At this, Monseigneur went scarlet in the face, lost his temper, and with the sharp retort that that would be a fine way to punish the Duc d'Orléans for his misconduct in Spain, got up and left the room. Adelaide, pretending to be astonished, turned to Mme de Maintenon with a look of alarm, exclaiming, 'Aunt, have I said something stupid?' It was the King who answered angrily that if the Duchesse de Bourbon continued to spread rumours and influence Monseigneur, she would find herself in trouble. The subject, says Saint-Simon, was then allowed to lapse, but was taken up again and again. The discussion ended with great indignation all round, and reflections that did Mademoiselle de Bourbon's cause far more harm than any benefit she might have gained from her mother's attachment to Monseigneur.

Saint-Simon thereupon concluded that no time should be lost in convincing the King that Madame la Duchesse's influence was likely to make Monseigneur even harder to manage; that if their children were to marry he might be obliged to grant demands from Monseigneur that originated from her, and that in his old age he might become the slave of both of them.

Adelaide, after that brilliant start, did little more. She was too confident of becoming Queen of France before many years had passed, too busy in her daily round of duties and pleasures to realise the full dangers of her situation. Her main contribution was to take Mademoiselle under her wing, to protect and prepare her for the great position that would be hers after marriage, and here Adelaide showed less than her usual sagacity, for although her young cousin was barely fifteen, she was known to be utterly depraved, a glutton and a drunkard, physically extremely unattractive, and generally suspected of an incestuous passion for her father, which he was believed to reciprocate. She was, in fact, though the King and Mme de Maintenon may not, at that time, have been aware of the worst of her vices, the very picture of a younger generation whose morals and manners elderly ladies condemned. 'I must confess,' wrote Mme de Maintenon to the Princesse des Ursins, 'that I find the young women of today quite intolerable. The outrageous, immodest way in which they dress, their smoking habits, their drunkenness, their greed, their laziness and vulgarity, I find utterly disgusting. They seem to me so disinclined to listen to reason that I cannot endure them.'

The King, tired, worried, and feeling his age, spent more and more time in the comfort of his old wife's society. Versailles, where they had to be on their best behaviour, became such a bore to the younger set that they sought every excuse to enjoy themselves in Paris, where they were safe from royal disapproval. Even Marly was not what it had been, for, in response to news that the people of Paris were grumbling at the huge sums spent there when the armies lacked for food and ammunition, the King announced that he could no longer afford to feed the ladies, on Marly excursions, or pay for any entertainment, except for his own diversion.

In the end, Saint-Simon's efforts were successful (supposing him to have been as dominant in the affair as he would have us think). Mme de Maintenon and Adelaide made, under his direction, the final move that brought success, by an indirect approach to Monseigneur's unofficial wife, Mlle Choin, in response to whose pressure, Monseigneur at last gave his consent. Everyone, except Madame la Duchesse, was delighted. The Orléans called on Monseigneur, when he was still at table with the Bourgognes. He kissed the Duchesse d'Orléans five or six times; the Duc d'Orléans embraced Monseigneur; there were toasts to the father-in-law to be, to the betrothed's mother, and to the daughter herself. 'The Duchesse de Bourgogne, perfectly radiant, enlivened the whole party, and the Duc de Bourgogne, so glad of the marriage, and to see it so happily arranged, lifted the elbow with such joyful utterances that next day he could hardly believe he had made them.'

There was still more joy when, later that evening, Madame was told the splendid news, and quickly wrote to the Duchess of Hanover. 'This evening, about seven o'clock, when I was sitting by my window, writing to the Queen of Spain and the Duchess of Savoy, the Duchesse de Bourgogne with her ladies and her husband came running in, exclaiming, "We are bringing you the Duc de Berry, because the King has just announced that he is to marry Mademoiselle. The King is coming to tell you, and Monseigneur also. We have come on ahead." I at once replied, "As soon as I too may speak, let me assure you, Madame, that I shall always be grateful for all the trouble you took to bring this affair to a happy conclusion. I also know," said I, turning to the Duc de Bourgogne, "that you too have wished for it; and for that I thank you a thousand times." To the Duc de Berry, I said, ' Come and kiss me. Now you are more than ever Madame's boy, as the Dauphine used to say. I shall keep you close in my heart and love you dearly; but I am too old to see you often, for I can no longer assist you. Be merry and contented, and I shall rejoice in your happiness."

This took place at the end of May. On 2 June, the King announced the betrothal, which was considered a triumph for Adelaide, who was busying herself with the selection of the new Duchesse de Berry's household, including, much against her will, Mme de Saint-Simon as the first lady-in-waiting. It had been that lady's dearest wish to succeed the Duchesse du Lude, who was nearing retirement, and thus to reign supreme as lady-in-waiting to the next Dauphine—the highest post open to a lady of the Court. Adelaide's private apartments were much in demand for the wedding festivities,and it was in her bedroom that the bridal couple signed the marriage contract. Dangeau said that never, at any function, had he seen the ladies so bejewelled.

Next day was the wedding, and a touching scene followed, when the bride's new rank entitled her to take precedence over Madame, her grandmother. 'Push me forward, Madame,' she said very graciously, 'so as to propel me in front of you. I need time to grow accustomed to that honour.' Twenty-eight places were set for the supper, and later the couple were escorted to their new apartments. All the ladies entered the bride's room. Cardinal de Janson blessed the bed. The Duchesse de Bourgogne handed the new Duchesse de Berry her nightgown, and when all the guests had departed and the couple were in bed, it was left to Mme de Saint-Simon, as lady-in-waiting, and the solemn Duc de Beauvilliers, as the bridegroom's one-time governor, to draw the curtains together, on either side, 'not without a little laughter,' said Saint-Simon, 'at the idea of performing such a function together.'

The marriage from the start was a total failure. The Duc de Berry, at first, fell too ardently in love, and fell out again almost as quickly. Adelaide blamed him, saying that he was unfeeling; but soon afterwards she had cause to rue the day when she had found him such a wife. Mademoiselle who, before her marriage, had deceived everyone with an appearance of shyness and modesty, now showed herself for what she was. At one of the first parties given by Adelaide in her honour she became so drunk that the witnesses were inexpressibly shocked.¹ Her husband, also present, received such comfort as was possible in the circumstances, but the after-effects 'both above and below', as Saint-Simon delicately put it, were embarrassing to witness, and the bride was sent back to Versailles in a most sottish condition. Mme de Saint-Simon was fortunately absent.²

The sad words with which Saint-Simon closes the long catalogue³ of his efforts to bring about the Duc de Berry's marriage now become understandable: 'The more this princess allowed her true nature to appear, and she kept nothing back, the more we lamented our success in an enterprise which, had I known the half, nay the thousandth part of what we were so tragically to witness, I should have done everything possible to prevent.'⁴

¹ 'The Duchesse de Berry,' wrote Madame, on 14 December 1710, 'fainted dead away. We thought it was a stroke, but when the Duchesse de Bourgogne poured some vinegar over her face she returned to her senses and began to vomit most abominably. Who could wonder? After hours of continuous stuffing during the play—glazed peaches, chestnuts, a confection of red currants and cranberries, dried cherries with quantities of lemonade, and then fish for supper and wine on top of that. She had felt sick, had tried to restrain herself, and had fainted. She has recovered today; but though I tell her that she will be really ill one day, if she over-eats so gluttonously, she will not heed me.'

² In the *Souvenirs*, Mme de Caylus writes that not only was the bride still tipsy two days after the wedding; but that on the very next day she showed herself for what she was, La profligate, with ambition such as drunkards do not ordinarily possess.

³ Filling nearly half a volume of his *Mémoires*, in the Chéruel edition of 1856.

⁴ For the subsequent history of the Duc and Duchesse de Berry, see the *Historical Memoirs of the Duc de Saint-Simon*, Vols II and III. Edited and translated by Lucy Norton, Hamish Hamilton, 1968, 1972.

The Death of Monseigneur

ADELAIDE, NOW twenty-five years old, was taking life more seriously, accepting her responsibilities as the future queen, and taking her place as arbiter of the manners and modes of the Court, but she did not cease from those childish pranks and liberties that so amused and touched the hearts of the King and Mme de Maintenon. Saint-Simon says that in public her manner towards them was serious and formal, reverential to the King, to Mme de Maintenon, a charming mixture of affection and respect. When they were alone, it was a different story. Alone with them she was never still. She treated the King's study as though it were her boudoir, coming and going as she pleased even during his Council meetings, and welcomed by the ministers, whom she was always ready to oblige, smoothing away misunderstandings, and doing them small kindnesses, except for those whom she profoundly disliked, Jérôme Pontchartrain the Chancellor's son, for example, whom she often called 'your one-eyed monster', when speaking of him to the King. She was indeed daringly outspoken, for one evening, when the King and Mme de Maintenon were talking affectionately of the English Court at Saint-Germain (it was at a time when they hoped to make their peace with Queen Anne), she exclaimed, 'You say, Aunt, that English queens are better than their kings. Do you know why?' and, dancing about, she continued, 'It is because under kings the women rule; but, with a queen, the men do so.' It was a wonder that neither of them was angry; but they both burst out laughing and agreed that she was right.

She had, of course, no love for Monseigneur, or the Cabal at Meudon; but she strove to hide her feelings, taking great pains to appear on good terms with him, and looking serenely happy whenever she was at Meudon, Nonetheless, she felt deeply embarrassed by her relationship with the King's daughters, and was determined to be revenged on them after Monseigneur's death. One evening, at

Fontainebleau, when the three princesses[1] and their ladies were with the King after his supper, and she had been making him laugh with baby-talk, she noticed Madame la Duchesse and Mme la Princesse de Conti eyeing one another and scornfully shrugging their shoulders. When the King had risen and gone to feed his dogs,[2] she seized Mme de Saint-Simon and Mme de Levis by the hand, and pointing to those same princesses, only a few feet away, cried out, 'Did you see them? Did you see them? I know that I behave absurdly and must appear very silly; but he needs to have a bustle about him, and that kind of nonsense diverts him.' Then, swinging upon their arms, she cried out in fits of laughter, 'How absurd they are! How they make me laugh! I can mock them because I shall be their queen. I need not mind them now or ever; but they will have me to reckon with, for I shall be their queen.' And she skipped and hopped, and laughed out loud, even though Mme de Saint-Simon whispered, begging her to be quiet lest the princesses hear her, and the whole *assemblée* think she had gone mad. But she laughed and danced all the more, and did not cease until the King's return.

She truly had many excellent qualities that made her much beloved, especially by her household and the people who knew her best. Saint-Simon, who was luke-warm in his praise of the Princesse de Conti, and positively vitriolic about the other two royal ladies, loved her devotedly, and knew her well, since his wife had been, from the very beginning, one of her ladies. He loved her for her grace and kindness; but, above all, he saw in her the embodiment of his most cherished dreams. She knew her place in the hierarchy, and respected the place of others, according to their rank, age, and appointments. This pyramidal structure topped by the King, of noble landowners, prelates, and ordinary people, Saint-Simon fervently believed would protect and support the best interests of the whole nation, since the well-being of rich and poor, lords and peasants, would be equally dependent on the prosperity of the land. Adelaide's willingness to accept her responsibilities, and put up cheerfully with the constraints that rank and etiquette

[1] Adelaide's cousins, the King's legitimated daughters: the Dowager Princesse de Conti, aged forty-five; Madame la Duchesse and the Duchesse d'Orléans, aged thirty-eight and thirty-four, respectively.

[2] The King had a dog-room, next to his study, in which he kept his pet shooting-dogs, Bonne, Ponne, and Nonne. Feeding them was a pleasure which he enjoyed every day after his own meals.

demanded of her, filled him with gratitude and respect. His praise of her, in his memoirs, reveals deep affection, and when he tries to be fair and to show her faults, his criticism is singularly free from any trace of his customary waspishness.

He begins by saying of her that, despite her many good and agreeable qualities, she had another side to her nature, both as a princess and as a woman. This did not imply any tendency to be treacherous, he hastens to add, for in the keeping of secrets, or in loyalty to friends, she was as silent as a deep well, nor did she ever make mischief. There were, however, 'certain small human failings that marred her perfection. She was apt to give her friendship to mere acquaintances, if she saw them often and they amused her, or if she felt the need to use them, and she admitted to this dangerous defect with a grace and candour that made it seem almost like a virtue. The root of the matter was that she wished at all times to please, and could thus hardly be blamed if others pleased her, in return, especially if they happened to be good-looking'. She was sociable by nature, and very ready to be fond of the people, old and young, with whom she spent her life. She also loved gossip and scandal and in her early years, with the younger members of her household, had allowed herself altogether too much liberty.

That she was greatly loved is not in doubt. Her warm smile, and touching gratitude when people showed her affection won the devotion of those who came near to her. From the King, Mme de Maintenon, and Louis her husband, from her dear Tessé and that most critical observer Saint-Simon, from her Spanish gentleman servant Domingo, who would not marry for fear of dividing his affection, and died of grief in less than a year after her death, she received a love only equalled by that felt for her captivating grandmother, whom she so closely resembled.

It must be said, however, that not everyone took a charitable view of her failings. The Venetian ambassador and Madame were especially severe. He had written, in 1698, that Adelaide was sly and malicious. 'She fawns most abjectly on Mme de Maintenon, calls her Aunt in public, but in private mocks her as Grandmamma.'[1] Madame, who had never cared for her, always found much to criticise. In September 1708 she wrote, 'The Duchesse de Bourgogne attends mass wrapped up in a nun's hood in the hope of appearing devout, and pretends to weep at the *Salut*; but she

---

[1] 'Grandmamma' was, strictly speaking, correct, or 'Grandmamma-in-law', since Mme de Maintenon's husband was Louis's grandfather.

drinks two bottles of strong wine without ill effects, and is such a flirt that she makes eyes even at her equerry ... She is rude to me every day at the King's table and, when I am about to help myself, sweeps the dishes away from under my very nose. She looks past me when I visit her, and says nothing or giggles about me with her ladies. It is all the old ragbag's doing. She wants me to complain, so that she may say there is no living with me, and get me sent to a convent; but I am saying nothing and never complain. I laugh at all they do, and tell myself that she is not immortal, that nothing lasts, and that they cannot get rid of me unless I die.'

In later years Madame appreciated the change that came over Adelaide after her victorious struggle with Vendôme, for several years later, looking back to that time, she wrote, 'The Duchesse de Bourgogne changed entirely for the better. She gave up playing pranks and drinking too much. Instead of behaving like an unruly child, she became polite and sensible, conducting herself in a manner befitting her rank, and no longer allowing her young ladies to be familiar or stick their fingers into her dish.'

At that period, there was one quite insignificant lady at the Court for whom Adelaide felt a healthy respect, not untinged by jealousy. This was Mme de Maintenon's protégée, Jeanette Pincré, whose marriage, in 1711, would have passed unnoticed, had not her circumstances been so extraordinary. When she was a very small child, her father had died, leaving her mother penniless with a swarm of children to bring up. The poor woman had made her way to Versailles with her whole brood, and had flung herself upon her knees at the door of Mme de Maintenon's coach, as that lady was leaving for Saint-Cyr. No one can deny that Mme de Maintenon was charitable. She took the entire family under her wing, gave them money, found places for all the children, as suited their ages, and Jeannette, a pretty little girl, she took into her own household to be brought up by her ladies until she was old enough to be sent to Saint-Cyr. Jeannette was a tiny and most attractive child; she amused Mme de Maintenon's women with her chatter, and pleased their mistress also. One day, the King encountered her and caressed her. She showed no fear of him, which greatly pleased him; he grew into the habit of playing with her, and when the time came for her to go to school, he would not hear of it.

As Jeannette grew up, she became still more amusing and even prettier, showing signs of developing a witty and most agreeable character, treating the King always with a freedom which he never found ill-timed or tedious. She conversed with him on all manner of subjects, joking and teasing when she found him in the mood, even playing with the papers on his desk. Yet she was never indiscreet or familiar; and to Mme de Maintenon she was equally pleasant; in fact everyone in that household became attached to her. Even Adelaide treated her with respect, and feared her too, thinking that she might carry tales to the King, although in fact she never harmed anyone. At last, however, Mme de Maintenon began to think her too clever, and feared that the King was becoming altogether too fond of her. Thus, from a mixture of fear and jealousy, she decided to get rid of Jeannette by way of honourable marriage although, at first, the King would not hear of it. Finally, a match presented itself with Villefort, whose mother was another of Mme de Maintenon's protégées,[1] and to this the King did consent. He had already given Jeannette many presents of money, and now gave her a generous dowry, while to her husband he presented the governorship of Guérande, in Brittany, and the promise of the next colonelcy to fall vacant in an infantry regiment.

If Mme de Maintenon thought herself safely delivered of Jeannette's presence by this marriage, she was vastly mistaken. At the last moment the King said firmly that he would refuse his consent unless Jeannette returned to live, as before, with her household. Who could ever have foreseen, Saint-Simon says, that in later years,[2] she would be their comfort and sole support in their leisure hours, and so remain until the King's death? The marriage was a happy one, Mme Voysin, wife of the Secretary of State, gave the wedding breakfast, and the couple were publicly bedded at the house of Mme de Villefort, the bridegroom's mother. Adelaide was there and presented the bride with her nightgown. In later years the bridegroom was appointed a *gentilhomme de la manche* to her son Louis XV, and distinguished himself honourably in the wars.

This quiet wedding was an event of disproportionate interest in an otherwise dull season. Versailles was very empty, for although

[1] Mme de Villefort had gained an audience of Mme de Maintenon, after her husband was killed in the war. She was 'spirited and adventurous, but virtuous and innocent of any flightiness'; she was also most appealingly sad and lovely, in her widow's weeds. Neither the King nor Mme de Maintenon could ever resist a charming face. They took her under their protection, called her 'their lovely widow' and, since she was well bred, made her an under-governess of the children of France. Thus her fortune was made.

[2] He meant, after Adelaide's death.

the King insisted on holding the usual winter balls and plays, as well as the weekly receptions, and although the wives of many ministers gave magnificent balls and other entertainments in honour of the Duchesse de Bourgogne, the younger set preferred to go to Paris, and Monseigneur, for much of the time, was away at Meudon.

He was fifty years old, and becoming elderly, spending the daylight hours hunting with his wolfhounds, and the evenings quietly at home with Mlle Choin, whom he was supposed to have married. 'They make funny marriages in this family,' said Adelaide, referring to Monseigneur's choice, and the King's unofficial marriage to his bastards' governess. Indeed there was a certain resemblance between the courts of Versailles and Meudon; with Mme de Maintenon tucked away in her *niche* at the former,[1] and Mlle Choin, at Meudon, disappearing to her attic when there were official visitors. In private, she queened it in Monseigneur's drawing-room, sitting in an arm-chair, and allowing all other royalty, including Adelaide, to accommodate themselves on *tabourets*. Yet she was a good-hearted, respectable woman with no malice in her; discreet, and unself-seeking. When Monseigneur, one day, brought her his will, showing a very large bequest in her favour, she had torn it up with her own hands, and after the Flanders campaign she had done her limited best to reconcile him with Louis. It had been of no avail, for Monseigneur continued to treat his eldest son with marked aversion, reserving all his affection for the Duc de Berry, who shared his love of hunting and good eating, and endeared himself by a cheerfulness, quick temper, and energy that were not in his father's nature.

Monseigneur, at this time, seemed in excellent health, and took great care of himself. Some years previously he had had a bad attack of apoplexy, brought on by over-eating; but this had so much disturbed him that he had ever since followed a strict diet, and there had been no recurrence. No one else was alarmed for him; his accession appeared a certainty, and the only question was how soon that would be. The King's health, on the other hand, gave cause for serious concern. He was visibly and rapidly ageing. The worries

[1] Mme de Maintenon's *niche*, or 'nook', was famous. Madame thought it very silly and self-indulgent, and described it thus. 'It is a silly thing about French-women that they always want to lie about in dark corners. Mme de Maintenon has had regular little kennels made for her, where she goes when she wants to lie down. She has built a little house round her day-bed, a kind of tent of boards which can be completely closed. The Duchesse de Bourgogne has one too, and so has the Princesse de Conti. I should die of suffocation if I had to use such contraptions.' Marly, 13 November 1710.

and anxieties so courageously borne during the last disastrous years, the long hours spent working with his ministers on ever more discouraging problems, had affected his magnificent constitution, and the regular bleedings and purgings insisted on by his doctors had weakened rather than improved his health. Thus what most occupied people's minds was not the future tenancy of the throne, notwithstanding an astrologer's prediction; 'King's son, king's father, never king himself', but the changes that would take place, and the plight in which every individual would find himself when Monseigneur removed his court from Meudon to Versailles.

It was a nerve-racking time for Mme de Maintenon. She need expect no harm from Mlle Choin in the next reign; but with the Princesse de Conti, and Madame la Duchesse, her avowed enemy, queening it at Versailles, she foresaw endless annoyance and disrespect to herself and the Bourgognes. She was seventy-six years old; very tired by her struggles to support the King and Adelaide, and longing for a quiet life in retirement at Saint-Cyr. For the moment, the hostility between the two factions, though it did not diminish, was held in check by the King's authority; and so things continued, until the sudden, shattering event of Monseigneur's death changed the entire situation.

On Saturday 11 April 1711, news came to Saint-Simon, spending the Easter fortnight at his country house, that Monseigneur had been taken ill. He had been driving home to Meudon from Versailles, accompanied by Adelaide, when he had seen a priest taking the Sacraments to a sick person, and had stepped down from his coach to kneel in prayer. After making inquiries, he had been informed that it concerned a man dying of smallpox, which so much upset him that he had told his doctor he would not be surprised if he contracted the infection, of which an epidemic, raging in Europe, had caused many deaths in France.

Next day, as he dressed to go hunting, he fell backwards out of his chair, and his doctor immediately had him put to bed. The King was informed by Fagon, but in so casual a fashion that he thought little of it, and went to Marly where, after his dinner, he received several messages from Louis and Adelaide, who were at Meudon, and did not leave Monseigneur's side, not even for a moment. Adelaide, Saint-Simon says, 'cannot have been deeply grieved by what her mind must have told her was a possibility, but she fulfilled all the duties of a daughter-in-law, with the enhancement of her natural grace and charm, and fed him with her own hands'. Her husband, 'always careful to do his duty, did it now in full measure, and despite grave suspicions of smallpox, which he had not had, refused to leave Monseigneur's bedside until it was time to attend the King at his supper'.

When the King heard the news, he announced that whatever the illness he would go to Meudon next day, and remain there. He forbade his children to follow him, kindly issued a general interdiction covering all those who had not had smallpox, and gave permission to all who had already had it to pay their court at Meudon, or to stay away if they felt nervous. Mme de Maintenon joined him there, where she received a letter from Louis, and another from Adelaide, both expressing more concern for the King's health than for that of Monseigneur. Louis wrote, 'I have taken the liberty to write to the King regarding something of even greater importance to the State than the health of Monseigneur. You will readily understand that I mean his own well-being. There is no one who does not tremble when he considers that the King is all the time in danger from bad airs, not only of smallpox, but of other diseases that are equally malignant and even more to be feared. I realise, Madame, that the King has a duty to his family; indeed I am only too well aware of it by the order he gave me not to approach him. But I know also that he owes still more to his subjects, and that if their vote were taken he would not unnecessarily expose himself to a risk, from which God, I trust, will protect him, but which nonetheless is very real ... After these public considerations, I feel ashamed to mention something personal. I speak of Mme la Duchesse de Bourgogne. Pray, Madame, reflect on all that I must think and fear, loving her as I do, if I see her going to Meudon, and believe that only the King's gratification could prevail over my disquiet.'

Adelaide wrote, 'I am beside myself with worry, much more for the King than for Monseigneur, for I have a feeling that he will happily recover ... I am delighted, dear Aunt, that you are coming here to dine, for then we shall be at ease. We can devise together some means by which I may see the King here, for to tell you the truth I have no desire to enter that house. My opinion regarding myself is the same as for you, namely that if I contract a disease no one will be grateful; but on the contrary I shall be blamed for it. Yet I must see the King; I cannot endure Versailles without him; you have no idea what it is like. The plain truth is that when he is absent all places are dead.'

The King did not send for Adelaide. The only people he summoned, except for those who had had smallpox, were the members of his council for the morning meetings. Mlle Choin was confined to one attic, and Père Tellier, Monseigneur's confessor, to another. Both were kept hidden from view, their meals were sent up to them, and their treatment was identical, save only that Mlle Choin was allowed to see Monseigneur, and Père Tellier saw no one but the King.

On the 13th, Monseigneur seemed better, the pocks had appeared, and Fagon[1] assured the King that all was going well, better even than he had dared to hope. The fishwives of Paris, with whom Monseigneur had always had a warm relationship, arrived at Meudon, as they had done at the time when a bad attack of indigestion was mistaken for apoplexy. Monseigneur insisted on seeing them, and they flung themselves on their knees at the foot of his bed, kissing it again and again, vowing that they would make the city of Paris ring with *Te Deums* in gratitude for his recovery. Monseigneur, however, was not so sanguine. He said that it was not yet time to rejoice but, always touched by popular support, he ordered them to be shown over the house, given dinner, and sent away with a present of money.

The next day, at Meudon, began quietly enough; but at four o'clock in the afternoon there was a sudden worsening. Monseigneur lost consciousness and Boudin,[2] his personal physician, suggested sending to Paris for other advice, because he and Fagon, being Court physicians, never saw infectious fevers and had no experience of smallpox. At this, Fagon flew into a rage, refusing to consult anyone or listen to arguments, and insisting that they would do best without interference. Thereupon both doctors lost their heads, trying remedy after remedy, without waiting to see the effect. A priest was then sent for; but he had time only to take Monseigneur's hand and extract something in the way of a confession, before the poor prince touched his breast and, after receiving absolution, sank into a coma.

---

[1] Here is Madame's description of him: 'You cannot imagine what Dr Fagon looks like; thighs like birds' legs, a mouth full of teeth, the upper row black and rotten, and large thick lips that make his mouth jut out.'

[2] Jean Boudin, doctor to Monseigneur, and after him, to Adelaide, was Dean of the Faculty of Paris. Saint-Simon says, 'He was like a pudding in figure as well as name, son of one of the King's apothecaries. He had studied medicine, was careful, hard-working, learned. Had he confined himself to work and study, he might have developed a sound, even an excellent mind. . . .'

The King meanwhile had been told nothing by Fagon. Had not Molière died twenty years before Fagon's appointment in 1693, he might have used him as a model for the doctors in his plays, as it was, Fagon might almost be said to have based himself upon them. He was old, and his judgement was no longer infallible. Nonetheless, among Saint-Simon's praises of him there must have been a grain of truth, for the memoirist had, in his own view, abundant reason to detest him, Fagon being a favourite of Mme de Maintenon. 'Fagon,' says Saint-Simon, 'had one of the best and cleverest brains in all Europe. He was interested in every facet of his calling, a great botanist, a good chemist, a skilful surgeon, an excellent doctor and an outstanding practitioner ... He could be dangerous because, although generally well-informed, he was easily biased and, having made up his mind, could hardly ever be shifted. Once convinced, however, he became so in all sincerity and did everything possible to repair the harm caused by his former prejudices. He was the implacable enemy of those he called "quacks", that is to say claimants to secret knowledge and dispensers of cures, and there he certainly went too far ... According to him, the only way to cure was by the methods recommended by the faculties, whose laws were sacred to him.'[1]

The doctors' decision not to tell either the King or Mme de Maintenon of Monseigneur's state does seem extraordinary. They let him go to his supper, imagining his son to be no worse, though he had been anxious about him earlier in the day. When he rose from table, he nearly fell backwards with astonishment at the appearance of Fagon quite distraught, crying out that all was lost. One may imagine the horror that seized him in this sudden change from calm confidence to the last degree of despair. He tried to enter his son's bedroom, but the Princesse de Conti prevented him, saying that Monseigneur would not know him. She even went so far as to press him back with her hands and to tell him that he must now think only of himself.

At this the King finally gave way, and sank down upon a sofa, near the door of the anteroom, remaining there for nearly an hour, waiting until death should come. He remembered nonetheless to send for Père Tellier, who had already gone to bed, but rose and dressed hastily, to go to Monseigneur's bedroom. By that time, it was too late, at least according to what the servants said, 'but that

---

[1] 'Showing piety in medicine' was what Molière called it.

Jesuit,' relates Saint-Simon, 'perhaps to reassure the King, maintained that he had found good and sufficient grounds for giving absolution'.

Mme de Maintenon had joined the King on the sofa, and was making an effort to weep. She tried to persuade him to leave, but he would not do so until Monseigneur had expired, which did not occur until eleven o'clock, when Fagon's departure made it known that all was over. 'What a sight met my eyes, Madame!' wrote Mme de Maintenon to the Princesse des Ursins. 'The King was sitting on a day-bed, dry-eyed, but shaking from head to foot, surrounded by the weeping members of his family and their people. It seems that before my arrival he had entered his dying son's bedroom three or four times, terrified lest he expire before Père Tellier was able to give him Extreme Unction.'

Only then did the King call for his coach; but, by some mistake, a servant brought Monseigneur's carriage, and the King asked for another, because the sight of it grieved him. Even at that moment, he had sufficient self-command to see and speak to Pontchartrain, telling him to arrange with the other ministers to come to Marly next day for the Wednesday Council meeting. But Pontchartrain replied that there was nothing urgent, and that it could very well be postponed. The King then with some difficulty stepped into his coach, supported on either side; Mme de Maintenon stepped in after him and, as they drove away, a crowd of officers and servants, belonging to Monseigneur's household, flung themselves down on their knees the entire length of the courtyard on either side, imploring him with terrible howls to have compassion on them, for they had lost their master and would starve to death.

While Meudon provided this scene of horror, everything at Versailles was going on as usual. Saint-Simon was chatting with his wife, as she undressed to go to bed, when one of their footmen, whom they had lent to the Duchesse de Berry, entered in a state of great agitation, saying that bad news must have come from Meudon, for he had seen the Duc de Bourgogne whispering to his brother with his eyes full of tears. Saint-Simon thereupon hurried to the Berrys' apartment, but found it deserted, everyone having gone to Adelaide's room, and he followed after them as quickly as he could.

Madame, at Saint-Cloud, had been about to say her prayers and go to bed thinking that all was well at Meudon, when the Maréchale de Clérambault appeared looking quite stunned, to tell her that Monseigneur was dying and the King, at that very moment, was passing through Versailles on his way to Marly. She added that the Duchesse de Bourgogne had ordered her carriage, so as to follow him. Immediately afterwards a message came that the Grand Dauphin was dead.

'You may imagine the shock to me,' wrote Madame. 'I quickly dressed and rushed over to see the Duchesse de Bourgogne, where I found the most harrowing scene imaginable. The Duc and Duchesse de Bourgogne looked stunned and deathly pale; neither of them saying a word. The Duc and Duchesse de Berry lay on the floor leaning their elbows on one of the day-beds and sobbing so loud that the noise could be heard three rooms away. My son and his wife wept silently,[1] and did what they could to quieten the Duc and Duchesse de Berry. Ladies were sitting on the floor all around the Duchesse de Bourgogne, and they too were weeping. I accompanied the Duc de Berry and his wife to their apartments, and they went to bed, but did not cease to weep. As I left, the Duchesse de Bourgogne told me that the King had forbidden any of his family to go to Marly that night; we were to wait until next morning. It was half-past two by the time I was back to my room and in bed; but I slept only a couple of hours and at seven o'clock rose again and returned there at half-past eight.'

At Versailles, after Madame's departure, the noise and disorder continued, with the footmen and valets groaning and sobbing aloud, showing, said Saint-Simon, 'how much people of that kind stood to lose'. Adelaide waited for orders from the King, who had sent to tell her that she was to meet him in the avenue, near the stables, as he wished to see her when he passed through the grounds. At about half-past midnight, another message came, and Saint-Simon saw her gather up her shawl and head-scarves from the dressing-table and, followed by her ladies, go down the grand staircase and out to her carriage. 'She bore herself with her usual grace, erect and

---

[1] Saint-Simon was shocked to see the Duc d'Orléans crying. He thought that his friend was affecting a sorrow he did not truly feel; and, when they were alone together in the prince's study, he expostulated. ' "Monsieur," I exclaimed, rising to my feet. He understood me at once and answered in a broken voice, now weeping in earnest, "You may well be surprised; but such scenes are moving. He was a good man, and when they let him alone, he was kind to me. I know that my grief will be short ... but at present, kinship, pity, humanity are all involved, and one does feel sad.' " Saint-Simon praised his sentiments, but expressed his intense astonishment. 'At this he rose, put his head in a corner with his nose to the wall, and sobbed most bitterly, something I never would have believed, had I not seen it with my own eyes.'

resolute, her eyes scarcely moist, but betraying her inner turmoil by the stealthy glances which she cast around her.'

Adelaide had only a short time to wait in the avenue before the King appeared. She stepped down to greet him at the door of his coach, but Mme de Maintenon, who was seated at that side, cried out, 'What are you thinking of, Madame? Do not come near us, we are pest-ridden!' Saint-Simon did not hear what the King said, if anything; but he did not kiss her, on account of the contagion. The fact of the matter was that Fagon had kept the nature of Monseigneur's illness such a profound secret that not even the Duc de Beauvilliers, who had slept at Meudon, was aware of the danger, and he had returned to Versailles immediately after the Council meeting. He had gone to bed early, but had been awakened by a servant summoning him to the Duchesse de Bourgogne's apartment, where he arrived shortly before her return.

He found the two royal princes and the Duchesse de Berry waiting in the anteroom. When she appeared and the first greetings were over, he saw that the heat was stifling in that small room, and suggested that they should all go through the bedroom, and into the large drawing-room that separated it from the great gallery. There, Adelaide sat down on a sofa beside her husband, and set herself to comforting him. 'And she had far less trouble in doing that,' said Saint-Simon, 'than in summoning the need for comfort herself, although, without any parade of false feeling, one could see that she did her best to produce the tears which she thought that decency required.' She responded with a frequent use of her handkerchief to the sobs and cries and howling of her brother-in-law the Duc de Berry, 'who was sometimes quiet, but only because he choked, and then again would break out into cries so monstrously loud that they resembled the bellowings of deep despair. At last he drove himself into such a paroxysm of grief that they were obliged to undress him on the spot, to summon doctors, and have remedies prepared . . . The Duchesse de Berry was beside herself. The bitterness of despair showed in her face; but you might see as plainly as though it were written there, that her frenzy of uncontrollable misery came not from love or sorrow, but from blighted self-interest.'

So passed the greater part of the night, until, at length, the Duc de Beauvilliers announced that it was time to deliver the young princes from such distressing publicity, and proposed that they should each go to their own rooms. Before going, the Duchesse de Bourgogne had a word with Mme de Levis, who said that, since the princes had no cause to be sorrowful, it would be dreadful to see her making a pretence. She answered quite simply that, without any pretence, compassion and the whole spectacle had moved her, and that good manners, nothing more, had given her self-control. After these few words, 'which expressed her true feelings with dignity and truth, she retired to her private rooms, and rested there until morning'.

The attitude of her husband was very different. At first, he was stunned by the suddenness of the blow. He saw how enormously Monseigneur's death had elevated him in rank, above all, he was overcome by the vast responsibilities he would now have to bear. His scrupulous conscience-ridden nature, weakened by lack of purpose, quailed at the very thought. Saint-Simon, who had caught a glimpse of him when he first heard the news, 'could detect no tender feelings, only the intense preoccupation of a man utterly absorbed in his thoughts'. He saw the prince again in the great gallery, when he was, in all sincerity, 'weeping tears of compassion, piety, and exhaustion'. But the impression of his being in a state of shock was what dominated. Madame describes him as looking 'overwhelmed, deathly pale, saying not a word,' and it was several days before he recovered. His letters to his brother Philip tell us what he was feeling.

Writing on the day when Monseigneur fell ill, he said, 'You will no doubt be extremely anxious, my dearest brother, when you read this letter; but I trust that by that time we shall be free from worry'. The day after Monseigneur's death, he wrote only a few lines: 'The subject of this letter is so dreadful, my dear brother, that I have not the strength to tell you of it. I share your grief, which will be only too much like my own.' He took up his pen again a few days later: 'I wrote only a brief word to you, my dearest brother, on the fifteenth of this month, regarding the tragedy that has come upon us. I do not doubt that, with your kind heart, you have been deeply afflicted, and I am sure that you have felt for me also. I have been shocked and profoundly stirred, and was unwell for several days, that is to say I was listless, and without appetite. God be thanked, I am better now. This is a blow from the hand of Him, whom we must submissively adore. You will have heard that the King thinks it best that I should assume the title of Dauphin, which reminds me, at all moments, of the loss I have sustained. I know, my dear brother, that you were well-assured of Monseigneur's affection; it was not by my intention that I did not enjoy the same

love, and I cannot sufficiently impress on you my pleasure at seeing
our hearts united . . .' This letter honestly expresses the sentiments
proper to the occasion; but there is no sign of personal grief, nor
could that have been expected from a son who for many years had
been cordially disliked. Adelaide did not feel the bond of blood
relationship, and was thus able to speak more freely. 'I was truly
moved by the death of Monseigneur,' she wrote to the Duc de
Noailles, the husband of her childhood's friend Françoise d'Aubigné,
'but, like everyone else, I shall soon recover; and, I believe with
better reason. You have not been away so long as to have forgotten
the situation at the Court, and may therefore imagine much of what
I feel.' Saint-Simon had good cause to say that 'no sorrow was ever
more fleeting than that felt for the death of Monseigneur'.

19

Dauphin and Dauphine

WHEN THE King and Mme de Maintenon reached Marly they found themselves not expected, and in considerable discomfort. No one had warned the staff of their coming; the house was shut, the keys mislaid, there were neither fires nor candles, nothing but a few used nightlights. They were thus obliged to sit for an hour in the cold, in Mme de Maintenon's little ante-room, waiting until her room was made ready, and they could be alone. Madame la Duchesse and the Princesse de Conti followed them from Meudon, where horror reigned. They stood, at first, in the drawing-room, in the midst of all the confusion of servants struggling in the darkness to prepare the room, and they wept loudly for long stretches of the time. They then went into the ante-room, where the King sat dry-eyed in a distant corner beside Mme de Maintenon.

Meudon, when they had left it, was like a desert. There remained only the officers and servants of Monseigneur's household staff, who spent the night wandering in the garden, for Monseigneur's body had blackened and putrefied so rapidly that, although the windows and door of his room were left wide open on to the terrace, the whole house stank so abominably that it was impossible to remain indoors. At that point, someone remembered poor Mlle Choin, shut away in her garret-room. No one had thought to tell her the sad news, and she had realised the situation only when she heard the lamentations. Two of her friends, Mlles de Lillebonne and de Melun, went to her, brought her quickly downstairs and, bundling her into a hired coach which chanced to be available, carried her off to Paris.

Regarding the body of Monseigneur, it was considered useless as well as dangerous to open it, and it was taken next day, without any kind of ceremony, straight to Saint-Denis, in one of the King's ordinary coaches, with part of the front window removed to allow room for the end of the coffin.

That same morning, Thursday, 16 April, the King, worn out after his wretched night, slept later than usual. When he awoke, Adelaide, who had arrived very early from Versailles, visited him with Mme de Maintenon. He then rose, went to his study, and immediately sent for his ministers, in order to make the necessary arrangements, and the changes required by Monseigneur's death in the established forms of ceremony, that crazy structure of etiquette on which his rule at the Court was maintained. The first question was how the Duc de Bourgogne, who was the grandson, not the son of the reigning monarch, should be addressed. His father had been the Dauphin, but no one had ever called him anything but Monseigneur. It had begun as a joke, when he was a baby; but the King had taken it up, and had used no other name even after he became a man. It may have been affectionate informality, but on the other hand Louis XIV had a strong dislike of any suggestion that he was not immortal, and was never heard to refer to Monseigneur as 'my son', preferring to regard him as 'a mere genealogical incident at his Court'.[1]

However that may have been, the old King was, if only for a short time, stricken by Monseigneur's death. To everyone's astonishment he had remained controlled and tearless through all the agonies of the previous day; but on the day after, when his ministers arrived, he broke down. He had taken Beauvilliers and the Chancellor into one of the window-recesses of his study; but his eyes had overflowed with tears, and his voice was so choked with sobs that he could hardly speak. The ministers, at the table, wept too, until Torcy, deciding that the time had come to be a little firm, said that there would be no difficulty in giving the title of Dauphin to the Duc de Bourgogne, since it was impossible for any man to come between him and the King to deprive him of his rights. The King stated that such was his opinion also, and the Chancellor agreed. Thereupon the question was settled, and the King made the announcement at midday, during his dinner. 'I had been displeased with myself,' wrote Torcy in his *Journal*, 'for what I thought showed hardness of heart, but when I saw the others laughing as they left the study, I felt I had been more compassionate than they who had wept in the King's presence, and I ceased to reproach myself.'

One last question remained; in speaking to the new Dauphin,

[1] Extracted from the article on Bossuet in the *Encyclopaedia Britannica*, 13th edition.

should people say *Monseigneur* or *Monsieur*, and in speaking of him and his wife, *Monsieur le Dauphin* and *Madame la Dauphine*, or more simply, *le Dauphin* and *la Dauphine*? It took a week to come to the decision that he should be referred to as *Monsieur le Dauphin*, written to as *Monseigneur le Dauphin*, and addressed in speaking as *Monsieur*. This ruling was more important than it might appear, for the bastards and princes of the blood had been quietly raising their status by causing their friends and dependants to call them *Monseigneur*, thus bringing their treatment nearer to equality with the sons of France. The Duc de Bourgogne had always disapproved of such encroachments; as for Saint-Simon, they made his blood boil. Louis seized the opportunity to make his views known. He made a point of insisting on the *Monsieur*, and correcting those who forgot and called him otherwise; the bastards, however, did not follow his example, and continued to allow the *Monseigneur*. Nonetheless, a hint had been given that in the course of time a different mode would be established. In the case of Adelaide, there was no question to be decided; she was *Madame la Dauphine*, and beyond competition.

As may be imagined, no one slept well on the night after Monseigneur's death; but, very early on the Thursday morning, Louis and Adelaide went to hear mass. Saint-Simon joined them there before the end, and followed them back to their apartments. He says that very few courtiers were present, because no one had expected her to be so early at Marly; but Adelaide had wanted to be with the King when he woke. The little duke was surprised to see them tearless, quite obviously giving more thought to their new rank than to mourning the death of Monseigneur, for now and then a smile escaped them as they talked; yet he did not find it in his heart to blame them, having regard to all the circumstances.

Their first task was to persuade the Berrys to accept the new order gracefully, for etiquette demanded that Adelaide's rank should be marked with greater state than that of her sister-in-law. But the Duchesse de Berry did not take kindly to the second place. When Monseigneur was alive, she and Adelaide had been treated as equal in rank; but that could not continue. Three days after the Grand Dauphin's death, the King ruled that the Duc de Berry should attend his brother's *coucher*, and hand him his nightshirt, and that the Duchess should do the same for Adelaide. The Duc de Berry made no fuss about this; not so the Duchess. She was jealous of Adelaide's popularity; there were tantrums; she had involved her husband in her fault-finding, and the King had sometimes been obliged to intervene to prevent a public scene.

Now that Monseigneur was dead, the command to wait on Adelaide filled her with rage, more especially since she set such great store by her privileges as a granddaughter of France that one day, when her mother came to visit her and the footman inadvertently opened both sides of the door (an honour due only to herself and the Duchesse de Bourgogne) she had flushed crimson, and, after the Duchesse d'Orléans's departure, had furiously ordered Mme de Saint-Simon to dismiss the man. To wait on Adelaide would be to mark the present difference in their rank, and that the Duchesse de Berry refused to accept gracefully. She wept, sobbed, and screamed so loud that her husband, who had the firm intention of attending his brother's *lever* on the following day, was obliged to send an excuse, for fear of a quarrel. In the end they had to get her father the Duc d'Orléans to speak to her; only then did she consent to obey the King's command. Even so, she delayed in going for a further three days, and remained extremely sulky. Saint-Simon describes the occasion: 'She attended the *toilette* of Madame la Dauphine; handed her her petticoat and, finally, offered her *la sale*.[1] Madame la Dauphine pretended to have heard nothing, and not to have noticed the inexcusable delay. She received the Duchesse de Berry's services with all the kindness imaginable, and the most unaffected signs of fondness. Her great desire for a happy relationship with her sister-in-law persuaded her to overlook this latest prank as though it were she, and not the Duchesse de Berry, who had everything to gain and nothing to lose by forgetfulness.'

The King, meanwhile, had been concerning himself with arrangements for his Court. He and Mme de Maintenon were alone for four days after Monseigneur's death. On 19 April, he came out of retirement, announcing that he would be in residence at Marly for the next three months, in order to escape the foul air of Versailles, and he published a list of those of his family and courtiers to whom he would give lodgings. On Monday the 20th, he received the silent condolences of his courtiers, wearing long black mantles, and the ladies with mantillas. The King saw them in his study, standing in ordinary morning dress, his hat under his arm, and his hand resting on his writing table. The ladies, as they passed him, curtseyed, and

[1] *La sale* was the name given to the little red tray on which the queens and princesses were offered their watches, fans, handkerchiefs, and other small objects of adornment.

the gentlemen bowed very low. He returned their salutations with
marked politeness to all those of rank, but noticed no one else. There
was a great crowd, for not only did all Versailles and Marly attend,
but all Paris also, dressed in funeral black, for it was a unique opportunity to appear at Court before the King. A great number of people
took advantage of the opportunity, notwithstanding that many of
them had no right to wear long mantles, which used to be the
prerogative of men of rank. Some of them looked supremely ridiculous, and the King found it hard to keep from smiling 'when some
nonentity filed past him, in a state of losing most of his mourning
garments'.

There were other receptions, 'to receive silent condolences',
given by the princes of the blood and, to Saint-Simon's fury, by
the King's bastards, who managed by a trick to insinuate themselves,
thus once more staking their claim to equality with the princes and
princesses of royal blood. Despite his vituperation, Saint-Simon
called, like the other courtiers, on his bitter enemy the Duc du
Maine; for in life he was never quite so unconforming as his
Mémoires would have us believe. After the royal receptions, there
were many others for the diplomatic corps; the Parlement; the
Chamber of Commerce, and the Provost of the Merchants, representing the people of Paris, to mention only a few. They read
lengthy addresses before the King, and then went to read them all
over again to the Dauphin and Dauphine, who complained a little,
because that custom had been in abeyance since the reign of Henri II.
All these harangues were delivered on 27 April, and the King went
to Versailles to hear them. Dangeau says that Louis and Adelaide
reached Marly an hour after his return, and that both were 'much
fatigued by listening to the great number of speeches, although they
said that many had been extremely eloquent'.[1]

Gradually the Court came to life again; but with certain restric-
tions, on account of mourning. No gambling or cards were allowed,
and poor Adelaide was reduced to playing goose with her household.
By 7 May, however, there were quiet card-parties in Mme de
Maintenon's room, and soon afterwards all games, with the exception of *lansquenet*, were once more permitted in the Marly drawing-
rooms. It was very dull, for a time, without plays or balls, but soon
the hunting began again for, in France, in those days, there was no

[1] It is typical of Louis's primness that he refused to receive the deputation
from the players, on the grounds that they were people of no service to the
State. 'He is all piety and religion,' said the Marquise d'Huxelles.

close-season. All through the spring and summer the princes and courtiers galloped through the forests of Marly and Fontainebleau, in pursuit of deer, wild boar or wolves, the King following at a great pace with his four-in-hand of racing ponies. They had one particularly enjoyable day, after the Court returned to Versailles, when the meet was in the Bois de Boulogne, and a large crowd drove out from Paris. Adelaide, on horseback, took the opportunity to speak to many of them, and, Dangeau recounts, 'said so much that was civil and kindly that they went home charmed by her appearance and simple-hearted friendliness'.

They had a good day's hunting, and afterwards Adelaide rode on to Passy, where the Duchesse de Lauzun had a magnificent hunt breakfast prepared. They were at table until eight in the evening, and so many people came that Mme de Lauzun was obliged to arrange for a second sitting. 'It was a most happy occasion,' says Dangeau. 'They played *brelan, lansquenet, and papillon*, and did not return to Versailles until after midnight.' That was on 23 September, little more than five months after Monseigneur's death, and already the Court had returned to normal—except in dress, for the year of mourning decreed by the King had still over six months to run. In every other way, the unhappy Dauphin seemed to be forgotten. The Meudon Cabal, feeling the blow to their ambitions, may have regretted his absence; but the only people likely to have grieved for him were his friend and sister the Princesse de Conti, and poor Mlle Choin,[1] and even her grief, says Saint-Simon, 'was less prolonged and less violent than was expected, which astonished people, and made them think that she had not been such an influential figure as was generally supposed'.

In Europe, Monseigneur's death was regarded as of considerable importance because it brought Philip V a step nearer to the throne of France. In the view of the Allies, it created a dangerous gap. But, only eleven days later, a courier from Nancy brought news of far greater moment: the thirty-two-year-old Emperor had died suddenly of smallpox and, by a curious coincidence, had fallen ill on the same day as Monseigneur. There was no direct male heir to the

[1] One of the King's first actions on the morning after his son's death was to send a gentleman with a comforting message to Mlle Choin, assuring her of his protection and a pension of ten thousand livres, for which she had not asked. One of the strange contradictions in the nature of Louis XIV was the kindness and consideration that he often showed to the members of his family and his servants, and his insensitive cruelty to people in general; for instance his disregard of the 100,000 men who died in the making of the Versailles gardens.

Holy Roman Empire, and his brother Charles, who, in Barcelona, had recently declared himself to be King of Spain, thus became Emperor. The Protestant members of the Alliance immediately took fright. The prospect of a union between the two great Catholic Empires of Austria and Spain was altogether too formidable; it could be foreseen that they would never allow the Archduke Charles to retain the Spanish throne.

Torcy brought the great news to Louis XIV, as the King was getting into bed, and then went to tell it to the Duc de Bourgogne. He recounts that 'they hailed it as though it had been a great victory, although M. le Duc de Bourgogne's conscience prevented him from appearing to rejoice'. Next day, letters were sent to King Philip and the Princesse des Ursins, and it was thus that Philip received the news that, after his father's death, his traditional enemy had died also, and that his rival, the Archduke Charles, had been summoned to a higher destiny. Everything must now be done to free Spain by assisting him to become Emperor.

The Queen of Spain was gravely ill with the tuberculosis that caused her death three years later. The doctors would not allow her to be disturbed; thus Mme des Ursins, when she went to her with the letters in her hand, told her only of the Emperor's death, and not that of her father-in-law. The little Court at Saragossa had been genuinely saddened and alarmed by Monseigneur's demise, for he had supported King Philip, and had so firmly opposed the policy of forcing him to abdicate, that he had roused himself from his habitual torpor to speak for him at the Council. Now that the Grand Dauphin no longer lived, they feared lest the King of France revert to his original plan, and abandon Spain. The Princesse des Ursins comforted them with her optimism, and set herself to distract Philip from his sorrow, and inspire him to make fresh plans. Vendôme was sent for, and arrived post-haste, on horseback, having heard the news at his headquarters. He confirmed that every effort should be made to secure the Archduke's accession, and to obtain for him the votes of the Catholic Electors of Bavaria and Cologne; the Pope's support could be taken for granted, since Rome was sure to desire a Catholic Emperor. 'This death,' said Philip, 'is a sign from heaven'; and he offered to compose a letter to be sent to the Archduke, at Barcelona. 'It would be the most noble manner of signifying my intentions.'

Assisted by Vendôme, he did, indeed, write a very lengthy letter, appealing to the noble heart of his enemy, and offering him a fair settlement, to be agreed in advance, by which the Archduke would have the Empire and Philip the kingdom of Spain. This letter was greatly admired at Versailles, more especially so because Vendôme, when sending a hand-written copy to the King, made a note that it was the work of King Philip himself. There remained, nonetheless, some doubt at the Court of the entire truth of that statement. The Archduke sent no reply, returning the letter unopened, for although he had every intention of accepting the Empire, he chose to do so without the help of King Philip and still continued, at Barcelona, to style himself King of Spain. Nonetheless, to the Spanish people, the Emperor's death was a clear sign of the beginning of the long road to peace.

At Versailles, also, the courtiers saw with deep thanksgiving the not too distant possibility of peace. 'Last night, around midnight,' wrote Madame on 25 April, 'we received news that the Emperor had died of smallpox on the 17th of the present month. What a miracle it would be if this event should bring us peace; but time will tell. Here only the sadness is felt.'[1]

There was also a great sense of relief. Despite his victory at Malplaquet, Marlborough's huge losses in men and money had prevented his bringing the war to a successful conclusion. What is more, a change of government in England, where the Whig hawks were succeeded by Tory doves, had brought public opinion to side with Lord Peterborough, when he said, 'We are all great fools to get ourselves killed for two such boobies' (meaning King Philip and Charles VI, the new Emperor). In April 1711, England seceded from the Alliance and, in the following December, the Duke of Marlborough, on a charge of misappropriating public funds, was deprived of all his offices by Queen Anne, and relieved of his command. 'This will do for us everything that we could desire,' said Louis XIV.

The old King's valiant refusal to accept defeat or admit to discouragement now appeared justified. Money to pay and feed the armies had begun to trickle into the treasury, in the shape of bullion from the New World; and, in Spain, Vendôme was re-establishing

[1] Saint-Simon says that 'few lamented the Emperor, a prince with a most violent temper, below the average in wit and intelligence; who showed little esteem for his mother the late Empress, no tenderness for his wife, and scant respect or affection for his brother the Archduke. . . . For France, his death was a great event and a piece of quite unexpected good fortune that finally led to peace and the preservation of the Spanish monarchy.'

King Philip by winning several important victories.[1] The Court took on a new life, adapting to the important changes in ceremonial caused by the change in the succession. Adelaide's new status, in particular, was marked by a number of innovations in etiquette, of the kind which the King and his courtiers believed to be immensely important to the glory of the Court. Hitherto, when she had attended services in the Versailles chapel, she had shared a small square of red velvet carpet with the Duchesse de Berry. Now her place in the chapel was far nearer the altar, and she had a large and comfortable cushion to kneel on alone.

Besides doubling the cavalry escort that rode around her coach, the King added to her staff an officer of the royal bodyguard, ten men and a corporal of the French Guard, and two of the hundred Swiss, normally attached to the monarch alone. He also provided her with an officer of his bodyguard, to stand outside the door of her apartments, and escort distinguished visitors to her audience chamber.

The ceremonial attending her public dinners became more elaborate than when she and Louis had been no more than the Duc and Duchesse de Bourgogne, for the King, to whom ceremony was a matter of symbolic importance, decided to revive for her all the dignities hitherto belonging only to Queens of France which, after the death of Maria Theresa, had not been transferred to the unfortunate Dauphine. Thus her table was dignified by the three symbols of royalty, the Ship, the Padlock, and the Wand. The Ship, a beautiful silver cruet-holder, contained her salt-cellar, napkin, and dishes; the Padlock, a small padlocked case, enclosed the late Queen's knife, fork, and spoon; and the Wand, a staff of office, borne by her major-domo.

It was on 8 August, 1711, that the new Dauphin and Dauphine first dined in state, in the presence of most of her ladies (the duchesses among them seated on *tabourets*, the rest standing) and a great crowd of spectators. Every step of the ritual was performed strictly in accordance with tradition. First appeared the major-domo, marching at the head of a solemn procession to the door of her buttery, where a basin was presented to him, in which he ceremoniously washed his hands. He was followed by the comptroller of the house-

[1] It is extraordinary, in view of Saint-Simon's claim to speak nothing but the truth, that he gives Vendôme no credit for his brilliant generalship. 'The fact of the matter is that, when his emotions overcome him, the little duke is not to be trusted.'

hold and the first gentleman-in-waiting. A silver tray with sops of bread was offered to him by the chief officer of the buttery, to whom he gave one of them, which the officer gracefully devoured. He then proceeded with another to touch all the dishes to be offered to the royal couple. Lastly, taking the wand of office from the master of ceremonies, he returned to the dining-room in procession with an armed guard, the officers of the household, the gentlemen-in-waiting, and the servants belonging to the buttery, carrying various dishes. At that point he announced that dinner was served and the Dauphin and Dauphine entered and took their seats. The next step was for the major-domo to free his hands by entrusting his hat and staff to the officer of the Goblet, and to present a golden dish, holding a towel, one end of which was dipped in water, so that the royal couple might wash and dry their fingers. Thereafter he recovered his hat and wand and, returning under escort to the buttery door, he inspected and tasted the various courses before they were offered. His duty thereafter was to station himself behind the Dauphin's chair, on the right-hand side, and to remain there until the meal was at an end.

Thus the King showed his pride in Adelaide, by giving her prematurely all the honours of her future rank. He had already endowed her, as a supreme mark of his trust, with absolute authority over her household, and permission to choose her officers and ladies, without first asking his approval. Such authority had been invested in no other princess but, when he gave it, the King was in no doubt of Adelaide's capabilities. Nonetheless, she thought it wisest never to use this privilege. Her attitude to the King was one of genuine affection, combined with wariness and tact. She knew his sudden changes too well to do anything to arouse his distrust, and that was one reason for his loving her so much. When she wanted something, she showed her wishes by a smile or a nod, but she never asked for anything outright, or misused her power, and although she was capable of standing up to the King on behalf of others—her husband, for example, or her dear Tessé—she asked nothing for herself; yet the King's love was such that she obtained all her wishes. Guided by Mme de Maintenon, she showed a wisdom in dealing with him extraordinary in one so young (she was in her twenty-seventh year in 1711), and in all the fifteen years she had spent at his Court, his love and trust in her, and his delight in her companionship had never flagged. Had she made demands on him, said Saint-Simon, she would have lost his confidence forever.

Louis XIV did indeed detest being asked for favours. In 1710, for example, the early death of the Marquis de Bellefords left vacant the lucrative post of Captain and Governor of Vincennes, and the King was inundated with requests, some from the most distinguished of his courtiers, which he refused even to read. Then, at a gentle hint from Adelaide, supported by Mme de Maintenon, he presented the appointment, unsolicited, to the poverty-stricken Marquis du Châtelet, a very capable and gallant gentleman, the husband of one of the gentlest and best-esteemed of her ladies-in-waiting, and it was much remarked that this most modest and retiring lady was the one to benefit by royal favour. The affair made a great impression, showing as it did that, where the Dauphine was concerned, genuine virtue and merit had higher claims than intrigue or corruption.

Of all the honours showered upon Adelaide, the only one that appeared to give her pleasure was her promotion to riding on horseback beside Louis, when the King reviewed his troops in the great courtyard of Versailles. For the rest, she had no pride in them, and no gratification. She was so small, so lively and volatile, that the constraint of tight bodices and stays bore down most heavily upon her, and the endless ceremonies, that required her to stand or sit motionless for long periods, were near torture, though she did not let them affect her temper. Like Madame, she preferred the comparative ease of riding clothes, or the loose morning dresses in which she ran about at the Ménagerie. Her lack of interest in her appearance soon became noticeable, and Mme de Maintenon was seriously disturbed when the King complained. She wrote to Mme des Ursins, 'Madame la Dauphine is adored by everyone; if she would only go to bed earlier and take a little more care of her dress she would be quite perfect. The casual style which she favours is not becoming to her, nor does it suit her rank.' To Adelaide herself she wrote, admonishing her 'to dress with greater care, since your untidiness displeases His Majesty. It is important for you to wear jewels, so as to draw attention to the clearness of your complexion and the neatness of your figure'.

Adelaide was duly impressed by this warning, and at once proceeded to smarten herself up. The question of jewellery was another matter, for all of this occurred only a few weeks after Monseigneur's death, when the Court, but not the King, was still in mourning (by tradition, he did not wear mourning for his descendants). Adelaide, however, felt that it would cause offence and show poor taste, were she to appear in full fig, decked out with jewels, when all the rest wore black or grey, the highest in rank draping their rooms and carriages in mourning covers.

It is a manifestation of her desire to avoid unpleasantness, and of her reliance on Mme de Maintenon's help, that they together devised a scheme, by which her jewellery was taken secretly to the old lady's room. Adelaide arrayed herself there in royal magnificence, before the King's visit every afternoon, and after he had gone, removed the greater part of it before returning to play cards in her own apartments.

There is no doubt that, at this time, she was not well enough dressed to suit her rank, and she may have felt guilty at displaying so little interest in clothes. On the other hand, she was conscious of being ill-served and neglected by her wardrobe mistress. Thus, when the sad disgrace of Mme de Mailly occurred a few months later, the princess most uncharacteristically did little to defend her.

Mme de Mailly had been a member of Adelaide's household from the very beginning, when, to everyone's surprise, for she was without experience, she was appointed Mistress of the Wardrobe, largely, it was supposed, because, as a cousin of Mme de Maintenon, and brought up in her apartments, her loyalty to that lady could not be doubted. By tradition, the post should have gone to a princess of the blood, and much jealousy was aroused; but the King, in his concern for Adelaide's happiness, wished her to be surrounded by friends and play-fellows, and kept away from proud and ambitious princesses, deep in Court intrigues. Mme de Mailly and Adelaide were soon on friendly terms, and had many happy times together, as when, on the day after the little princess's arrival at Versailles, the King sent the crown jewels to the Mistress of the Wardrobe, and they sat down merrily together to choose the ones that Adelaide liked best.

On the other hand, Mme de Mailly, though she liked the glory, was not enamoured with the idea of work or responsibility. A country-girl from Provence, she had been as poor as a church-mouse when Mme de Maintenon took her to live at Versailles; and she had been married 'partly by compulsion, partly by desire' to the Comte de Mailly, who inherited a vast fortune. She was a dear friend of both Saint-Simons. He describes her as 'never losing the inelegance of her provincial upbringing; but covering it with the lustre of Mme de Maintenon's all-powerful favour'. She was not ill-natured, and was a loyal friend—when she made a friend; but to the rest of the world she seemed excessively proud and disagreeable. Incompetent herself, and fiercely critical of others, people at the time had considered her a very bad choice, but they could do nothing about it, and were forced to accept her.

At the start, she did not do badly, and the princess's appearance excited admiration; but she grew lazy, and bored with the labour involved, and before long handed over her responsibilities to one of the waiting-women. As a result, the costs had risen to more than double those of the late Queen, and yet Adelaide's wardrobe contained little that was new, and nothing either fashionable or elaborately embroidered. Indeed, she was reduced to borrowing from her ladies such accessories as tippets, muffs, and ribbons. Desmaretz, the Treasurer, had scene after scene with Mme de Mailly, as she haughtily presented him with her quite outrageous bills; but at length even his patience was exhausted, and he told both the King and Mme de Maintenon, who together spoke to Adelaide. Notwithstanding her gentle nature, she felt that after suffering in silence for so many years she had endured enough, and the outcome was that Mme de Mailly was divested of the Wardrobe, which was given into the care of Adelaide's trusty old friend Mme Quentin. As for the waiting-woman involved, who had been enriching herself at the King's expense, she was dismissed with ignominy.

Mme de Mailly went into hysterics, weeping, screaming, protesting at the stain on her honour, creating so loud a rumpus that Mme de Maintenon, after enduring it for a fortnight, produced some kind of an excuse for her; but the Wardrobe she never recaptured. No one pitied her, for her arrogance and vanity had alienated all her friends, and people had been shocked to see the Dauphine so ill-clad.

While Adelaide was thus settling down to becoming a sedate young matron, responsible for the running of her own establishment, holding Court in her private apartments, playing with her little boys, and no longer careering about the country in a wild pursuit after pleasure, an extraordinary change had come over Louis. Since his father's death he had gained amazingly in self-confidence and, encouraged by the King's kindness and increased respect, he had become like a different man.

'One saw,' said the rapturous Saint-Simon, 'that prince, once so shy, uncouth, abstracted, so finicky in his morals, so drawn to unworthy studies, that stiff and awkward figure, a stranger in his own home, lacking always in ease and perpetually embarrassed—one saw this man, I say, gradually opening out, composedly taking his place in Society, and there showing himself as free, dignified, agreeable, acting host at times in the Marly drawing-rooms, presiding over a circle of courtiers like a god in his temple, graciously receiving from mere mortals the homage to which he was well accustomed, and rewarding them with the lustre of his exalted smile.' Louis indeed became extremely popular, 'people flocked to him whenever he appeared, not only to pay their court, but for the pleasure of hearing his talk, discovering his deep knowledge in many branches of learning, and his strong grasp of the questions current in State affairs'.

'Most pleasing to many of his hearers,' continues Saint-Simon, was that, although gracious and polite to all, he showed himself fully acquainted with the gradations of rank in French Society, and the degree of respect due to age, birth, and station, which was something his grandfather thought unworthy of notice. Even the King saw the change that had come over him, and treated him with ever-growing affection and esteem. He instructed the generals and Ministers of State to meet for conferences in the new Dauphin's apartments,[1] and to keep him fully informed of their deliberations. Louis attended all the meetings of the Councils, continued to receive reports from the governors and intendants of provincial cities, and generally worked hard to prepare himself for the enormous task that lay ahead. The courtiers, enchanted, 'admired his unstudied eloquence, the good sense in all that he said, and, more even than that, derived from him the much-needed and yearned-for comfort of seeing before them a future master, eminently capable of sovereignty because of his great benevolence and the good use to which he showed that he would put it'.

Mme de Maintenon was less exuberant regarding Louis. All that she could find to say of him, in a letter to the Princesse des Ursins, was, 'M. le Dauphin has done much better since the death of Monseigneur; Madame la Dauphine makes everyone adore her'. To the Duc de Noailles, she wrote, 'M. le Dauphin applies himself to

[1] According to Saint-Simon, the King's instructions caused considerable discomposure to the ministers involved. 'It came on them like a thunderbolt, and left them so stunned that they were unable to hide their mortification.' Perhaps he exaggerates, for Dangeau barely mentions the order.

Moreover, those powerful ministers, whom Saint-Simon calls 'the hammers of the State', believed that they would before long be dependent on the approval of the new Dauphin. It can scarcely be thought that they would not welcome an opportunity to know him better, and show him their quality.

affairs of State, and is more affable with the courtiers'. Meanwhile, from distant Cambrai, Fénelon was writing to the Duc de Chevreuse, 'I hear that our little prince[1] is doing better, that his reputation is rising, and that he is to have more power. He needs your support to gain practice in State affairs, thus learning to see things for himself and make his own decisions. He needs to work with other men, in order to discover their good qualities, and learn how to use them, despite their faults. You must encourage him to give reports to the King, so as to lighten his burden, and assist him in coming to decisions by tactfully offering advice. If he can do this with deference, and a show of zeal, he will give no offence and soon come to be trusted.'

Fénelon, homesick, conscious of the fame he had won in his archbishopric, and bitterly resentful of his continued, and unjust exile,[2] had some months earlier sent Beauvilliers, in a burst of anger, a paper for Louis's reading, entitled *Examen de conscience sur les devoirs de la Royauté*. It was less a letter than a diatribe against Louis XIV, accusing him, somewhat unfairly, of being the sole cause of his country's disasters, and proceeding to reproach the young prince for failing to shake off his uncritical veneration for his grandfather. The paper was addressed to the Dauphin, but whether or not Beauvilliers showed it to him is unknown. He may well not have done so, since it might have served to set Louis against the King, whom in other letters Fénelon enjoins him to comfort and support. One paragraph, however, does apply to Louis himself, and shows a concern which Saint-Simon had earlier shared, although he did not express himself with such severity. 'Sending out dispatches from your study, in which you perpetually confine yourself, is wasting precious time which you owe to the State. Do you not avoid acquaintanceship with other men out of laziness? Is it not arrogance that leads you to shun Society, trumping up excuses that are mere quibbles in comparison with your duty to study men? Is it not self-indulgence to amuse yourself alone in your study, on the pretext of being engaged in secret work?'

This was written at the time of Monseigneur's death; by midsummer, the great change had come over Louis, and he was taking

[1] Writing to Beauvilliers or Chevreuse, Fénelon always spoke of Louis as, *le petit prince*.

[2] The King would never forgive Fénelon. To him Jansenism was but a short step from republicanism, and Fénelon's early history and sympathy with that doctrine made his disgrace permanent.

his place in Society. What is more, he had found a friend in Saint-Simon, and was using him as a kind of unofficial private secretary. The idea had first come from the Ducs de Beauvilliers and Chevreuse. They had spoken of it to the little duke, with a warning that the first moves would need to be made with infinite caution, remembering the many times when he had been near disgrace, and the jealousy which would be caused by any sign of his advancement.

Saint-Simon's happy marriage to a lady in their own set, whom everyone, including the King and Mme de Maintenon, liked and esteemed, confirmed the dukes' high opinion of him. Moreover, they had been much impressed by the essay on Louis's character which he had unwillingly consented to write at their request;[1] and they had not forgotten his amply justified prophecy that the combination with Vendôme would bring disaster. They saw in Saint-Simon a man of wisdom and integrity, a loyal friend whose views on religion and politics were similar to their own,[2] thus an excellent assistant and friend for the young Dauphin, and for the future, a valuable counsellor in the next reign.

As for Saint-Simon, it is not too much to say that he seized the opportunity with abounding joy. He listened to Beauvilliers's advice to be secret and very prudent, but he could not resist 'taking some soundings', in order to discover the prince's feelings for him. He describes every step of the way, in his *Mémoires*. 'One evening, in the Marly gardens, I joined the Dauphin, when he had only a small following. Emboldened by his gracious smile, I whispered into his ear that events, of which he had known, had hitherto kept me from him, but that I now hoped to show my devotion more openly, trusting that this would not displease him. He replied, also in a whisper, that he "looked forward with pleasure to seeing me more often".' 'I quote,' says Saint-Simon, 'his exact words, because his ending was so particularly gracious.' Thereafter he looked for opportunities to join Louis in his evening walks, when no one of special note happened to be with him, but he was infinitely careful not to be seen with him in Society.

During the lifetime of Monseigneur, Louis and Saint-Simon had

---

[1] Saint-Simon probably felt deeply thankful for his stipulation that the prince should on no account see his essay. What he wrote was just and discerning regarding Louis's good qualities; but hard and most outspoken on his faults and petty weaknesses—not a good basis on which to build a friendship.

[2] Saint-Simon's devotion to M. de Rancé, the famous reformer of La Trappe, was well known.

seen little of each other; but, since his death, Adelaide's fondness
for Mme de Saint-Simon, and the efforts of the Ducs de Chevreuse
and Beauvilliers had been bringing them more often into the same
company. They knew little of one another's opinions; but the prince
was deeply grateful to the little duke for publicly supporting him
against Vendôme, and had shown his gratitude when they met on
his return from Flanders. Moreover no one more abominated, or
was more disliked by, the prince's enemies in the Meudon Cabal
than Saint-Simon, whose refusal to associate with the King's
bastards was well known, even although his furious attacks upon
them were confined to the memoirs. In real life, prudence demanded
that he should pay them the proper official calls.

At last the moment came which Saint-Simon had so patiently
awaited. He happened to overhear, in the drawing-room at Marly,
the end of an animated conversation between Louis and Adelaide,
which appeared to concern a question of etiquette, and he ventured
to ask the difficulty. The Dauphin replied that a State visit to the
English Court, at Saint-Germain, would require a complete change
in seating arrangements, on account of the coming of age of Princess
Louisa.[1] On the occasion of their mourning visit, after Monseigneur's
death, the whole party had stood the entire time, because the princess, who should have allowed precedence to the new Dauphine by
giving up her armchair and taking a *tabouret*, had shown no inclination to do so, and no one had liked to protest.

As Louis explained the reasons for their all remaining unseated,
and earnestly asserted the need for gradation and order in matters of
rank, especially where his own rightful superiority was involved,
Saint-Simon was in ecstasies. It was his own cherished opinion.
rank, especially where his own rightful superiority was involved,
'What a joy to hear you speak in this way!' he exclaimed. 'How
right to be meticulous in ceremony, for when that is neglected,
nothing remains to inspire respect.' The prince agreed with enthusiasm, and Saint-Simon cleverly managed to turn the conversation to
the subject nearest his heart, the precautions which the dukes and
peers of France were compelled to take in order to safeguard their
hereditary rights. One thing led to another, and a few days later he
received a summons to attend the Dauphin, in his private apartments.

At this point, the Duc de Beauvilliers took fright, and laid down

[1] Princess Louisa Maria Theresa (1692–1712), daughter of James II and
Mary of Modena. She died of smallpox.

strict instructions. Saint-Simon was to enter by the back way, to visit the prince publicly only at the times when he received other courtiers, and then only for a very short time, and on rare occasions, 'often enough for the visits not to appear unusual, yet not so often as to suggest any suspicion of favour'. Louis himself was enjoined to take no notice of Saint-Simon at such times; yet, ever and again, the little duke relates, the prince managed to give him a stealthy smile that was all the encouragement he desired. Discretion was no doubt essential; but they do seem to have gone to conspiratorial lengths; it was, however, typical of the methods of the Duc de Beauvilliers, than whom a more secret man never existed. Had he been less so, he could never have enjoyed the King's uninterrupted trust and favour for the past twenty-five years at a Court where the least rumour of forming a party, or holding secret meetings, might easily result in permanent disgrace.

The first interview was a success. Louis told Saint-Simon that he knew from M. de Beauvilliers that he might be trusted, and then proceeded to attack the ministers for the boundless power which they had wrested from the King, of whom he spoke with love and gratitude. Saint-Simon was in raptures; but, fearing lest these excellent sentiments should degenerate into blind adoration, he ventured to say that the King was ignorant of many things that would deeply disturb him, had he not made it impossible for people to speak to him. Louis was impressed. He allowed the truth of all Saint-Simon had said, then, returning affectionately to the subject of the King, he blamed his bad upbringing, and the pernicious influences under which he had fallen. His mind, said Louis, essentially just and virtuous, had been led astray into practices that had brought much unhappiness to his country.

Saint-Simon spoke once more of the encroachments of the ministers and the King's bastards on the established rights of the dukes[1] and royal princes; whereat Louis exclaimed in indignation, mentioning with particular heat the title *Monseigneur*, which they denied to the dukes.

To hear his future sovereign expound his own most cherished

---

[1] In the old coronation service, there was a moment symbolising the rôle played by the dukes and peers as the monarch's supporters. The great crown of Charlemagne, when the king left the altar to proceed to his throne, was held over his head by a circle of dukes. The result was that, at a certain moment, he seemed to disappear within a hedge of dukes. When this moment was deliberately omitted at the coronation of Louis XV, Saint-Simon refused to attend.

beliefs was music in the ears of Saint-Simon. It will be seen that his sole concern was for rank, precedence and the upholding of the rights of the dukes and peers of France. Nothing else mattered much to him; but there was reason behind his apparent snobbishness. He was deeply concerned for the welfare of his country, and it was his confirmed opinion that this depended on France being governed, not by an absolute monarch, subject to human weakness and temptations, nor by one assisted by professional administrators, whose ruling passions would be for personal advancement and personal wealth; but by a king advised and supported by the peers of the realm, the great landowners, whose prosperity depended on the well-being of the country as a whole. Looking at eighteenth-century England, he thought he saw near-perfection. But it would not quite do for France, and Saint-Simon spoke sadly of '*Les funestes charmes d'l'Angleterre*'.

After a second interview, Saint-Simon was even more gratified. All his doubts of the prince had vanished; he now saw him as 'pious, tolerant, just, and enlightened, ever striving to improve his mind . . . I savoured the pleasure of enjoying his full and most precious trust at our very first interview. I clearly foresaw the destruction of those hammers of the State [the Ministers], and other enemies of the high nobility, whom they had crushed to dust beneath their feet, and who, revived by this prince would be restored to their rightful status. This general longing for the restoration of rank and order was my heart's desire, far outweighing any hope of personal advancement. I felt the joyful hope of deliverance from a servitude, so intolerable to me that, despite my best endeavours, my exasperation often became apparent.' Yet despite these noble sentiments, Saint-Simon's personal ambition was certainly aroused: 'a brilliant and not too distant future unfolded before my eyes; but I resolved to proceed with the utmost caution. Above all, I determined to cherish my hopes in secret . . . yet I should have thought it both thankless and disloyal not to express my gratitude to the one person to whom my joy was due. Thus, knowing that the Duc de Beauvilliers held the key to the Dauphin's heart and mind, I considered it no treachery to go at once to him, and tell him all.'

In the months that followed, there were many other sessions at Fontainebleau, Versailles, and Marly, all of them conducted with the same deadly secrecy. Saint-Simon's pockets were always stuffed with notes, and he tells us that as he hurried past the courtiers in the salon, on his way to the Dauphin's back door by the privies, he could not help chuckling as he observed the people, whose characters were hidden under his coat, and who were very far from imagining what important conversations were taking place concerning them. His admittance to the Dauphin's study was always arranged in the same way. Duchesne, Louis's confidential servant, was waiting for him by the back door, and let him in when no one was there to see. Yet, in spite of all precautions, he was on one occasion caught red-handed.

It happened when the King was at Marly, where the Dauphin was lodged in one very large room that served as his bedroom, study, and reception-room. The prince and Saint-Simon had been there, working together for some considerable time, in strictest privacy, but not in security, for Louis had firmly refused, despite Saint-Simon's advice, to draw the bolt across the door. 'The Dauphine never comes at this time,' he had said, to which Saint-Simon had replied that it was not so much the Dauphine whom he feared, as the crowd of courtiers who followed her everywhere. Louis, however, remained adamant, and Saint-Simon did not dare to press him. It was a long session, for both had made pages of notes on the subjects under discussion, and these were spread about on a small writing-table and the top of a chest of drawers. They were deep in conversation, their hands full of papers, when suddenly the door burst open, and Adelaide walked in. 'Our eyes glazed, our bodies remained as still as statues, our silence, our utter consternation lasted fully the time of a slow *pater*. The princess spoke first. She was perhaps a little disconcerted to find that her husband, whose every secret she thought she knew, had been concealing something from her. Turning to the prince, she said in a quavering voice that she had not expected to find him in such good company, and then she smiled, first at him, then at me. I had just sufficient time to return her smile and lower my eyes before the prince replied, smiling also, but rather less warmly, "Well, Madame! Since you do find me so well occupied, perhaps you will have the goodness to leave me".' Adelaide did not need to be told twice. She looked at him for a moment; gave a truly sunny smile to them both, and left the room, closing the door behind her.

'Now, Sir,' said Saint-Simon, 'had you only consented to bolt the door!' 'You were right and I was wrong,' replied the prince, 'but there is no harm. Fortunately she was alone, and I can vouch for her silence.' Saint-Simon, however, was not so confident, and the

Duc de Beauvilliers when he was told went quite pale with fright. But they misjudged Adelaide; who told no one at all, not even her crony Mme de Saint-Simon. It might have been different in the early days, when she never ceased to chatter; but adversity had taught her discretion and, as Saint-Simon himself said of her, 'where other people's secrets were concerned, she was like a deep well'.

The Duc de Beauvilliers had never been able to win her friendship. He would have liked to gather her into the pious set of his wife's friends; but she found them altogether too high-minded and, despite Saint-Simon saying that she enjoyed the society of serious ladies, their sober lives were ill-suited to her frivolous nature. Of Beauvilliers himself she was mortally afraid because he knew too much of her affair with Nangis, which might, even then, have brought her into serious trouble with her husband, and probably also with the King. She need not have feared him for, apart from being kind-hearted, he was well aware of her powerful influence over the Dauphin, and was anxious, above all, to gain her trust. Chevreuse, by a fortunate chance, had managed to break the ice in a totally unexpected manner. Life, at the Court, had become very dull owing to the ban on *lansquenet* and play-acting, and Adelaide, searching for some new diversion, wished to revive *hoca*, an old game, on the lines of bingo, which had been the rage in Mazarin's time, and long since passed out of fashion. The trouble was that no one remembered the rules, until it was recalled that the Duc de Chevreuse had been much addicted to it in his youth. He was sought for in the other drawing-rooms and, when found, came to settle down, almost alone, with Adelaide, to teach her the game. Thereafter they remained so long together that people made a jest of it, saying that Mme de Chevreuse should be forewarned, lest she begin to think her husband lost to her.

It was a beginning; but Adelaide still did not trust them, wrongly supposing that they might turn Louis against her, 'not knowing,' says Saint-Simon, 'that the effect of true piety, virtue, and wisdom is to suppress and most carefully conceal anything likely to impair the peace and happiness of a marriage'. Where the little duke himself was concerned, she had no fears; but they were not on terms of friendship, although certainly not ill-disposed. He was a close friend of the ladies she cared for most, but she seldom conversed with him because he did not play cards, which was the only way to closer acquaintanceship. After surprising him with Louis, however, she took more interest and often smiled at him, as though to remind him that they shared a secret.

Adelaide spent the remainder of that dismal summer of 1711, when the Court was still in mourning, in trying to divert the King, whose spirits had sunk very low because of continual bad news from the armies, and the apparent failure of peace negotiations. She had time to reflect on her life and future responsibilities, and Mme de Maintenon was pleased for, writing to the Duc de Noailles, she said, 'Madame la Dauphine, has accepted her elevation, and becomes politer and even more discreet. She gives all the appearance of the highest rank, and that it does not displease her.'

At Versailles, on the day of Candlemas, when she was alone in her bedroom with Mme de Saint-Simon, her other ladies having gone before her to the chapel, she began to speak, rather sadly, of the numbers of people she had known since coming to the Court, so many of whom were now dead; of what she should do when she, too, grew old; of how only Mme de Saint-Simon and Mme de Lauzun would remain from the days of her childhood; and she had run on in this fashion until it was time to go to the sermon. That was on 2 February. Ten days later, she was dead. The rest is pitiful.

20

The Death of Adelaide

O N 18 JANUARY, there was an excursion to Marly. Adelaide reached there very early, intending to welcome the King on his arrival; but that was not to be, for her teeth ached so badly, and her face was so dreadfully swollen that they immediately put her to bed. She was up again at seven that evening, because the King desired her presence in the drawing-rooms; but she played cards with her head enveloped in a hood, and she did not dress. She saw him afterwards in Mme de Maintenon's room, but very soon returned to eat her supper in bed. Next day, she felt better, and during the remainder of the holiday was able to lead her ordinary life. Not much attention was paid to her indisposition, for her constitution was never robust, and people were used to her being unwell. She had needed in adolescence the quiet, well-ordered life, to which she was used in Savoy. In France, indeed, it was one of Mme de Maintenon's chief complaints that the little girl was taken from her care a year too soon, when the King had decided to advance her marriage. But, if Adelaide had one outstanding quality, it was an acceptance of her duty, as she saw it, and a determination to do it well. To please the King and Mme de Maintenon had been instilled into her by her father and beloved grandmother as her whole duty, and she eagerly embraced that task, regardless of fatigue, pain, or personal troubles. By demanding too much of her, by giving her no rest, they probably undermined a constitution, further weakened by a number of miscarriages before she reached the age of fourteen. When serious illness came, she had not the stamina to resist it, and her exhaustion was made worse by the succession of purgings, bleedings, and emetics prescribed by the royal doctors.

On 30 January, while they were still at Marly, an accident to Monsieur le Duc may have served to distract attention from Adelaide's state of health. He had gone out shooting with the Duc de Berry, in freezing weather, and a shot, ricocheting on the ice, had lodged in one eye and blinded him. He was ill for some weeks, and suddenly developed measles. The royal family left him with Madame la Duchesse at Marly when they returned to Versailles on Monday, 1 February.

On Friday, 5 February, Adelaide was taken ill with a high fever. It was not thought serious at first, for most people suffered from such attacks, and, in Adelaide's case the immediate cause was believed to be various stews cooked in the Italian way, which she had been eating for some days past. Moreover, she had spent the morning making cheesecakes, at the Ménagerie, and had consumed more of them than was good for her. Attacks of indigestion were nothing new to her; and Mme de Maintenon had said that there was no reason to 'blame her stomach', only herself for greed.

Next day, she was up again, but towards evening the fever returned and increased, and the night was much disturbed. She nonetheless insisted on rising early next morning to go to mass, it being Sunday; but at six o'clock, that same evening, she was seized with a most violent pain in her head below the temples in an area not larger than a six-sous piece, but so agonising that when the King came to see her before his supper she implored him not to enter. This terrible pain lasted without intermission all through that night and the whole of Monday the 8th, and was not relieved by any of the sedatives then known, though they made her inhale tobacco smoke and chew the leaves, and imbibe a quantity of opium. They also bled her twice from the arm. The pain diminished, and Adelaide, feeling at last some relief, said that in all her life she had never suffered so much, not even in childbirth. But the fever returned with even greater fury, and so it continued throughout the night of Monday the 8th. On Tuesday the 9th, they bled her again, this time from her foot. During the whole of that day, she was in a state of prostration. The King came to her many times, but she was in a high fever, with short interludes of muzziness that caused renewed anxiety, since the opium she had taken was judged insufficient to justify that condition, broken as it was by signs of delirium. Marks appeared on her skin that gave Boudin, her head doctor, reason to hope that the illness might turn out to be measles, for there was known to be much of it about, both at Versailles and in Paris. It was thought that when the rash came out in abundance her head would clear; but this did not happen.

Tuesday night was very bad indeed; the spots vanished, and the doctors ceased to believe in measles; but her mind still remained cloudy. On the morning of Wednesday the 10th, the King came to her early. They had given her a strong emetic; the effect was very violent, but it brought no relief. The Dauphin who had not left her bedside was persuaded to go into the garden for some fresh air; but they could not prevent his returning almost immediately. He himself was unwell and feverish, but that was put down to fatigue from having watched three nights in her room.

The night of Wednesday was worse than all the others. She was consumed by a raging fever, going from exhaustion to delirium, with short intervals of lucidity. The King came at nine o'clock next morning to her room, which Mme de Maintenon had not left since the start of the illness, except when he was with her. By that time, the princess was so bad that they found it necessary to prepare her to receive the last sacraments, and Mme de Maintenon undertook that sad task. The poor young girl was for a moment taken by surprise, although, even on the first day, she had known herself to be gravely ill; 'I have an idea that there will be a peace, and that I shall not see it,' she had said. At that moment, however, she did not feel so badly, and she questioned the doctors regarding her condition. They reassured her as best they might, but continued to press her gently, urging her not to delay. She thanked them for their frankness, saying that she would prepare herself, but she did no more.

Somewhat later, fearing lest she should again lose consciousness, her confessor Père de La Rue, a Jesuit of whom she had always appeared very fond, came to her bedside and urged her to delay her confession no longer. She looked at him, replied that she perfectly understood him, but nothing more, and when he offered to hear her then and there, she did not answer. Being a man of intelligence, he saw at once what was the matter, and kindly and honest as he was, he stopped immediately, saying that she might perhaps feel some dislike of making her confession to him, and entreating her to be frank and, above all, to have no fear, for he would bear all the responsibility. He begged her to say whom she would prefer, promising to go himself to fetch him. The Dauphine then said that she would like M. Bailly, a priest of the mission, in the parish of Versailles. He was regarded as severe, even slightly Jansenist, and he confessed the more pious ladies of the Court, including Mmes du Châtelet and de Nogaret, of the princess's household. Père de La Rue left at once to find him; but unfortunately he was away, in

Paris. The Dauphine appeared distressed by that news, and wished to wait for his return; but Père de La Rue told her she had best not waste precious time which the doctors could put to good use after she had received the Sacraments. She then requested a Franciscan friar, Père Noël by name, and Père de La Rue immediately brought him to her.

Meanwhile, she prepared herself to confess, asking for the assistance of Mme de Maintenon because she felt very weak. When Père Noël arrived she was left alone with him, and the King and the doctors seized that moment to persuade the Duc de Bourgogne to go to his room. He had a raging fever, and did not resist, but sent every moment to ask for news of the princess, and they could keep him from going to her only by concealing the rapid progress of her illness.

When her confession (which took a long time) was finished, and Mme de Maintenon had returned to the bedroom, the princess was disturbed by a scruple. 'I have done wrong, Aunt, have I not,' she said to Mme de Maintenon, 'in taking a different confessor?' 'No,' replied Mme de Maintenon. 'It is always permissible. One needs full liberty of conscience.' During this interval, they had sent to the parish church of Versailles for everything necessary to give her Extreme Unction and Communion, and the King went to salute the Holy Sacraments at the foot of the grand staircase. The Dauphine received them most piously, and afterwards said to Mme de Maintenon, 'Aunt, I feel quite different; as though I were entirely changed.' 'That,' said Mme de Maintenon, 'is because you have come close to God, and He gives you comfort.' 'My only grief,' said the Princess, 'is to have offended against God.' 'That sorrow,' continued Mme de Maintenon, 'suffices to obtain pardon for your sins, provided you are firmly resolved to commit them no more, if God gives you back your health.' 'Yes, indeed,' said the Princess, 'but I fear that if I recover I may not do sufficient penance.'

An hour later, she asked for the prayers for the dying; but was told that the moment had not yet come and, to comfort her, they urged her to try to sleep. At this time the King and Mme de Maintenon were in the drawing-room, next door, to which the doctors had been summoned to confer in their presence. There were seven of them altogether, some attached to the Court, others from Paris. They unanimously directed that she should be bled from the foot before the fever returned, and that an emetic be given her in the early hours, if the bleeding had produced no beneficial result. When the fever returned it was less violent than before, but the night was cruel. One thing worried her especially, for she said to Mme de Maintenon, 'Aunt, I have only one anxiety, the matter of my debts.'[1] 'You have trusted me so fully, until now,' replied Mme de Maintenon, 'will you not trust me to deal with them?' 'Monsieur le Dauphin knows about them,' continued the Princess, 'I should like to see him.' 'That cannot be,' said Mme de Maintenon, 'because you have measles; but tell me about them, I promise that, if you recover, they will never be mentioned.' The Dauphine then asked for her writing-case which she opened herself, fingering some of the papers in an effort to find those concerned with her debts; but, wanting the strength, she closed the case, and had it put near the foot of her bed. She asked again to see the Dauphin, repeating that he had knowledge of her debts; but, as the King had expressly forbidden him to enter her room, for fear of the bad air, Mme de Maintenon tried to distract her, saying, 'If he knows about your debts, you may rest assured that in his love for you he will pay them immediately;' and, with that the Dauphine appeared satisfied.

Next day, the King came very early, and the Dauphine was given an emetic at nine o'clock, but it had no effect. As the day wore on fresh symptoms appeared, each one more distressing than the last. She was conscious only at rare intervals. Mme de Maintenon remained in the *ruelle*, beside the bed, weeping bitterly. 'Oh! Aunt, you are making me cry,' said the Princess, for she wanted to keep up her courage. The King came every hour to see her, and they drew her attention to the fact that she did not speak to him. 'I am afraid of crying,' she replied. With her ladies, she was less constrained. She asked to see her favourites, so as to bid them farewell, and when the Duchesse de Guiche approached, she said, 'My lovely duchess, I am dying'; to which the weeping duchess replied, 'No! No! God will restore you, in answer to Monseigneur le Dauphin's prayers.' 'I think quite the opposite,' said the Princess, with something of her old fire. 'It is because God loves him that he sends him this affliction.' She then said these words, the last of which she was fully conscious, to the people standing round her bed: 'Princess today, tomorrow nothing, and in two days forgotten.'

Meanwhile the King and the Dauphin (who was still in a high fever, and forbidden by royal command to leave his room) refused to give up hope. They did what has always been, and is still, the

[1] The rest of this chapter is taken largely from the *Souvenirs sur Mme de Maintenon*, by Mlle d'Aumale, her secretary, at Saint-Cyr.

:ustom in desperate cases, they summoned the doctors to a consul-
ation. Seven appeared, headed by Fagon, the King's chief physi-
:ian, Dodart, the Dauphin's head doctor, Boudin, first physician
:o the Dauphine, and La Carelière, the Duc de Berry's doctor. The
:onsultation took place in the presence of the King and Queen of
England, who had come in haste from Saint-Germain, and was held
in the Dauphine's drawing-room. Five of the seven doctors advised
bleeding her once more (for the fifth time). The two others said that
'although bleeding might be beneficial on some occasions, it would,
at that particular time, be dangerous'. They bled her from the foot,
at seven in the evening. She almost fainted during the process; but
came to herself and appeared, for a moment, to feel some relief.
Yet the fever rose again that night (Thursday the 11th) just as it
had done on the previous nights. They gave her three more glasses
of an emetic; the effect was violent, but did not restore her to
consciousness. Her strength was leaving her.

Mme de Maintenon, seeing that she no longer recognised anyone, went to pray in the Chapel. The King, on the other hand,
would not leave the bedroom; but notwithstanding his presence, the
servants became so distraught that many strangers were allowed to
enter. In the midst of the confusion, a gentleman-in-waiting
advanced with a powder, which was said to be admirable, and,
since no hope remained, the doctors agreed to risk her being given
it. This powder did, indeed, cause her to regain consciousness to the
point where she said, 'Oh! how bitter that tastes.' Mme de Maintenon, informed that she was once more conscious, appeared at that
moment, and they said to the Princess, 'Here is Mme de Maintenon;
do you recognise her?' 'Yes,' she replied. Mme de Maintenon said,
'Madame, you go to God.' 'Yes, Aunt,' the Princess obediently
murmured, falling back in a state of complete insensibility. The
King left her just after eight o'clock, only a few minutes before she
died.[1] Stepping into his carriage, at the foot of the grand staircase,
he drove away to Marly, accompanied by Mme de Maintenon. Both
were so deeply affected that they did not have the strength to visit
even the Dauphin.

Next day Tessé wrote to the Princesse des Ursins, 'That unhappy
lady, whom God made my mistress, has died, as you might say, in
my arms. I saw her draw her last breath, and despite the general

---

[1] According to etiquette, the King might not be where there was death,
except on the battlefield.

custom of avoiding the sight of death, I gazed so long on that dreadful scene that the sight still remains with me.'

The Dauphin, grief-stricken and ill, remained in his room at Versailles, refusing to see anyone except the Duc de Berry and the Duc de Beauvilliers, who also had been ill in bed but rose to spend a few moments with his pupil. 'He was thus able to admire the great qualities with which God had endowed him; for never had the Dauphin shown himself so noble as on that fearful day.'[1] Although they did not know it, this was the last occasion on which they were to meet in this world. It is not known who broke the news of Adelaide's death, but we do know how Louis received it. 'Oh God! save the King,' he exclaimed, as though, writes the Abbé Proyart, he had a presentiment that he himself would never reign.

On the following day, which was a Saturday, they persuaded him to follow the King to Marly, in order to spare him the anguish of hearing noises from the room above, where the Dauphine had died. He left at seven in the morning, and was borne in a carrying-chair to his coach, though that did not spare him the salutations of a few tactless courtiers, to whom he courteously responded. The King was not yet awake when he arrived, and he had himself set down at the chapel, where he heard mass. He was then carried to his room, which he entered by one of the windows, and Mme de Maintenon went to him at once. Their suffering was so intense that they cut the interview short; but he still had to endure visits from the princes and princesses, as well as those of his intimate friends. They spoke in his presence, of the treatment which the Princess had received, and they blamed the doctors for her death. 'Whether the doctors have killed her; or whether God has called her back to Him,' he gently replied, 'we must adore alike what He permits and what He commands.'

At that moment Saint-Simon entered the room, and was inexpressibly moved by the kind look which Louis turned upon him. Otherwise, he was horrified by the Prince's appearance. His eyes were wild and glazed, his face had changed colour, and there were spots upon it, livid rather than red. He was standing, and the tears he was holding back filled his eyes. Soon afterwards, they came to tell him that the King was awake. He turned at the announcement; but made no other move. His pages once or twice urged him to go to the King, but he neither moved nor spoke. Then Saint-Simon approached and, motioning him to go, spoke softly to him, but

[1] Saint-Simon, *Mémoirs*.

seeing that he still made no move took him gently by the arm, saying that sooner or later he must go to the King, and that it would be kinder not to delay. 'He gave me,' said Saint-Simon, 'such a look as nearly broke my heart, and at once left the room. I never saw him again. God grant that I may meet him in that eternal life, to which his virtues will surely have brought him.'

The King, being by then awake, all those persons who had the *grandes entrées* were collected in his bedroom. It was nearly full by the time the Dauphin entered by the back door. The King called to him as soon as he perceived him, and they embraced long, tenderly, and repeatedly, their words broken by tears and sobs. When he had had time to look closely at him, the King was horrified by his appearance, and ordered the doctors present to take his pulse. It was alarmingly weak, or so they afterwards said; at that moment they merely remarked that although it was not quite normal, there was nothing to worry about, but that he would do well to go to bed. He obediently retired to his room, and that day saw only his confessor, his familiar friends, and the Duc de Chevreuse. That night he had a high fever.

The next day was Sunday. He made an effort, following the King's example, to resume his ordinary life, for the King, in accordance with his policy of not allowing either death or disaster to disturb his routine, had given orders for a shoot, after dinner. When the time came, however, he said he had a headache and cancelled the carriages, though it did not prevent his holding a meeting of his council, after which Torcy went to the Dauphin, and worked with him three hours, despite his being overwhelmed with grief.

Meanwhile, at Versailles, preparations were in train for Adelaide's lying-in-state. On the Saturday morning, they had combed and dressed her hair, placed on her a plain linen gown with black and white ribbons, and, so attired, she lay all day in public. A great concourse of viewers came to see her. That same evening, the doctors conducted a post-morten examination in the presence of the Duchesse du Lude, her lady in waiting, and the Marquise de Mailly, lately her Mistress of the Robes, whose offices forced them to witness the distressing scene. No traces were found of measles, smallpox, or of purple blotches. Her brain, and other organs, showed no deterioration. They reported only that her blood was quite dried up,[1] and that, since a few weeks, she had been pregnant. In the

---

[1] This may show that, had poor Adelaide been left alone and not bled so often, she might have had a chance to recover.

evening, her body was placed in a coffin by the Duchesse du Lude
and the Marquise de Mailly, one holding her head and the other
her feet. It was then set on a dais, three steps high, with no other
pomp than six wax candles, and was left there throughout the whole
of Sunday. On Monday the 15th, it was removed to a Bed of State,
where, according to etiquette, it would lie exposed for several days.
Two altars were arranged in the room, and on all the days that
followed masses were said hourly, from six in the morning until
midnight.

At three o'clock on the first day, the guard of honour was set.
Four bishops, in rochets and capes, and six ladies kept watch in
relays; and immediately there were quarrels over rights and
precedence from the bishops and the ladies alike. The bishops
required chairs with backs, and hassocks to kneel on, and when
these were refused them, their loud complaints distracted those
who came to sprinkle Holy Water. With the ladies, the trouble was
caused by the claim of the Princesse d'Elbeuf (a Duchess of Lorraine) to take the honour of the first watch, in preference to the
Duchesse de Sully.[1]

At Marly, the Dauphin's condition was deteriorating. On the
Monday, he had seemed better, although full of foreboding. On
Tuesday, he said several times to Père Martineau, 'Father, I shall
not leave this place'. Martineau replied that all who knew of his illness were praying for his recovery, and that he should join his
prayers to theirs, for the sake of France. 'Would there be no vanity,'
said the Prince, 'in my asking God to spare me for the good of
France?' Père Martineau having reassured him, he continued, 'Ah!
well, God knows what plans He has for me. He is the master. His
will is mine. For life or death, let Him decide. *Fiat, Fiat.*' And in
the days that followed he was heard often to repeat those two words.

On that Tuesday afternoon the red blotches reappeared, and he
was again feverish. His ordinary physician took fright and asked for
assistance; but Fagon, in bad odour since the Dauphine's death,
refused to intervene. Then Desmoulins, the King's second doctor,
was called in; but, he found symptoms similar to those he had
encountered in the Dauphine's illness, and no doubt remembering
the disastrous failure of the remedies then prescribed, he would not

---

[1] The Princes of Lorraine ranked as Foreign Princes because the principality
had not originally been part of France. They ranked after the dukes and peers,
and were always making rows about precedence.

order any treatment. That night and the next day were bad. Red blotches vanished and reappeared; but the rash peculiar to measles (which they still suspected) was not seen.

The King and Mme de Maintenon visited him several times, and an effort was made to hearten him. When he wished to make a general confession, in preparation for the last sacraments, Père Martineau said, 'Why, Monsieur, are you giving up hope, when the doctors are full of confidence? You must assist their remedies by thinking happier thoughts.' 'Thank God,' said Louis, 'the thought of death does not sadden me. Pray that if God wishes me to live, it may be to serve Him better. If I am to die, pray that I may live with Him eternally.' And he added, 'Since I may not make my confession today, I had best turn my mind to other things, for there is not much time left'.

He then sent for all his household servants, and asked them whether he owed money to any of them. They all, weeping, said no. He thanked them for their service, and promised to recommend them to the King, hoping that they might be placed with his sons. To the officers of his household, he asked if they would name anyone to whom he had done harm or humiliated, so that he might make atonement. Someone exclaimed, 'Ah! Monseigneur, you have done nothing but good in this world, and all Frenchmen would gladly give their lives for you'. 'Yes,' said the Dauphin, 'Frenchmen do indeed deserve the love of their princes. The King will achieve his heart's desires if he can end this exhausting war, and I truly believe that he will succeed in that before long.'

He then had brought to him a list of the poor families whom he assisted, and considered how they would fare after his death. While so doing, he suddenly remembered that the Dauphine had left him some pieces of jewellery, and he ordered them to be sold for their benefit. Thereupon, his friends, some wishing to share in his charity, others to possess something that had belonged to him, bid for them, at the sale, far above their real value.

The rest of that day passed quietly enough, and the doctors were again misled regarding his condition; but the night and the following day were bad. Red blotches again appeared, and his extremities were cold as ice; yet he complained of feeling hot as fire. 'This is a dreadful fever,' he said. 'I feel as though I were burning inwardly.' Then, thinking perhaps that he might have sounded impatient, or cowardly, he added, 'Perhaps I think this fever so bad only because I have never before been ill, and am not used to suffer pain. After all, what is this pain compared to the flames of Purgatory, where we must expiate our smallest sins?' 'I answered him,' continued Père Martineau, 'that one effect of divine mercy might be to let the heat of his fever secure him against the fires of Purgatory, if he would bear it patiently and offer it to God, in penitence.' 'Most willingly,' he answered. 'How grateful we should be to God for giving us such an easy means of atonement!'

As his pain increased, he thought constantly of his approaching death, and once again expressed his desire to receive extreme unction and communion *in viaticum*; but, even in such tragic circumstances, the King's rule over his family was so absolute that they dared do nothing without his permission. On the first occasion, the King had consulted the doctors, and hearing from them that the prince would undoubtedly be able to go to church before long, he had refused permission. 'In that case,' he had said, 'there is no need to spread alarm.' '*Fiat, Fiat,*' replied the Dauphin, on learning of the King's refusal; but, still being convinced of the approach of death, he applied a second time to be allowed to take communion in his room, without pomp or spectators. He was, this time, so insistent that they spoke to Mme de Maintenon; but she evaded them. 'Monsieur le Dauphin,' said she, 'has lived like a saint, and wishes to die like one. I must commend his sentiments, but I cannot judge of his condition.' The doctors, again consulted, persisted in their view that the prince was not in imminent danger. They then attempted to open the King's eyes to his longing; but he was inflexible. 'I am not surprised,' said he, 'that Monsieur le Dauphin, who communicates so often when he is well, wishes to do so in his illness. But he must be reminded that the laws of the Church (which he would not wish to break) forbid communion *in viaticum*, except in cases of extreme danger. He must trust the doctors rather than to his own feelings.'

The Prince accepted that ruling quietly enough; but when he heard that his plea for extreme unction had also been refused by the doctors, he felt it as a cruel blow. 'Oh! Saviour,' he cried. 'Since no one will believe me, I must leave this world without the consolations which you provide for the dying. You know what my heart desires. Your will be done.' At this point a kinder, more Christian will prevailed, for Père Martineau broke into the discussion on the Church's laws, by telling the Prince that he might take communion, fasting, immediately after midnight. This suggestion was readily accepted by those who wished to spare the King the distress of witnessing a tragic scene, for it granted the desires of the dying man and at the same time shielded them from the reproach of allowing a Dauphin to die without the Sacraments.

The King was willing to allow a compromise that avoided all publicity and, relieved by the doctors' apparent belief in there being no danger, he went to bed. A few minutes before midnight Père Martineau gave Louis absolution; then, as the clock struck, the mass began, in his bedroom. He communicated with intense ardour, and at once, says Père Martineau, 'all his anxieties left him, and his mind was at peace.'

Nonetheless, the pain like a consuming fire increased all that day, becoming more and more agonising, and in his suffering he thought of his wife. 'Oh! my poor Adelaide,' he exclaimed, 'how you must have suffered! O! Lord, may it have been for her soul's salvation!' He then spoke of his children, and wished to see them; but, reflecting on the possibility of contagion, he thought it best to leave them at Meudon, where they had been taken. 'I shall see them very soon,' he said. His words were repeated to Mme de Maintenon, as a sign that he hoped to recover; but she replied, 'You do not understand. It is in the life to come that he hopes to see them. He says "very soon", because, in the eye of faith, the longest life is no more than a dream.' When she had last seen him, he had spoken of his sons, saying that he had no anxiety concerning them, for he knew that the King and she would do everything to give them the best possible education. He spoke later of the King, 'I know how well he loves me. My death will distress him deeply. Tell him to be of good cheer, for I die full of joy.'

He expired next day, Thursday, 18 February, at a quarter to eight in the morning. Saint-Simon and Madame, two people who had known him well, were in no doubt of the cause. 'He passionately loved his wife,' says the former. 'His grief at losing her broke his heart, and only by a most prodigious effort did his faith survive the blow. It was a sacrifice he offered without reserves, and it killed him . . .'

Madame reported to her aunt as follows: 'The virtuous prince, showed his great love for his wife by dying heartbroken at her loss, indeed he always said that he would not survive her. An astrologer of Turin, in a horoscope cast long ago, predicted that she would die in her twenty-seventh year, and she used often to speak of it. One day, she said to her husband, "The time is coming when I am supposed to die. Your rank will not allow you to remain unmarried, pray whom will you choose?' He answered, "I trust that God will never punish me so harshly as to let me see you die; but should that awful calamity befall me, I shall not need to remarry, for within a week I shall have followed you to the grave." And that, indeed, is exactly what has occurred.'

Mme de Maintenon, writing on the 29th to the Princesse des Ursins, simply said: 'The King is overwhelmed by grief, and all France is stunned.'

21

After Their Deaths

THE KING was indeed stunned by his grief, the only real
sorrow he had ever been called upon to bear. With Adelaide's
death the light and laughter were abruptly extinguished, for
she was his darling, the person he had loved best in all his life. On
her he had depended for his joy and comfort; but she would never
again warm his cold heart with her funny loving ways, restore his
youth in her companionship, and strengthen and support him by
the deep respect of her public attitude. He was old, tired, and
depressed by years of disaster; his old wife needed all the faith and
devotion she could muster to sustain him in his almost intolerable
pain. For once, even Madame felt compassion for her. 'Although
the old woman is our worst enemy,' she wrote, 'I still wish her a
long life for the King's sake; everything would be much worse were
she to die, and he loves her so dearly that he would certainly not
survive her.'

The Dauphin's death had been so sudden that there was no time
to summon the King. He had gone to bed, and they had not dared,
or perhaps had not had the heart, to wake him, and next morning at his
reveil, no one had the courage to speak. Sourches relates that it was
by their mournful faces that he learned the tragic news. Very
deeply moved, he embraced the Duc de Berry tenderly and
repeatedly, saying over and over again, 'Now I have no one left but
you!'

They had thought that because the door to the Dauphin's room
opened into the King's ante-chamber, he would wish to leave Marly
and go for a time to Trianon; but that he would not do, merely
moving into the room of Madame la Duchesse. He was not long
disturbed, however, for that same afternoon while he walked in
Marly gardens, the Dauphin's body was taken without ceremony to
Versailles, and he was able to sleep in his own room. As always, he
found strength by clinging to the rhythm and pattern of his regular

life. He continued, as had lately become his custom, to eat his dinner privately in Mme de Maintenon's room, but he held his usual councils and, on the 26th, resumed his daily sessions with his confessor. That same afternoon, he went out shooting.

On the day after the removal of the Dauphin's body, an autopsy was performed. His heart was taken out and embalmed, and later placed beside that of the Dauphine, to be conveyed with hers to the church of Val de Grâce. His body was then put into a coffin, to lie in state on the dais beside the Dauphine, presenting, says Sourches, 'a spectacle so unlooked for, so tragic, that none of those who had the pain of witnessing it could afterwards recall the scene without shuddering'.

In the evening the two hearts were taken to Val de Grâce, and immediately there were quarrels over precedence, which the King was obliged to settle. The King's almoner, attached to the household of the Dauphin, claimed the right to carry the Dauphine's heart, on the grounds that his household took precedence over hers. The Bishop of Senlis, the Dauphine's chief almoner, demanded the same privilege, on account of his superior rank in the Church, and because Cardinal de Janson had appointed him Grand-Almoner for that especial ceremony. When applied to, the King would not reverse the Cardinal's ruling; but he had a note made on the register that the decision was 'in compliance with the King's particular orders'. He had, at the same time, to appoint a prince and princess to accompany the hearts. The Duchesse d'Orléans should by rights have escorted the heart of the Dauphine, but she pleaded extreme languor, having been most tenderly attached to her niece. Her great-aunt, the Grand-duchess of Tuscany,[1] who should have replaced her, replied that no one thought of her, except for funerals; that, being allowed none of the pleasures of the Court, she need not endure its fatigues, and that therefore she regretted being indisposed. Failing both these ladies, the King appointed the Princesse de Condé to act as escort.

The two hearts were borne in a coach, drawn by eight horses, draped in black cloth reaching to the ground, and decorated with immense silver crosses. The Bishop of Senlis, in cape and rochet; the Princesse de Condé; the Duc de Maine; the Duchesse de Ven-

---

[1] Marguerite Louise d'Orléans (1645–1721). She was married, in 1661, to Cosimo III de Medici; but fourteen years later was returned to France because of her unedifying conduct. She lived, supposedly in a state of penitence, in the Abbey-convent of Montmartre.

dôme; Mademoiselle de Conti, and the Duchesse du Lude stepped
in at the foot of the grand staircase, to the mournful beating of the
muffled drums of the French and Swiss regiments of the guard. This
coach was followed by several others containing the ladies and
officers of the two households. A forest of white wax candles,
borne by a mounted bodyguard of pages and footmen, illuminated
the procession, which left Versailles at half-past six in the evening,
and reached Val de Grâce only at midnight. The abbess read a
deeply moving address, and all was over by two o'clock. On the
return there was no ceremony, and the ladies who were tired spent
the night in Paris.

Meanwhile, at Versailles, preparations had been going on for the
ceremonies attendant on the removal of the bodies. The two iron
gates of the courtyard were draped in black, unrelieved by any
heraldic adornments. The steps to the entrance of the château, the
grand staircase, the first guardroom, and all the rooms of the
Dauphine's apartment were draped from ceiling to floor with black
cloth, and two strips of it, embroidered with their coats of arms,
were hung from the outer door to the door of the room in which
were the coffins. The bodies lay in state for three days, beginning on
Saturday, 20 February. They were guarded, on the right-hand side
by young noblemen of the Dauphin's household, and on the left by
the Dauphine's ladies. There were also four bishops, two on either
side.

The traditional etiquette for royal obsequies required that all the
princes of the blood, and after them all the princesses, should come
in two processions to sprinkle holy water. Since there were two
coffins, there should rightly have been four processions; but to
Saint-Simon's disgust, all that was given was the merest shadow of
the lengthy ritual. A desire to relieve the King of visible signs of
mourning, and his own wish not to listen to official addresses,
caused a shortening and simplification of the ceremonial, and a
reduction in the numbers of persons taking part. 'Nothing,' said he,
'was ever so much abridged or so foreign to tradition.' But if something was lacking in grandeur it was made up for by the vast crowd
of weeping spectators who gathered in such great numbers to file
past the coffins that barriers were erected to prevent accidents.

The two bodies lay in state until the three days had elapsed. At
nightfall on Tuesday the 23rd, a long procession was formed to
escort them to Saint-Denis. The Duc d'Orléans, whom the King
had charged with the arrangements, presented himself at five o'clock

in the state drawing-room, together with many of Adelaide's old friends—Dangeau her gentleman-in-waiting, Tessé her master of the horse, the Duchesse du Lude, and other ladies of her household. For the last time, they sprinkled holy water on the coffins, as did the bishops and other clergy, while the priests of the Versailles mission chanted a *miserere*. Ten soldiers of the bodyguard raised the two coffins, and four others the smaller urns that contained the entrails. While they descended the staircase and were loading them on to the funeral car (too grand a name, says Sourches, for what was no more than an ordinary waggon) the King's musicians sang the *De profundis*. A single pall was laid over both coffins, and the procession started on its way.

This, according to the *Mercure*, was the order of it. First, a hundred poor men, dressed in plain grey capes reaching to their feet, with cowls and leathern girdles, each carrying a torch. Then a company of the bodyguard, a hundred and twenty musketeers, sixty from each company, followed by detachments of the lifeguards and light cavalry. After them came the mourning coaches, the first five containing the princesses and their ladies. In the sixth rode the Duc d'Orléans alone with La Fare, the captain of his guard. Other coaches followed, containing the bishops and the two confessors, Père de La Rue and Père Martineau, and all of these were drawn by eight horses. Next came the King's pages holding candles, but not in mourning because the King never wore it for his descendants. After them rode the four mounted heralds with the King of Arms at their head, and finally the car itself, also with eight horses draped in black cloth down to the ground, surmounted by huge silver crosses of watered silk. Four mounted almoners, in cloaks, rochets, and square caps, held the four corners of the pall, on which the arms of France were embroidered on the right-hand side, and those of Savoy on the left. A vast number of footmen carrying torches, a hundred of the bodyguard, the King's lifeguards stationed at Versailles, all carrying torches, and three more coaches with six horses brought up the rear of the procession.

This long cortège, to which the darkness of the winter's night gave a still more mournful and majestic appearance, took nearly eight hours to reach Paris, entering by the Porte Saint-Honoré, on the road from Sèvres, at two in the morning; leaving, at four o'clock by the Porte Saint-Denis, and arriving at Saint-Denis itself between seven and eight o'clock. All the way the roads were lined by silent and respectful crowds; but even passing through Paris there were no incidents. When the glow from the torches became visible at Saint-Denis, the bells of the abbey-church rang out to summon the clergy of the other churches, whereupon the priests of the abbey, with the monks at their head, set out to join the front of the cortège, intoning as they went the prayers for the dead.

Those, including the poor, who had taken part in the procession then entered the church. The masters of ceremony had provided seats in the choir, with hassocks for the ladies; the Duc d'Orléans, Dangeau, and Tessé sat with them. In the chancel were two tables, on which the coffins rested, under the same canopy. The Bishop of Senlis, according to custom, delivered an address, to which the Abbot of Saint-Denis replied. The monks then sang a Requiem Mass, after which the congregation dispersed, leaving the coffins exposed in the church under a single pall, for, by tradition, forty days had to pass before they could be taken down to the Kings' burial chamber.

Yet that was not the end. On 16 April, rather later than the required forty days, the coffins were brought back to the chancel. Next day, which was Sunday, vespers for the dead were sung, in the presence of the Duchesse du Lude and the ladies of the household, after which the choir was opened to the public from half-past six until eight o'clock. It was on Monday the 18th that the final ceremony took place. The church had been most magnificently decorated to the design of Jean Berain, who had created so many of the fêtes, operas, and ballets, given for the delight of Adelaide in times past. The *Mercure* devoted a dozen pages to extolling the beauty of the scene. 'A wide band of black velvet extended all around the choir, with moulded lily-flowers, tears, dolphins, and crosses, painted gold and all in high relief. In every archway were curtains, with lilies on the upper part, and below a pattern resembling ermine. In the centre of each arch was a medal representing one of the virtues applicable to the Dauphin. It was a grand and splendid spectacle. In the middle of the choir, a construction of arches, hung with curtains, shielded a high dais. All within was white and gold, save for the pelmet, which was black velvet, emblazoned with arms. Above this, hung a frame, surmounted by a crown encircled by groups of candles, and all the length of the choir, clusters of candles gave the effect of acanthus leaves . . . On a platform raised by five steps had been erected a gilded tomb, supported on lions' feet. On this rested the coffins of Monseigneur le Dauphin and Madame la Dauphine, covered by a single goldan pall.' Only

Dangeau found a carping word to say of the setting. 'It was too glittering for such a sad occasion,' he noted in his journal.[1]

The service began at eleven o'clock with a funeral oration, delivered by the Bishop of Alet, that displayed both eloquence and good taste. It lasted an hour and a quarter. When it was over, High Mass was resumed, and did not finish until half-past two. The bishops then went to stand by the entrance to the vault. First the coronets were removed from the coffins, then the blue ribbon of the Order, and finally the golden pall. The Bishop of Metz, after the customary prayers, strewed a little specially prepared earth upon them, and they were gently lowered into the vault, while the monks sang the *Benedictus*.

One last ceremony still remained—a very ancient rite, dating back to the beginnings of the monarchy. The holders of the highest offices in the households of Monseigneur le Dauphin and Madame la Dauphine were called to place upon the coffins the emblems of their various functions. The King of Arms, with the heralds behind him, called out their names: 'Monsieur le Marquis de Maillebois, master of the King's wardrobe, bring here the royal robe of Monseigneur le Dauphin,' and the Marquis de Maillebois did so. 'Monsieur le Duc de Beauvilliers, first gentleman-in-waiting to Monseigneur le Dauphin, bring his coronet,' and the Duc de Beauvilliers brought it. 'Monsieur le Marquis de Villacerf, major-domo, and you the other stewards of Madame le Dauphine, bring here your wands of office.' Villacerf stepped forward, his wand bound with crepe, and the other stewards followed him, each of them handing his wand to a herald, standing at the entrance to the vault. The King of Arms continued with the list until he came to, 'Monsieur le Maréchal de Tessé, acting as first gentleman-in-waiting to Madame la Dauphine,[2] bring here her coronet.' Tessé stepped forward and yielded up the coronet; then, turning to the officers who had preceded him, he loudly announced, 'Madame la Dauphine is dead. Gentlemen, you may serve elsewhere, we have no further

[1] Berain was a theatrical designer, and might have been expected to live up to the greatest occasion for which his capabilities had been required. Everyone who worked for Adelaide seems to have been captivated by her, and perhaps Berain wished to give to her funeral something of the splendour of the coronation which she did not live to have. Perhaps he felt this was the last thing he could do for her.

[2] Dangeau was ill in bed, and Tessé was substituting for him in the highest office. In the same way, the Marquis d'O had taken Tessé's place as master of the horse.

duties.' The King of Arms proclaimed in a loud voice, 'The most high, mighty, and excellent prince, Monseigneur Louis, Dauphin, and the most high and virtuous princess Marie Adelaide of Savoy are dead. Pray God for their souls.'

With that the six-hour ceremony ended, and the congregation, very deeply moved, slowly dispersed, leaving the bodies of Louis and Adelaide to lie in the royal vault that had received the remains of Princes of France since Hugues Capet, the first king of their dynasty. Next morning Saint-Simon called on the Duc de Beauvilliers, already stricken by the illness that was to bring him to the grave two years later, and tenderly embracing him, said, 'So you come from burying France'.

Epilogue

THE DAUPHIN'S death was not the final blow. Only nine days later his sons, the five-year-old Duc de Bretagne (the new Dauphin) and the infant Duc d'Anjou were taken seriously ill with the same virulent form of measles that had carried off their parents. Both children had been sprinkled at birth with holy water, but neither had been christened, and the King, as much concerned for the welfare of their souls as for their bodies, instructed the Duchesse de Ventadour to appoint sponsors and arrange for an immediate ceremony, both children to be named Louis. They were accordingly christened on the evening of 7 March, though the little Dauphin's face was quite red with spots and he was sweating in a high fever. Next day the Court doctors summoned five others from Paris. Purges and emetics were administered, but they did not save him and he died that same night while they were bleeding him from the arm. The infant Duc d'Anjou was spared by the prompt action of his governess. 'While the doctors busied themselves with the elder child,' wrote Madame, 'the nurses locked themselves in with the younger prince. The doctors wished to open a vein because he had a raging fever; but the governess Mme de Ventadour and her deputy strongly opposed this and steadfastly refused to permit it; simply keeping him warm and comfortable. Thus the child was saved'—and lived to become Louis XV.

To the French nation the shock of the triple tragedy was overwhelming. Three members of the royal family dead in less than a month, three direct heirs to the throne wiped out in less than a year. The succession that eleven months ago had seemed secure down to the third generation now hung precariously on the life of one sickly infant, whom few people expected to survive.

People sought vainly for causes or explanations; Mme de Maintenon and the pious saw the hand of God outstretched to punish France for its pride and arrogance; but there were many at the Court who suspected murder. Not a few of the older generation remembered the dramatic affair of the poisonings in 1680; and the younger generation, though they had not known Brinvilliers and

Voisin, had heard of the *Chambre Ardente*[1] and the horrifying murders. All over Europe rumours of poison were in the air;[2] but there was never any certainty, for analysis was not then possible. Thus at every unexplainable death suspicions were aroused, those of the Dauphin and Dauphine being no exceptions.

Saint-Simon relates that when the royal family had gone to Marly on 18 January there were already sinister rumours. Boudin, Adelaide's head doctor, came to tell her that he had sure news of a plot to poison both her and the Dauphin. He did not give this information privately but blurted it out in the crowded drawing-room, looking so distraught that people were horrified, and going on to say that although he did not know the source of the rumour, he was fully persuaded of its accuracy. Which, Saint-Simon says, was an obvious contradiction; for how could he know that it was true if he was unaware of its origin. Twenty-four hours later the Dauphin received a similar warning in a letter from his brother King Philip, who spoke of the danger to him, but only vaguely mentioned the Dauphine. Such baseless rumours were generally discounted, but the royal family were, in this case, perturbed, and apprehension spread through the Court.

Shortly afterwards the Dauphine had fallen ill. On the morning of the day when the first symptoms appeared the Duc de Noailles had given her a very pretty box containing excellent Spanish snuff, which she had tried and found beneficial. She had remarked on it to her ladies, and after she had gone to bed, she feared lest the King should see it,[1] and asked Mme de Levis to bring it to her from the table in her boudoir, where she had left it lying. But it was nowhere to be found, though a search was made and, to cut a long story short, it was never seen again. Nothing was said of the loss lest the King should hear of it; but when the Dauphine died its strange disappearance was remembered, and there were dreadful rumours that pointed directly to the giver.

Next day was the customary autopsy, conducted by Fagon,

[1] The name given to certain courts of justice set up to try unusual crimes, such as heresy and poisoning. They were hung with black and, even in the daytime, lit by torches. The most famous of them was established to try the suspects arrested in the Affair of the Poisons in 1680.

[2] There had been strong rumours of poison, when the Queen of Spain (Charles II's wife; the daughter of Monsieur, and sister of Duchess Anne of Savoy) had died suddenly, in 1689, followed shortly afterwards by the young son of the Elector of Bavaria, to whom Charles II had recently bequeathed the Spanish throne.

Boudin, and Maréchal. The official report no longer exists, but it appears that Fagon and Boudin were in no doubt of her having been poisoned and said as much to the King. Maréchal, on the other hand, firmly stated that he had seen no sign of poison, or traces so slight as to be insignificant, and he added that he had seen similar appearances on bodies where there had been no suspicion of poison. Fagon and Boudin clung stubbornly to their opinion, Boudin in such a frenzy of agitation that he sounded like a madman; Maréchal alone remained calm. This dispute was carried on in the presence of the King and Mme de Maintenon, whose consternation may be imagined. It was not the last ordeal to which they were subjected.

On 10 February, the post-mortem examination of the Dauphin's body had taken place; it was Maréchal who performed the autopsy in the prince's bedroom, at Versailles. 'From head to foot,' wrote the Marquis de Sourches, 'the body was gangrenous, the heart was withered, and one lung entirely rotted by disease.' 'The opening of the body,' said Saint-Simon, 'was appalling. The organs had been reduced to pulp. The heart disintegrated when the Duc d'Aumont took it to place it in the urn, and flowed through his fingers down on to the ground. The blood had putrefied, and an intolerable stench filled the vast apartment.'

That same evening the doctors made their reports to the King in Mme de Maintenon's room; no details were spared them, and a similar dispute arose. Fagon, Boudin and some of the other doctors claimed to have found the violent effects of a very strong and subtle poison that had consumed like a raging fire the whole interior of the body, with the exception of the head. That had not been attacked, but had suffered in a manner very similar to that of the Dauphine. Maréchal, on the other hand, pronounced it as his opinion that the death had been natural; that there were no sure signs of poison; that he had opened other bodies in much the same condition, where there was no suspicion of foul play, and that the Dauphin's death was rightly attributable to a natural infection caused by the putrefaction of the blood, and inflamed by a raging fever so deep-seated that few signs of it had outwardly appeared. Thence had come the rotting of the various organs. No need to seek farther; that, in itself was sufficient to have caused death.

At this point both Fagon and Boudin had attacked Maréchal, becoming violently acrimonious until, out of compassion for the King, Maréchal had ended the dispute by turning to His Majesty and exhorting him for the sake of his health and peace of mind to put away dreadful fancies that, in his professional view, were wholly without substance.

The King accepted Maréchal's opinion; but the streets and coffee houses of Paris were alive with rumours to the contrary, pointing to the King's nephew the Duc d'Orléans as the murderer. There was not a shred of evidence against him, but in public opinion he was certainly guilty, and the accusations were not confined to Paris, but spread even to the drawing-rooms of Marly and Versailles, where he was not a popular figure. The King never thought him guilty.[1] He knew the Duc d'Orléans to be profligate, and deplored his dissolute way of life; but he knew also that his nephew was no black-hearted villain but, on the contrary, kind and easy-going, quite incapable of planning a series of murders to enable his grandchildren to ascend the throne.[2]

Today, the general opinion is that Maréchal was right, and that an epidemic of measles raging at that time, both at Paris and Versailles was a sufficient cause of the tragedy. A large number of courtiers contracted the illness and there had been many deaths, indeed, the *Gazette de Hollande*, published in February 1712, reported that five hundred people had died in those two places alone.

[1] Madame wrote, 'Certain wicked persons are spreading a rumour that my son poisoned Madame la Dauphine and Monsieur le Dauphin. I am convinced of his innocence—I would stick my hand in the fire for it. . . . That, however, was what was reported to the King; but he spoke kindly to my son, and promised him that he believed none of it.'

[2] 'Only a devil spewed out of Hell,' wrote Saint-Simon, 'could have imagined the idea of opening the way to the crown by so long a list of crimes, for he would have needed to dispatch not only the Duc de Bourgogne and both his children, but the Duc de Berry as well. The Duc d'Orléans's heart was not so black.'

Adelaide's Family in France

At the time of her arrival in France, aged 10 (1695)

Her grandfather Monsieur (so-called), Louis XIV's younger brother the Duc d'Orléans, aged 55

Her step-grandmother Madame (so-called), Monsieur's second wife, Elizabeth Charlotte of the Palatinate, Duchesse d'Orléans, aged 43

Her step-uncle, their son, Philippe Duc de Chartres, aged 21, and her step-aunt, his wife Françoise Marie de Bourbon, Duchesse d'Orléans, the King's legitimised daughter by Mme de Montespan, aged 18

Her step-aunt Elisabeth Charlotte d'Orléans, daughter of Monsieur and Madame, aged 17

Her great uncle Louis XIV, Monsieur's brother, aged 57

Her first cousin once removed Monseigneur (so-called), the Grand Dauphin, son of Louis XIV and Anne of Austria, aged 34

Her first cousins twice removed, sons of the above, Louis de France, Duc de Bourgogne (her future husband) aged 13; Philippe de France, Duc d'Anjou, aged 12; Charles de France, Duc de Berry, aged 10

Her legitimised cousins, children of Louis XIV
— by Mlle de la Vallière, Marie Ann, Dowager Princesse de Conti, aged 29
— by Mme de Montespan, Louis Duc de Maine, aged 25
— Louis Comte de Toulouse, aged 27
— Louise Françoise Duchesse de Bourbon (Madame la Duchesse, so-called), aged 22
— Françoise Marie married to the Duc de Chartres (see above), aged 18

Her distant cousin, Prince of the Blood, Henri Duc de Bourbon-Condé, Monsieur le Duc (so-called) aged 27

Index

Throughout this index, the subject of the book, Marie Adelaide of Savoy, Duchesse de Bourgogne, is referred to as Adelaide; her husband as Louis, and Louis XIV as the King.

'f' after a number indicates that the name occurs on two pages, 'ff' on three and 'fff' on four consecutive pages. Mentions on more than four consecutive pages are indicated e.g. 261-82 *passim*, discussion over a series of pages is indicated by the first page number followed by '*et seqq.*'